Re-Gifters

Written by Mike Carey

Art by Sonny Liew and Marc Hempel

Graytones by Jesse Hamm

Lettering by John J. Hill

re-gift (rē-**gift**)
—*verb*
1. to give an unwanted gift to someone else; to give as a gift something one previously received as a gift; also written *regift*

Example: *We have a neighbor who we know re-gifts, and we think that is very low class.*

Newcastle City Council

Newcastle Libraries and Information Service

☎ **0845 002 0336**

Due for return	Due for return	Due for return
2 0 SEP 2012		
25/05/2016		

Please return this item to any of Newcastle's Libraries by the last date shown above. If not requested by another customer the loan can be renewed, you can do this by phone, post or in person.
Charges may be made for late returns.

RE-GIFTERS

Published by Titan Books,

A division of Titan Publishing Group Ltd.

144 Southwark Street

London SE1 0UP

ISBN-10: 1 84576 579 6

ISBN-13: 9781845765798

Printed in Lithuania.

A CIP catalogue record for this book is available from the British Library.

This edition first published: July 2007

10 9 8 7 6 5 4 3 2 1

COVER BY SONNY LIEW AND MARC HEMPEL

Also available from Titan Books:

The Plain Janes (ISBN-13: 9781845765516)

What did you think of this book? We love to hear from our readers.
Please email us at: readerfeedback@titanemail.com, or write to us
at the above address.

To subscribe to our regular newsletter for up-to-the-minute news, great
offers and competitions, email: booksezine@titanemail.com

www.titanbooks.com

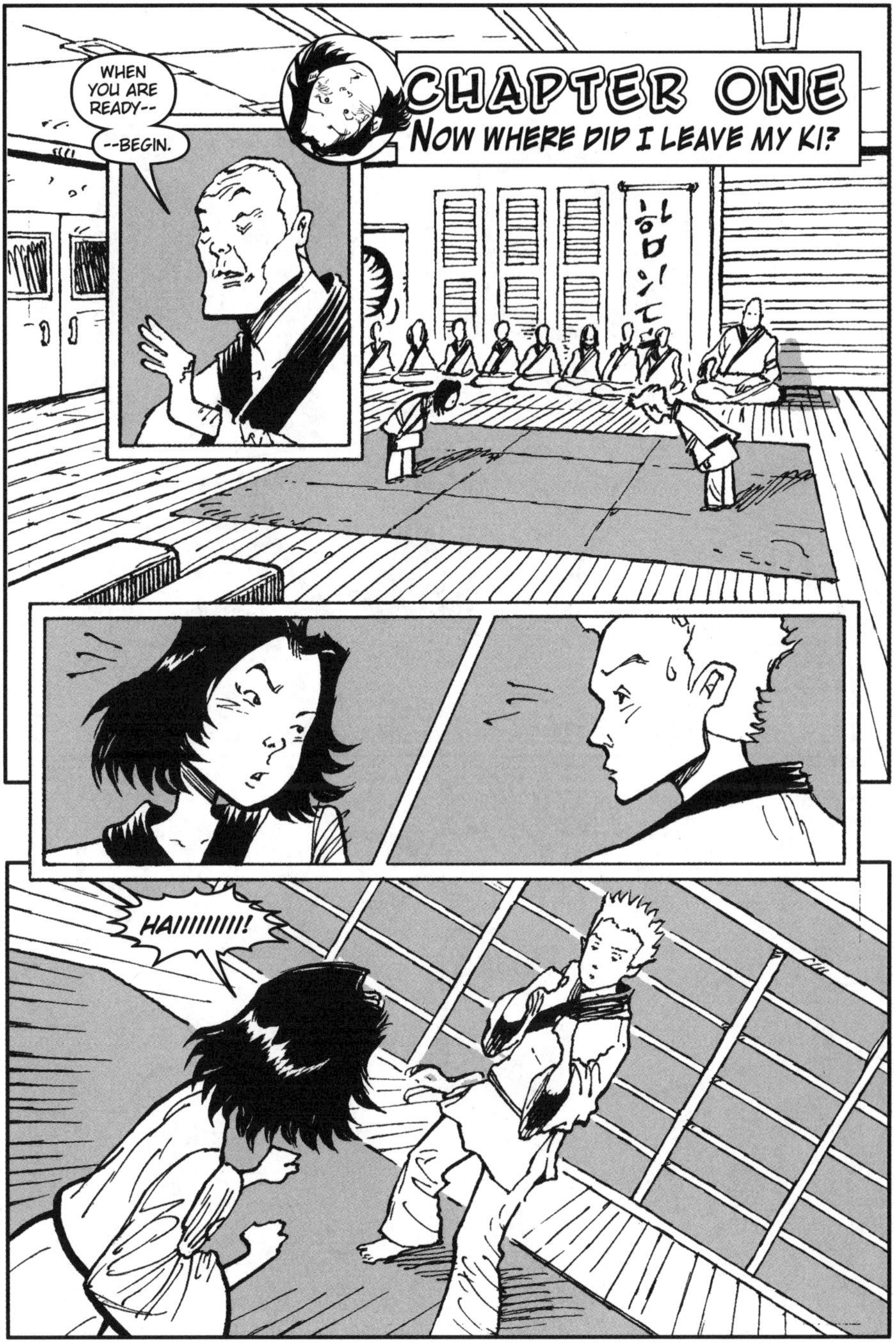
CHAPTER ONE
NOW WHERE DID I LEAVE MY KI?
WHEN YOU ARE READY--
--BEGIN.
HAIIIIIIIIII!

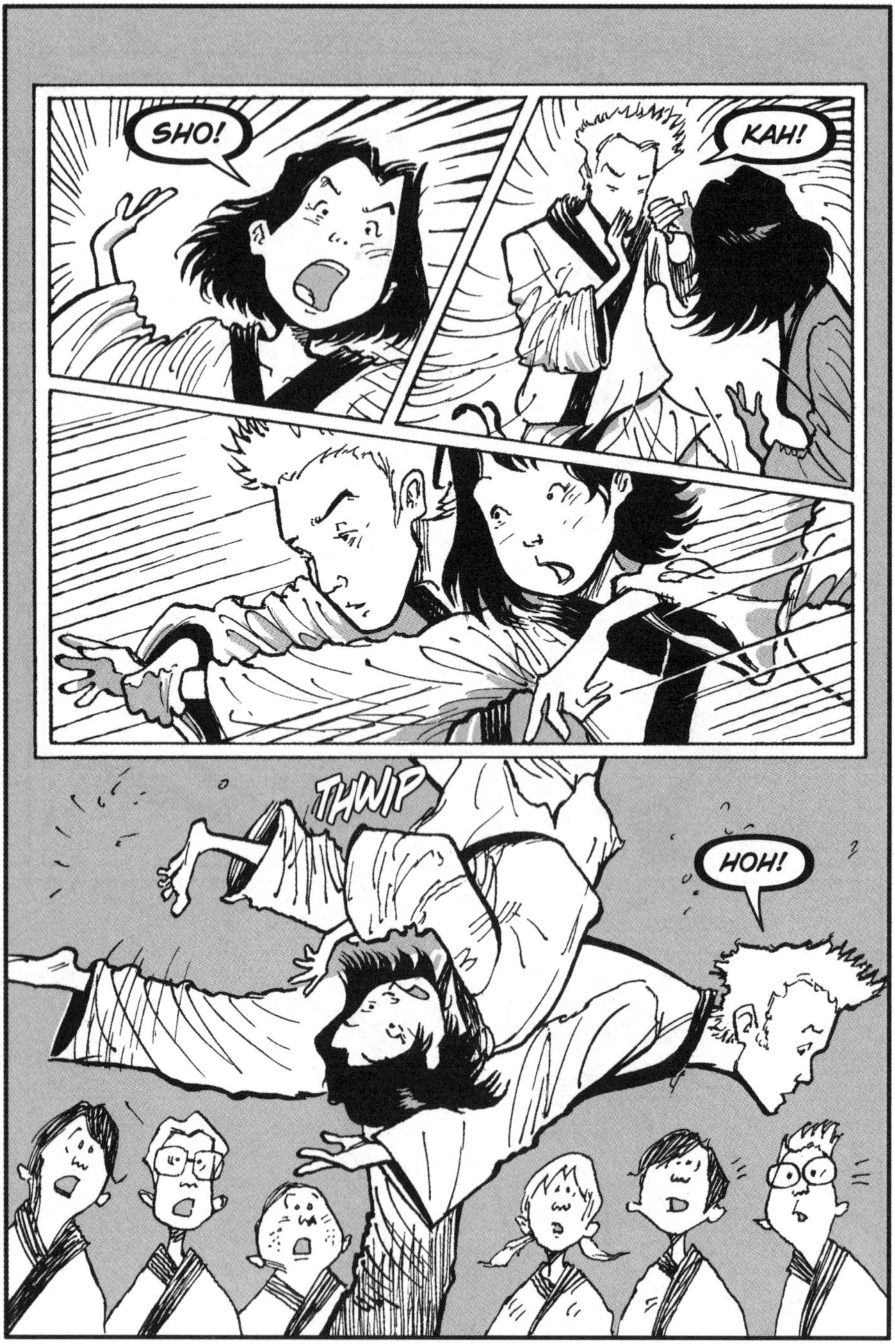
SHO!
KAH!
THWIP
HOH!

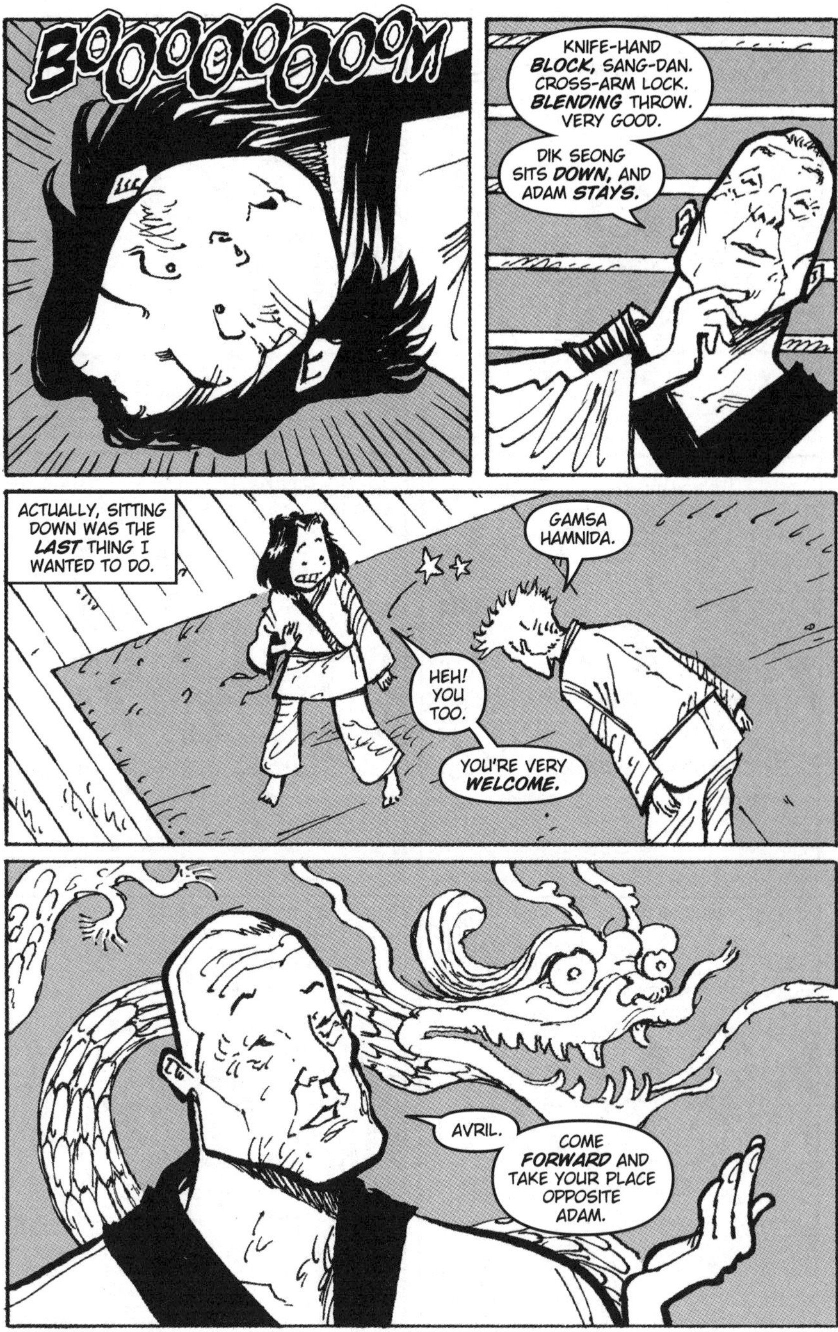
BOOOOOOOOOM
KNIFE-HAND BLOCK, SANG-DAN. CROSS-ARM LOCK. BLENDING THROW. VERY GOOD.
DIK SEONG SITS DOWN, AND ADAM STAYS.
ACTUALLY, SITTING DOWN WAS THE LAST THING I WANTED TO DO.
GAMSA HAMNIDA.
HEH! YOU TOO.
YOU'RE VERY WELCOME.
AVRIL.
COME FORWARD AND TAKE YOUR PLACE OPPOSITE ADAM.

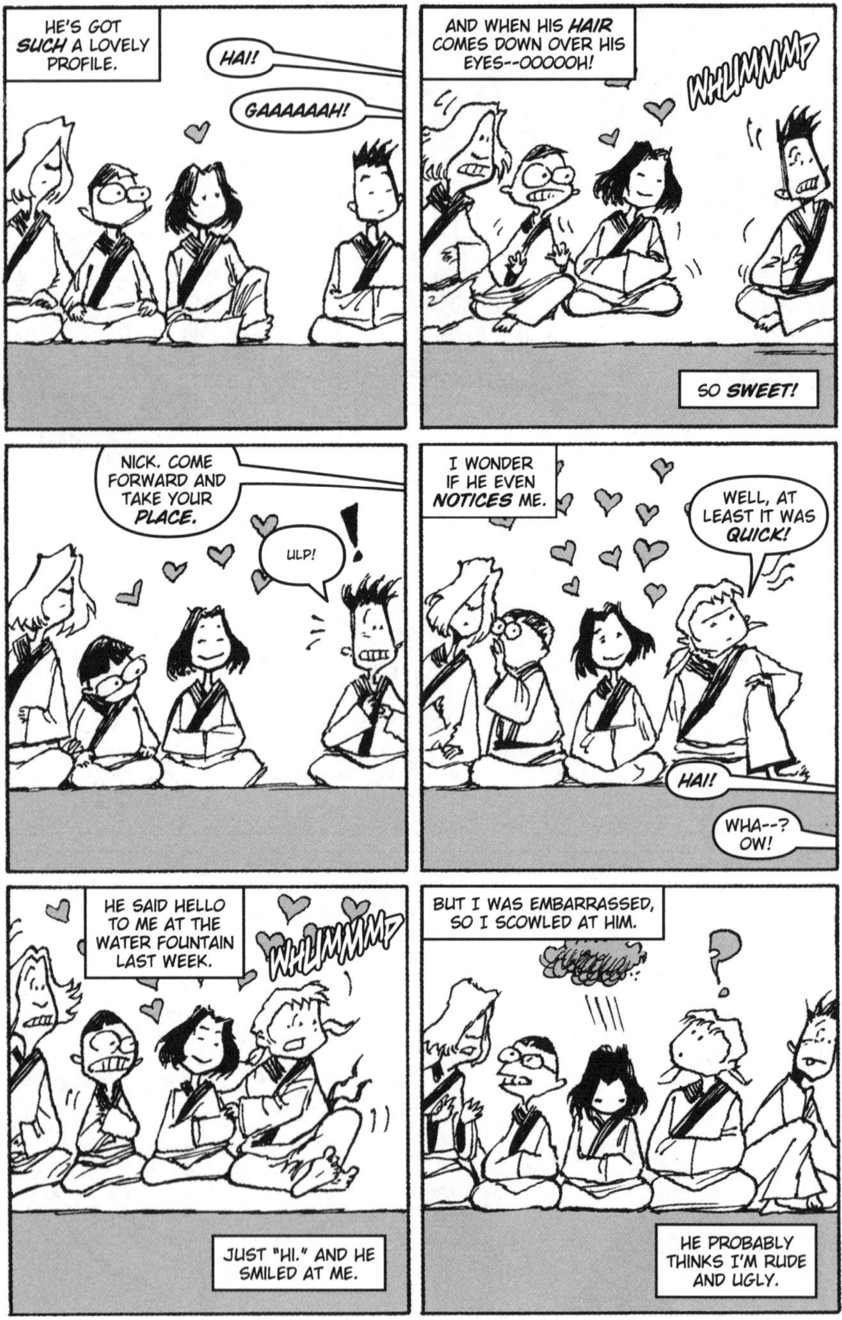

HE'S GOT *SUCH* A LOVELY PROFILE.
HAI!
GAAAAAAH!
AND WHEN HIS *HAIR* COMES DOWN OVER HIS EYES--OOOOOH!
WHUMMMP
SO *SWEET!*
NICK. COME FORWARD AND TAKE YOUR *PLACE.*
ULP!
!
I WONDER IF HE EVEN *NOTICES* ME.
WELL, AT LEAST IT WAS *QUICK!*
HAI!
WHA--? OW!
HE SAID HELLO TO ME AT THE WATER FOUNTAIN LAST WEEK.
WHUMMMP
JUST "HI." AND HE SMILED AT ME.
BUT I WAS EMBARRASSED, SO I SCOWLED AT HIM.
?
HE PROBABLY THINKS I'M RUDE AND UGLY.

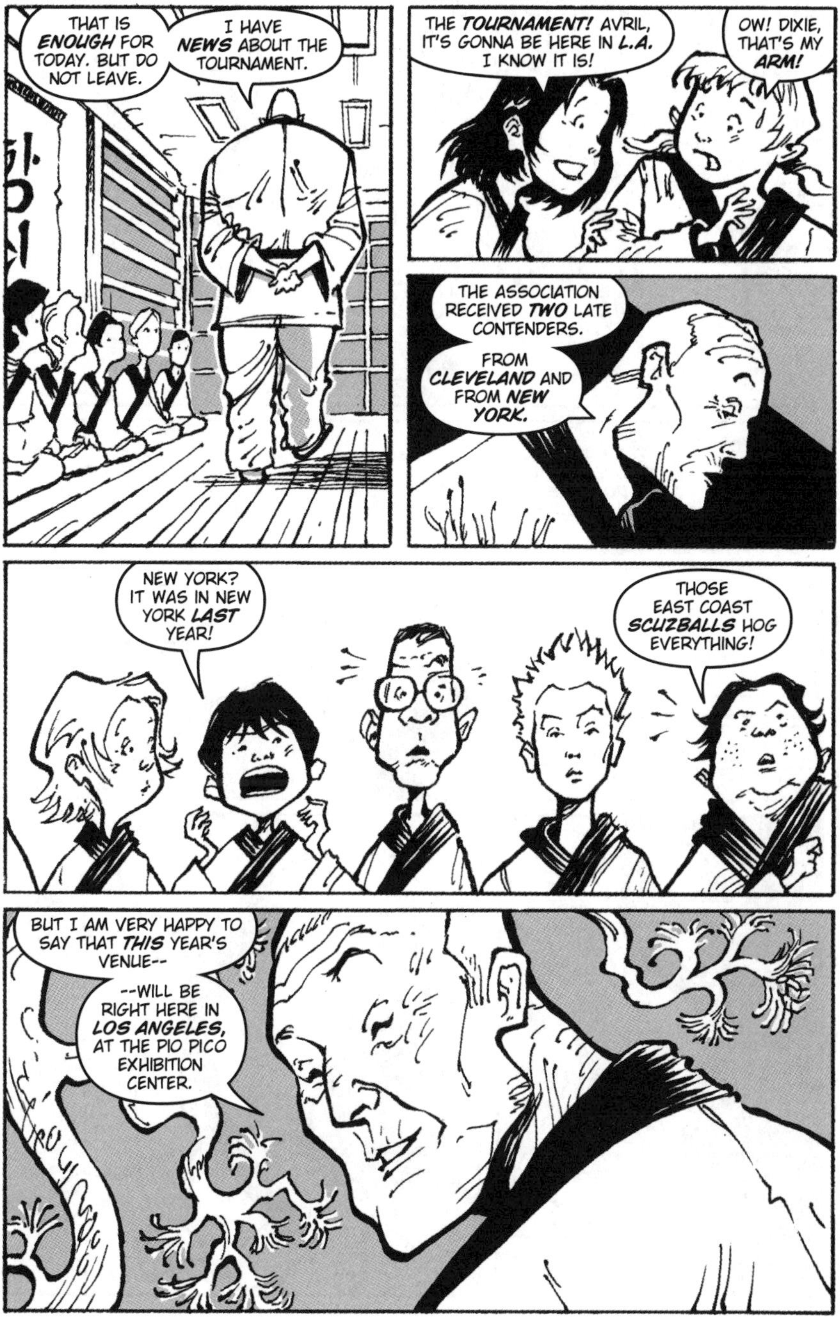
THAT IS ENOUGH FOR TODAY. BUT DO NOT LEAVE.
I HAVE NEWS ABOUT THE TOURNAMENT.
THE TOURNAMENT! AVRIL, IT'S GONNA BE HERE IN L.A. I KNOW IT IS!
OW! DIXIE, THAT'S MY ARM!
THE ASSOCIATION RECEIVED TWO LATE CONTENDERS.
FROM CLEVELAND AND FROM NEW YORK.
NEW YORK? IT WAS IN NEW YORK LAST YEAR!
THOSE EAST COAST SCUZBALLS HOG EVERYTHING!
BUT I AM VERY HAPPY TO SAY THAT THIS YEAR'S VENUE--
--WILL BE RIGHT HERE IN LOS ANGELES, AT THE PIO PICO EXHIBITION CENTER.

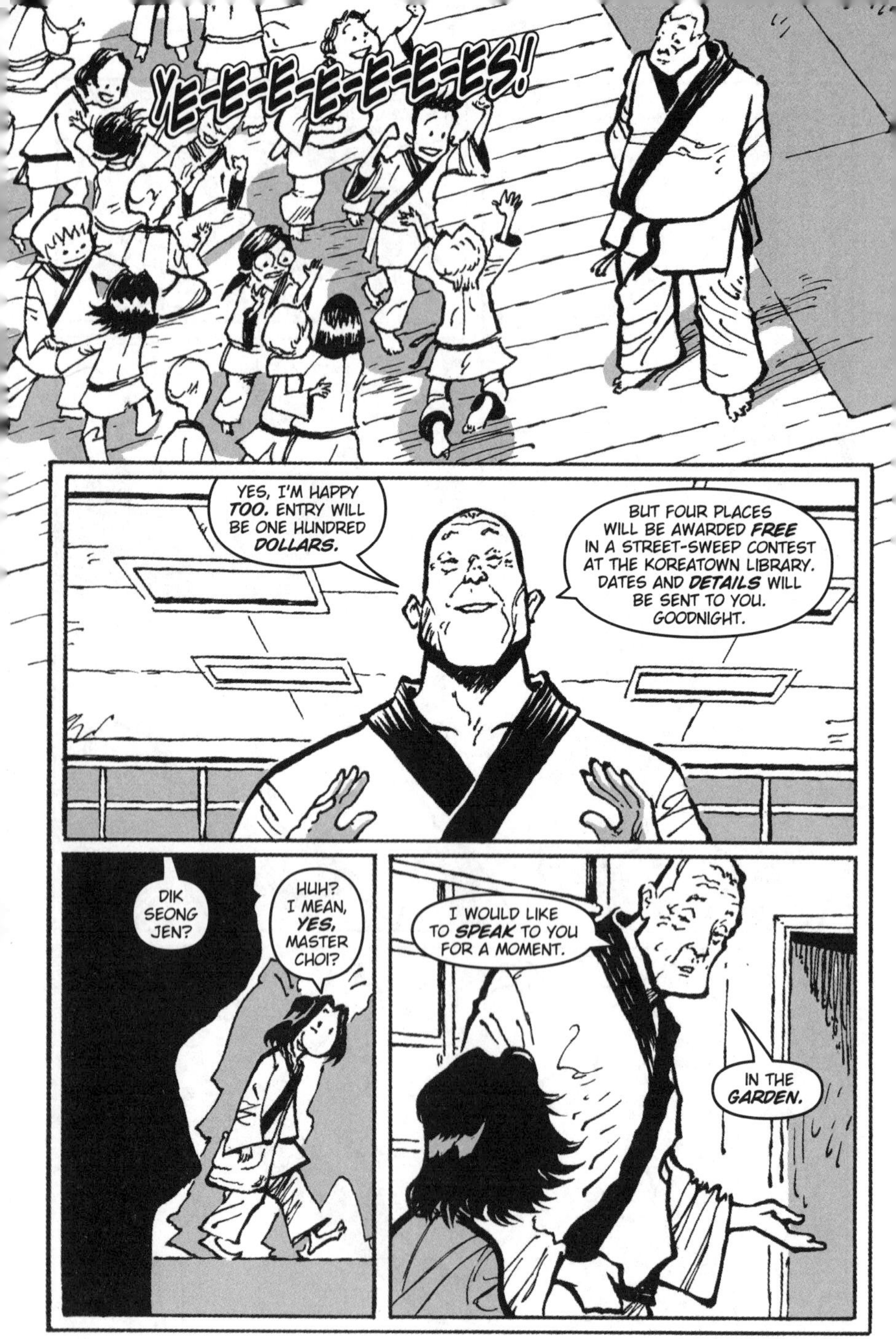
YE-E-E-E-E-E-ES!
YES, I'M HAPPY TOO. ENTRY WILL BE ONE HUNDRED DOLLARS.
BUT FOUR PLACES WILL BE AWARDED FREE IN A STREET-SWEEP CONTEST AT THE KOREATOWN LIBRARY. DATES AND DETAILS WILL BE SENT TO YOU. GOODNIGHT.
DIK SEONG JEN?
HUH? I MEAN, YES, MASTER CHOI?
I WOULD LIKE TO SPEAK TO YOU FOR A MOMENT.
IN THE GARDEN.

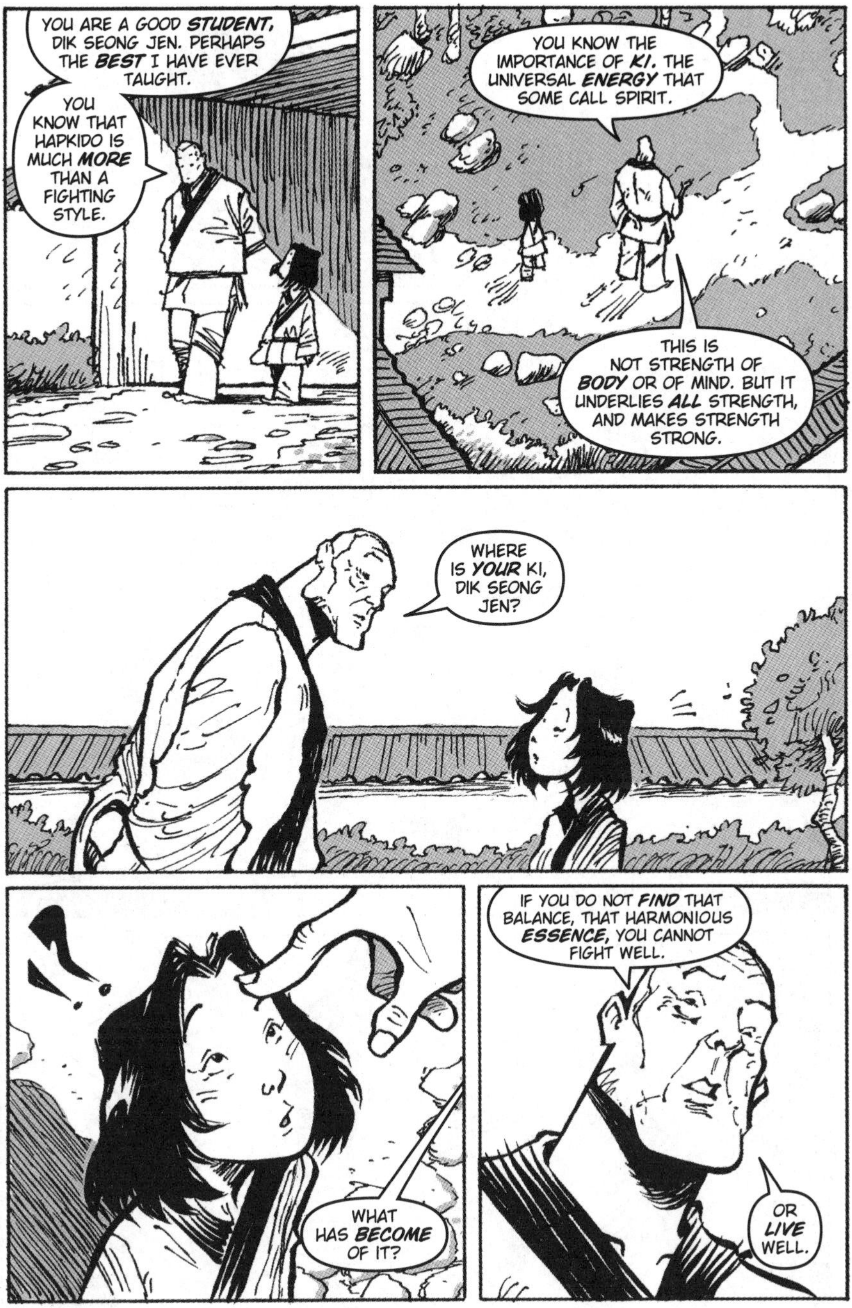
YOU ARE A GOOD STUDENT, DIK SEONG JEN. PERHAPS THE BEST I HAVE EVER TAUGHT.
YOU KNOW THAT HAPKIDO IS MUCH MORE THAN A FIGHTING STYLE.
YOU KNOW THE IMPORTANCE OF KI. THE UNIVERSAL ENERGY THAT SOME CALL SPIRIT.
THIS IS NOT STRENGTH OF BODY OR OF MIND. BUT IT UNDERLIES ALL STRENGTH, AND MAKES STRENGTH STRONG.
WHERE IS YOUR KI, DIK SEONG JEN?
WHAT HAS BECOME OF IT?
IF YOU DO NOT FIND THAT BALANCE, THAT HARMONIOUS ESSENCE, YOU CANNOT FIGHT WELL.
OR LIVE WELL.

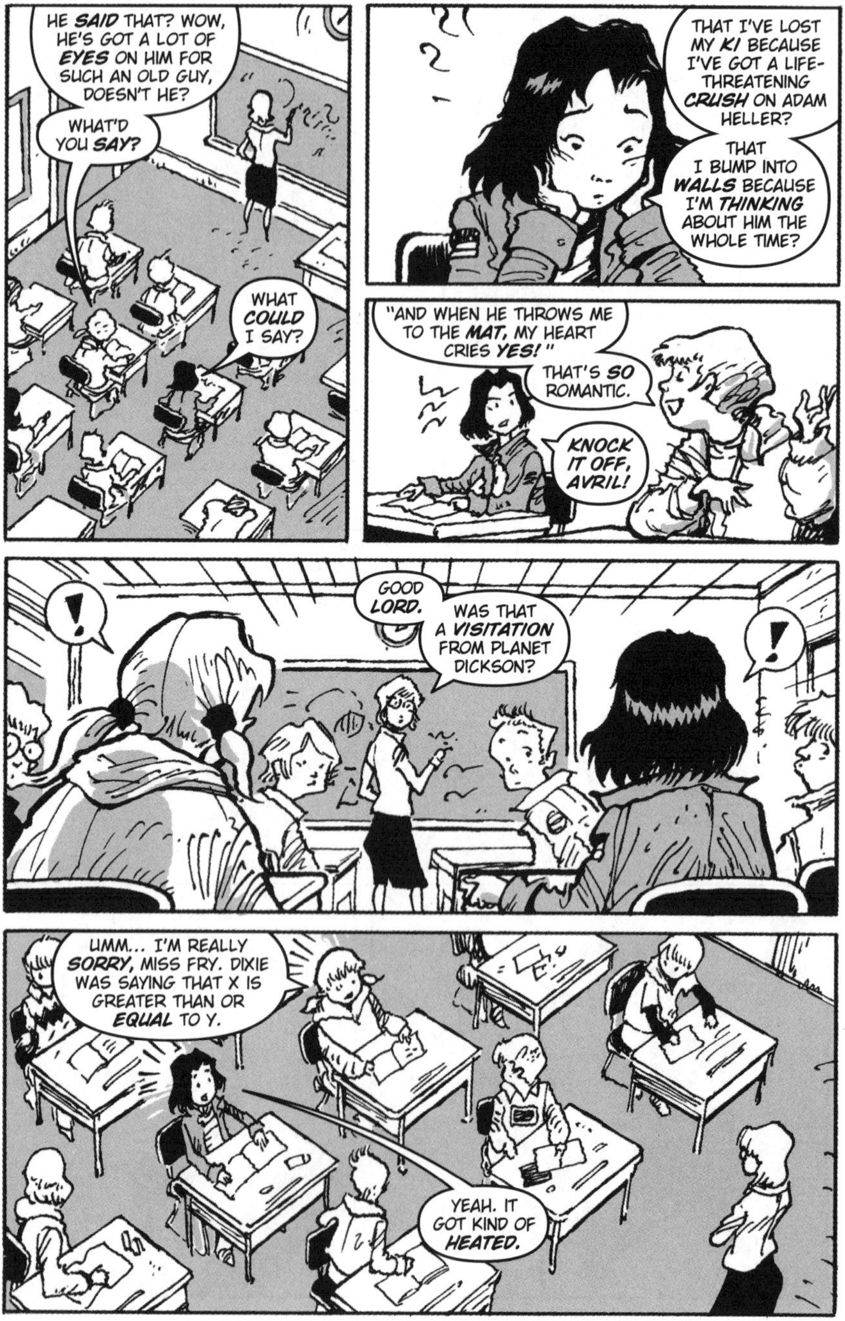
HE SAID THAT? WOW, HE'S GOT A LOT OF EYES ON HIM FOR SUCH AN OLD GUY, DOESN'T HE?
WHAT'D YOU SAY?
WHAT COULD I SAY?
THAT I'VE LOST MY KI BECAUSE I'VE GOT A LIFE-THREATENING CRUSH ON ADAM HELLER?
THAT I BUMP INTO WALLS BECAUSE I'M THINKING ABOUT HIM THE WHOLE TIME?
"AND WHEN HE THROWS ME TO THE MAT, MY HEART CRIES YES!"
THAT'S SO ROMANTIC.
KNOCK IT OFF, AVRIL!
!
GOOD LORD.
WAS THAT A VISITATION FROM PLANET DICKSON?
!
UMM... I'M REALLY SORRY, MISS FRY. DIXIE WAS SAYING THAT X IS GREATER THAN OR EQUAL TO Y.
YEAH. IT GOT KIND OF HEATED.

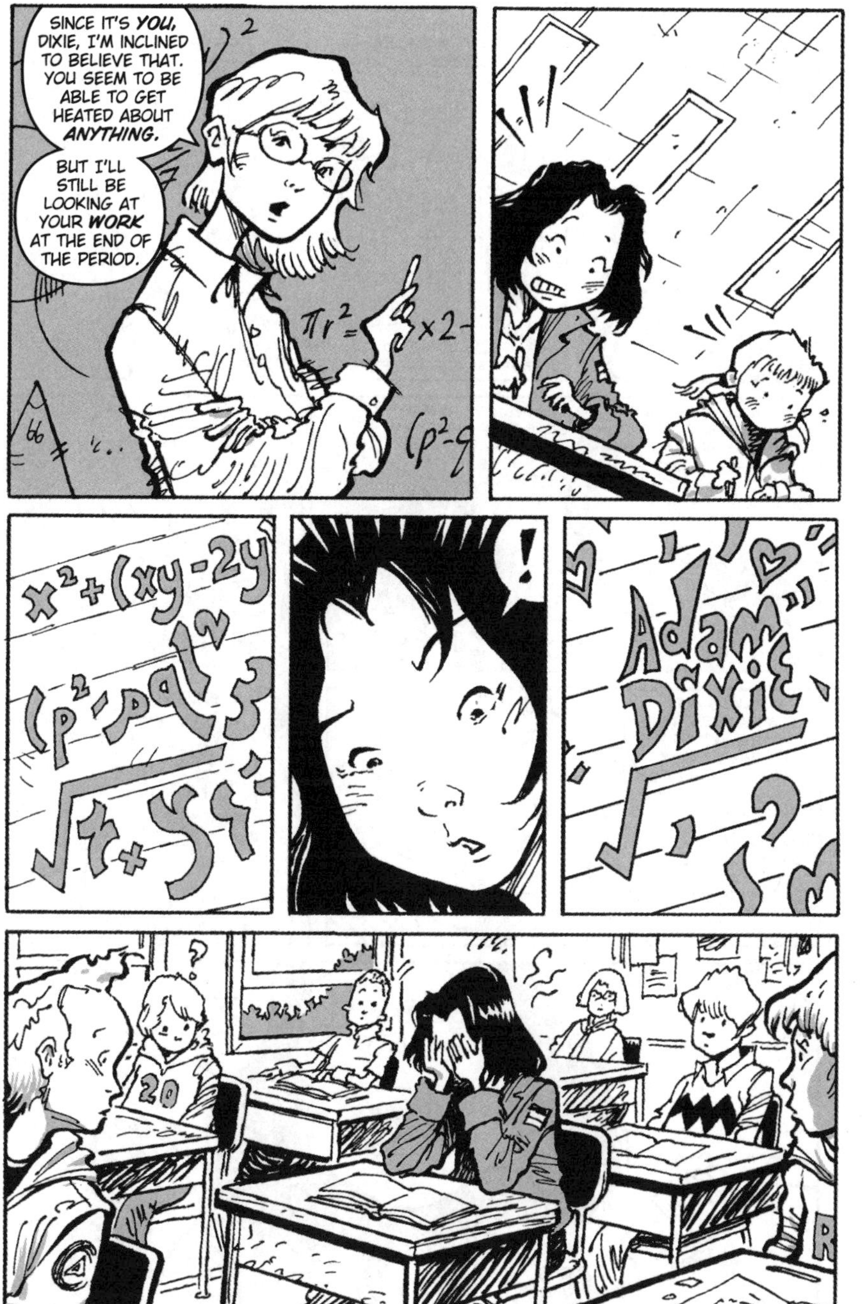
SINCE IT'S *YOU,* DIXIE, I'M INCLINED TO BELIEVE THAT. YOU SEEM TO BE ABLE TO GET HEATED ABOUT *ANYTHING.*
BUT I'LL STILL BE LOOKING AT YOUR *WORK* AT THE END OF THE PERIOD.
!
Adam
Dixie
20

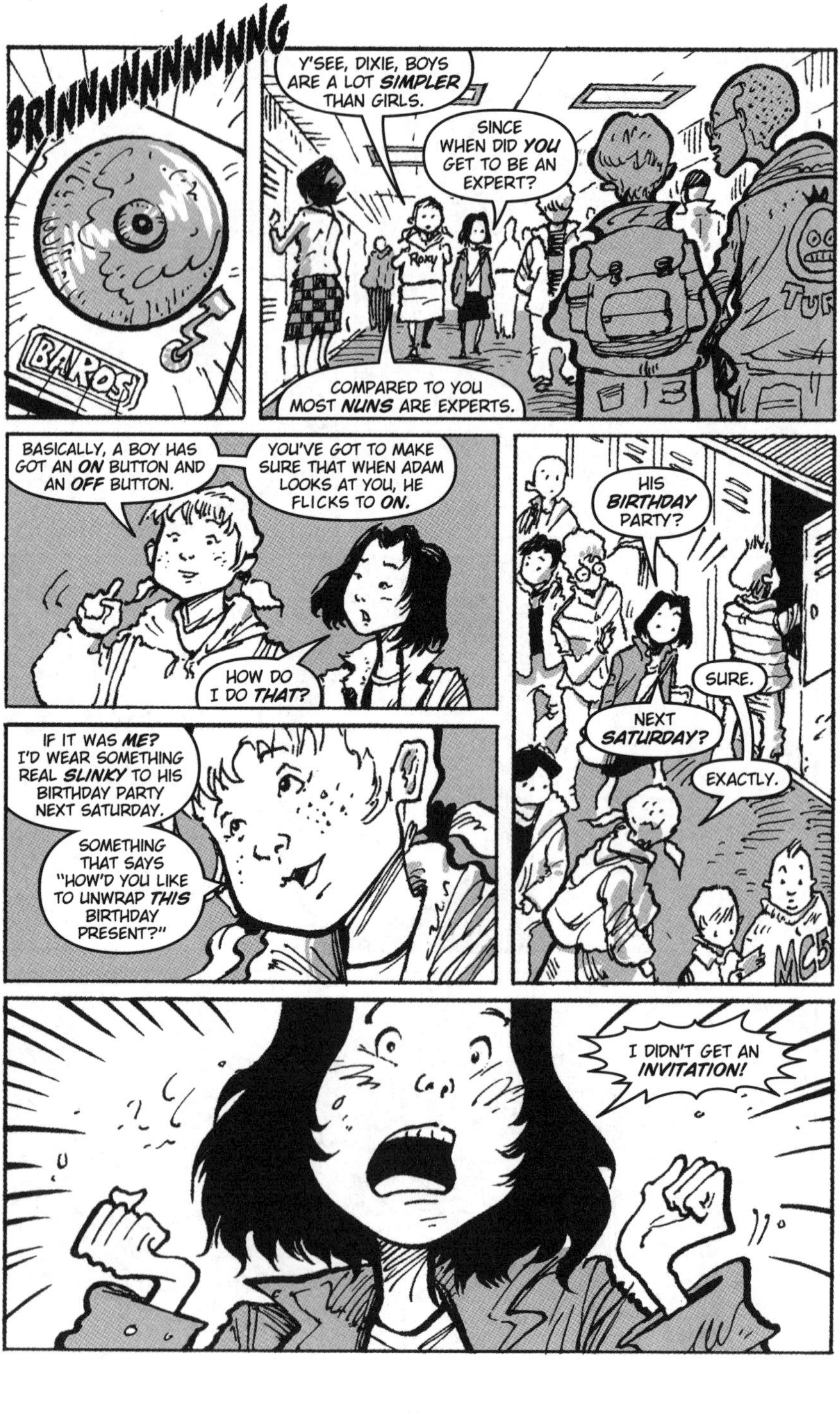
BRINNNNNNNNNNG
BAROS
Y'SEE, DIXIE, BOYS ARE A LOT SIMPLER THAN GIRLS.
SINCE WHEN DID YOU GET TO BE AN EXPERT?
COMPARED TO YOU MOST NUNS ARE EXPERTS.
BASICALLY, A BOY HAS GOT AN ON BUTTON AND AN OFF BUTTON.
YOU'VE GOT TO MAKE SURE THAT WHEN ADAM LOOKS AT YOU, HE FLICKS TO ON.
HOW DO I DO THAT?
IF IT WAS ME? I'D WEAR SOMETHING REAL SLINKY TO HIS BIRTHDAY PARTY NEXT SATURDAY.
SOMETHING THAT SAYS "HOW'D YOU LIKE TO UNWRAP THIS BIRTHDAY PRESENT?"
HIS BIRTHDAY PARTY?
SURE.
NEXT SATURDAY?
EXACTLY.
I DIDN'T GET AN INVITATION!

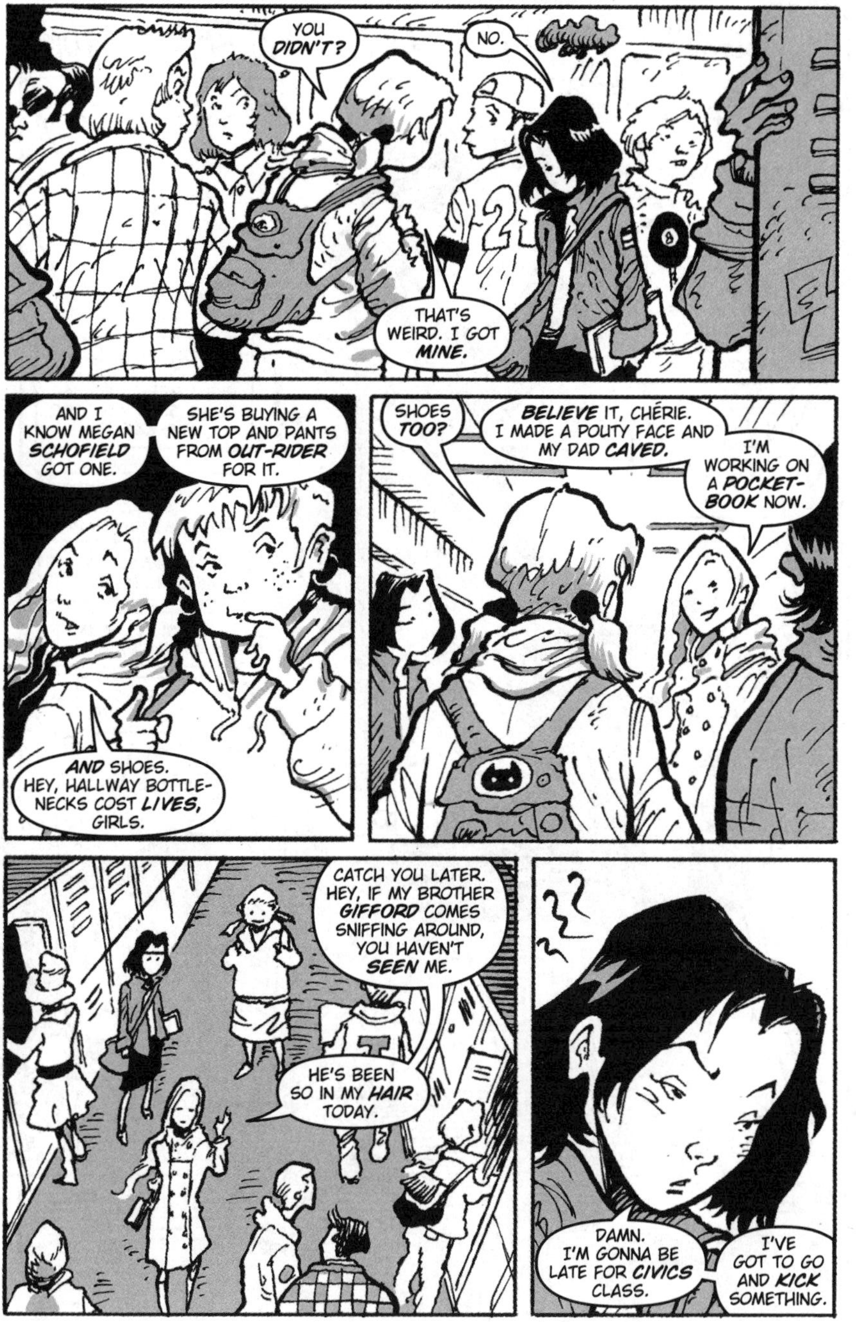
YOU DIDN'T?
NO.
THAT'S WEIRD. I GOT MINE.
AND I KNOW MEGAN SCHOFIELD GOT ONE.
SHE'S BUYING A NEW TOP AND PANTS FROM OUT-RIDER FOR IT.
AND SHOES. HEY, HALLWAY BOTTLE-NECKS COST LIVES, GIRLS.
SHOES TOO?
BELIEVE IT, CHÉRIE. I MADE A POUTY FACE AND MY DAD CAVED.
I'M WORKING ON A POCKET-BOOK NOW.
CATCH YOU LATER. HEY, IF MY BROTHER GIFFORD COMES SNIFFING AROUND, YOU HAVEN'T SEEN ME.
HE'S BEEN SO IN MY HAIR TODAY.
DAMN. I'M GONNA BE LATE FOR CIVICS CLASS.
I'VE GOT TO GO AND KICK SOMETHING.

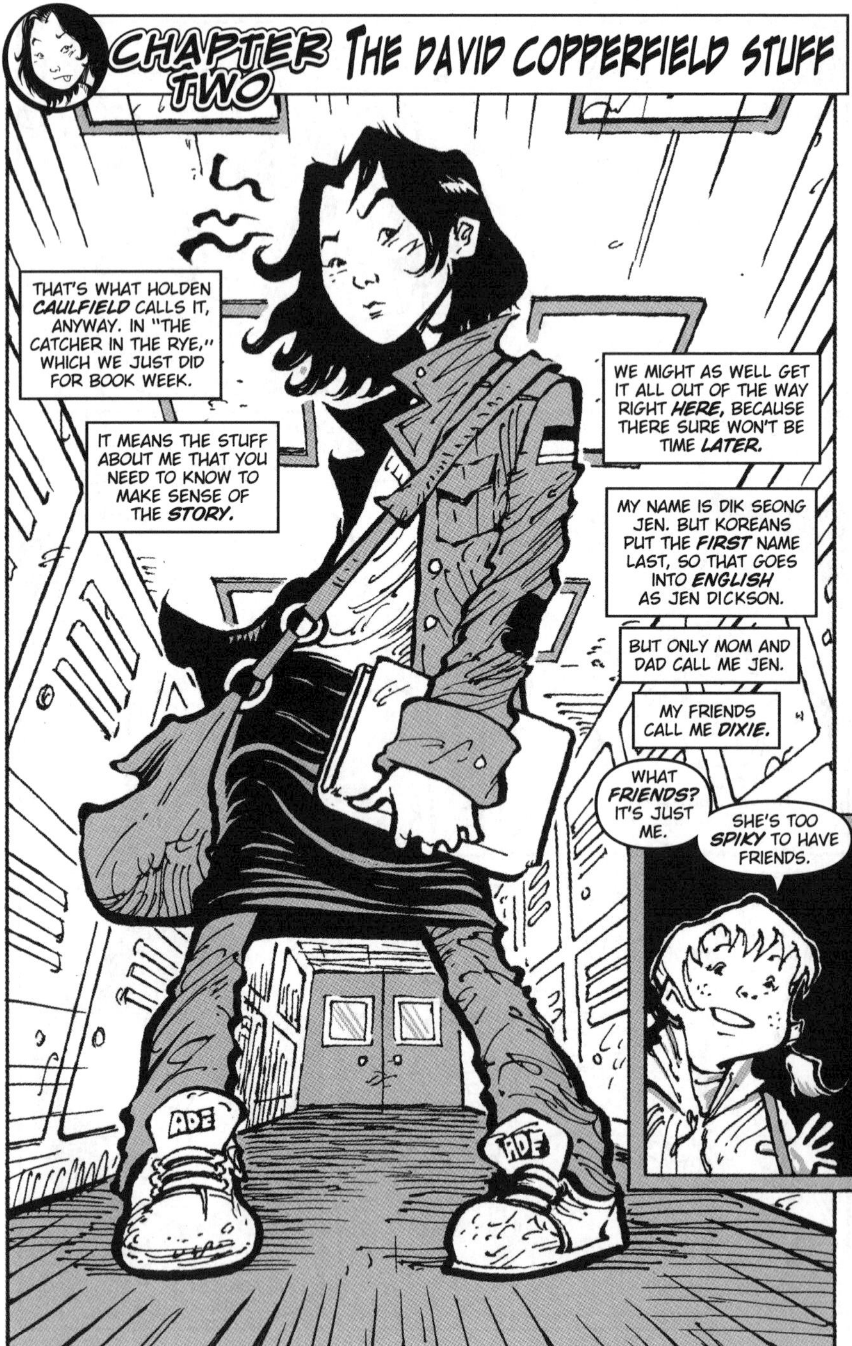
CHAPTER TWO
THE DAVID COPPERFIELD STUFF
THAT'S WHAT HOLDEN CAULFIELD CALLS IT, ANYWAY. IN "THE CATCHER IN THE RYE," WHICH WE JUST DID FOR BOOK WEEK.
IT MEANS THE STUFF ABOUT ME THAT YOU NEED TO KNOW TO MAKE SENSE OF THE STORY.
WE MIGHT AS WELL GET IT ALL OUT OF THE WAY RIGHT HERE, BECAUSE THERE SURE WON'T BE TIME LATER.
MY NAME IS DIK SEONG JEN. BUT KOREANS PUT THE FIRST NAME LAST, SO THAT GOES INTO ENGLISH AS JEN DICKSON.
BUT ONLY MOM AND DAD CALL ME JEN.
MY FRIENDS CALL ME DIXIE.
WHAT FRIENDS? IT'S JUST ME.
SHE'S TOO SPIKY TO HAVE FRIENDS.
ADE
ADE

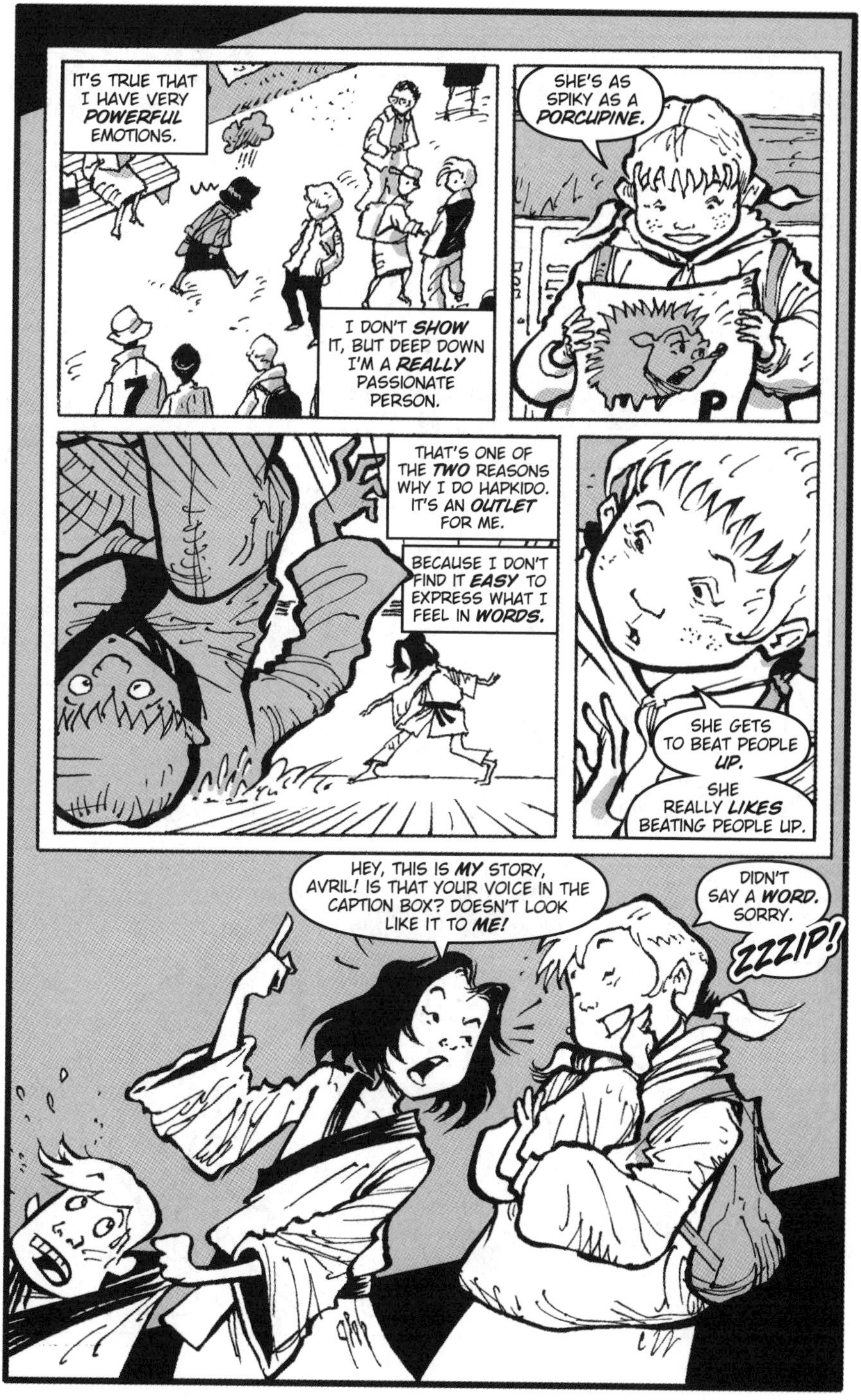
IT'S TRUE THAT I HAVE VERY POWERFUL EMOTIONS.
I DON'T SHOW IT, BUT DEEP DOWN I'M A REALLY PASSIONATE PERSON.
SHE'S AS SPIKY AS A PORCUPINE.
THAT'S ONE OF THE TWO REASONS WHY I DO HAPKIDO. IT'S AN OUTLET FOR ME.
BECAUSE I DON'T FIND IT EASY TO EXPRESS WHAT I FEEL IN WORDS.
SHE GETS TO BEAT PEOPLE UP.
SHE REALLY LIKES BEATING PEOPLE UP.
HEY, THIS IS MY STORY, AVRIL! IS THAT YOUR VOICE IN THE CAPTION BOX? DOESN'T LOOK LIKE IT TO ME!
DIDN'T SAY A WORD. SORRY.
ZZZIP!

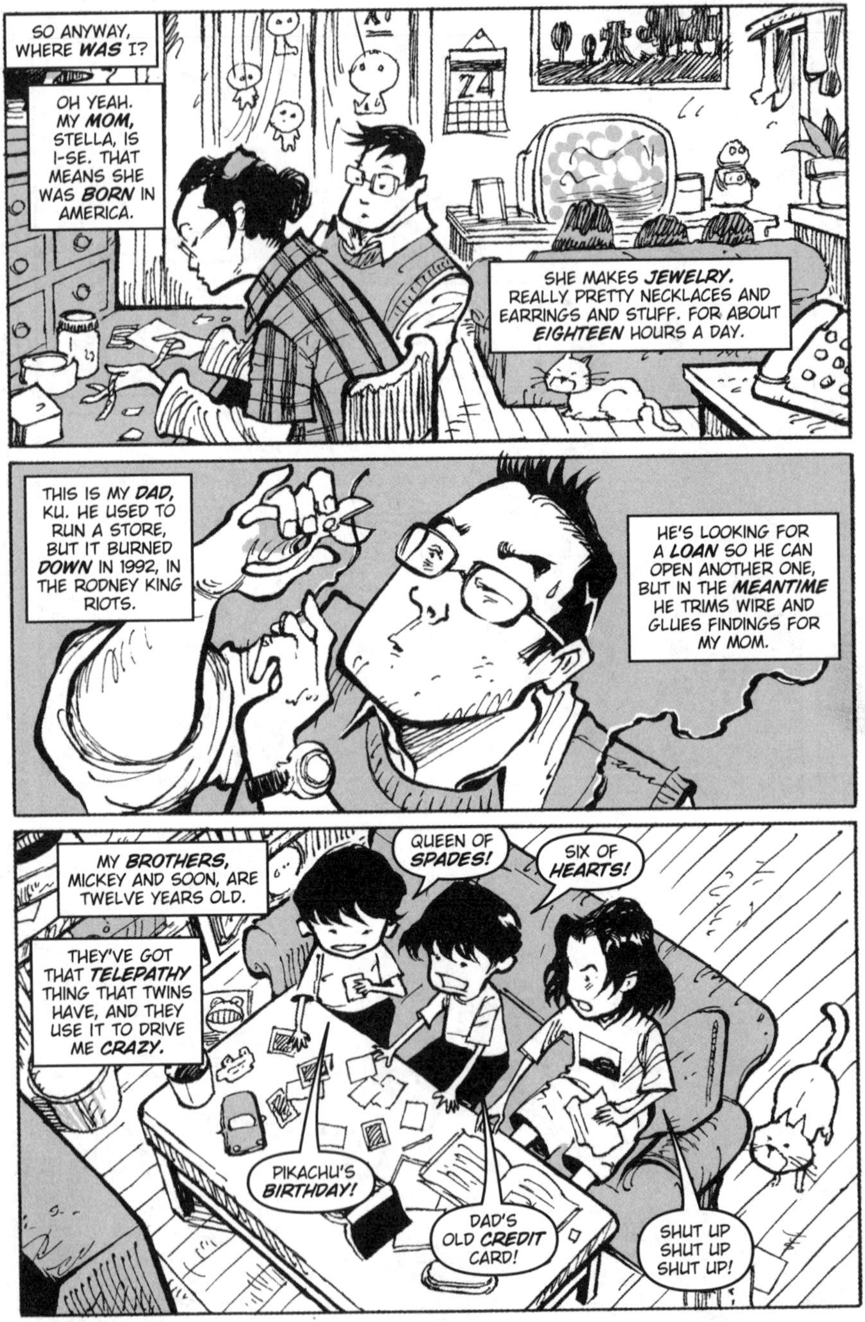
SO ANYWAY, WHERE WAS I?
OH YEAH. MY MOM, STELLA, IS I-SE. THAT MEANS SHE WAS BORN IN AMERICA.
SHE MAKES JEWELRY. REALLY PRETTY NECKLACES AND EARRINGS AND STUFF. FOR ABOUT EIGHTEEN HOURS A DAY.
THIS IS MY DAD, KU. HE USED TO RUN A STORE, BUT IT BURNED DOWN IN 1992, IN THE RODNEY KING RIOTS.
HE'S LOOKING FOR A LOAN SO HE CAN OPEN ANOTHER ONE, BUT IN THE MEANTIME HE TRIMS WIRE AND GLUES FINDINGS FOR MY MOM.
MY BROTHERS, MICKEY AND SOON, ARE TWELVE YEARS OLD.
THEY'VE GOT THAT TELEPATHY THING THAT TWINS HAVE, AND THEY USE IT TO DRIVE ME CRAZY.
QUEEN OF SPADES!
SIX OF HEARTS!
PIKACHU'S BIRTHDAY!
DAD'S OLD CREDIT CARD!
SHUT UP SHUT UP SHUT UP!

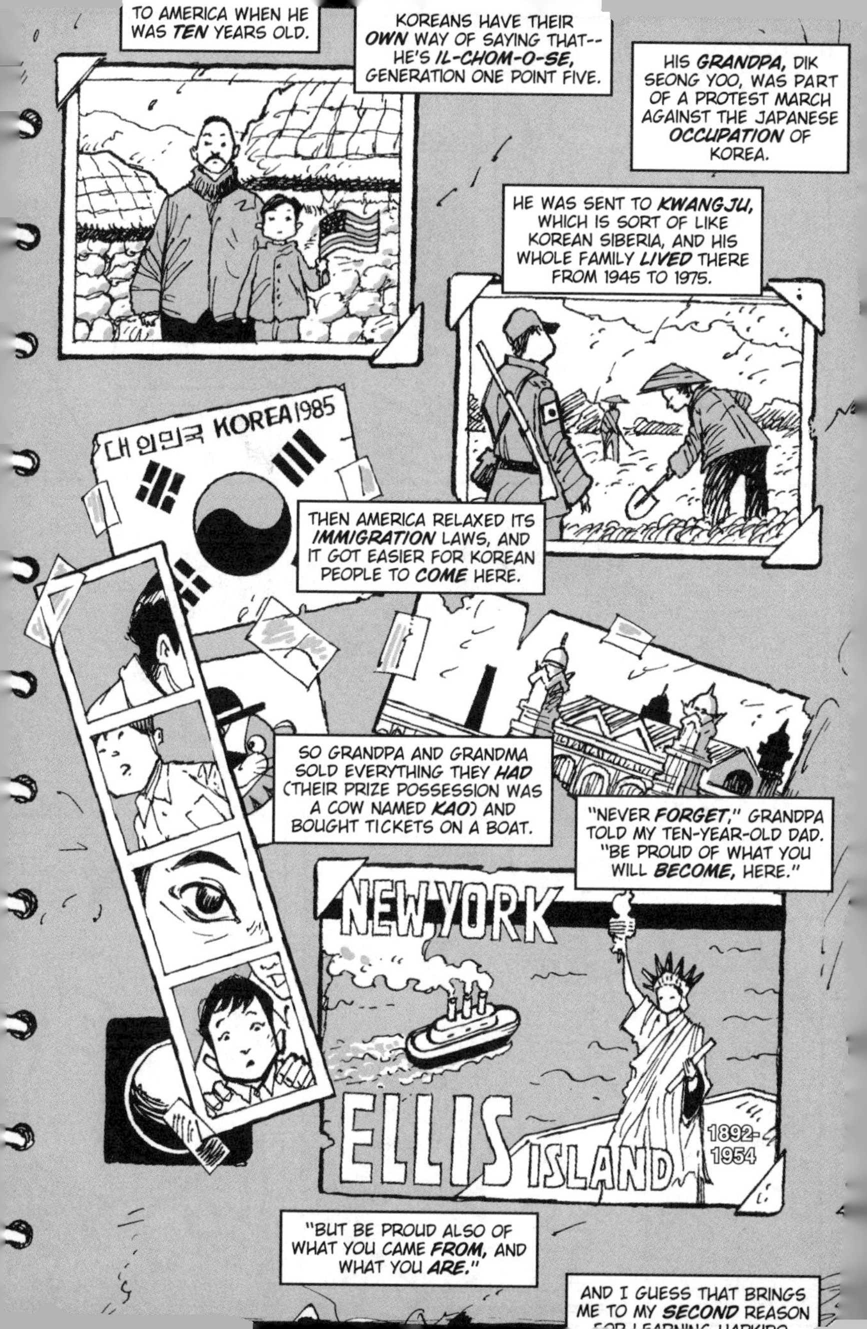
TO AMERICA WHEN HE WAS TEN YEARS OLD.
KOREANS HAVE THEIR OWN WAY OF SAYING THAT-- HE'S IL-CHOM-O-SE, GENERATION ONE POINT FIVE.
HIS GRANDPA, DIK SEONG YOO, WAS PART OF A PROTEST MARCH AGAINST THE JAPANESE OCCUPATION OF KOREA.
HE WAS SENT TO KWANGJU, WHICH IS SORT OF LIKE KOREAN SIBERIA, AND HIS WHOLE FAMILY LIVED THERE FROM 1945 TO 1975.
대의민국 KOREA 1985
THEN AMERICA RELAXED ITS IMMIGRATION LAWS, AND IT GOT EASIER FOR KOREAN PEOPLE TO COME HERE.
SO GRANDPA AND GRANDMA SOLD EVERYTHING THEY HAD (THEIR PRIZE POSSESSION WAS A COW NAMED KAO) AND BOUGHT TICKETS ON A BOAT.
"NEVER FORGET," GRANDPA TOLD MY TEN-YEAR-OLD DAD. "BE PROUD OF WHAT YOU WILL BECOME, HERE."
NEW YORK
ELLIS ISLAND
1892-1954
"BUT BE PROUD ALSO OF WHAT YOU CAME FROM, AND WHAT YOU ARE."
AND I GUESS THAT BRINGS ME TO MY SECOND REASON

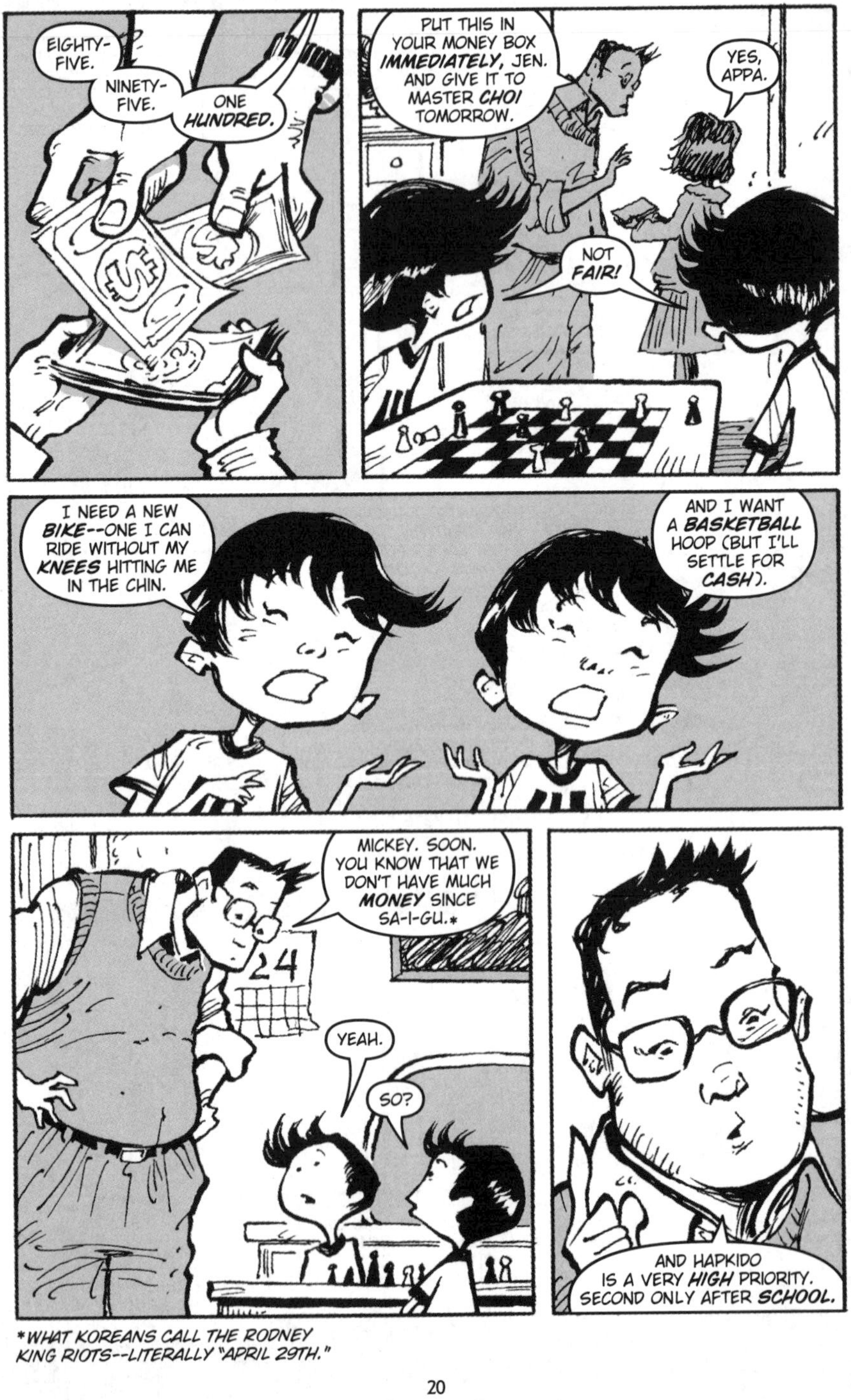
EIGHTY-FIVE.
NINETY-FIVE.
ONE HUNDRED.
PUT THIS IN YOUR MONEY BOX IMMEDIATELY, JEN. AND GIVE IT TO MASTER CHOI TOMORROW.
YES, APPA.
NOT FAIR!
I NEED A NEW BIKE--ONE I CAN RIDE WITHOUT MY KNEES HITTING ME IN THE CHIN.
AND I WANT A BASKETBALL HOOP (BUT I'LL SETTLE FOR CASH).
MICKEY. SOON. YOU KNOW THAT WE DON'T HAVE MUCH MONEY SINCE SA-I-GU.*
24
YEAH.
SO?
AND HAPKIDO IS A VERY HIGH PRIORITY. SECOND ONLY AFTER SCHOOL.

*WHAT KOREANS CALL THE RODNEY KING RIOTS--LITERALLY "APRIL 29TH."

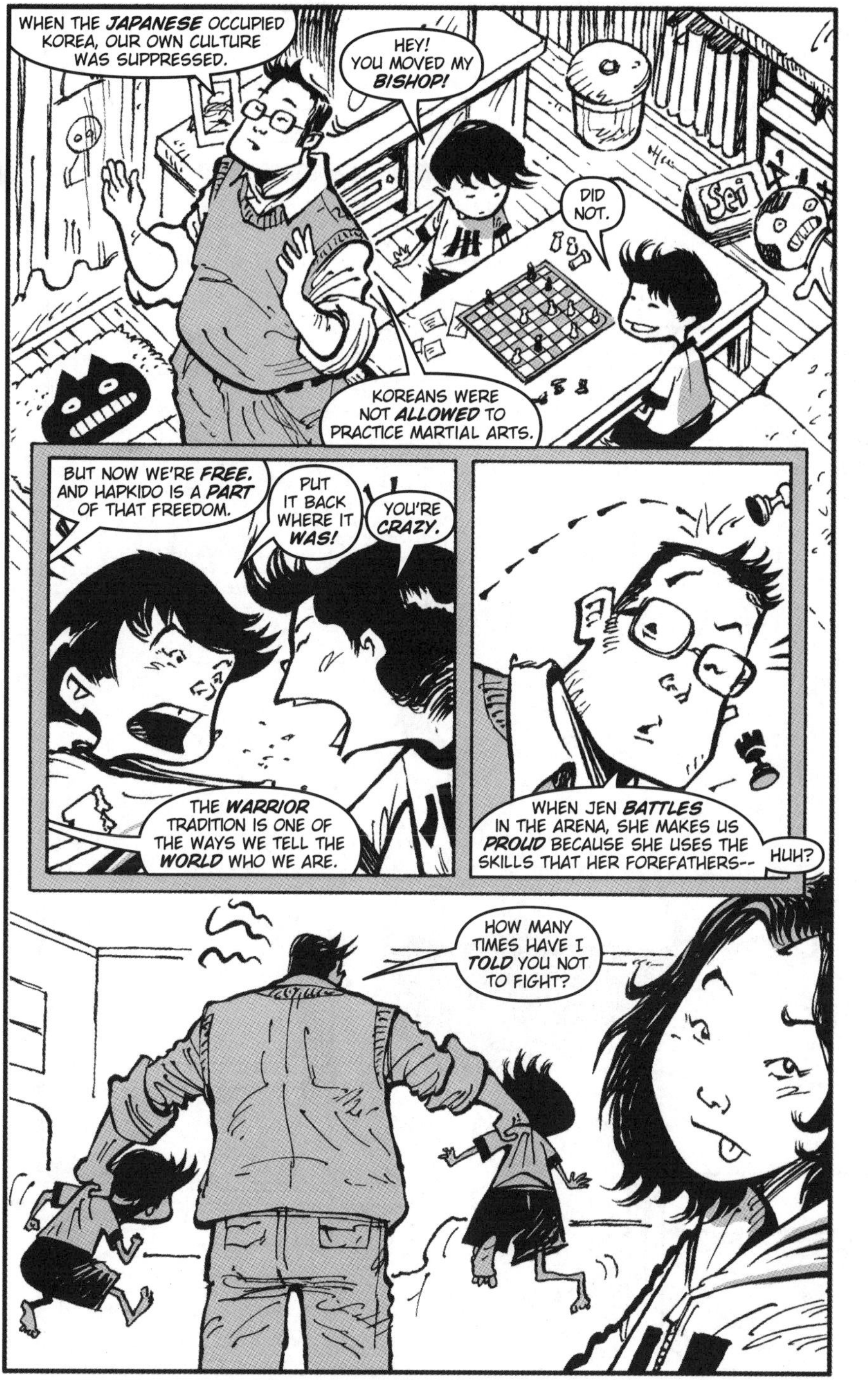
WHEN THE JAPANESE OCCUPIED KOREA, OUR OWN CULTURE WAS SUPPRESSED.
HEY! YOU MOVED MY BISHOP!
DID NOT.
KOREANS WERE NOT ALLOWED TO PRACTICE MARTIAL ARTS.
BUT NOW WE'RE FREE. AND HAPKIDO IS A PART OF THAT FREEDOM.
PUT IT BACK WHERE IT WAS!
YOU'RE CRAZY.
THE WARRIOR TRADITION IS ONE OF THE WAYS WE TELL THE WORLD WHO WE ARE.
WHEN JEN BATTLES IN THE ARENA, SHE MAKES US PROUD BECAUSE SHE USES THE SKILLS THAT HER FOREFATHERS--
HUH?
HOW MANY TIMES HAVE I TOLD YOU NOT TO FIGHT?

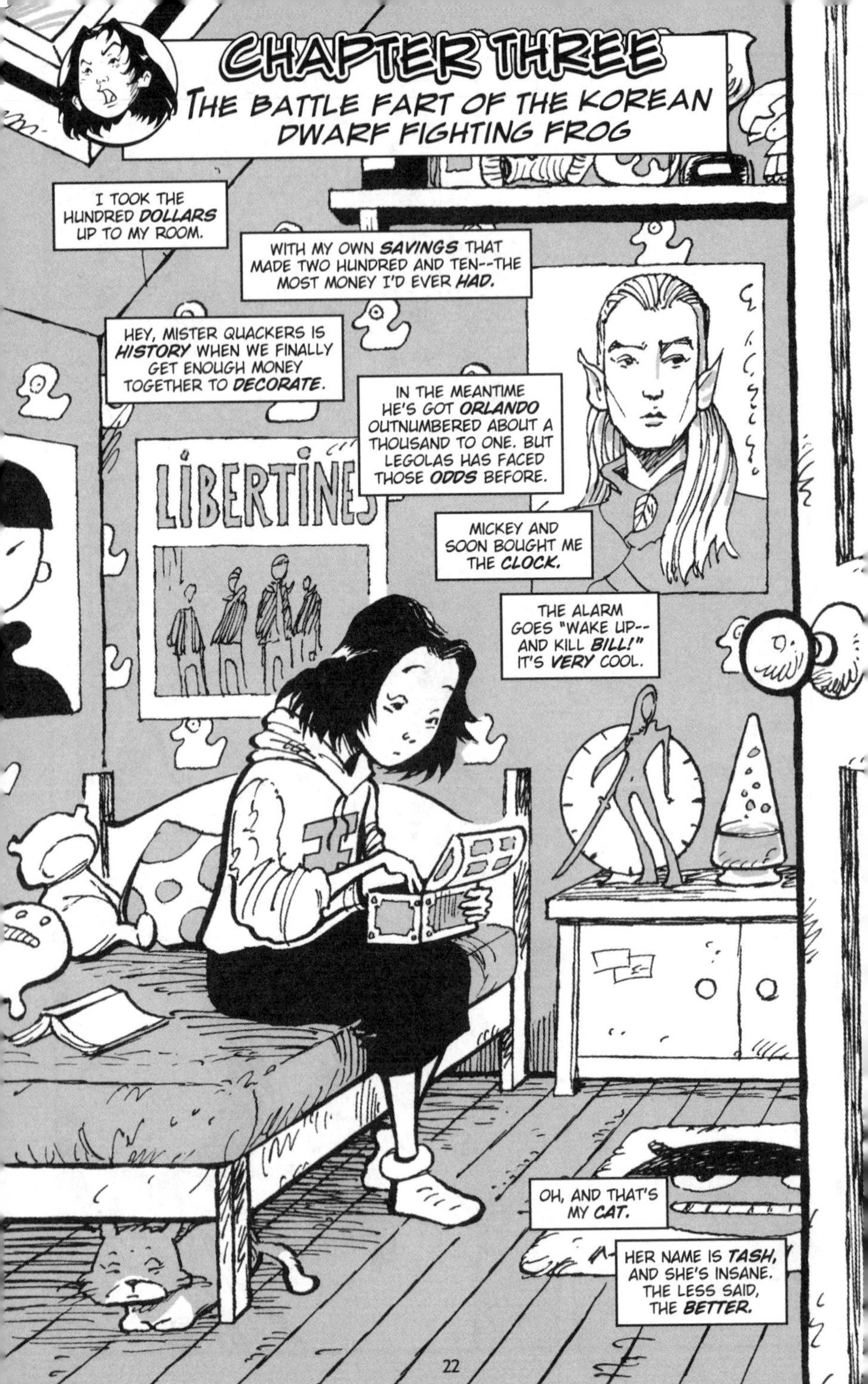
CHAPTER THREE
THE BATTLE FART OF THE KOREAN DWARF FIGHTING FROG
I TOOK THE HUNDRED DOLLARS UP TO MY ROOM.
WITH MY OWN SAVINGS THAT MADE TWO HUNDRED AND TEN--THE MOST MONEY I'D EVER HAD.
HEY, MISTER QUACKERS IS HISTORY WHEN WE FINALLY GET ENOUGH MONEY TOGETHER TO DECORATE.
IN THE MEANTIME HE'S GOT ORLANDO OUTNUMBERED ABOUT A THOUSAND TO ONE. BUT LEGOLAS HAS FACED THOSE ODDS BEFORE.
LIBERTINES
MICKEY AND SOON BOUGHT ME THE CLOCK.
THE ALARM GOES "WAKE UP--AND KILL BILL!" IT'S VERY COOL.
OH, AND THAT'S MY CAT.
HER NAME IS TASH, AND SHE'S INSANE. THE LESS SAID, THE BETTER.

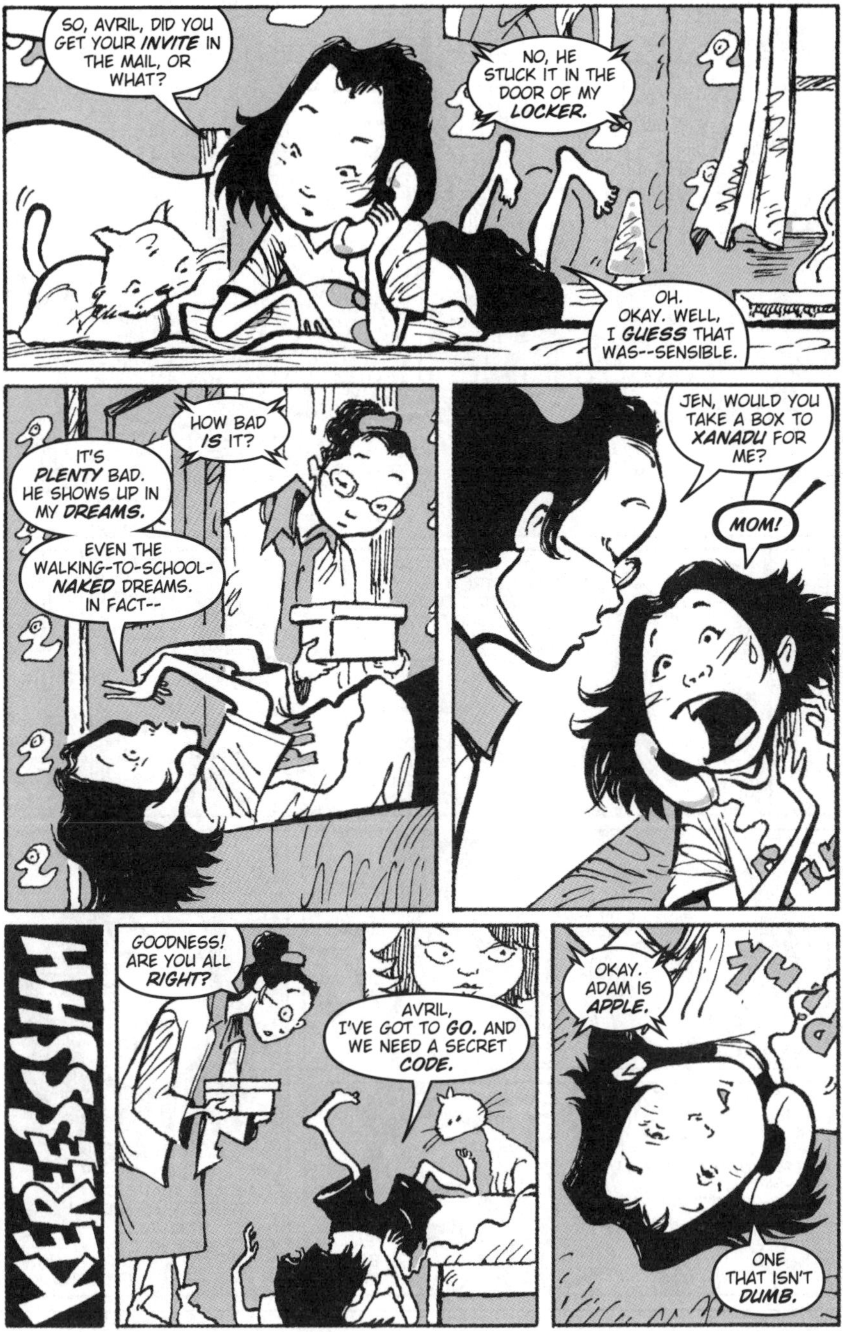
SO, AVRIL, DID YOU GET YOUR INVITE IN THE MAIL, OR WHAT?
NO, HE STUCK IT IN THE DOOR OF MY LOCKER.
OH. OKAY. WELL, I GUESS THAT WAS--SENSIBLE.
HOW BAD IS IT?
IT'S PLENTY BAD. HE SHOWS UP IN MY DREAMS.
EVEN THE WALKING-TO-SCHOOL-NAKED DREAMS. IN FACT--
JEN, WOULD YOU TAKE A BOX TO XANADU FOR ME?
MOM!
KEREESSHH
GOODNESS! ARE YOU ALL RIGHT?
AVRIL, I'VE GOT TO GO. AND WE NEED A SECRET CODE.
OKAY. ADAM IS APPLE.
ONE THAT ISN'T DUMB.

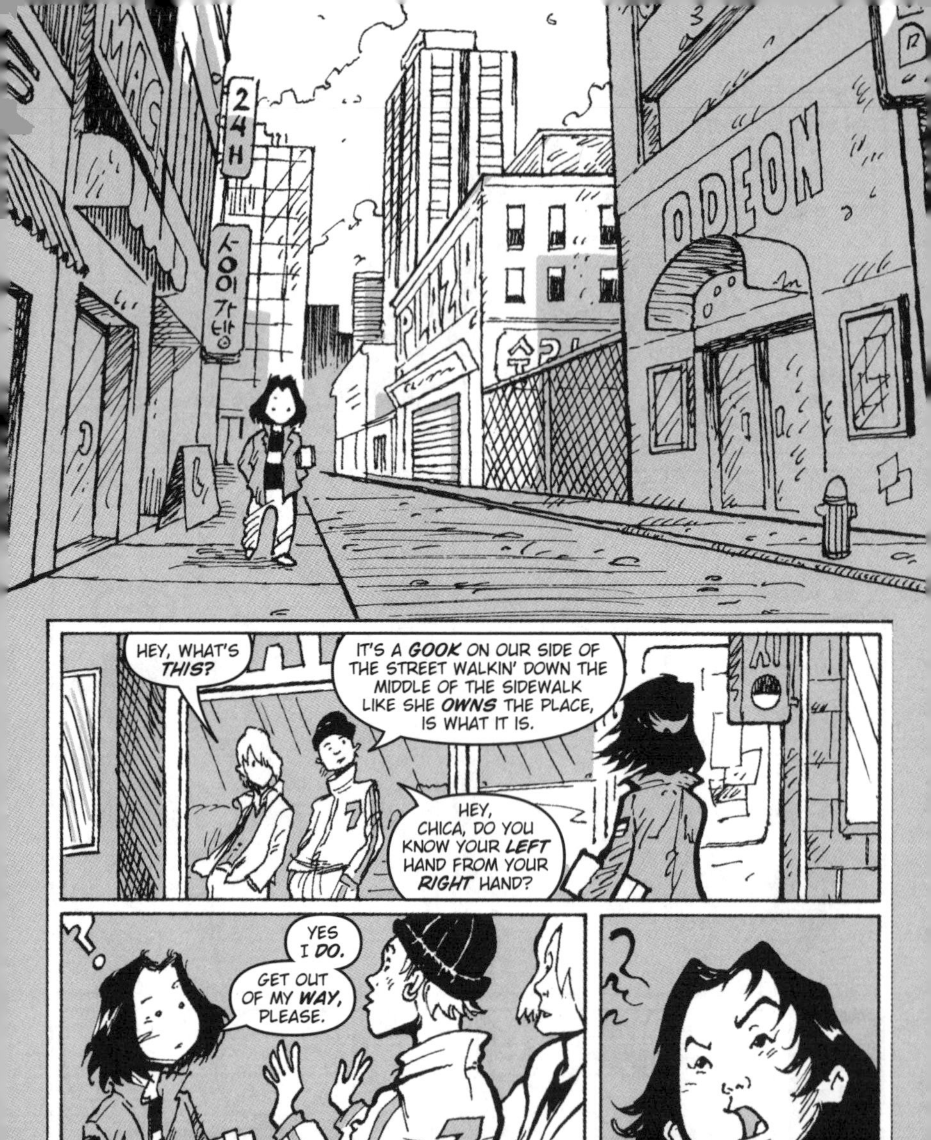
ODEON
HEY, WHAT'S *THIS?*
IT'S A *GOOK* ON OUR SIDE OF THE STREET WALKIN' DOWN THE MIDDLE OF THE SIDEWALK LIKE SHE *OWNS* THE PLACE, IS WHAT IT IS.
HEY, CHICA, DO YOU KNOW YOUR *LEFT* HAND FROM YOUR *RIGHT* HAND?
YES I *DO.*
GET OUT OF MY *WAY,* PLEASE.
SO YOU OUGHT TO BE ABLE TO TELL THE *GOOK* SIDE OF THE STREET FROM *OUR* SIDE...
COMPRENDE?
YEAH. *YOU* BELONG OVER THERE.
I'M GOING TO A STORE THAT'S ON *THIS* SIDE OF THE STREET.
AND YOU DON'T *OWN* THE SIDEWALK.

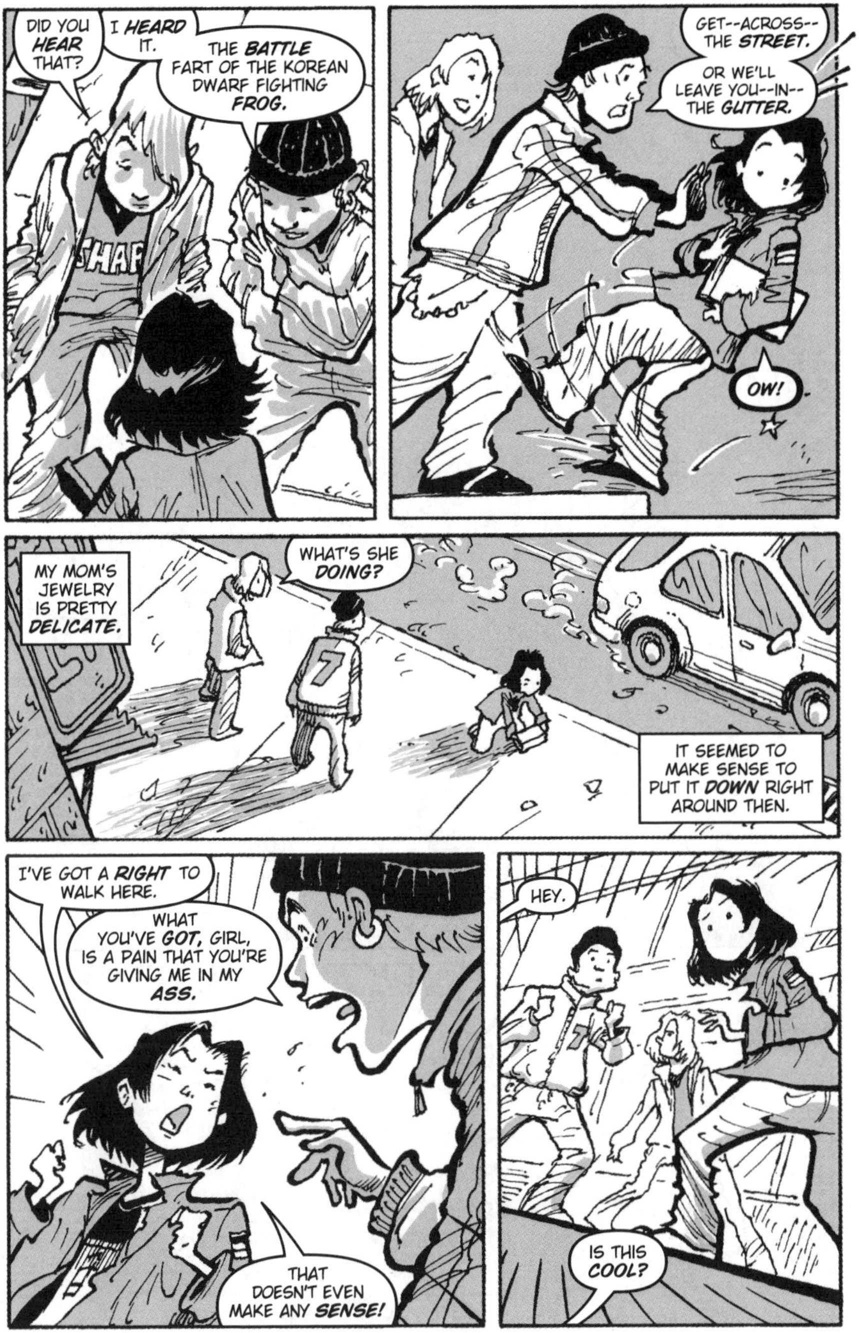
DID YOU HEAR THAT?
I HEARD IT.
THE BATTLE FART OF THE KOREAN DWARF FIGHTING FROG.
GET--ACROSS-- THE STREET.
OR WE'LL LEAVE YOU--IN-- THE GUTTER.
OW!
MY MOM'S JEWELRY IS PRETTY DELICATE.
WHAT'S SHE DOING?
IT SEEMED TO MAKE SENSE TO PUT IT DOWN RIGHT AROUND THEN.
I'VE GOT A RIGHT TO WALK HERE.
WHAT YOU'VE GOT, GIRL, IS A PAIN THAT YOU'RE GIVING ME IN MY ASS.
THAT DOESN'T EVEN MAKE ANY SENSE!
HEY.
IS THIS COOL?

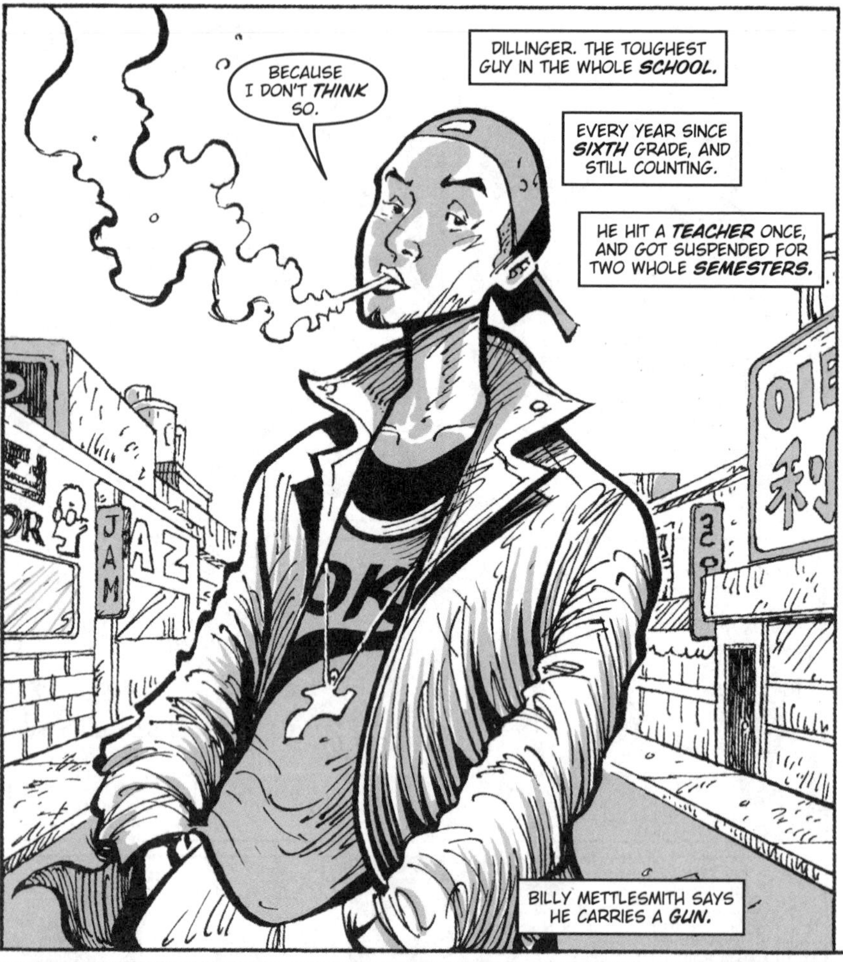
BECAUSE I DON'T THINK SO.
DILLINGER. THE TOUGHEST GUY IN THE WHOLE SCHOOL.
EVERY YEAR SINCE SIXTH GRADE, AND STILL COUNTING.
HE HIT A TEACHER ONCE, AND GOT SUSPENDED FOR TWO WHOLE SEMESTERS.
JAM
BILLY METTLESMITH SAYS HE CARRIES A GUN.

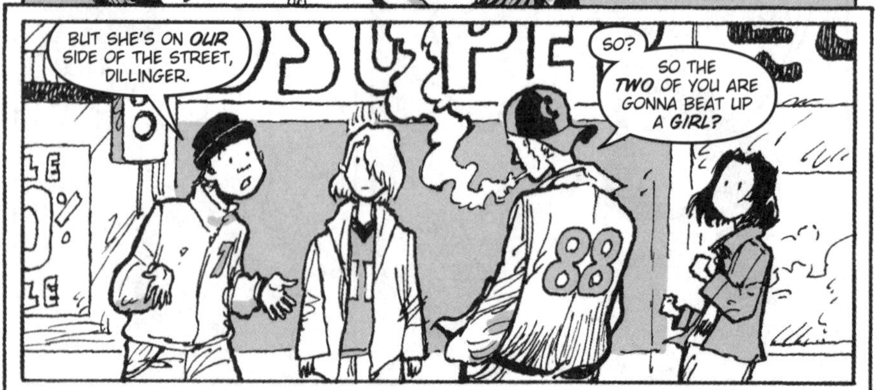
BUT SHE'S ON OUR SIDE OF THE STREET, DILLINGER.
SO?
SO THE TWO OF YOU ARE GONNA BEAT UP A GIRL?
88

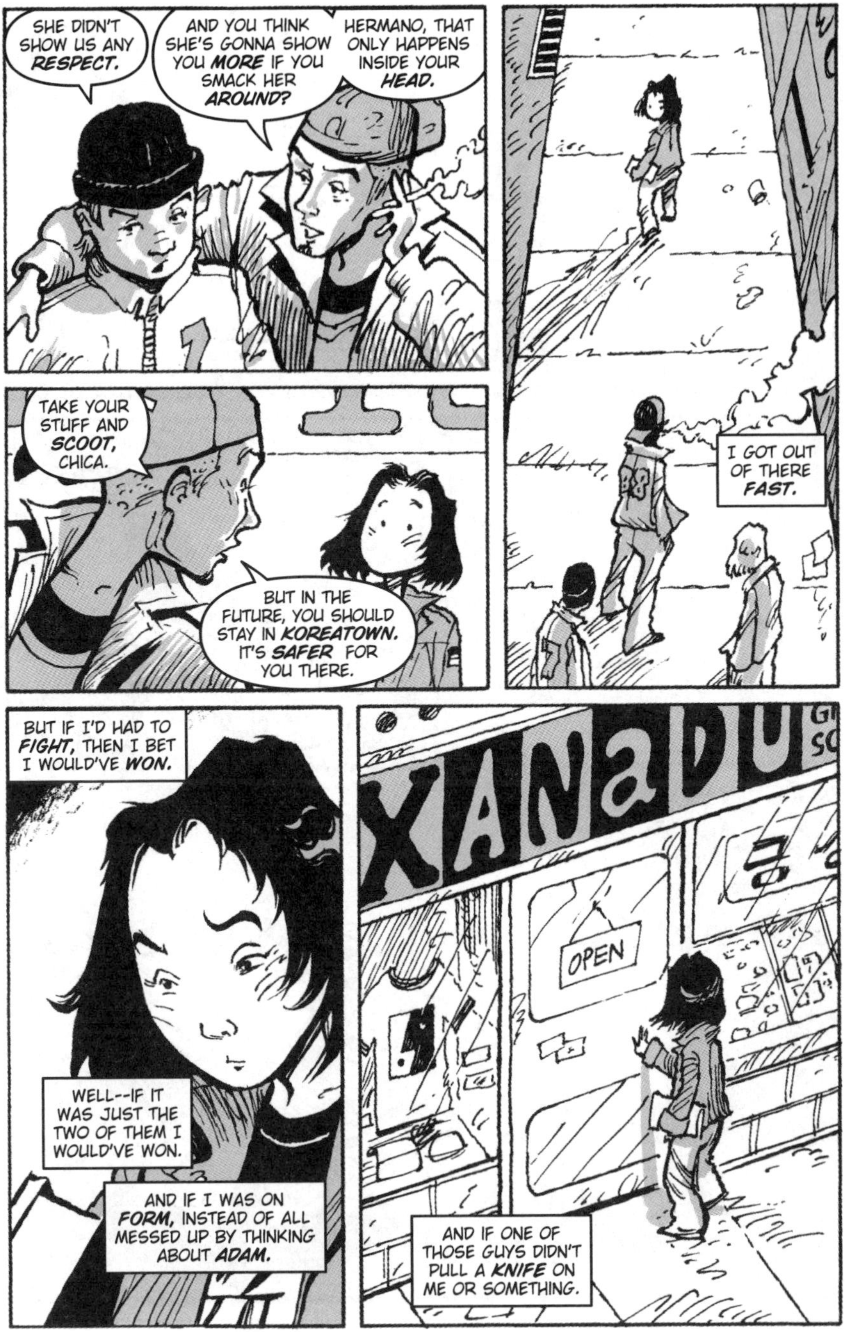
SHE DIDN'T SHOW US ANY RESPECT.
AND YOU THINK SHE'S GONNA SHOW YOU MORE IF YOU SMACK HER AROUND?
HERMANO, THAT ONLY HAPPENS INSIDE YOUR HEAD.
TAKE YOUR STUFF AND SCOOT, CHICA.
BUT IN THE FUTURE, YOU SHOULD STAY IN KOREATOWN. IT'S SAFER FOR YOU THERE.
I GOT OUT OF THERE FAST.
BUT IF I'D HAD TO FIGHT, THEN I BET I WOULD'VE WON.
WELL--IF IT WAS JUST THE TWO OF THEM I WOULD'VE WON.
AND IF I WAS ON FORM, INSTEAD OF ALL MESSED UP BY THINKING ABOUT ADAM.
XANADU
OPEN
AND IF ONE OF THOSE GUYS DIDN'T PULL A KNIFE ON ME OR SOMETHING.

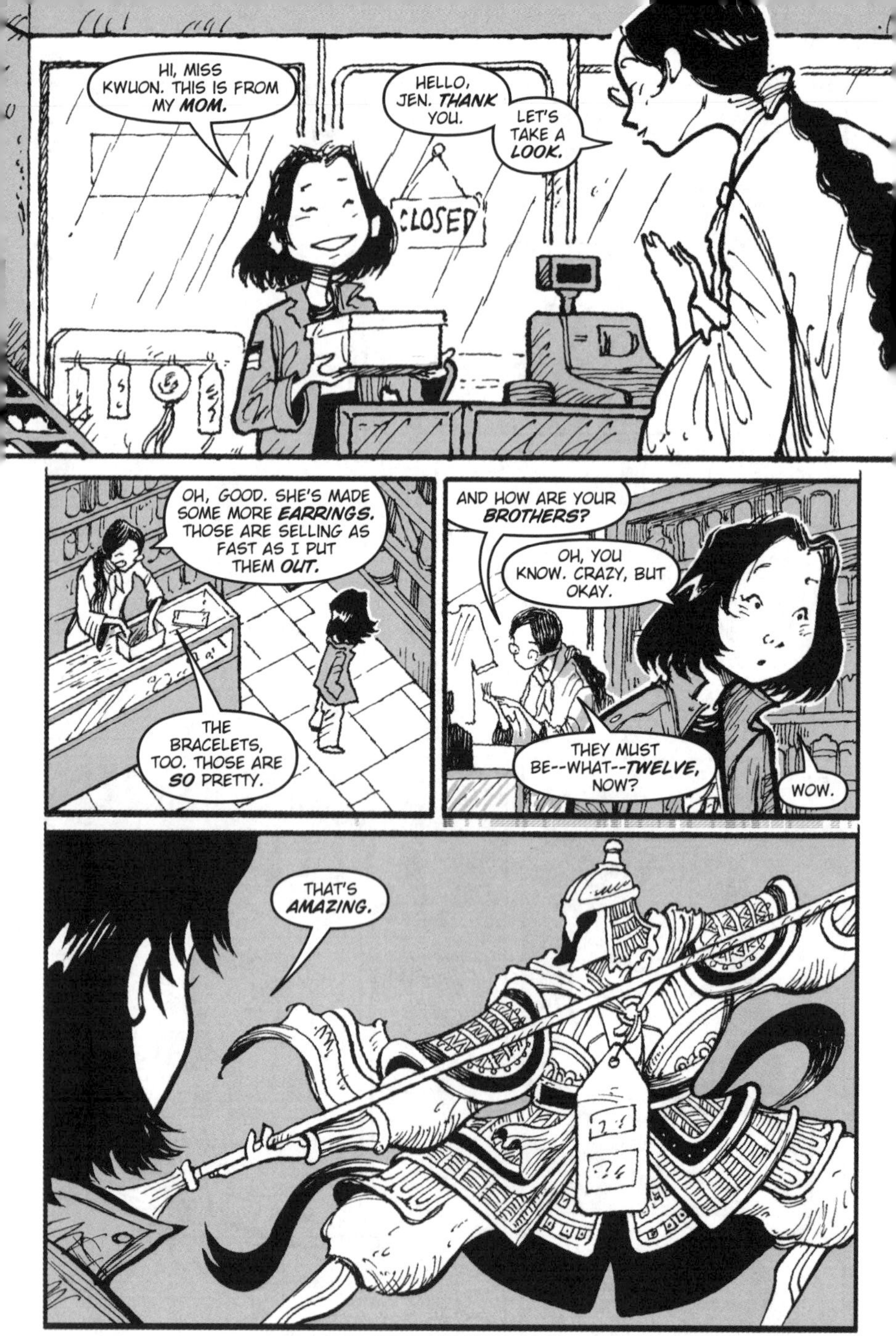
HI, MISS KWUON. THIS IS FROM MY **MOM.**
HELLO, JEN. ***THANK*** YOU.
LET'S TAKE A ***LOOK.***
CLOSED
OH, GOOD. SHE'S MADE SOME MORE ***EARRINGS.*** THOSE ARE SELLING AS FAST AS I PUT THEM ***OUT.***
THE BRACELETS, TOO. THOSE ARE ***SO*** PRETTY.
AND HOW ARE YOUR ***BROTHERS?***
OH, YOU KNOW. CRAZY, BUT OKAY.
THEY MUST BE--WHAT--***TWELVE,*** NOW?
WOW.
THAT'S ***AMAZING.***

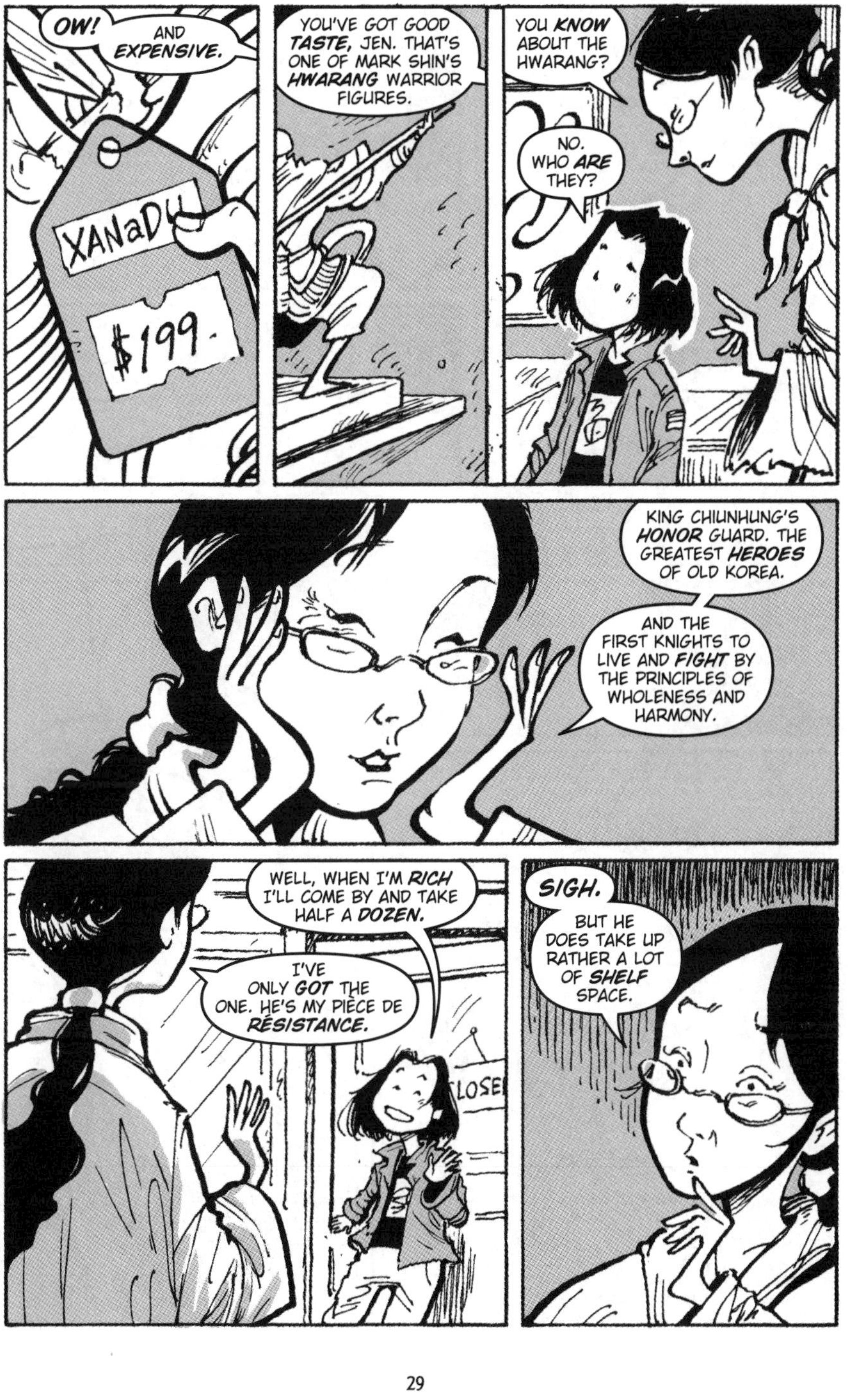
OW!
AND EXPENSIVE.
XANaDU
$199
YOU'VE GOT GOOD TASTE, JEN. THAT'S ONE OF MARK SHIN'S HWARANG WARRIOR FIGURES.
YOU KNOW ABOUT THE HWARANG?
NO. WHO ARE THEY?
KING CHIUNHUNG'S HONOR GUARD. THE GREATEST HEROES OF OLD KOREA.
AND THE FIRST KNIGHTS TO LIVE AND FIGHT BY THE PRINCIPLES OF WHOLENESS AND HARMONY.
WELL, WHEN I'M RICH I'LL COME BY AND TAKE HALF A DOZEN.
I'VE ONLY GOT THE ONE. HE'S MY PIÈCE DE RÉSISTANCE.
SIGH.
BUT HE DOES TAKE UP RATHER A LOT OF SHELF SPACE.

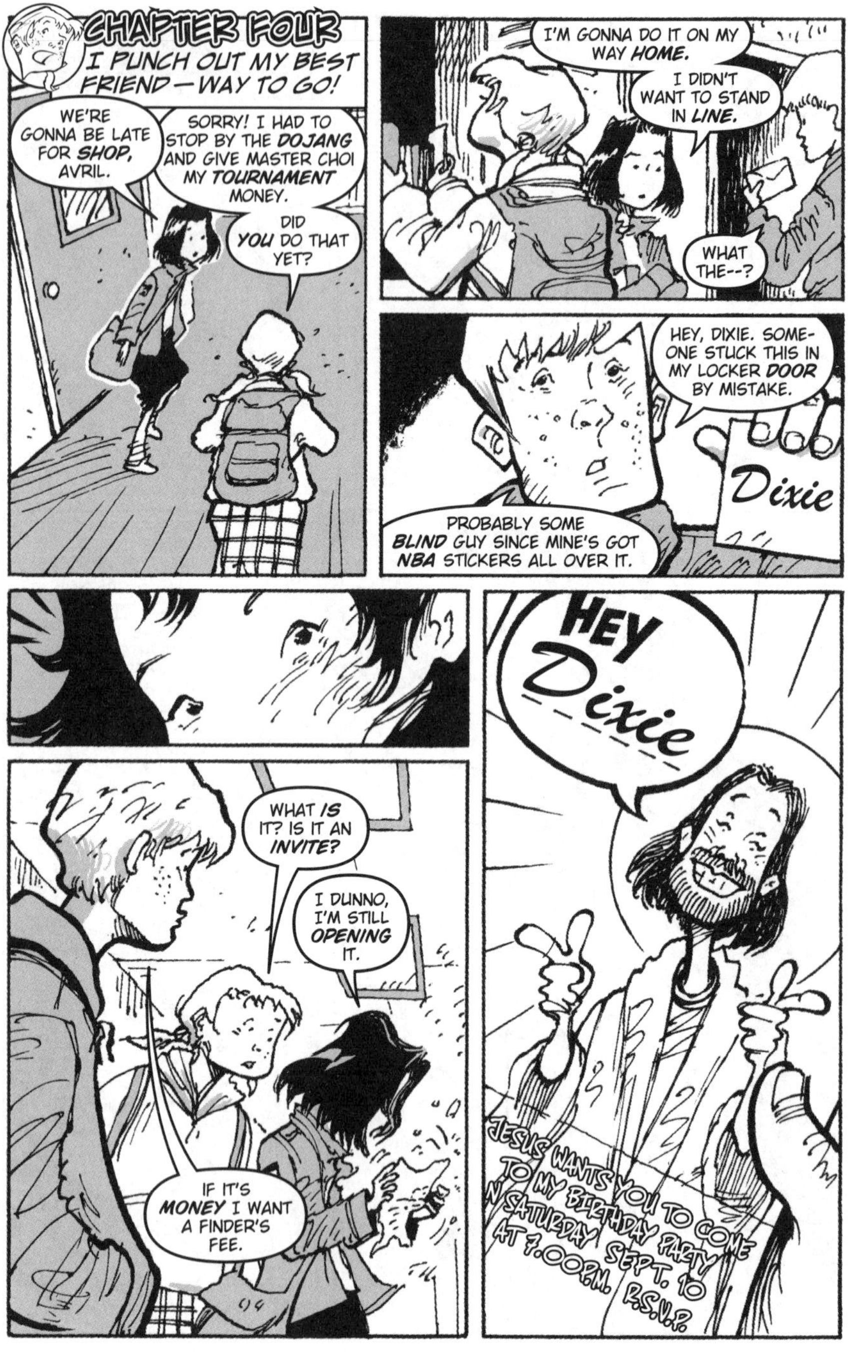
CHAPTER FOUR
I PUNCH OUT MY BEST FRIEND—WAY TO GO!
WE'RE GONNA BE LATE FOR SHOP, AVRIL.
SORRY! I HAD TO STOP BY THE DOJANG AND GIVE MASTER CHOI MY TOURNAMENT MONEY.
DID YOU DO THAT YET?
I'M GONNA DO IT ON MY WAY HOME.
I DIDN'T WANT TO STAND IN LINE.
WHAT THE--?
HEY, DIXIE. SOMEONE STUCK THIS IN MY LOCKER DOOR BY MISTAKE.
Dixie
PROBABLY SOME BLIND GUY SINCE MINE'S GOT NBA STICKERS ALL OVER IT.
WHAT IS IT? IS IT AN INVITE?
I DUNNO, I'M STILL OPENING IT.
IF IT'S MONEY I WANT A FINDER'S FEE.
HEY Dixie
JESUS WANTS YOU TO COME TO MY BIRTHDAY PARTY
N SATURDAY SEPT. 10
AT 7:00P.M. R.S.V.P.

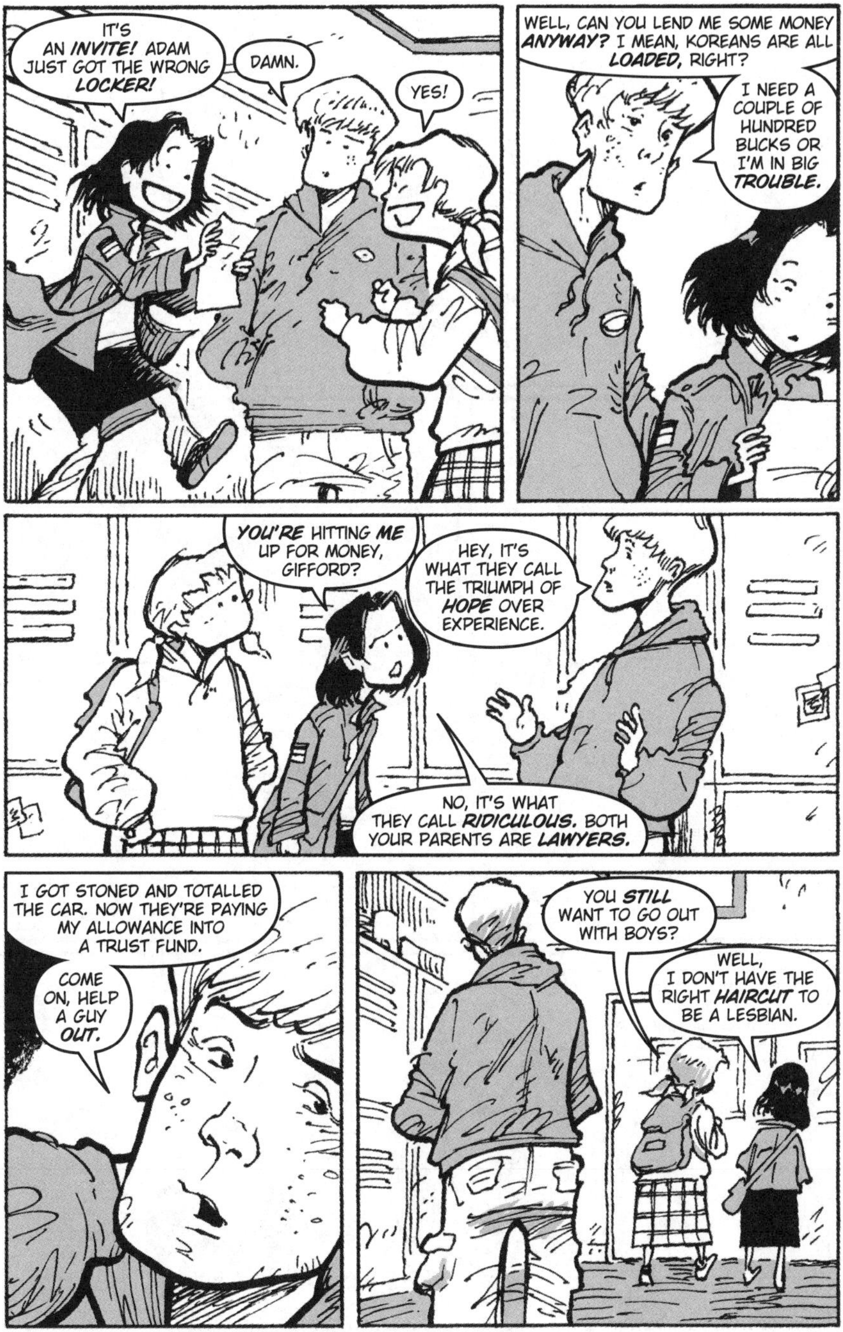
IT'S AN INVITE! ADAM JUST GOT THE WRONG LOCKER!
DAMN.
YES!
WELL, CAN YOU LEND ME SOME MONEY ANYWAY? I MEAN, KOREANS ARE ALL LOADED, RIGHT?
I NEED A COUPLE OF HUNDRED BUCKS OR I'M IN BIG TROUBLE.
YOU'RE HITTING ME UP FOR MONEY, GIFFORD?
HEY, IT'S WHAT THEY CALL THE TRIUMPH OF HOPE OVER EXPERIENCE.
NO, IT'S WHAT THEY CALL RIDICULOUS. BOTH YOUR PARENTS ARE LAWYERS.
I GOT STONED AND TOTALLED THE CAR. NOW THEY'RE PAYING MY ALLOWANCE INTO A TRUST FUND.
COME ON, HELP A GUY OUT.
YOU STILL WANT TO GO OUT WITH BOYS?
WELL, I DON'T HAVE THE RIGHT HAIRCUT TO BE A LESBIAN.

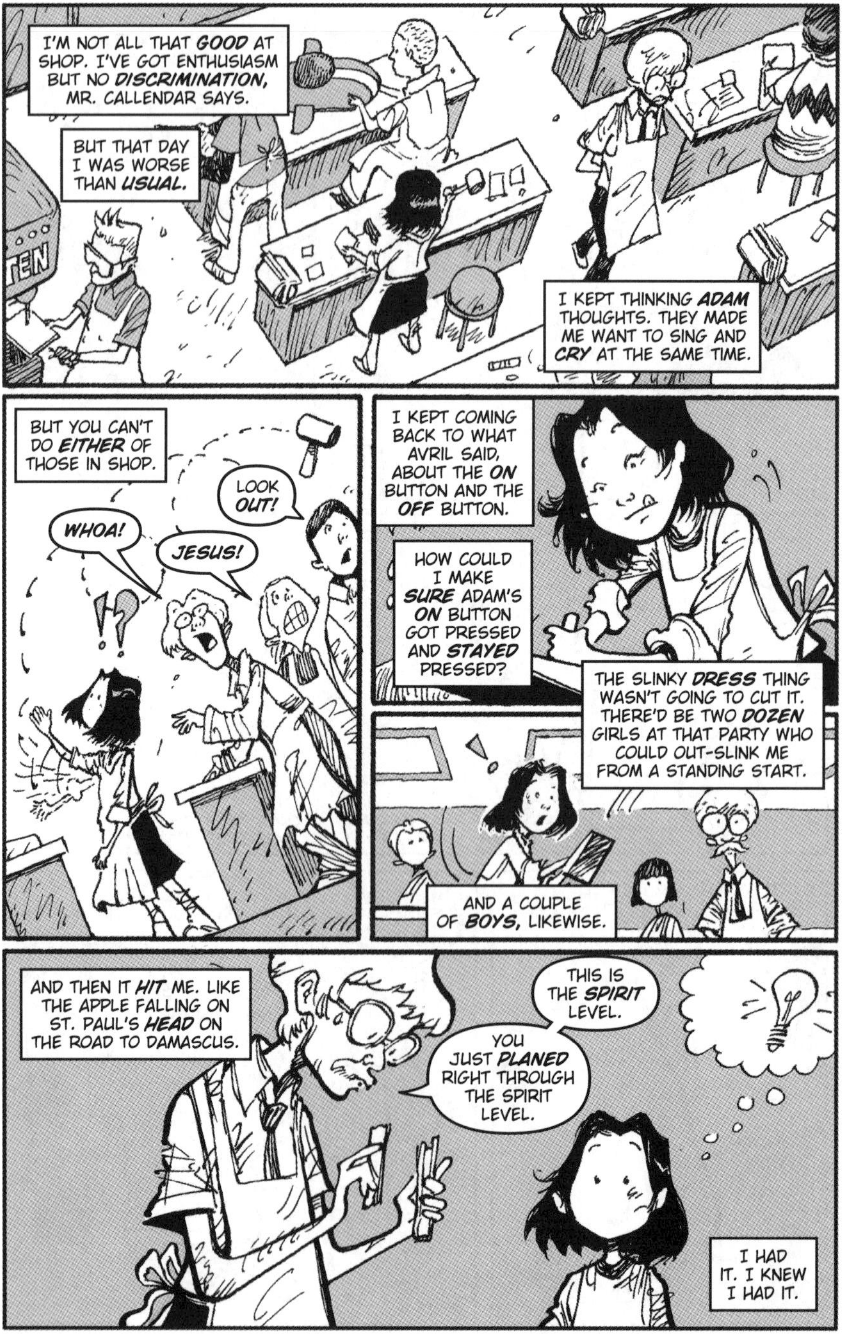

I'M NOT ALL THAT GOOD AT SHOP. I'VE GOT ENTHUSIASM BUT NO DISCRIMINATION, MR. CALLENDAR SAYS.
BUT THAT DAY I WAS WORSE THAN USUAL.
I KEPT THINKING ADAM THOUGHTS. THEY MADE ME WANT TO SING AND CRY AT THE SAME TIME.
BUT YOU CAN'T DO EITHER OF THOSE IN SHOP.
LOOK OUT!
WHOA!
JESUS!
I KEPT COMING BACK TO WHAT AVRIL SAID, ABOUT THE ON BUTTON AND THE OFF BUTTON.
HOW COULD I MAKE SURE ADAM'S ON BUTTON GOT PRESSED AND STAYED PRESSED?
THE SLINKY DRESS THING WASN'T GOING TO CUT IT. THERE'D BE TWO DOZEN GIRLS AT THAT PARTY WHO COULD OUT-SLINK ME FROM A STANDING START.
AND A COUPLE OF BOYS, LIKEWISE.
AND THEN IT HIT ME. LIKE THE APPLE FALLING ON ST. PAUL'S HEAD ON THE ROAD TO DAMASCUS.
THIS IS THE SPIRIT LEVEL.
YOU JUST PLANED RIGHT THROUGH THE SPIRIT LEVEL.
I HAD IT. I KNEW I HAD IT.

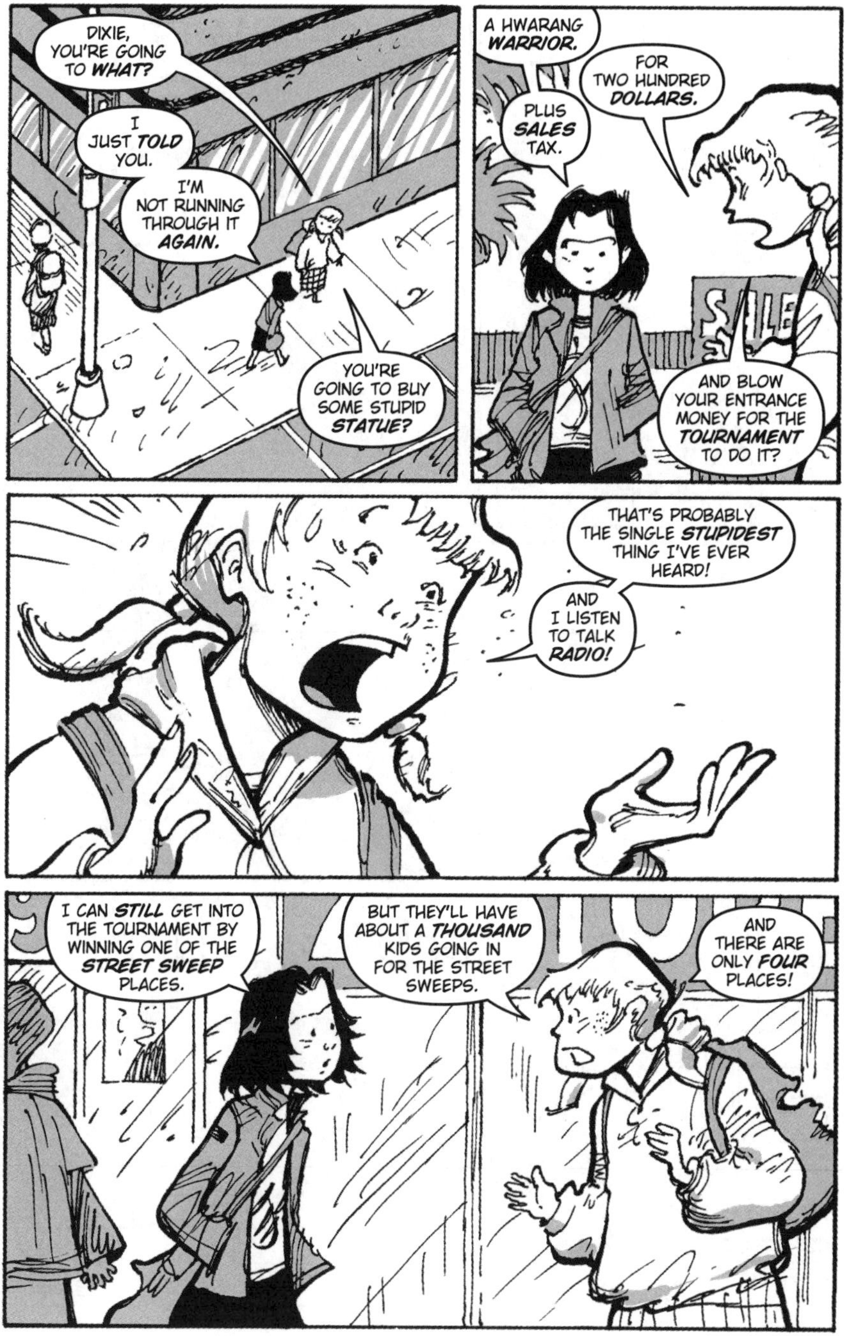
DIXIE, YOU'RE GOING TO WHAT?
I JUST TOLD YOU.
I'M NOT RUNNING THROUGH IT AGAIN.
YOU'RE GOING TO BUY SOME STUPID STATUE?
A HWARANG WARRIOR.
PLUS SALES TAX.
FOR TWO HUNDRED DOLLARS.
AND BLOW YOUR ENTRANCE MONEY FOR THE TOURNAMENT TO DO IT?
THAT'S PROBABLY THE SINGLE STUPIDEST THING I'VE EVER HEARD!
AND I LISTEN TO TALK RADIO!
I CAN STILL GET INTO THE TOURNAMENT BY WINNING ONE OF THE STREET SWEEP PLACES.
BUT THEY'LL HAVE ABOUT A THOUSAND KIDS GOING IN FOR THE STREET SWEEPS.
AND THERE ARE ONLY FOUR PLACES!

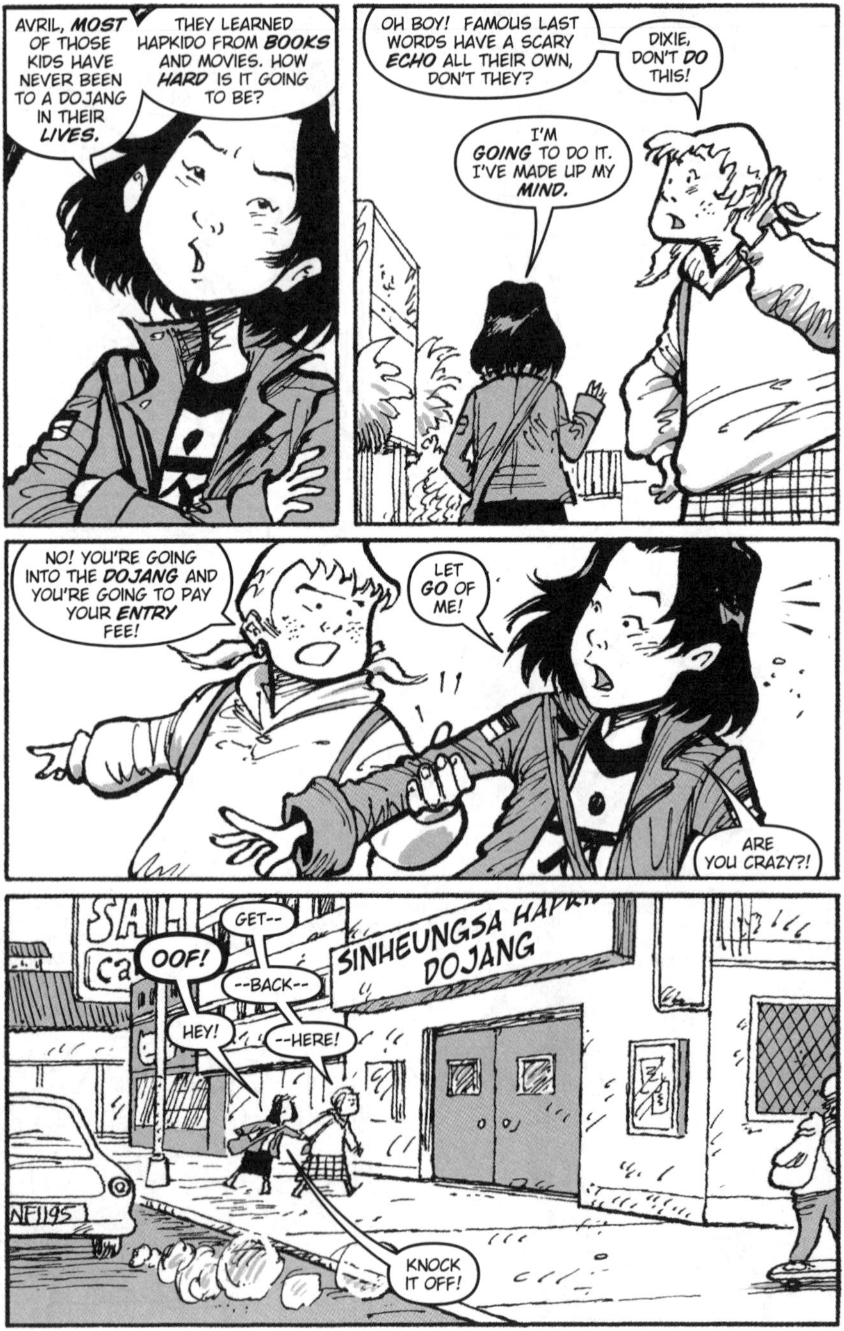
AVRIL, MOST OF THOSE KIDS HAVE NEVER BEEN TO A DOJANG IN THEIR LIVES.
THEY LEARNED HAPKIDO FROM BOOKS AND MOVIES. HOW HARD IS IT GOING TO BE?
OH BOY! FAMOUS LAST WORDS HAVE A SCARY ECHO ALL THEIR OWN, DON'T THEY?
DIXIE, DON'T DO THIS!
I'M GOING TO DO IT. I'VE MADE UP MY MIND.
NO! YOU'RE GOING INTO THE DOJANG AND YOU'RE GOING TO PAY YOUR ENTRY FEE!
LET GO OF ME!
ARE YOU CRAZY?!
SINHEUNGSA HAPKI
DOJANG
GET--
OOF!
--BACK--
HEY!
--HERE!
NF1195
KNOCK IT OFF!

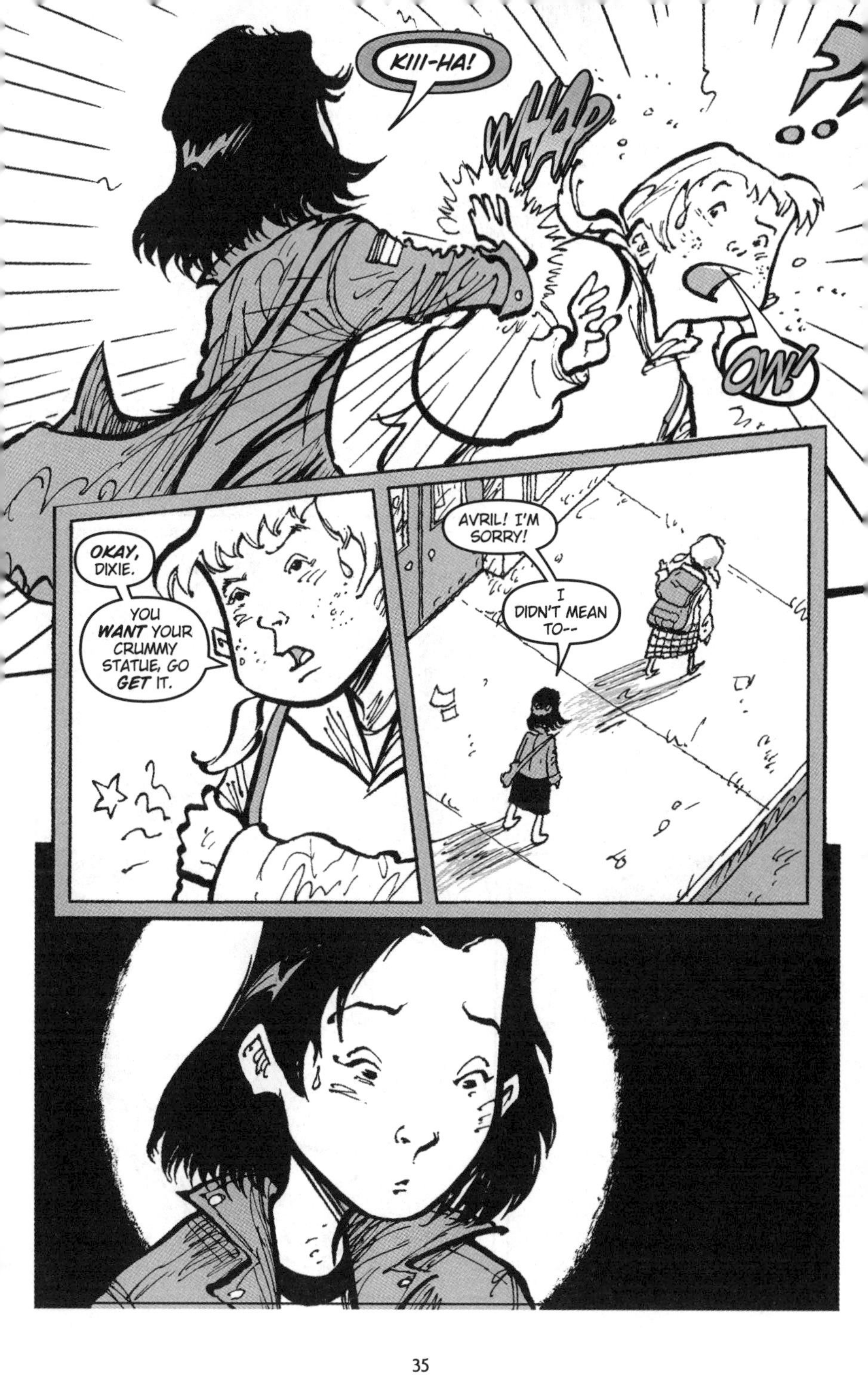
KIII-HA!
WHAP
?!
OW!
OKAY, DIXIE.
YOU WANT YOUR CRUMMY STATUE, GO GET IT.
AVRIL! I'M SORRY!
I DIDN'T MEAN TO--

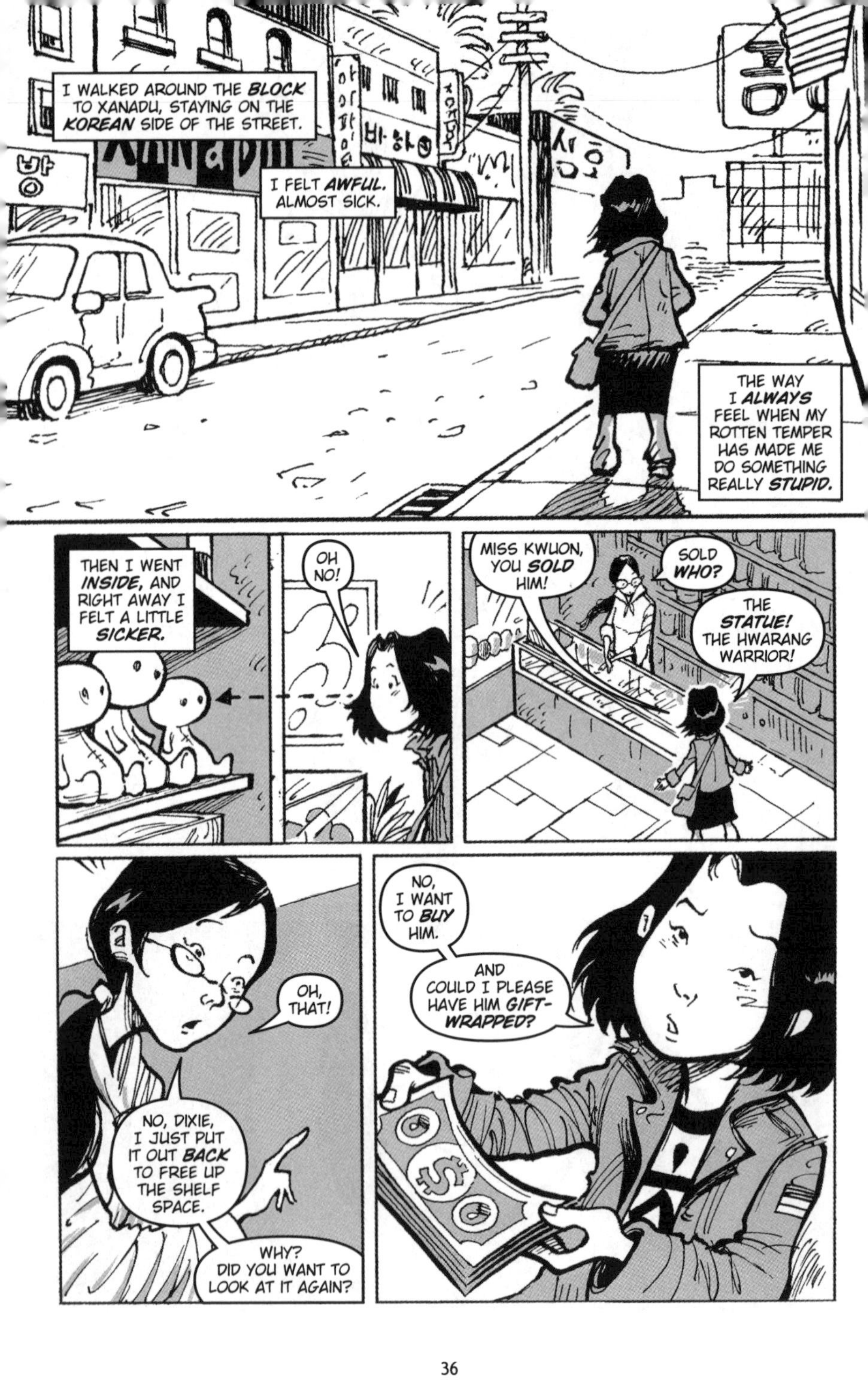
I WALKED AROUND THE BLOCK TO XANADU, STAYING ON THE KOREAN SIDE OF THE STREET.
I FELT AWFUL. ALMOST SICK.
THE WAY I ALWAYS FEEL WHEN MY ROTTEN TEMPER HAS MADE ME DO SOMETHING REALLY STUPID.
THEN I WENT INSIDE, AND RIGHT AWAY I FELT A LITTLE SICKER.
OH NO!
MISS KWUON, YOU SOLD HIM!
SOLD WHO?
THE STATUE! THE HWARANG WARRIOR!
OH, THAT!
NO, DIXIE, I JUST PUT IT OUT BACK TO FREE UP THE SHELF SPACE.
WHY? DID YOU WANT TO LOOK AT IT AGAIN?
NO, I WANT TO BUY HIM.
AND COULD I PLEASE HAVE HIM GIFT-WRAPPED?

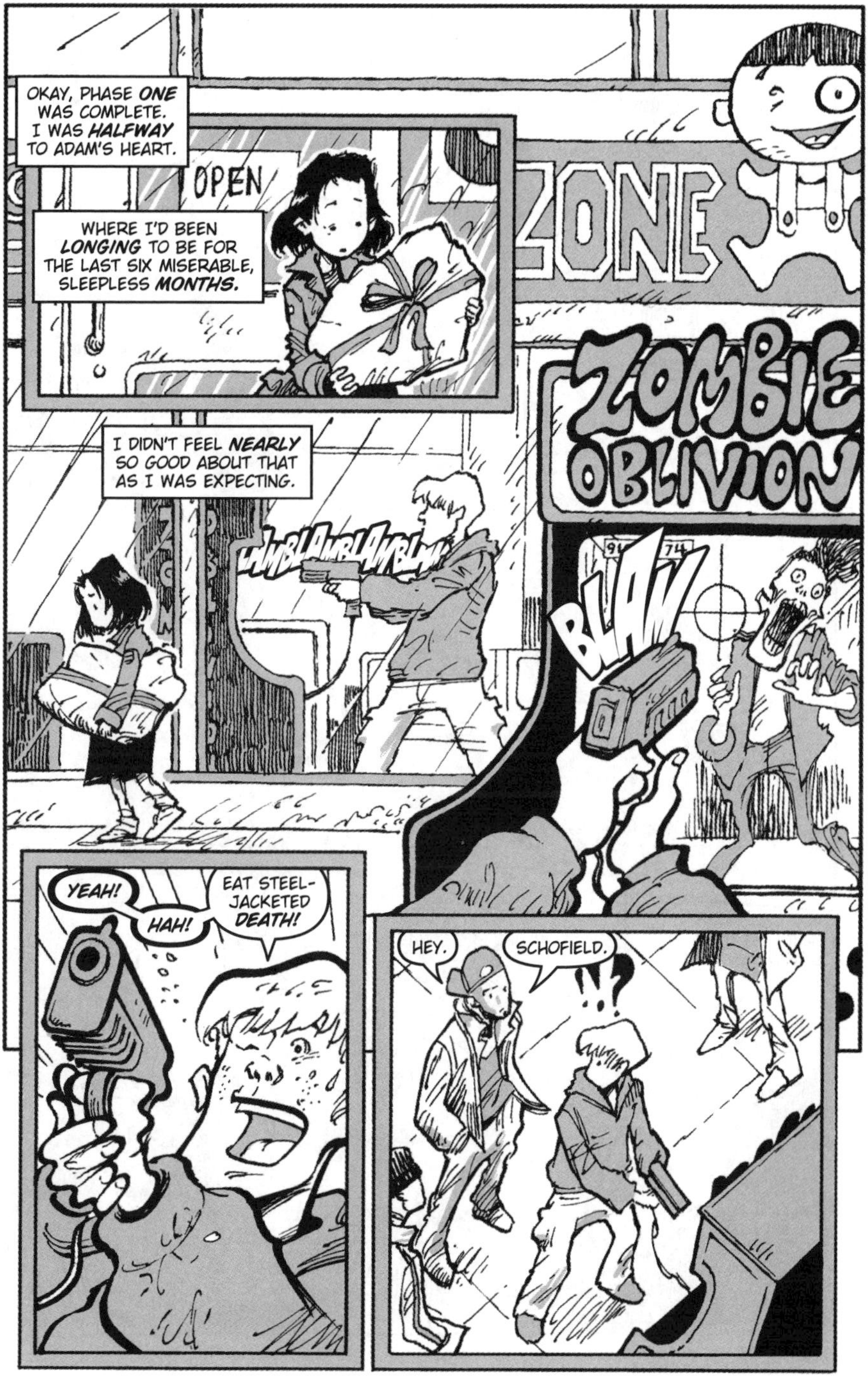
OKAY, PHASE ONE WAS COMPLETE. I WAS HALFWAY TO ADAM'S HEART.
OPEN
ZONE
WHERE I'D BEEN LONGING TO BE FOR THE LAST SIX MISERABLE, SLEEPLESS MONTHS.
ZOMBIE OBLIVION
I DIDN'T FEEL NEARLY SO GOOD ABOUT THAT AS I WAS EXPECTING.
BLAM
YEAH!
HAH!
EAT STEEL-JACKETED DEATH!
HEY.
SCHOFIELD.
!?

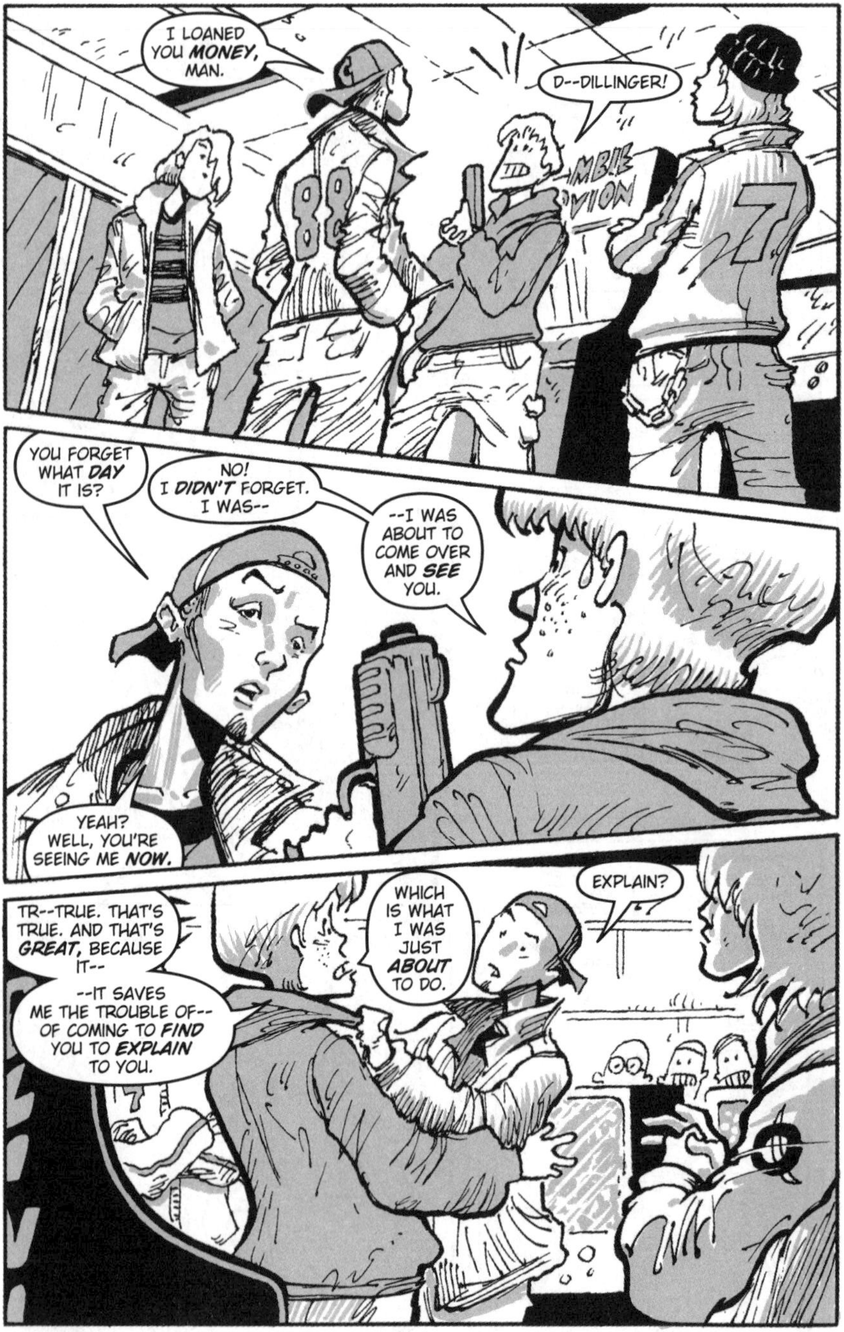
I LOANED YOU MONEY, MAN.
D--DILLINGER!
MBIE VION
YOU FORGET WHAT DAY IT IS?
NO! I DIDN'T FORGET. I WAS--
--I WAS ABOUT TO COME OVER AND SEE YOU.
YEAH? WELL, YOU'RE SEEING ME NOW.
TR--TRUE. THAT'S TRUE. AND THAT'S GREAT, BECAUSE IT--
--IT SAVES ME THE TROUBLE OF-- OF COMING TO FIND YOU TO EXPLAIN TO YOU.
WHICH IS WHAT I WAS JUST ABOUT TO DO.
EXPLAIN?

YEAH. YOU *SEE*, DILLINGER, THE FACT IS--I'VE GOT A *CASH* FLOW PROBLEM.

I NEED A COUPLE OF *DAYS* TO GET THE MONEY TOGETHER.

A WEEK. I NEED A *WEEK*.

OKAY, VATO, TODAY I'M THE *WISHING* FAIRY. YOU GOT SEVEN *DAYS*.

AFTER THAT-- WELL, I BET YOU KNOW WHAT *FORECLOSE* IS, SINCE YOUR FATHER IS A *LAWYER* AND ALL.

A *WEEK*?

YEAH.

ON TOP OF THE TIME YOU'VE *ALREADY* HAD?

Y--YEAH. I KNOW THAT'S--

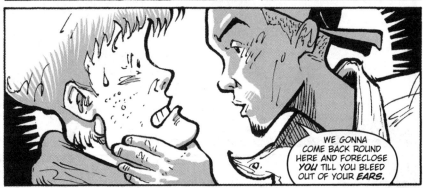

WE GONNA COME BACK ROUND HERE AND FORECLOSE *YOU* TILL YOU BLEED OUT OF YOUR *EARS*.

...

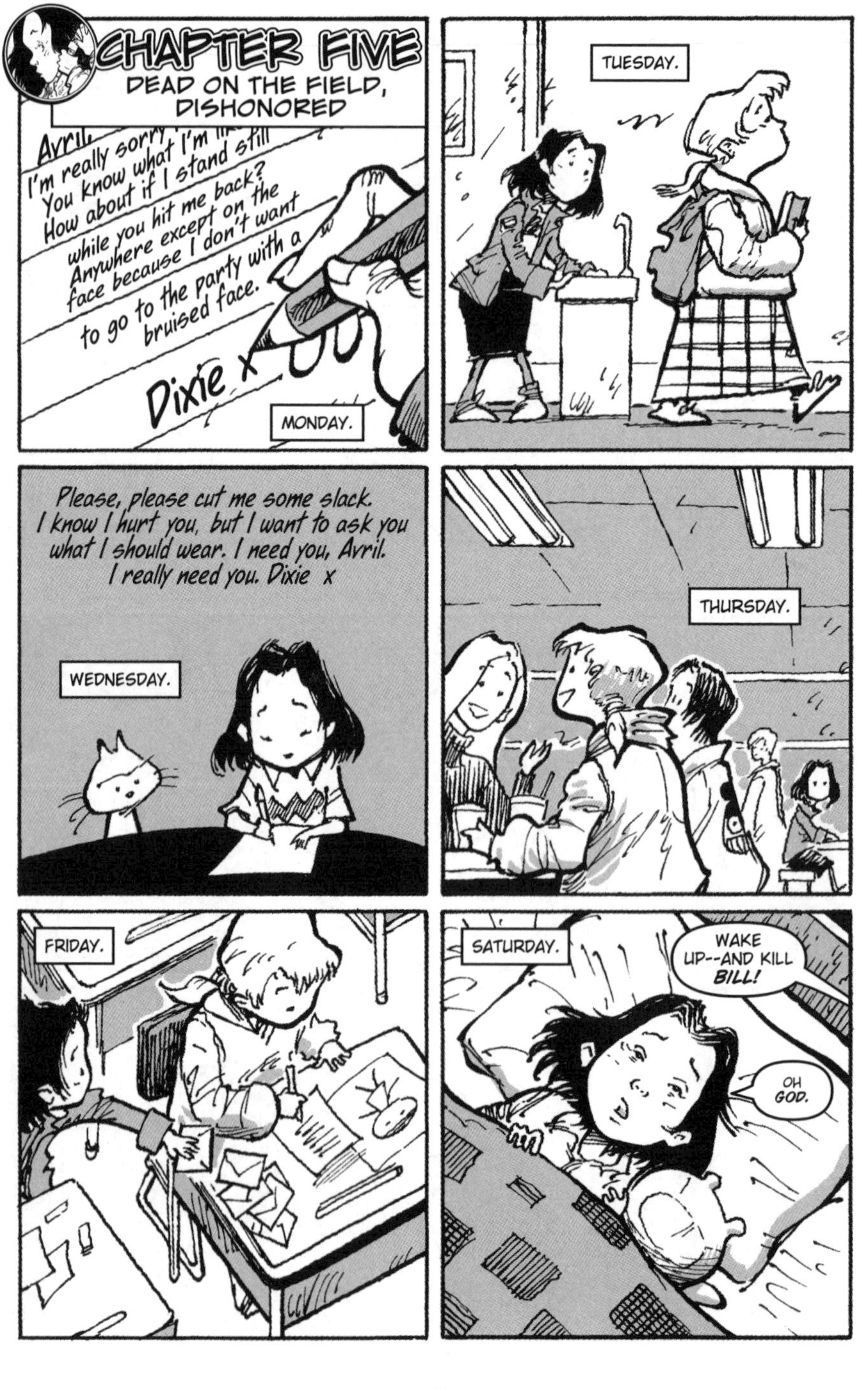
CHAPTER FIVE
DEAD ON THE FIELD, DISHONORED
Avril,
I'm really sorry
You know what I'm
How about if I stand still while you hit me back?
Anywhere except on the face because I don't want to go to the party with a bruised face.
Dixie x
MONDAY.
TUESDAY.
Please, please cut me some slack. I know I hurt you, but I want to ask you what I should wear. I need you, Avril. I really need you. Dixie x
WEDNESDAY.
THURSDAY.
FRIDAY.
SATURDAY.
WAKE UP--AND KILL BILL!
OH GOD.

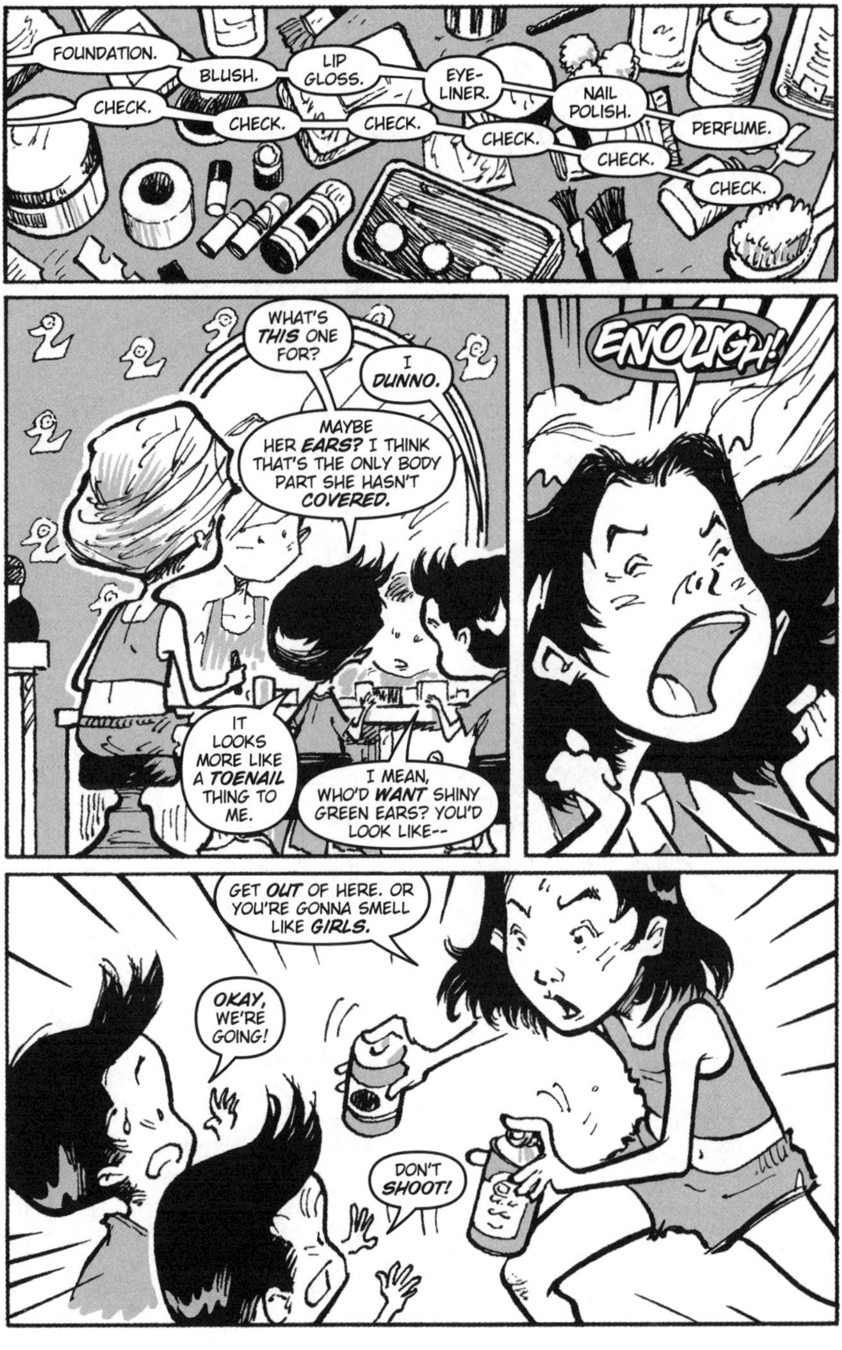
FOUNDATION.
CHECK.
BLUSH.
CHECK.
LIP GLOSS.
CHECK.
EYE-LINER.
CHECK.
NAIL POLISH.
CHECK.
PERFUME.
CHECK.
WHAT'S THIS ONE FOR?
I DUNNO.
MAYBE HER EARS? I THINK THAT'S THE ONLY BODY PART SHE HASN'T COVERED.
IT LOOKS MORE LIKE A TOENAIL THING TO ME.
I MEAN, WHO'D WANT SHINY GREEN EARS? YOU'D LOOK LIKE--
ENOUGH!
GET OUT OF HERE. OR YOU'RE GONNA SMELL LIKE GIRLS.
OKAY, WE'RE GOING!
DON'T SHOOT!

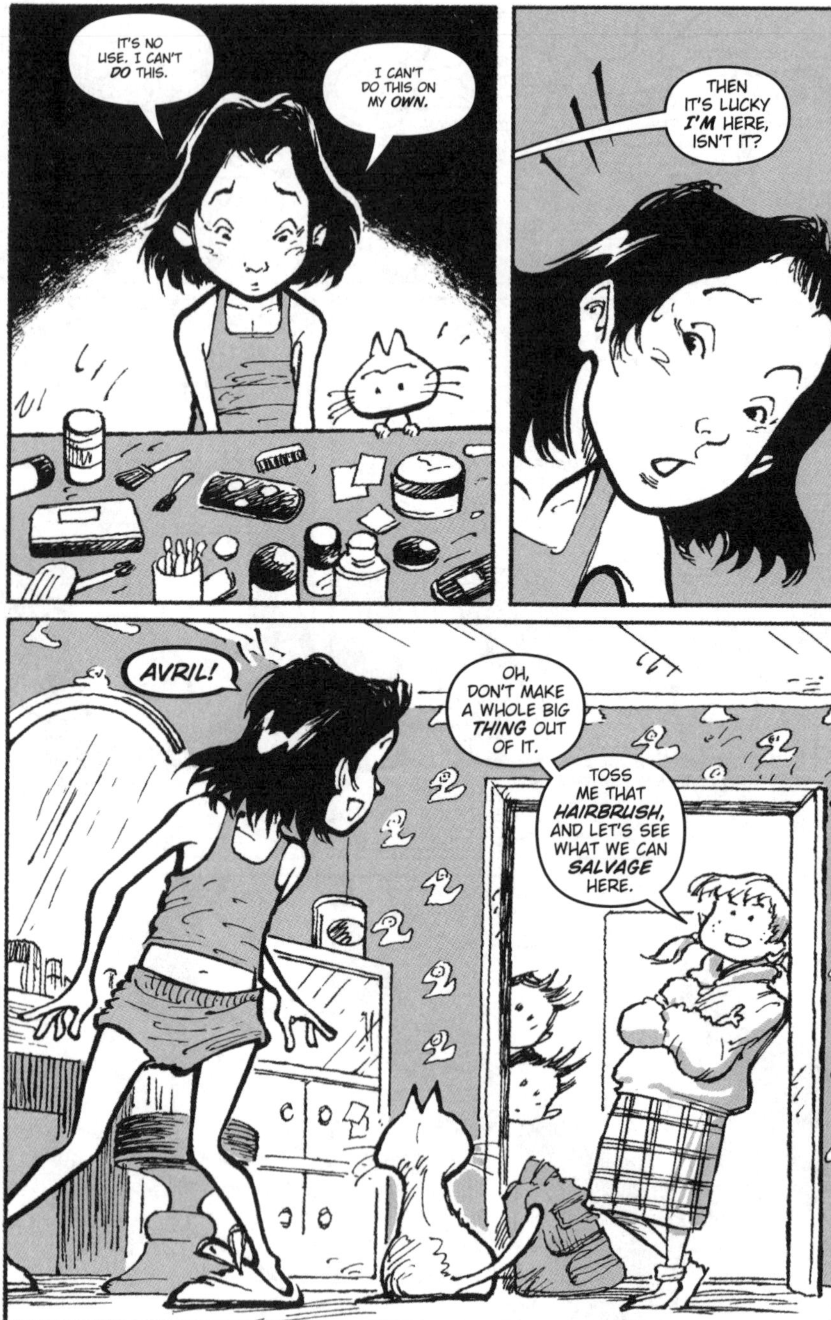
IT'S NO USE. I CAN'T DO THIS.
I CAN'T DO THIS ON MY OWN.
THEN IT'S LUCKY I'M HERE, ISN'T IT?
AVRIL!
OH, DON'T MAKE A WHOLE BIG THING OUT OF IT.
TOSS ME THAT HAIRBRUSH, AND LET'S SEE WHAT WE CAN SALVAGE HERE.

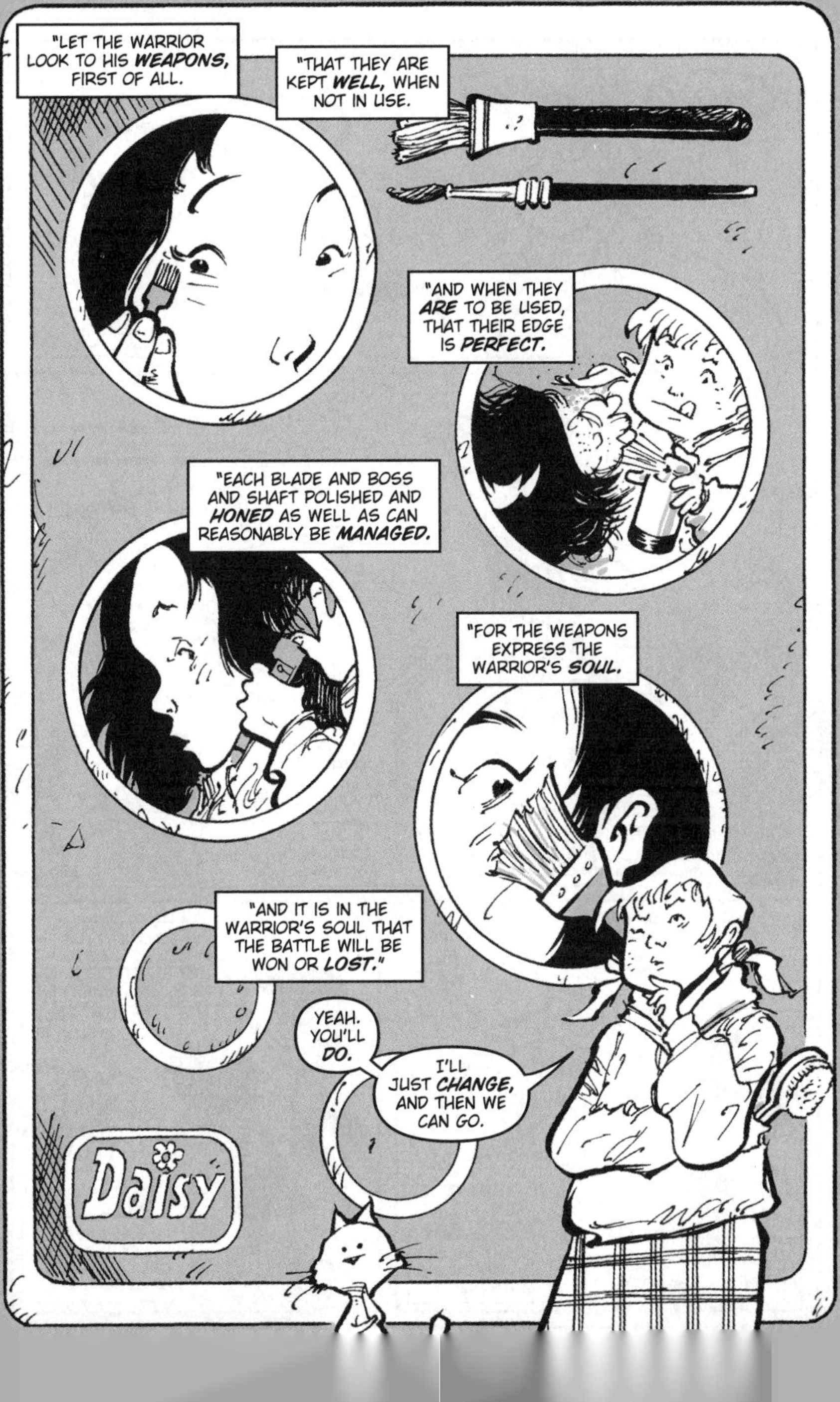
"LET THE WARRIOR LOOK TO HIS WEAPONS, FIRST OF ALL.
"THAT THEY ARE KEPT WELL, WHEN NOT IN USE.
"AND WHEN THEY ARE TO BE USED, THAT THEIR EDGE IS PERFECT.
"EACH BLADE AND BOSS AND SHAFT POLISHED AND HONED AS WELL AS CAN REASONABLY BE MANAGED.
"FOR THE WEAPONS EXPRESS THE WARRIOR'S SOUL.
"AND IT IS IN THE WARRIOR'S SOUL THAT THE BATTLE WILL BE WON OR LOST."
YEAH. YOU'LL DO.
I'LL JUST CHANGE, AND THEN WE CAN GO.
Daisy

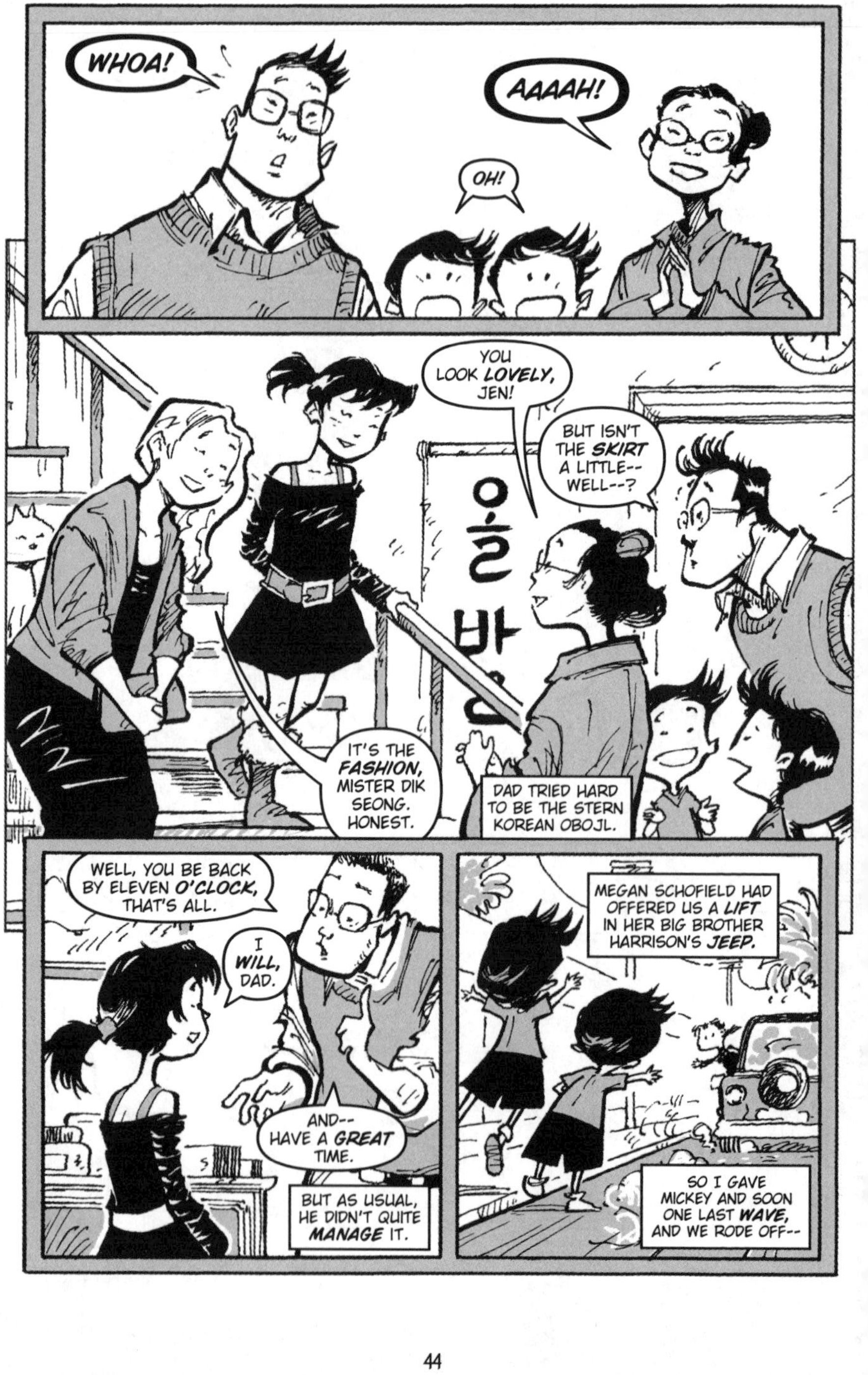
WHOA!
OH!
AAAAH!
YOU LOOK **LOVELY,** JEN!
BUT ISN'T THE **SKIRT** A LITTLE-- WELL--?
올
바
IT'S THE **FASHION,** MISTER DIK SEONG. HONEST.
DAD TRIED HARD TO BE THE STERN KOREAN OBOJI.
WELL, YOU BE BACK BY ELEVEN **O'CLOCK,** THAT'S ALL.
I **WILL,** DAD.
AND-- HAVE A **GREAT** TIME.
BUT AS USUAL, HE DIDN'T QUITE **MANAGE** IT.
MEGAN SCHOFIELD HAD OFFERED US A **LIFT** IN HER BIG BROTHER HARRISON'S **JEEP.**
SO I GAVE MICKEY AND SOON ONE LAST **WAVE,** AND WE RODE OFF--

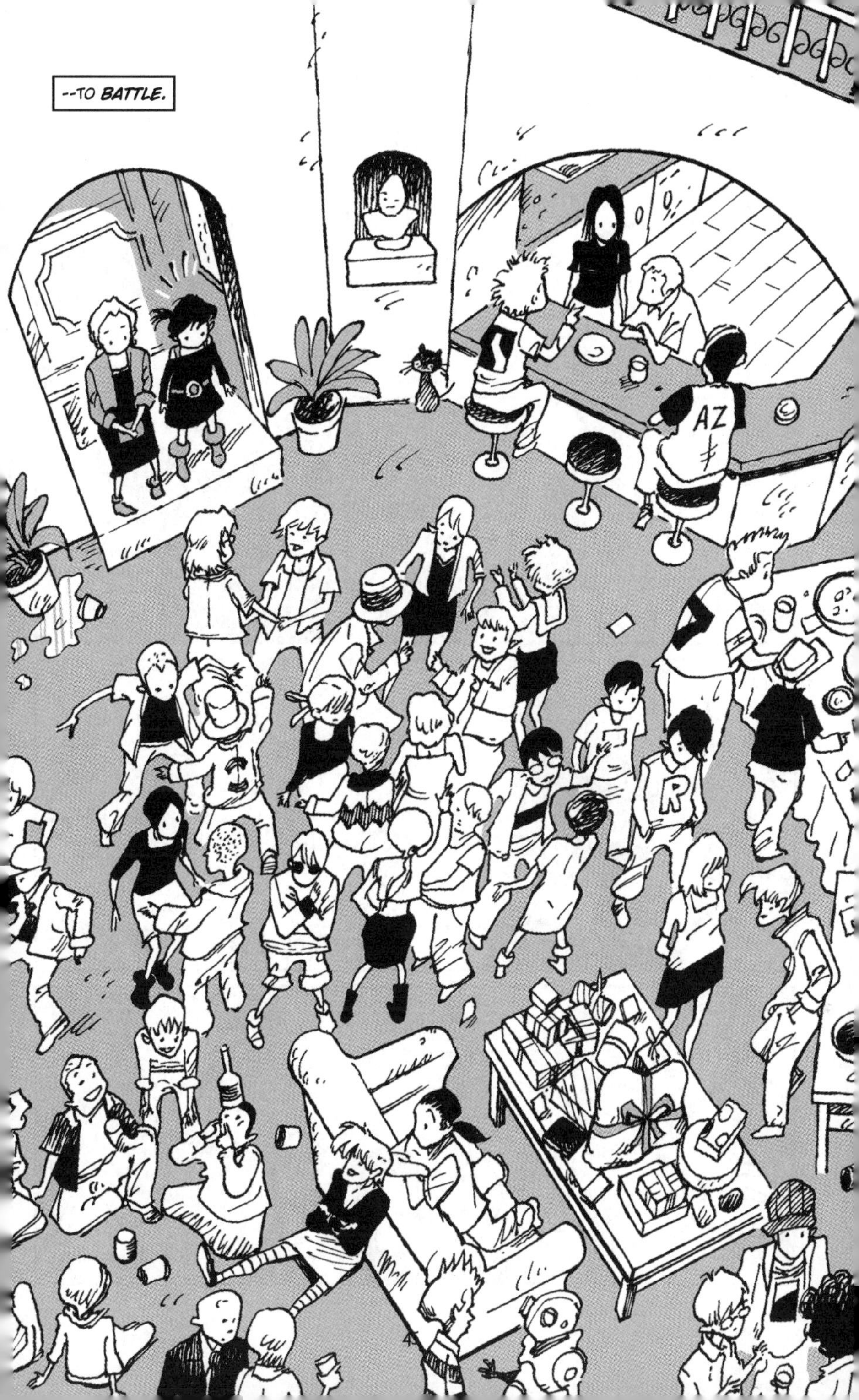
--TO BATTLE.

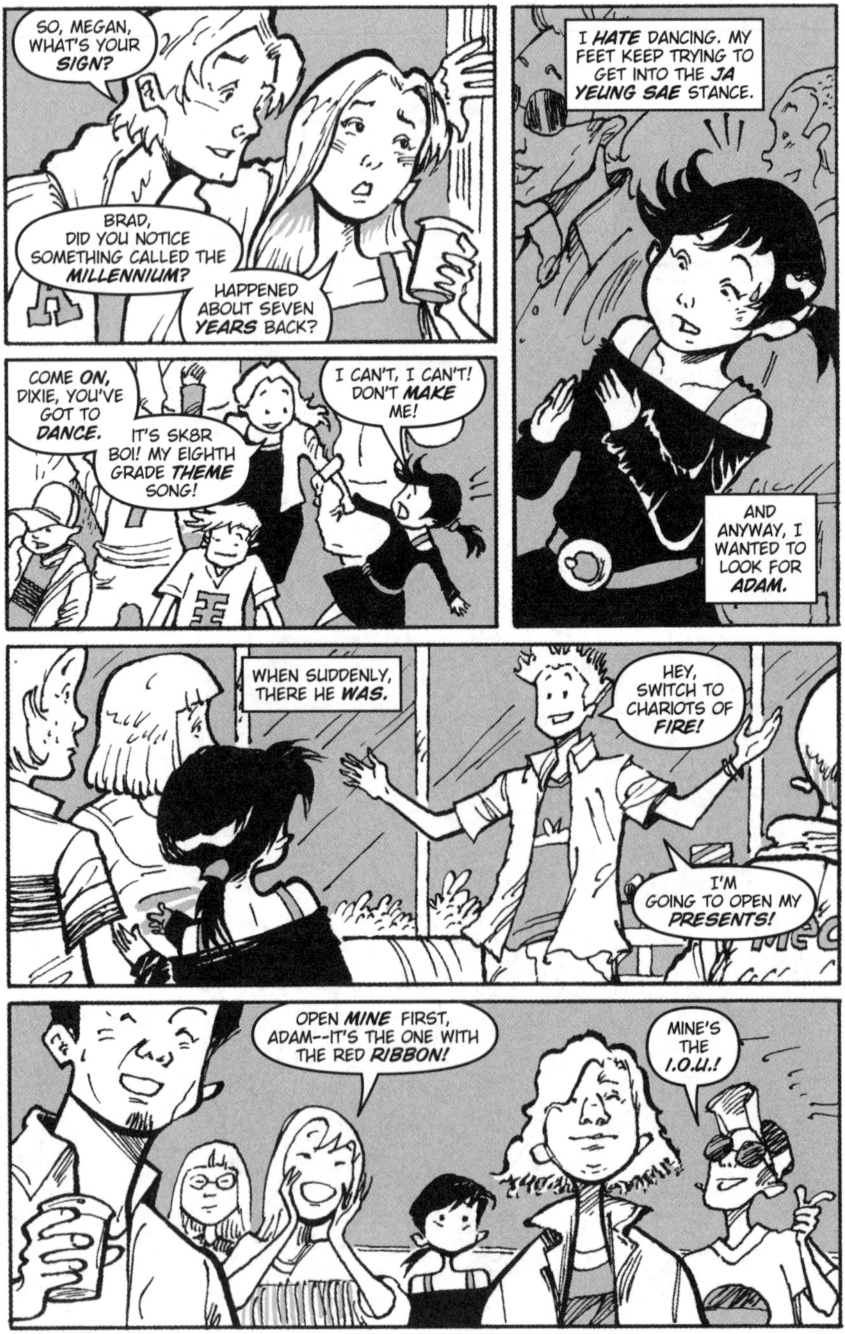
SO, MEGAN, WHAT'S YOUR SIGN?
BRAD, DID YOU NOTICE SOMETHING CALLED THE MILLENNIUM?
HAPPENED ABOUT SEVEN YEARS BACK?
COME ON, DIXIE, YOU'VE GOT TO DANCE.
IT'S SK8R BOI! MY EIGHTH GRADE THEME SONG!
I CAN'T, I CAN'T! DON'T MAKE ME!
I HATE DANCING. MY FEET KEEP TRYING TO GET INTO THE JA YEUNG SAE STANCE.
AND ANYWAY, I WANTED TO LOOK FOR ADAM.
WHEN SUDDENLY, THERE HE WAS.
HEY, SWITCH TO CHARIOTS OF FIRE!
I'M GOING TO OPEN MY PRESENTS!
OPEN MINE FIRST, ADAM--IT'S THE ONE WITH THE RED RIBBON!
MINE'S THE I.O.U.!

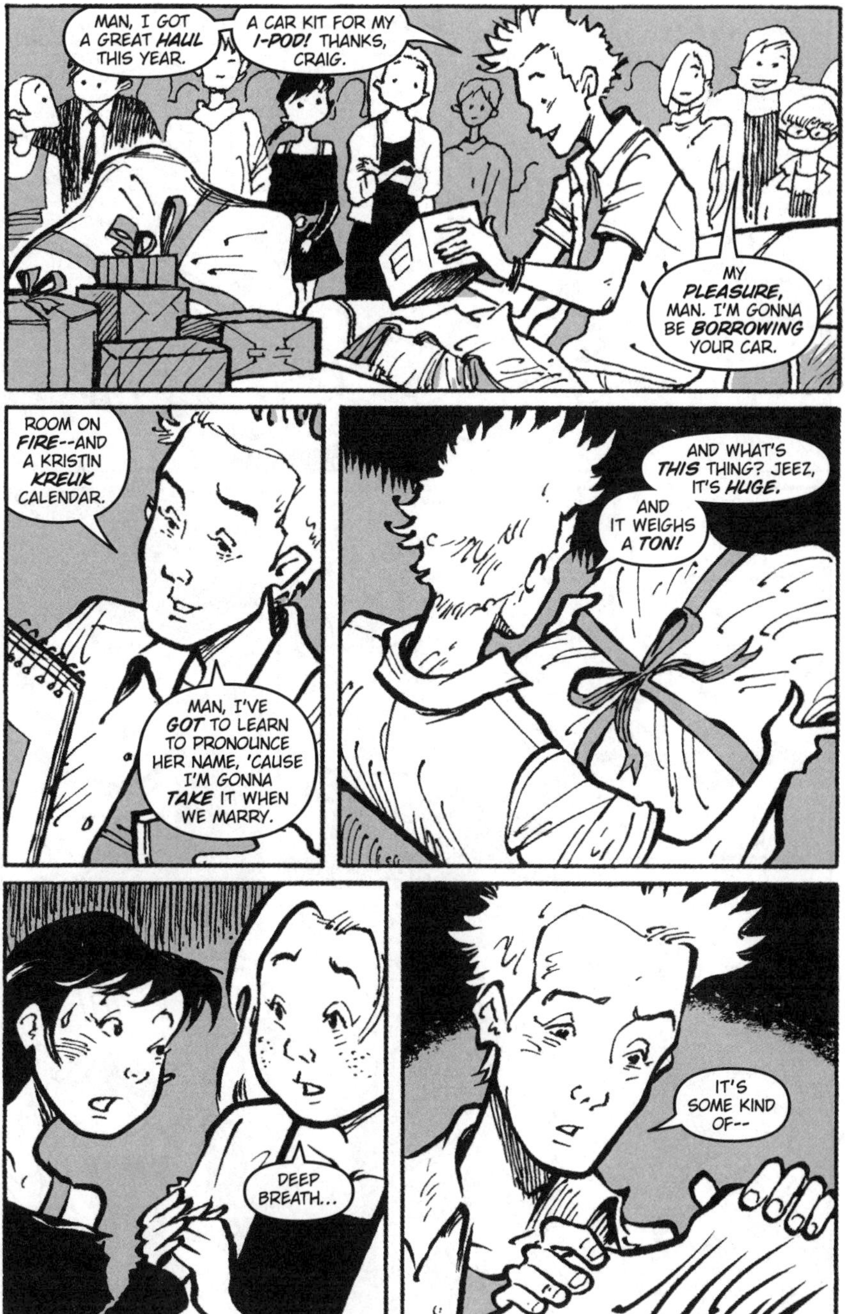
MAN, I GOT A GREAT HAUL THIS YEAR.
A CAR KIT FOR MY I-POD! THANKS, CRAIG.
MY PLEASURE, MAN. I'M GONNA BE BORROWING YOUR CAR.
ROOM ON FIRE--AND A KRISTIN KREUK CALENDAR.
MAN, I'VE GOT TO LEARN TO PRONOUNCE HER NAME, 'CAUSE I'M GONNA TAKE IT WHEN WE MARRY.
AND WHAT'S THIS THING? JEEZ, IT'S HUGE.
AND IT WEIGHS A TON!
DEEP BREATH...
IT'S SOME KIND OF--

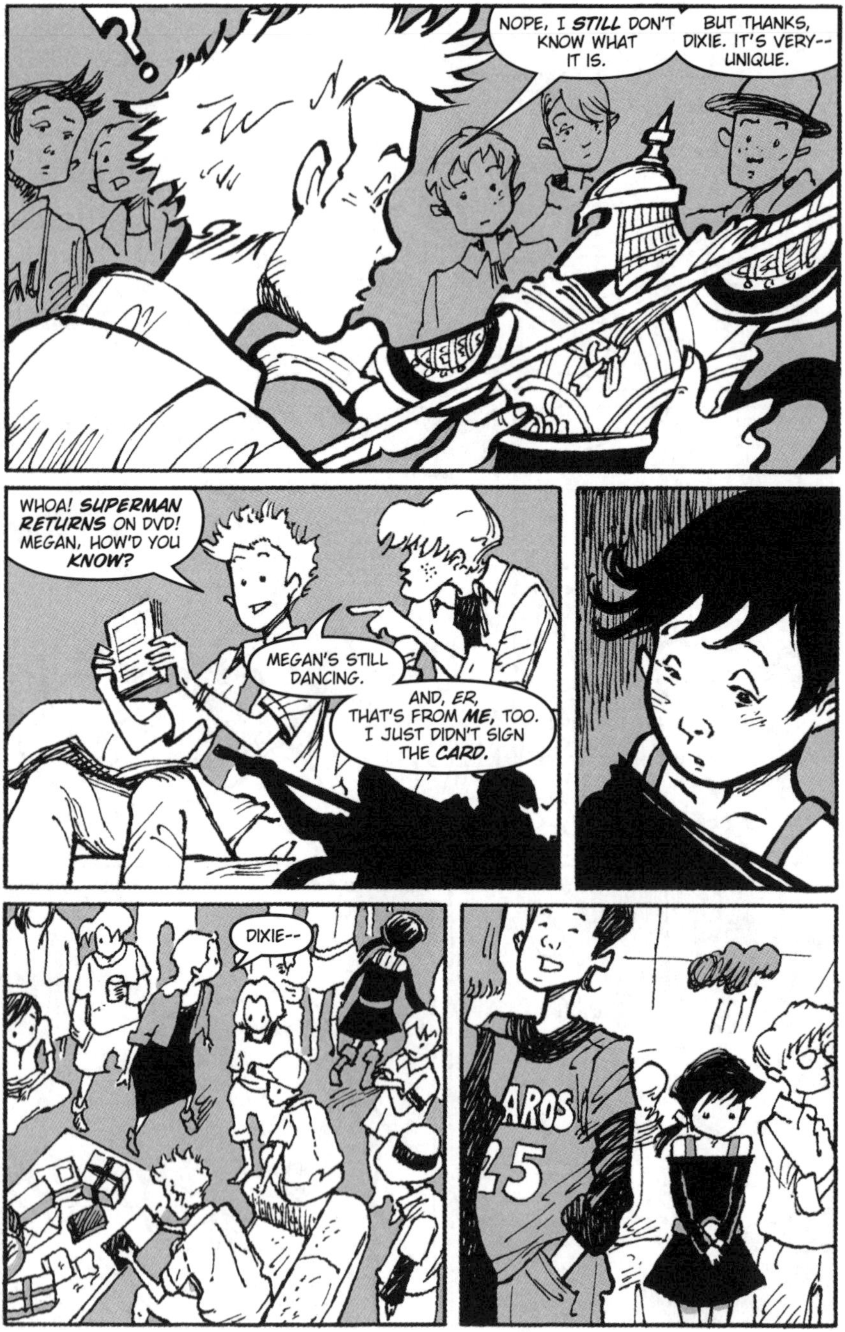
NOPE, I STILL DON'T KNOW WHAT IT IS.
BUT THANKS, DIXIE. IT'S VERY-- UNIQUE.
WHOA! SUPERMAN RETURNS ON DVD! MEGAN, HOW'D YOU KNOW?
MEGAN'S STILL DANCING.
AND, ER, THAT'S FROM ME, TOO. I JUST DIDN'T SIGN THE CARD.
DIXIE--
AROS
25

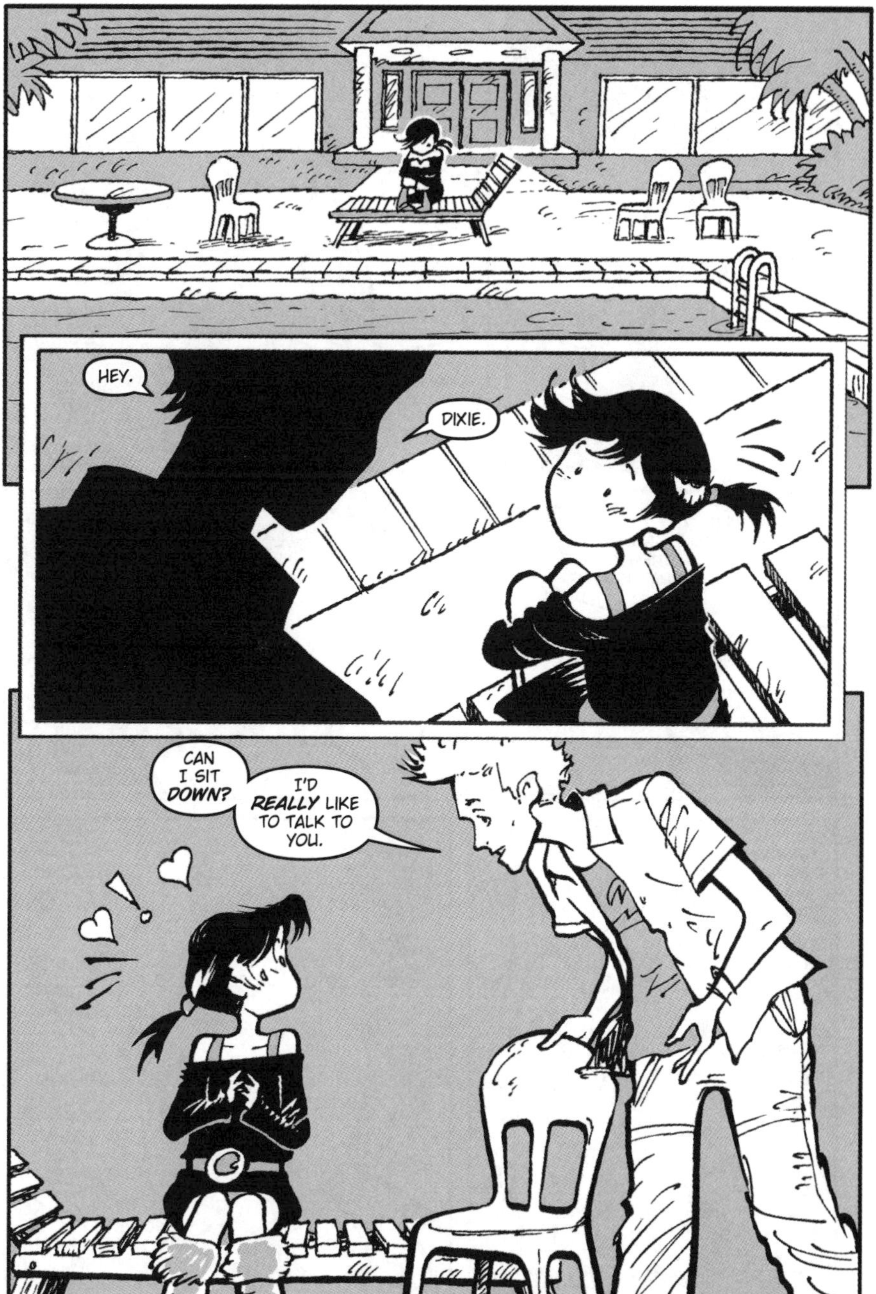
HEY.
DIXIE.
CAN I SIT DOWN?
I'D REALLY LIKE TO TALK TO YOU.

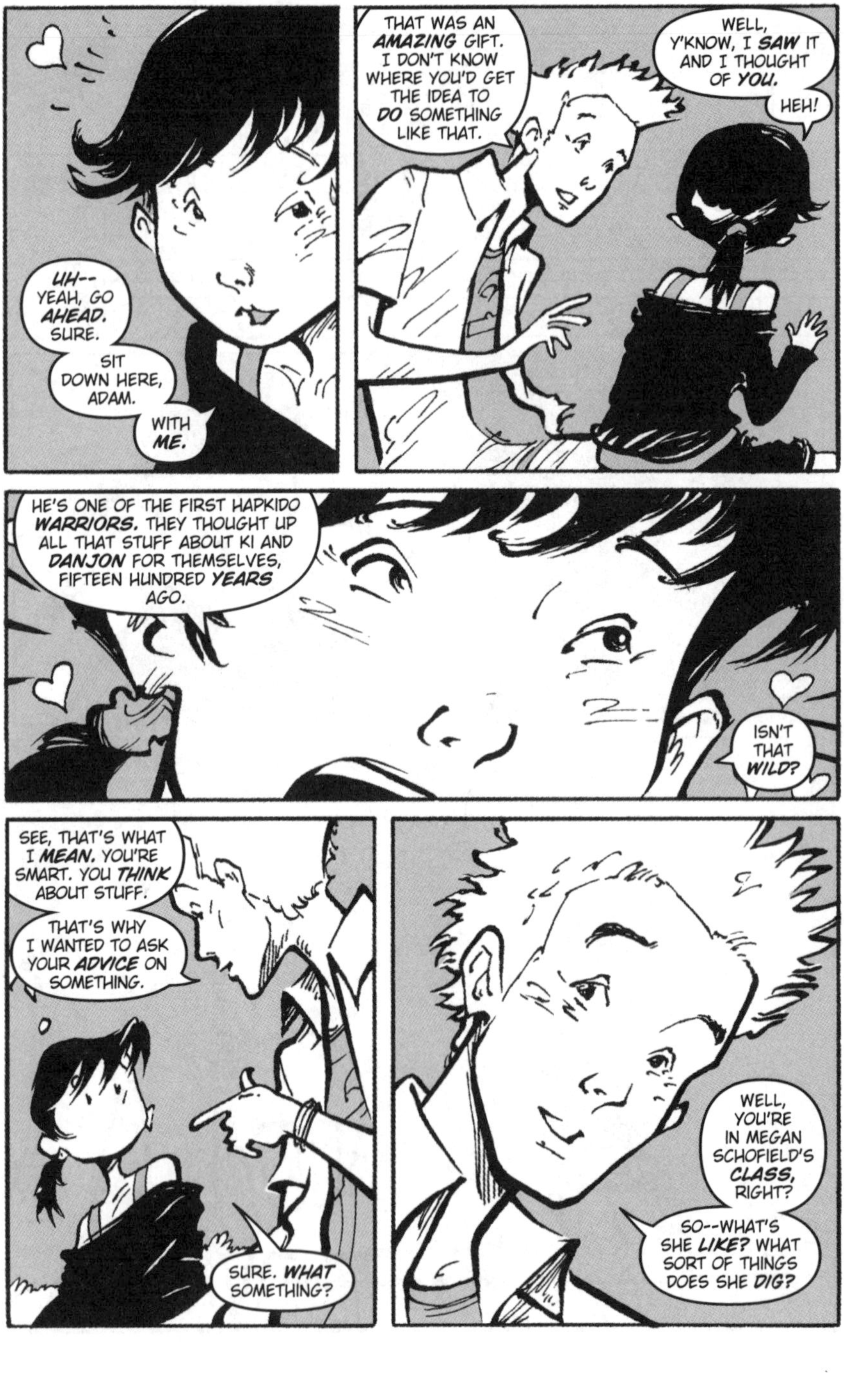
UH--
YEAH, GO AHEAD. SURE.
SIT DOWN HERE, ADAM.
WITH ME.
THAT WAS AN AMAZING GIFT. I DON'T KNOW WHERE YOU'D GET THE IDEA TO DO SOMETHING LIKE THAT.
WELL, Y'KNOW, I SAW IT AND I THOUGHT OF YOU.
HEH!
HE'S ONE OF THE FIRST HAPKIDO WARRIORS. THEY THOUGHT UP ALL THAT STUFF ABOUT KI AND DANJON FOR THEMSELVES, FIFTEEN HUNDRED YEARS AGO.
ISN'T THAT WILD?
SEE, THAT'S WHAT I MEAN. YOU'RE SMART. YOU THINK ABOUT STUFF.
THAT'S WHY I WANTED TO ASK YOUR ADVICE ON SOMETHING.
SURE. WHAT SOMETHING?
WELL, YOU'RE IN MEGAN SCHOFIELD'S CLASS, RIGHT?
SO--WHAT'S SHE LIKE? WHAT SORT OF THINGS DOES SHE DIG?

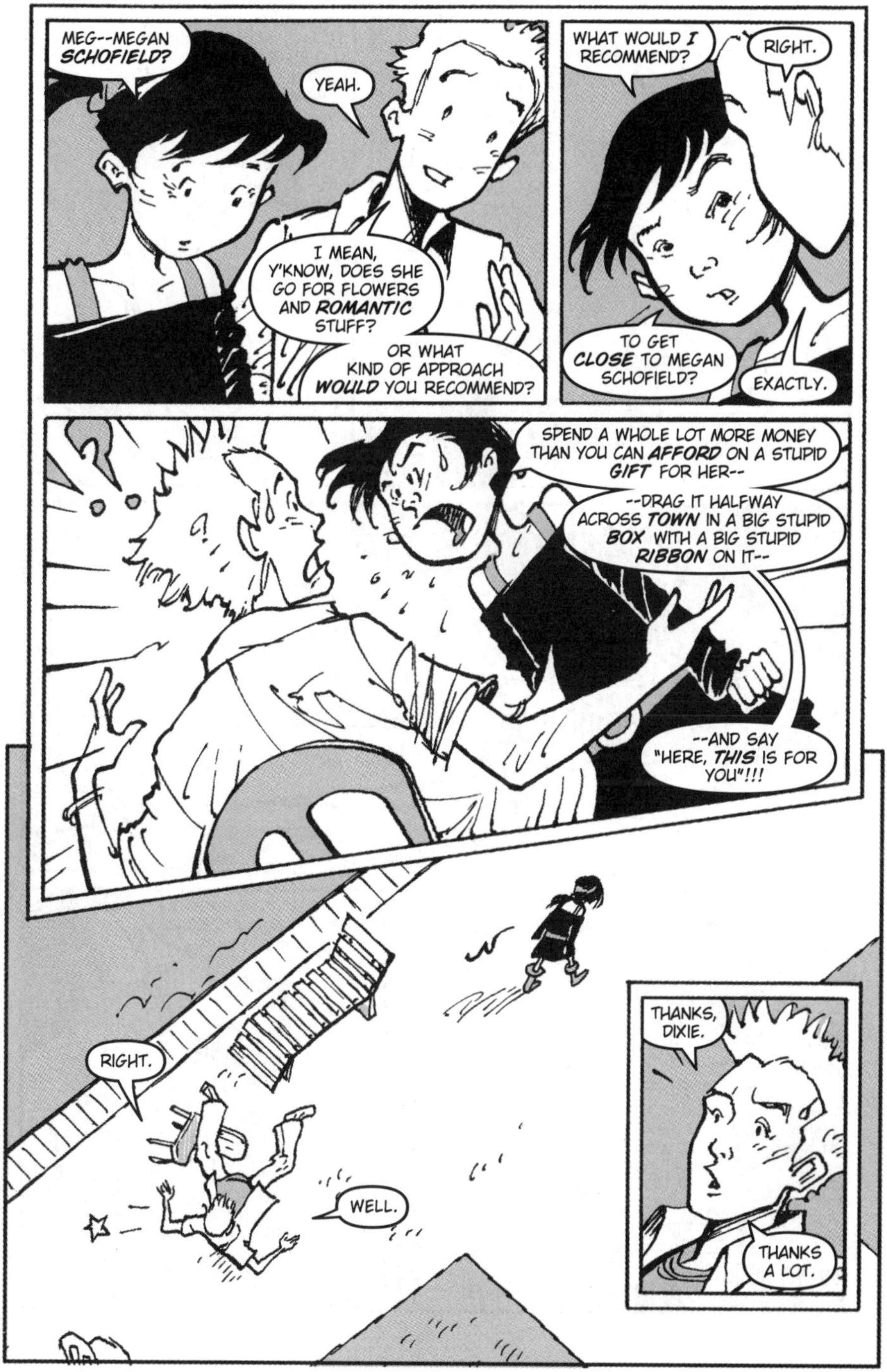

MEG--MEGAN SCHOFIELD?
YEAH.
I MEAN, Y'KNOW, DOES SHE GO FOR FLOWERS AND ROMANTIC STUFF?
OR WHAT KIND OF APPROACH WOULD YOU RECOMMEND?
WHAT WOULD I RECOMMEND?
RIGHT.
TO GET CLOSE TO MEGAN SCHOFIELD?
EXACTLY.
SPEND A WHOLE LOT MORE MONEY THAN YOU CAN AFFORD ON A STUPID GIFT FOR HER--
--DRAG IT HALFWAY ACROSS TOWN IN A BIG STUPID BOX WITH A BIG STUPID RIBBON ON IT--
--AND SAY "HERE, THIS IS FOR YOU"!!!
RIGHT.
WELL.
THANKS, DIXIE.
THANKS A LOT.

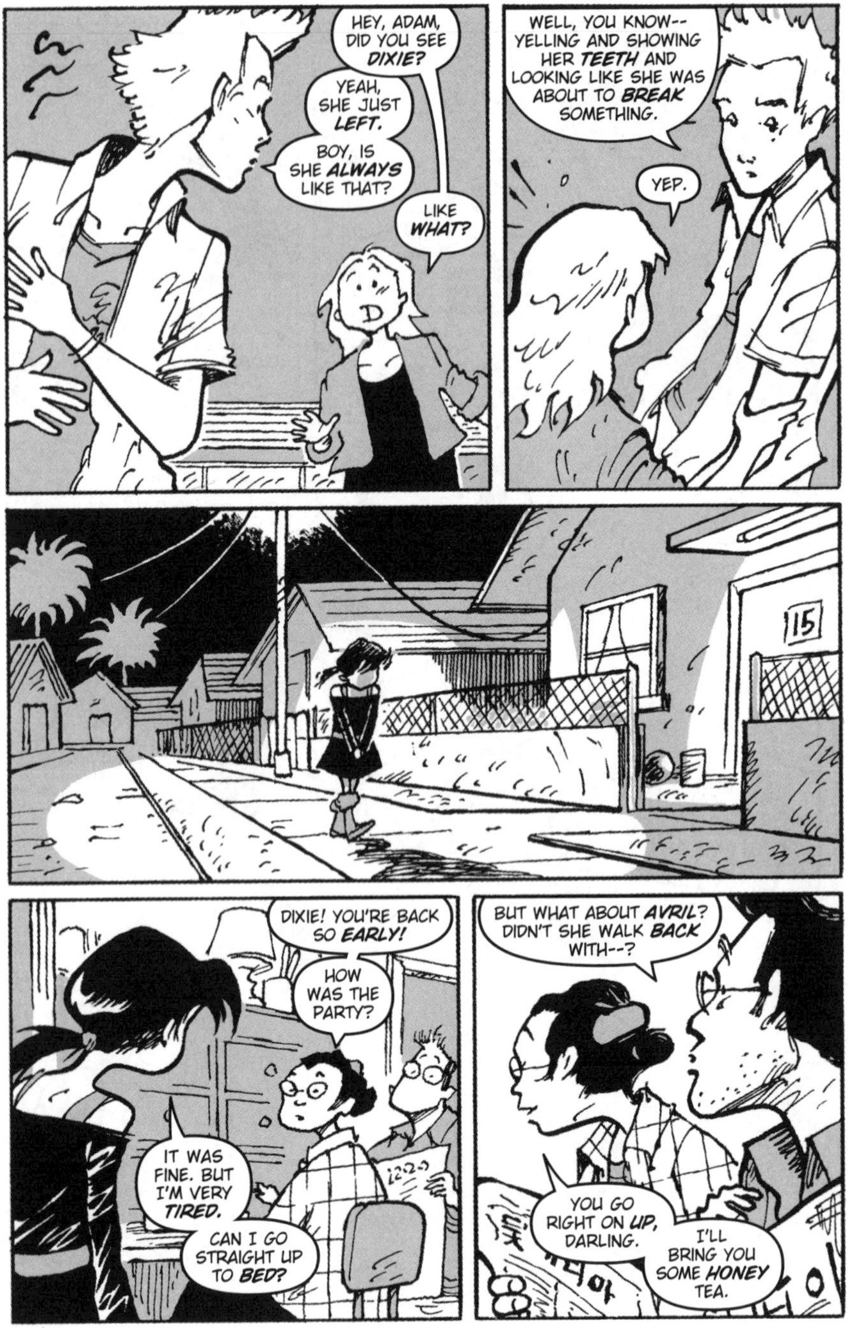
HEY, ADAM, DID YOU SEE DIXIE?
YEAH, SHE JUST LEFT.
BOY, IS SHE ALWAYS LIKE THAT?
LIKE WHAT?
WELL, YOU KNOW-- YELLING AND SHOWING HER TEETH AND LOOKING LIKE SHE WAS ABOUT TO BREAK SOMETHING.
YEP.
15
DIXIE! YOU'RE BACK SO EARLY!
HOW WAS THE PARTY?
IT WAS FINE. BUT I'M VERY TIRED.
CAN I GO STRAIGHT UP TO BED?
BUT WHAT ABOUT AVRIL? DIDN'T SHE WALK BACK WITH--?
YOU GO RIGHT ON UP, DARLING.
I'LL BRING YOU SOME HONEY TEA.

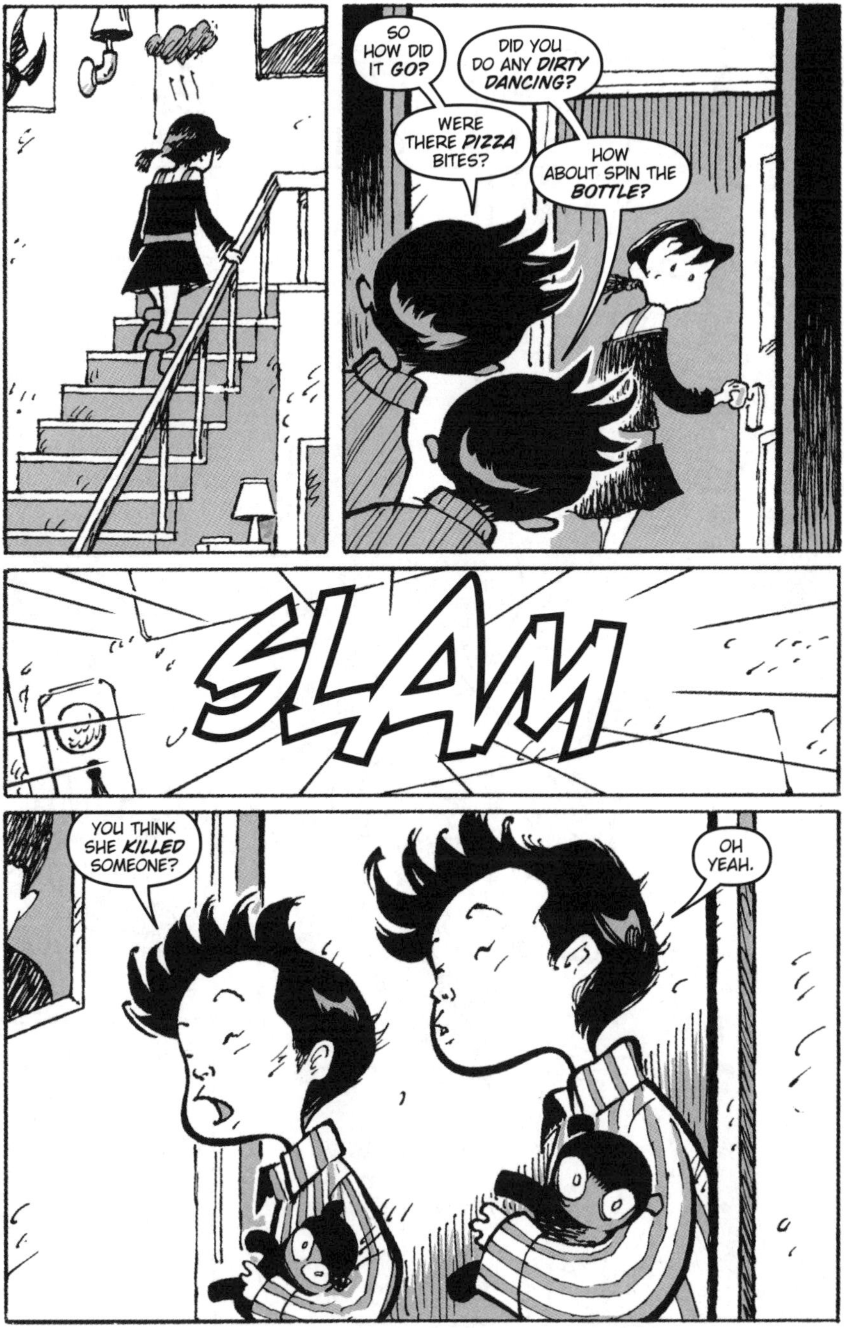
SO HOW DID IT GO?
DID YOU DO ANY DIRTY DANCING?
WERE THERE PIZZA BITES?
HOW ABOUT SPIN THE BOTTLE?
SLAM
YOU THINK SHE KILLED SOMEONE?
OH YEAH.

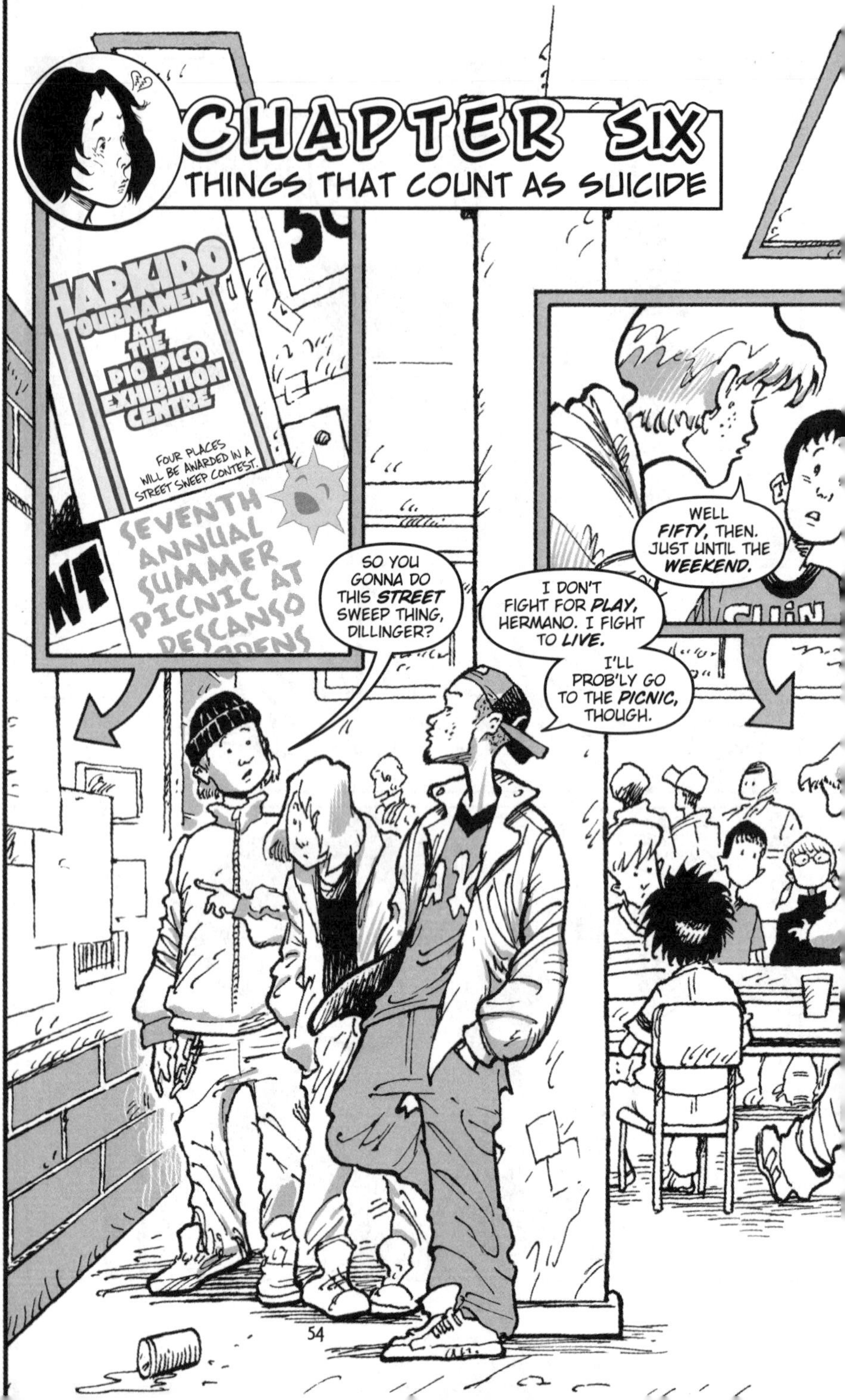
CHAPTER SIX
THINGS THAT COUNT AS SUICIDE
HAPKIDO TOURNAMENT AT THE PIO PICO EXHIBITION CENTRE
FOUR PLACES WILL BE AWARDED IN A STREET SWEEP CONTEST.
SEVENTH ANNUAL SUMMER PICNIC AT DESCANSO
SO YOU GONNA DO THIS STREET SWEEP THING, DILLINGER?
I DON'T FIGHT FOR PLAY, HERMANO. I FIGHT TO LIVE.
I'LL PROB'LY GO TO THE PICNIC, THOUGH.
WELL FIFTY, THEN. JUST UNTIL THE WEEKEND.

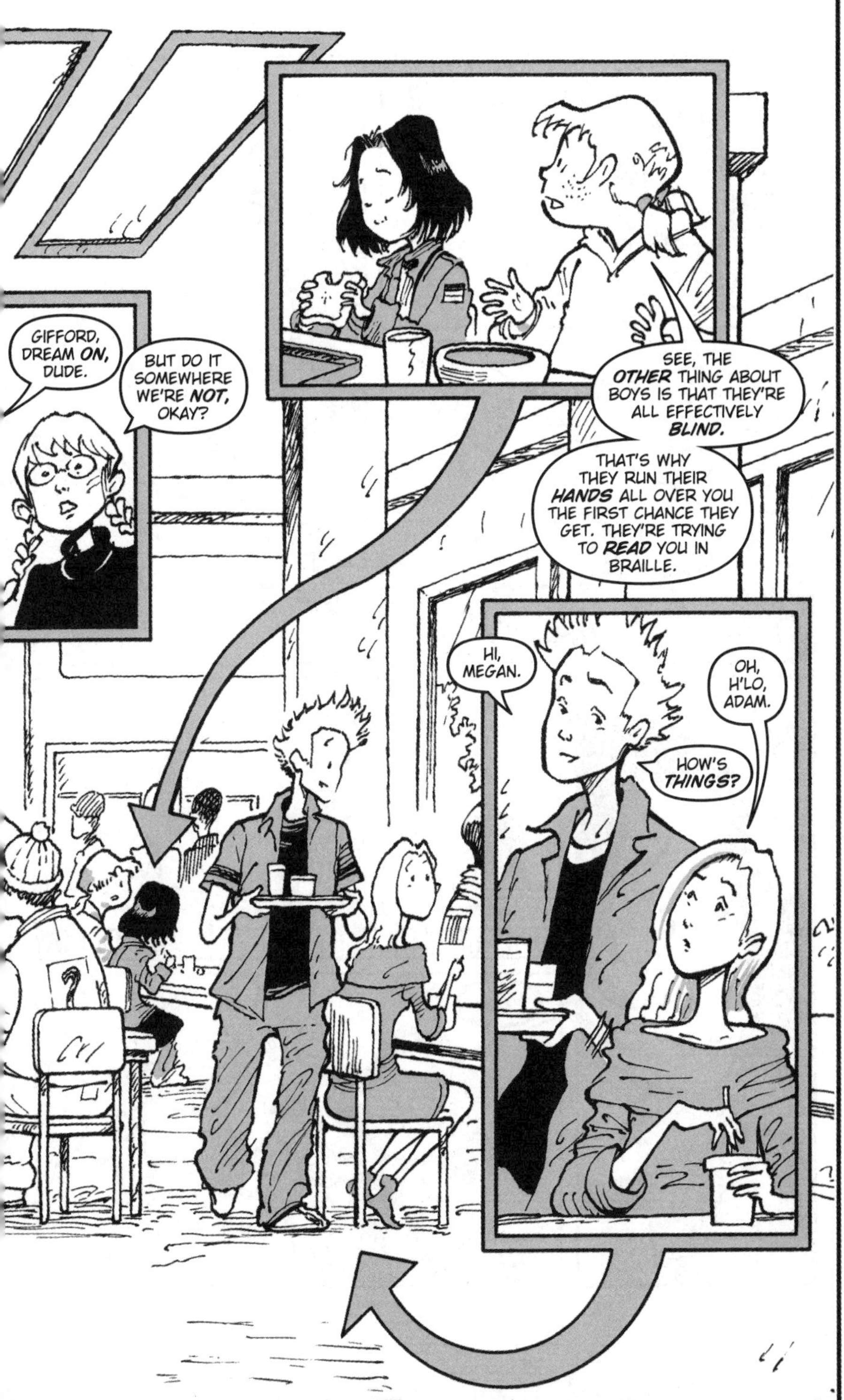
GIFFORD, DREAM ON, DUDE.
BUT DO IT SOMEWHERE WE'RE NOT, OKAY?
SEE, THE OTHER THING ABOUT BOYS IS THAT THEY'RE ALL EFFECTIVELY BLIND.
THAT'S WHY THEY RUN THEIR HANDS ALL OVER YOU THE FIRST CHANCE THEY GET. THEY'RE TRYING TO READ YOU IN BRAILLE.
HI, MEGAN.
OH, H'LO, ADAM.
HOW'S THINGS?

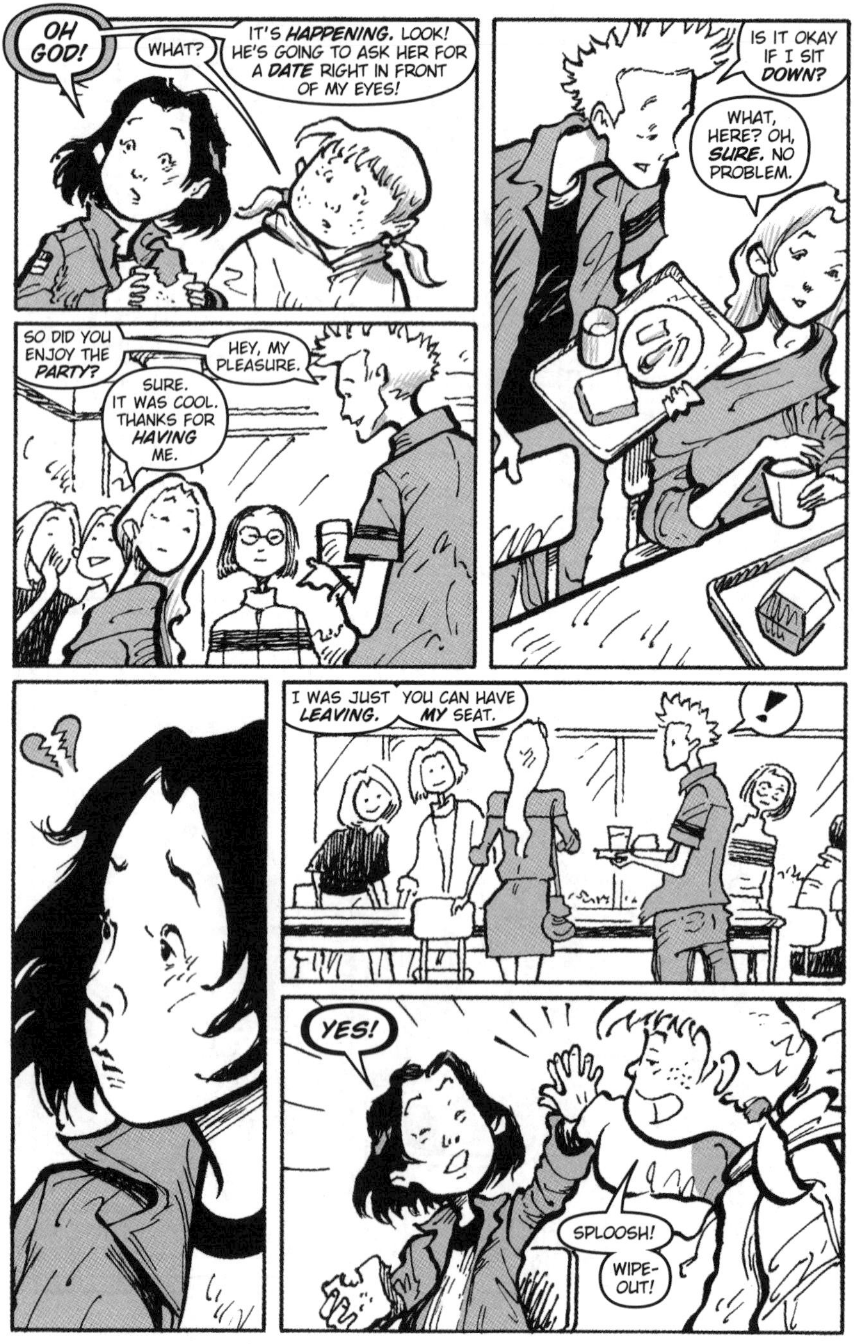
OH GOD!
WHAT?
IT'S HAPPENING. LOOK! HE'S GOING TO ASK HER FOR A DATE RIGHT IN FRONT OF MY EYES!
IS IT OKAY IF I SIT DOWN?
WHAT, HERE? OH, SURE. NO PROBLEM.
SO DID YOU ENJOY THE PARTY?
SURE. IT WAS COOL. THANKS FOR HAVING ME.
HEY, MY PLEASURE.
I WAS JUST LEAVING.
YOU CAN HAVE MY SEAT.
!
YES!
SPLOOSH!
WIPE-OUT!

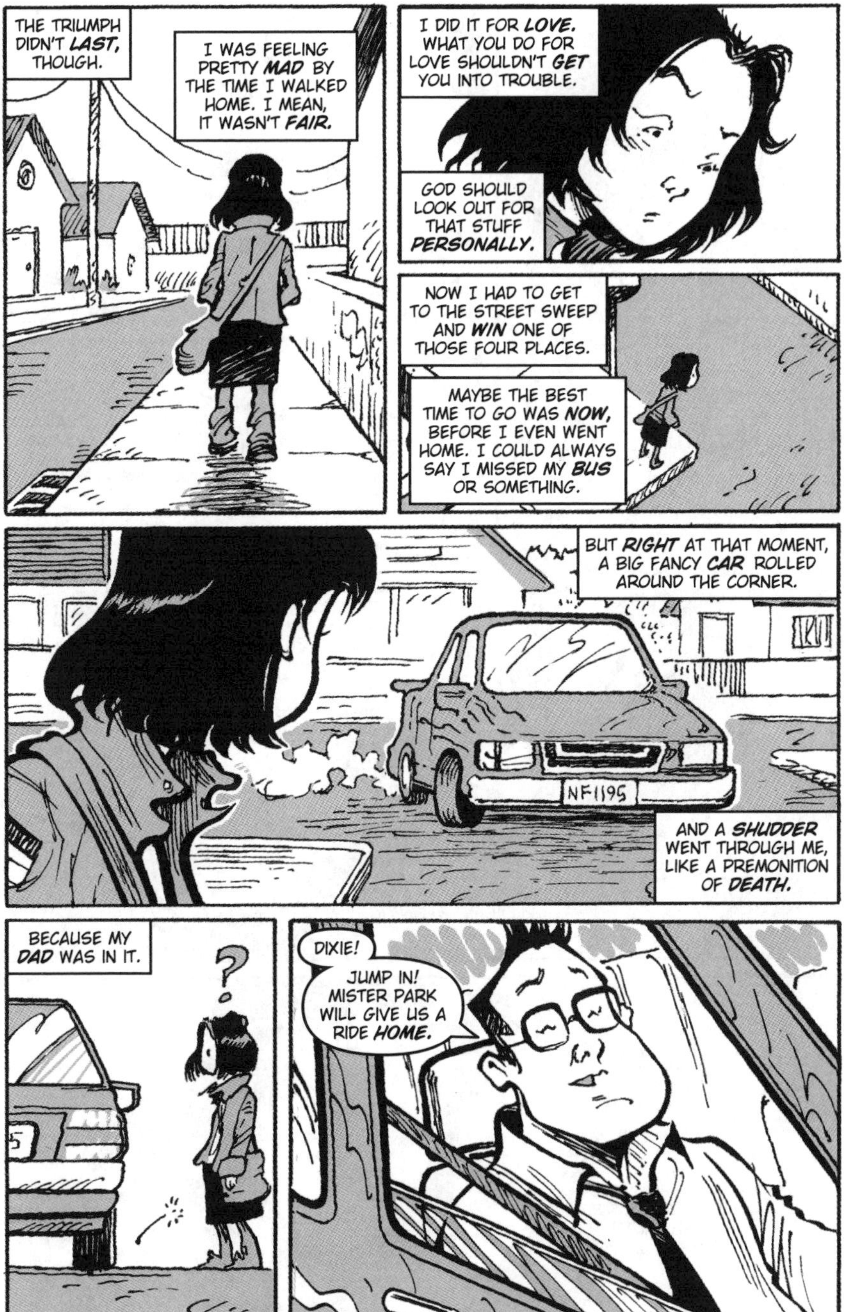
THE TRIUMPH DIDN'T LAST, THOUGH.
I WAS FEELING PRETTY MAD BY THE TIME I WALKED HOME. I MEAN, IT WASN'T FAIR.
I DID IT FOR LOVE. WHAT YOU DO FOR LOVE SHOULDN'T GET YOU INTO TROUBLE.
GOD SHOULD LOOK OUT FOR THAT STUFF PERSONALLY.
NOW I HAD TO GET TO THE STREET SWEEP AND WIN ONE OF THOSE FOUR PLACES.
MAYBE THE BEST TIME TO GO WAS NOW, BEFORE I EVEN WENT HOME. I COULD ALWAYS SAY I MISSED MY BUS OR SOMETHING.
BUT RIGHT AT THAT MOMENT, A BIG FANCY CAR ROLLED AROUND THE CORNER.
NF1195
AND A SHUDDER WENT THROUGH ME, LIKE A PREMONITION OF DEATH.
BECAUSE MY DAD WAS IN IT.
?
DIXIE!
JUMP IN! MISTER PARK WILL GIVE US A RIDE HOME.

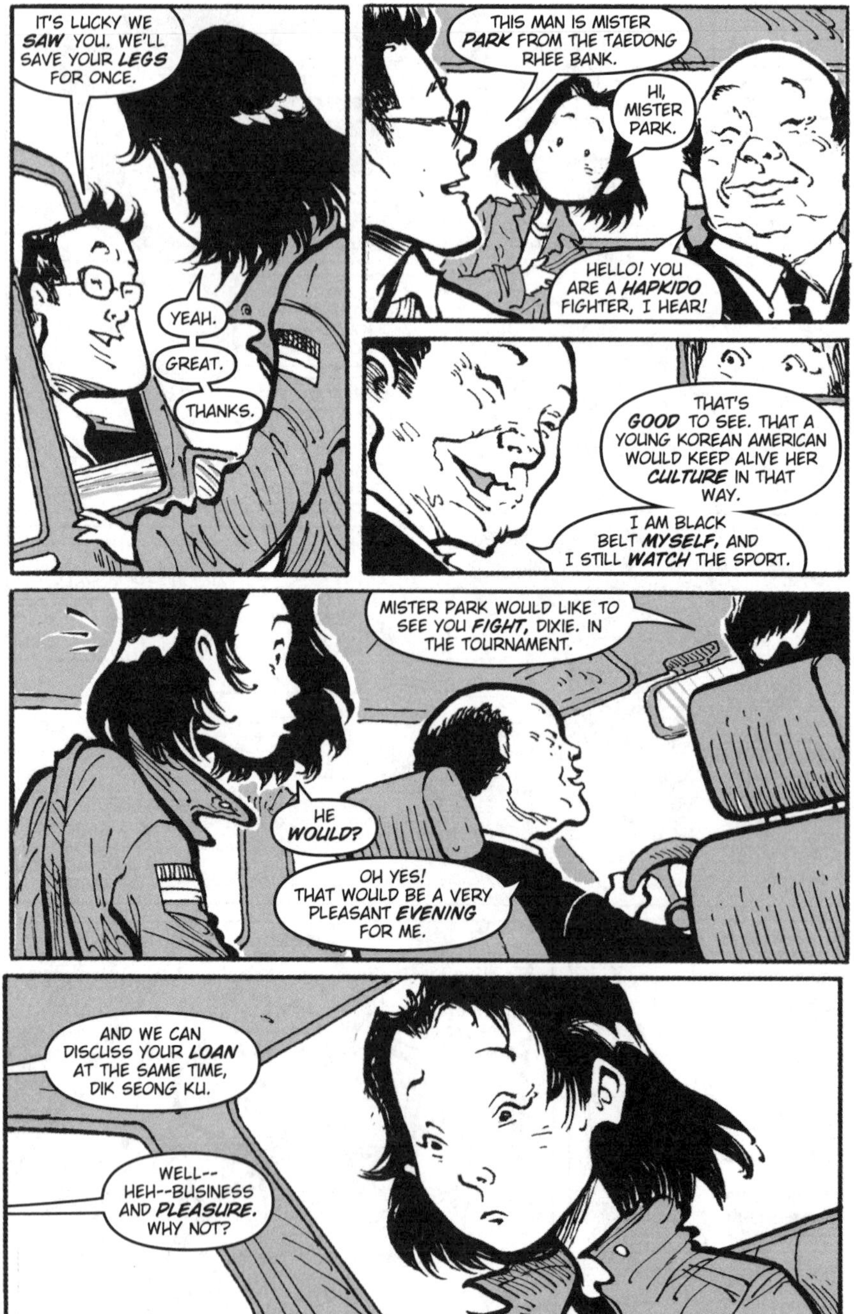
IT'S LUCKY WE SAW YOU. WE'LL SAVE YOUR LEGS FOR ONCE.
YEAH.
GREAT.
THANKS.
THIS MAN IS MISTER PARK FROM THE TAEDONG RHEE BANK.
HI, MISTER PARK.
HELLO! YOU ARE A HAPKIDO FIGHTER, I HEAR!
THAT'S GOOD TO SEE. THAT A YOUNG KOREAN AMERICAN WOULD KEEP ALIVE HER CULTURE IN THAT WAY.
I AM BLACK BELT MYSELF, AND I STILL WATCH THE SPORT.
MISTER PARK WOULD LIKE TO SEE YOU FIGHT, DIXIE. IN THE TOURNAMENT.
HE WOULD?
OH YES! THAT WOULD BE A VERY PLEASANT EVENING FOR ME.
AND WE CAN DISCUSS YOUR LOAN AT THE SAME TIME, DIK SEONG KU.
WELL--HEH--BUSINESS AND PLEASURE. WHY NOT?

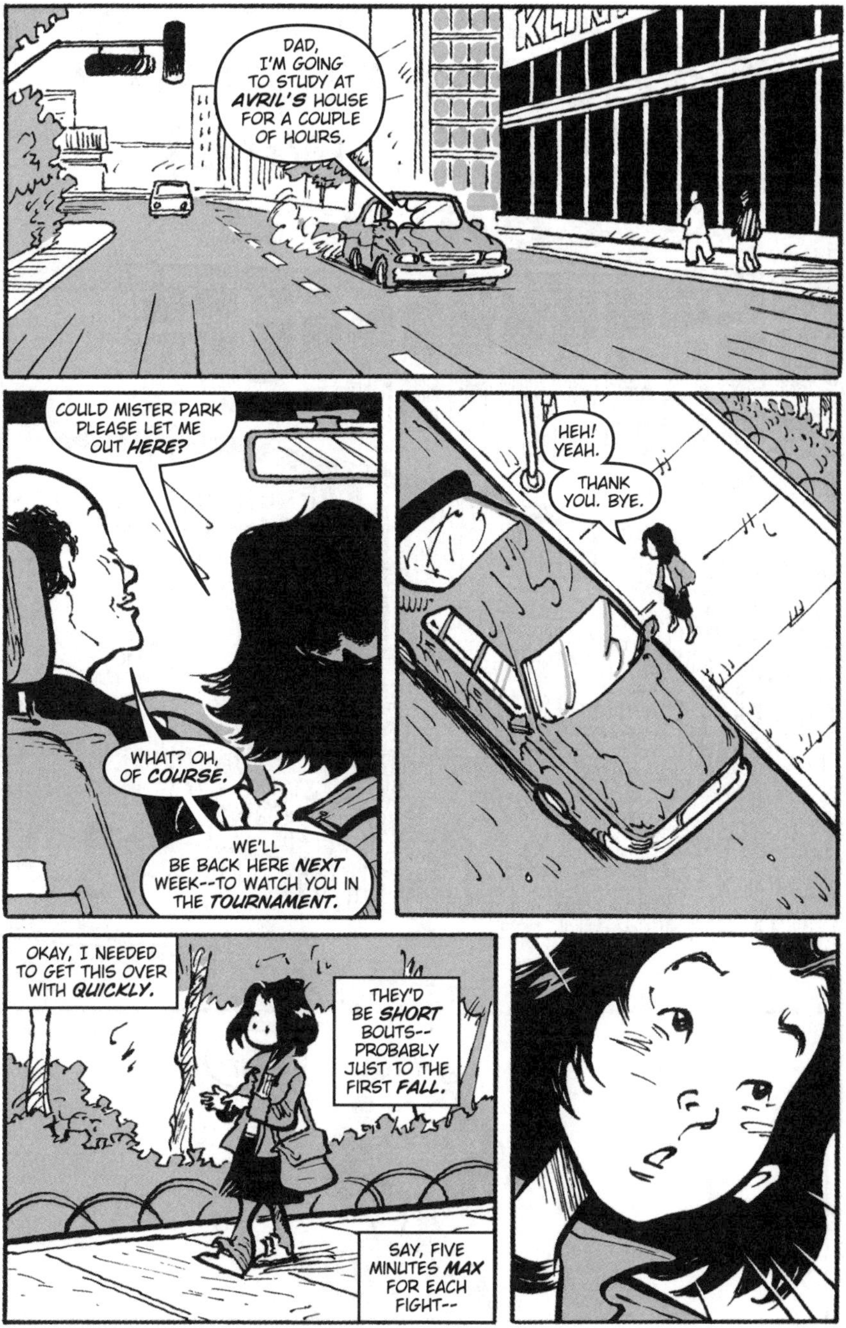
DAD, I'M GOING TO STUDY AT AVRIL'S HOUSE FOR A COUPLE OF HOURS.
COULD MISTER PARK PLEASE LET ME OUT HERE?
WHAT? OH, OF COURSE.
WE'LL BE BACK HERE NEXT WEEK--TO WATCH YOU IN THE TOURNAMENT.
HEH! YEAH.
THANK YOU. BYE.
OKAY, I NEEDED TO GET THIS OVER WITH QUICKLY.
THEY'D BE SHORT BOUTS--PROBABLY JUST TO THE FIRST FALL.
SAY, FIVE MINUTES MAX FOR EACH FIGHT--

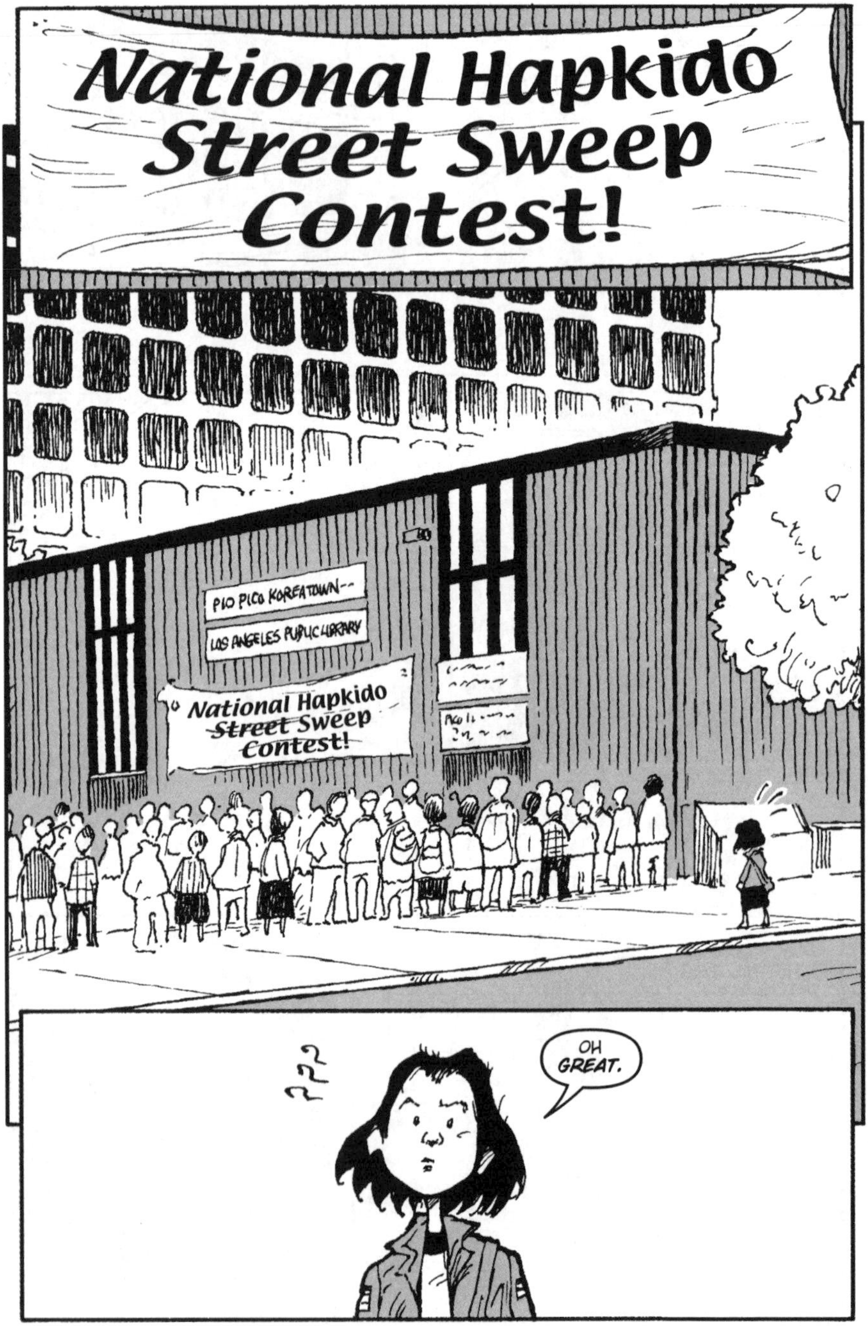
National Hapkido Street Sweep Contest!
PIO PICO KOREATOWN
LOS ANGELES PUBLIC LIBRARY
National Hapkido Street Sweep Contest!
OH GREAT.

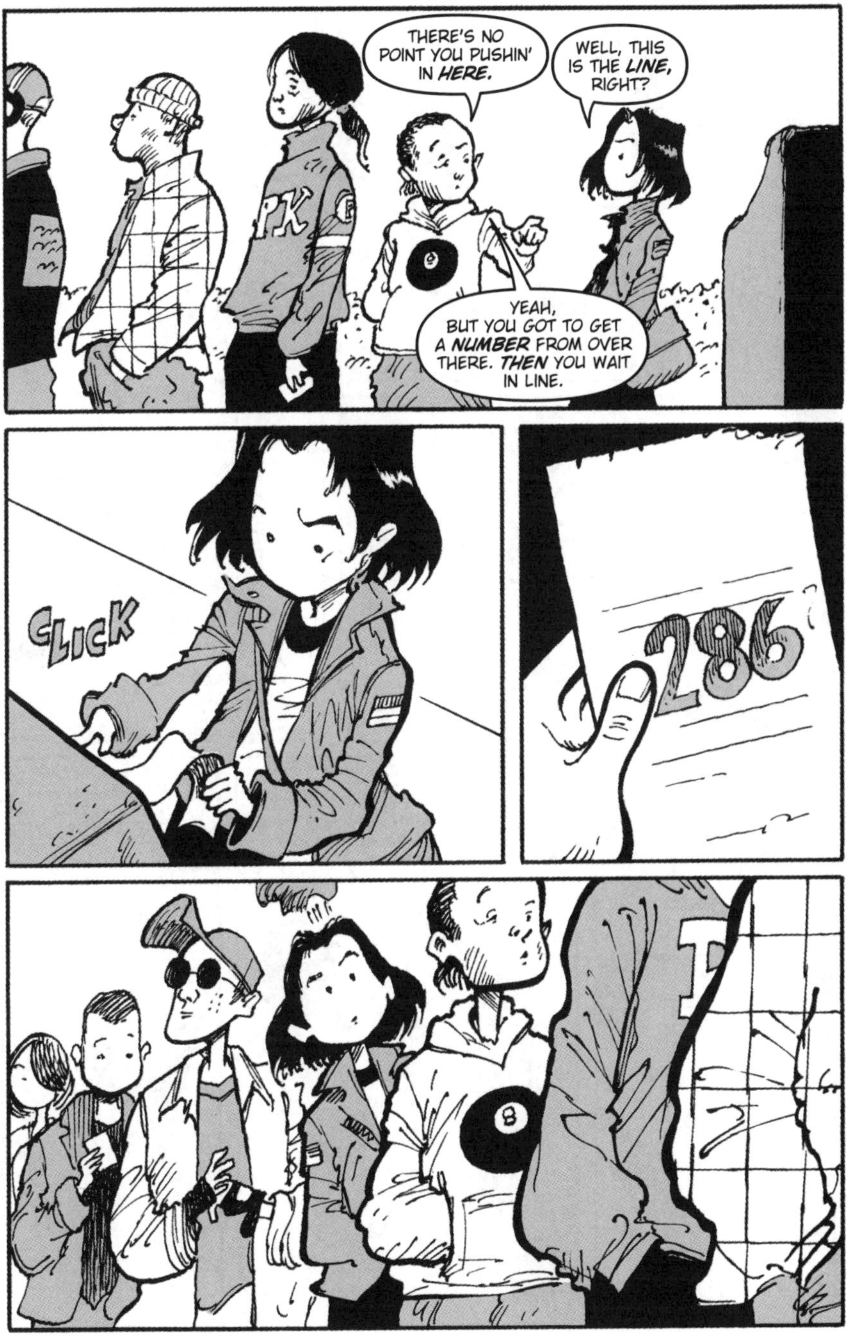
THERE'S NO POINT YOU PUSHIN' IN HERE.
WELL, THIS IS THE LINE, RIGHT?
YEAH, BUT YOU GOT TO GET A NUMBER FROM OVER THERE. THEN YOU WAIT IN LINE.
CLICK
286

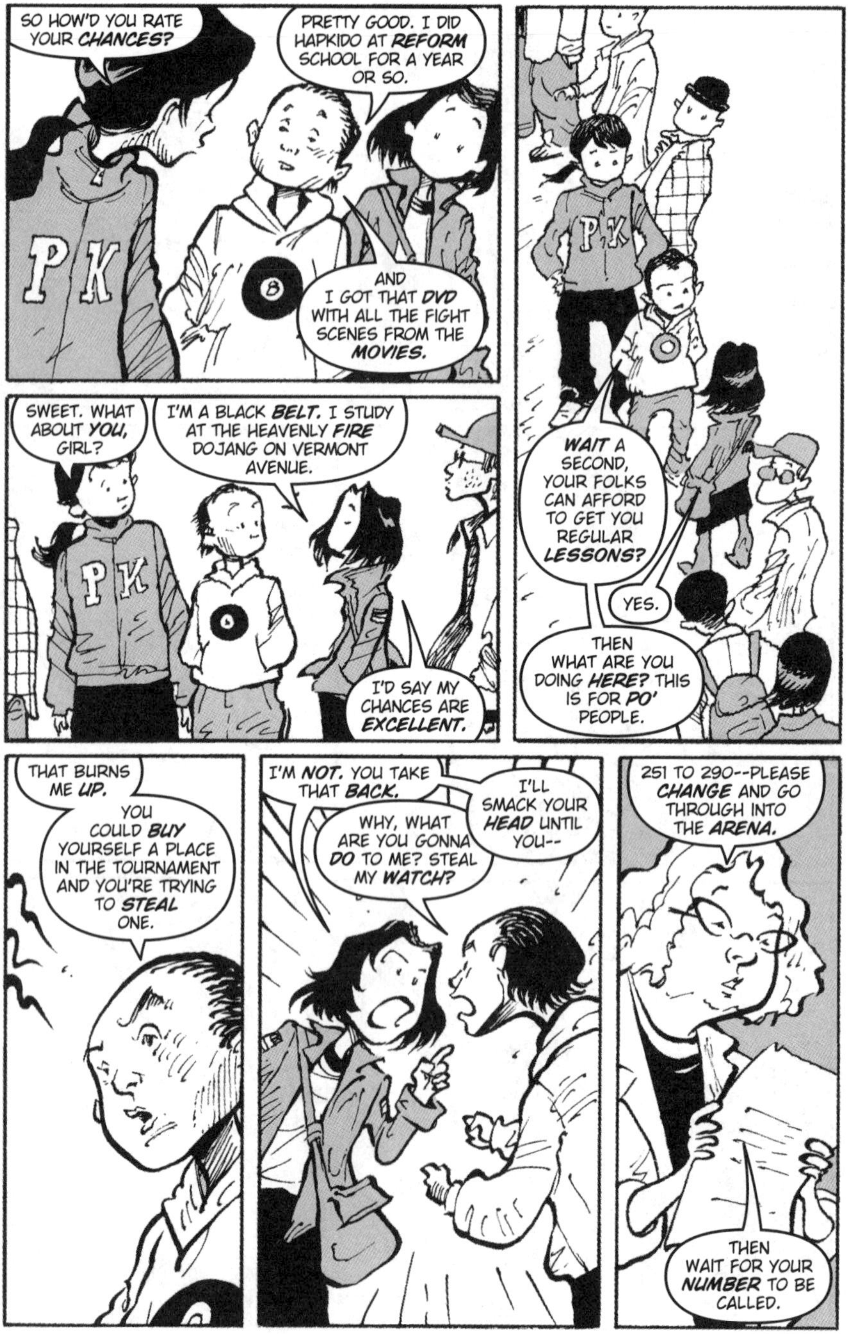
SO HOW'D YOU RATE YOUR CHANCES?
PRETTY GOOD. I DID HAPKIDO AT REFORM SCHOOL FOR A YEAR OR SO.
AND I GOT THAT DVD WITH ALL THE FIGHT SCENES FROM THE MOVIES.
PK
SWEET. WHAT ABOUT YOU, GIRL?
I'M A BLACK BELT. I STUDY AT THE HEAVENLY FIRE DOJANG ON VERMONT AVENUE.
I'D SAY MY CHANCES ARE EXCELLENT.
PK
PK
WAIT A SECOND, YOUR FOLKS CAN AFFORD TO GET YOU REGULAR LESSONS?
YES.
THEN WHAT ARE YOU DOING HERE? THIS IS FOR PO' PEOPLE.
THAT BURNS ME UP.
YOU COULD BUY YOURSELF A PLACE IN THE TOURNAMENT AND YOU'RE TRYING TO STEAL ONE.
I'M NOT. YOU TAKE THAT BACK.
WHY, WHAT ARE YOU GONNA DO TO ME? STEAL MY WATCH?
I'LL SMACK YOUR HEAD UNTIL YOU--
251 TO 290--PLEASE CHANGE AND GO THROUGH INTO THE ARENA.
THEN WAIT FOR YOUR NUMBER TO BE CALLED.

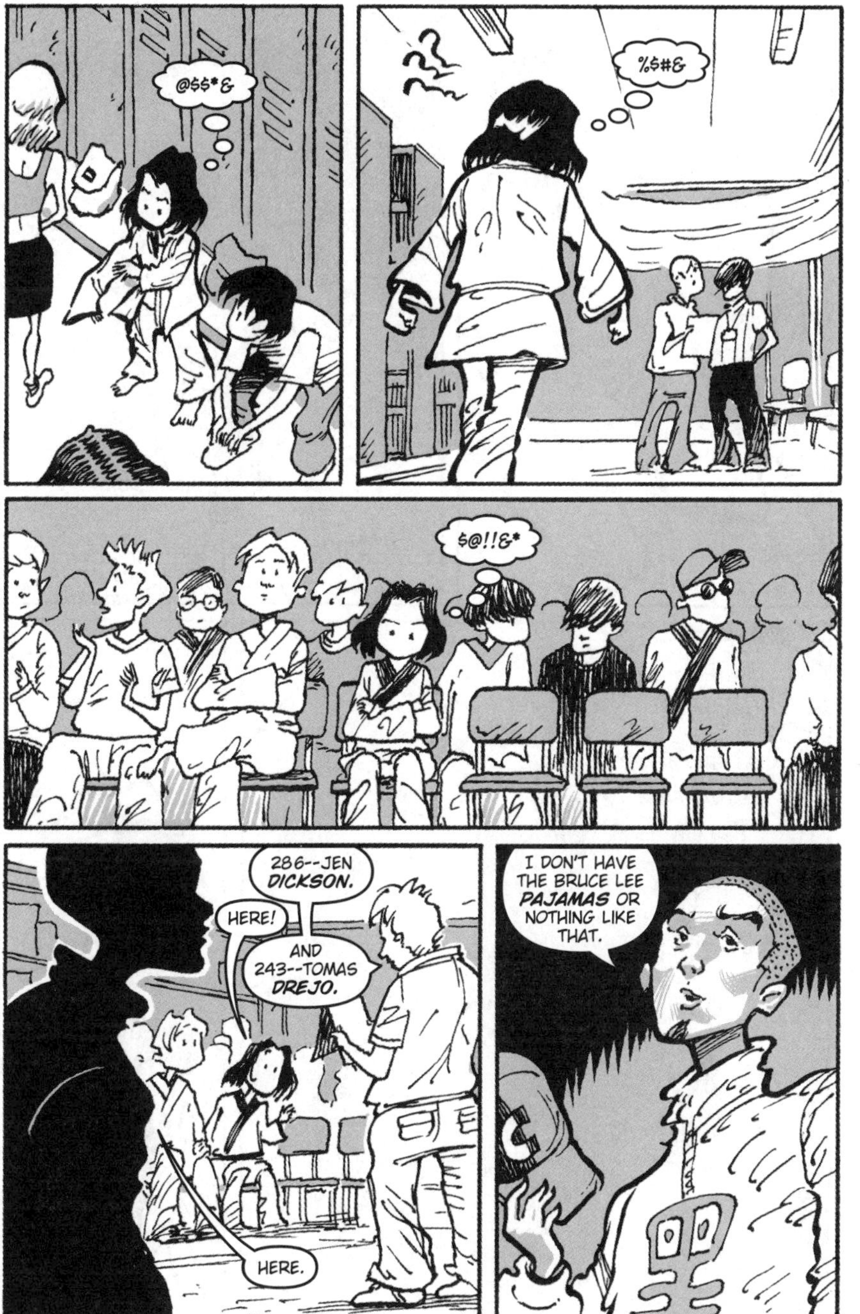
@$$*&
%$#&
$@!!&*
286--JEN
DICKSON.
HERE!
AND
243--TOMAS
DREJO.
HERE.
I DON'T HAVE
THE BRUCE LEE
PAJAMAS OR
NOTHING LIKE
THAT.

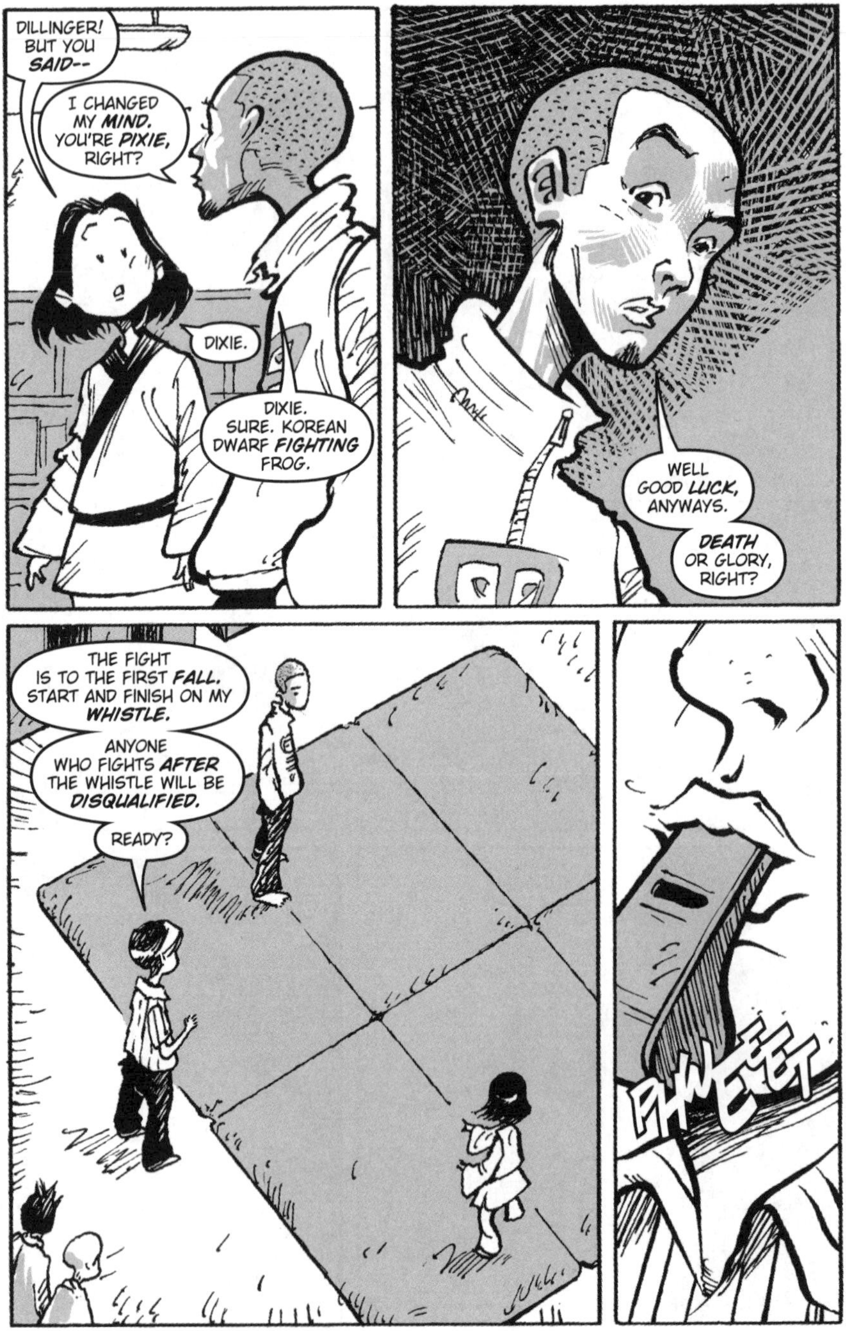
DILLINGER! BUT YOU SAID--
I CHANGED MY MIND. YOU'RE PIXIE, RIGHT?
DIXIE.
DIXIE. SURE. KOREAN DWARF FIGHTING FROG.
WELL GOOD LUCK, ANYWAYS.
DEATH OR GLORY, RIGHT?
THE FIGHT IS TO THE FIRST FALL. START AND FINISH ON MY WHISTLE.
ANYONE WHO FIGHTS AFTER THE WHISTLE WILL BE DISQUALIFIED.
READY?
PHWEEET

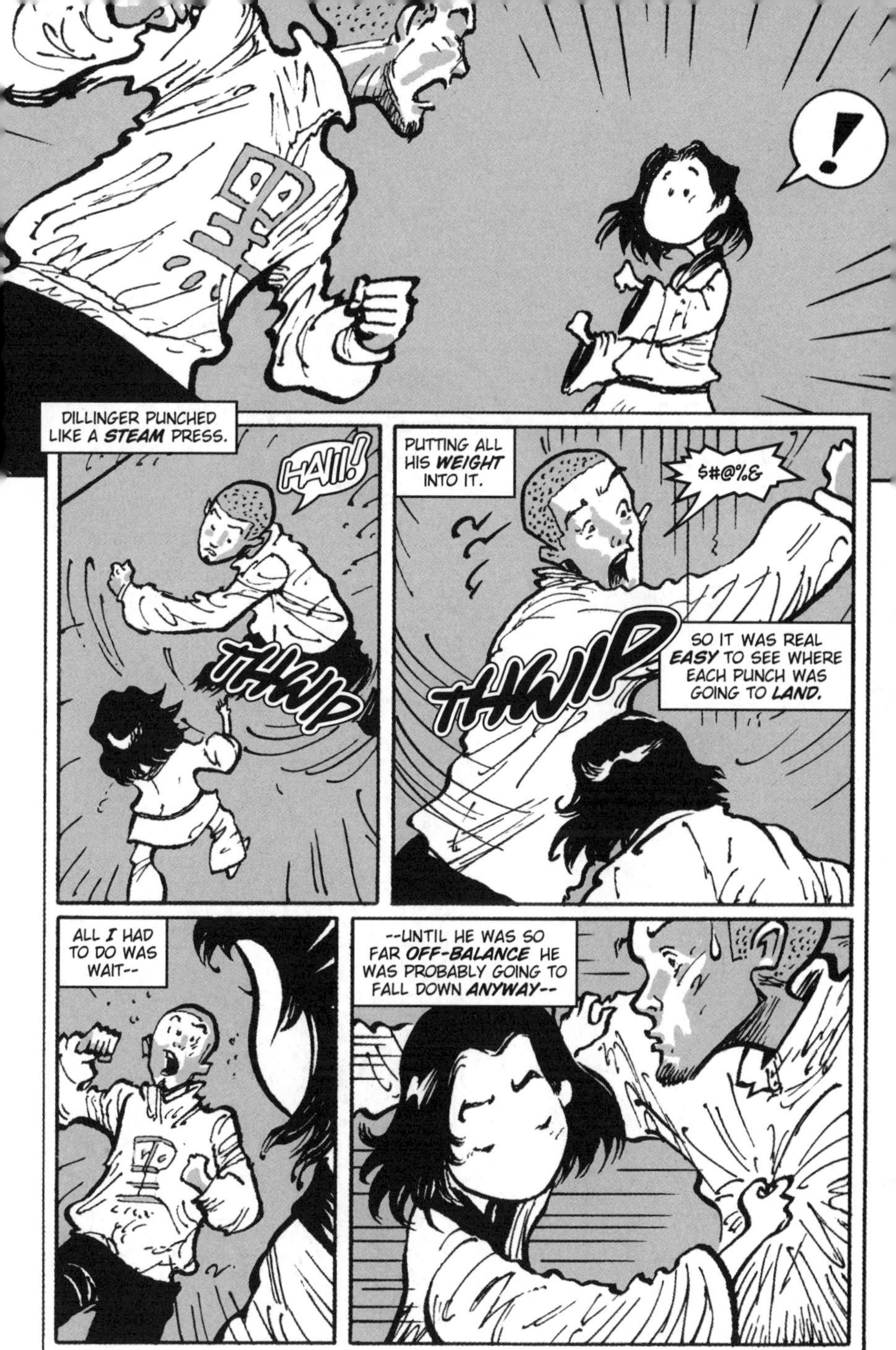
!
DILLINGER PUNCHED LIKE A STEAM PRESS.
HAII!
THWIP
PUTTING ALL HIS WEIGHT INTO IT.
$#@%&
THWIP
SO IT WAS REAL EASY TO SEE WHERE EACH PUNCH WAS GOING TO LAND.
ALL I HAD TO DO WAS WAIT--
--UNTIL HE WAS SO FAR OFF-BALANCE HE WAS PROBABLY GOING TO FALL DOWN ANYWAY--

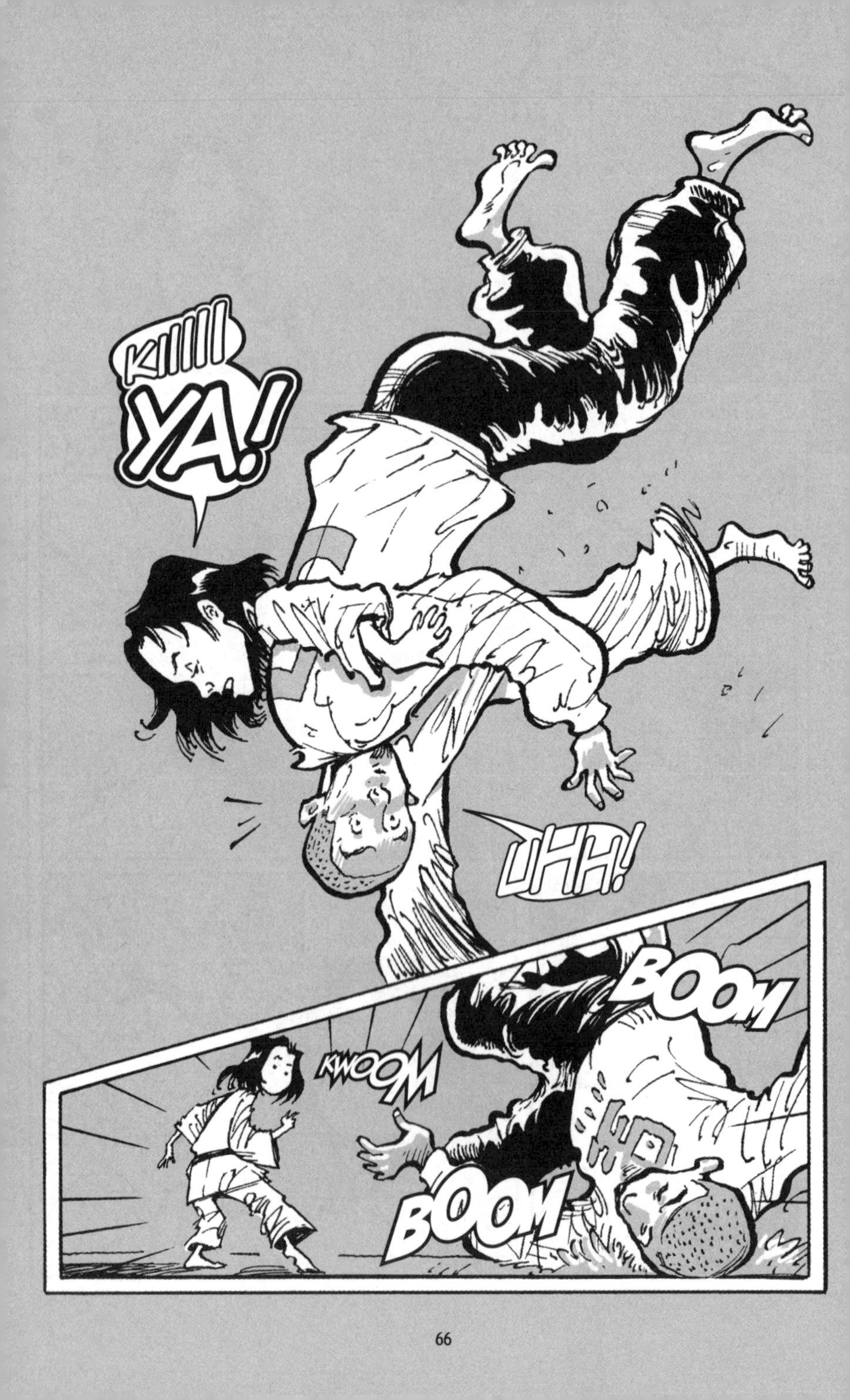
KIIIIII
YA!
UHH!
BOOM
KWOOM
BOOM

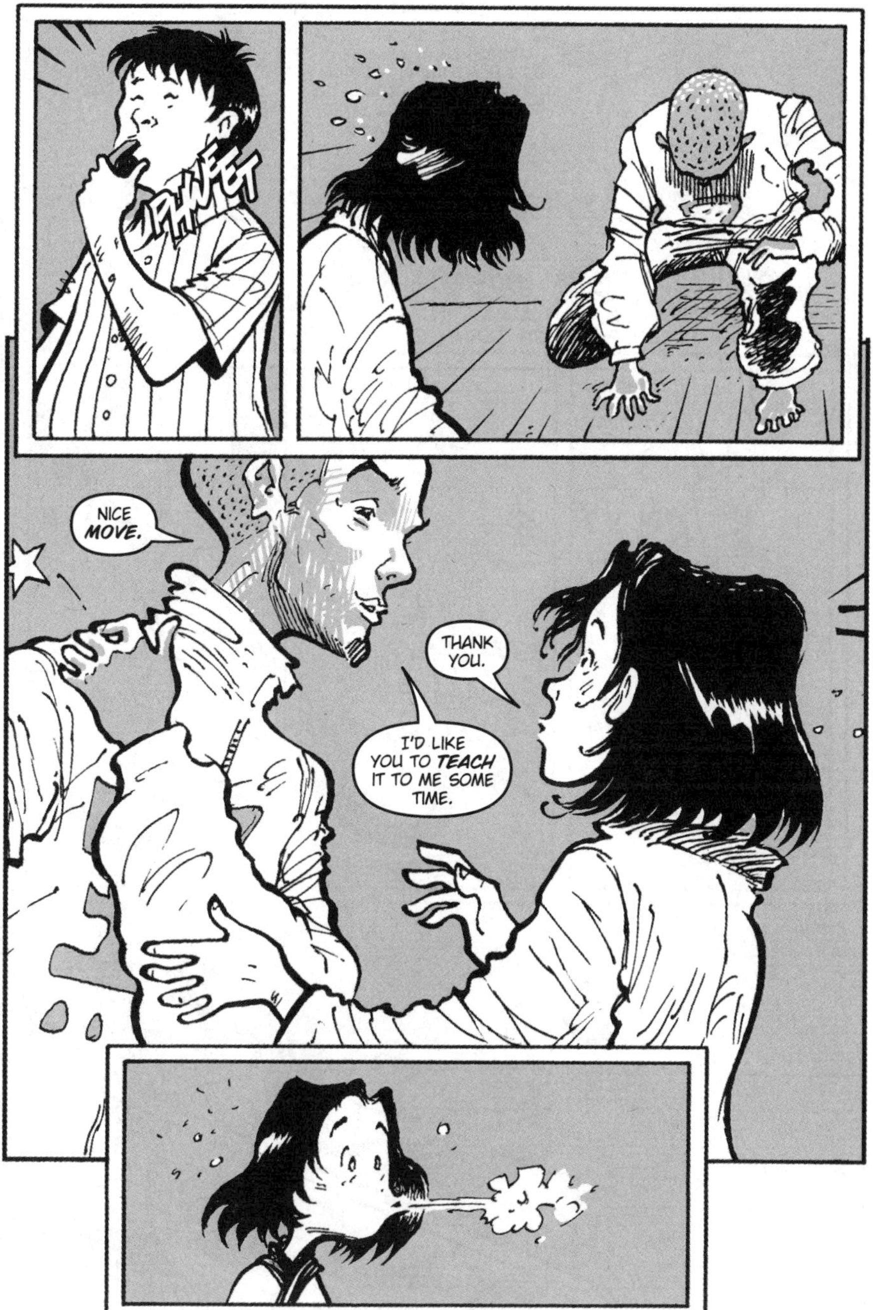
PHWEET
NICE *MOVE.*
THANK YOU.
I'D LIKE YOU TO *TEACH* IT TO ME SOME TIME.

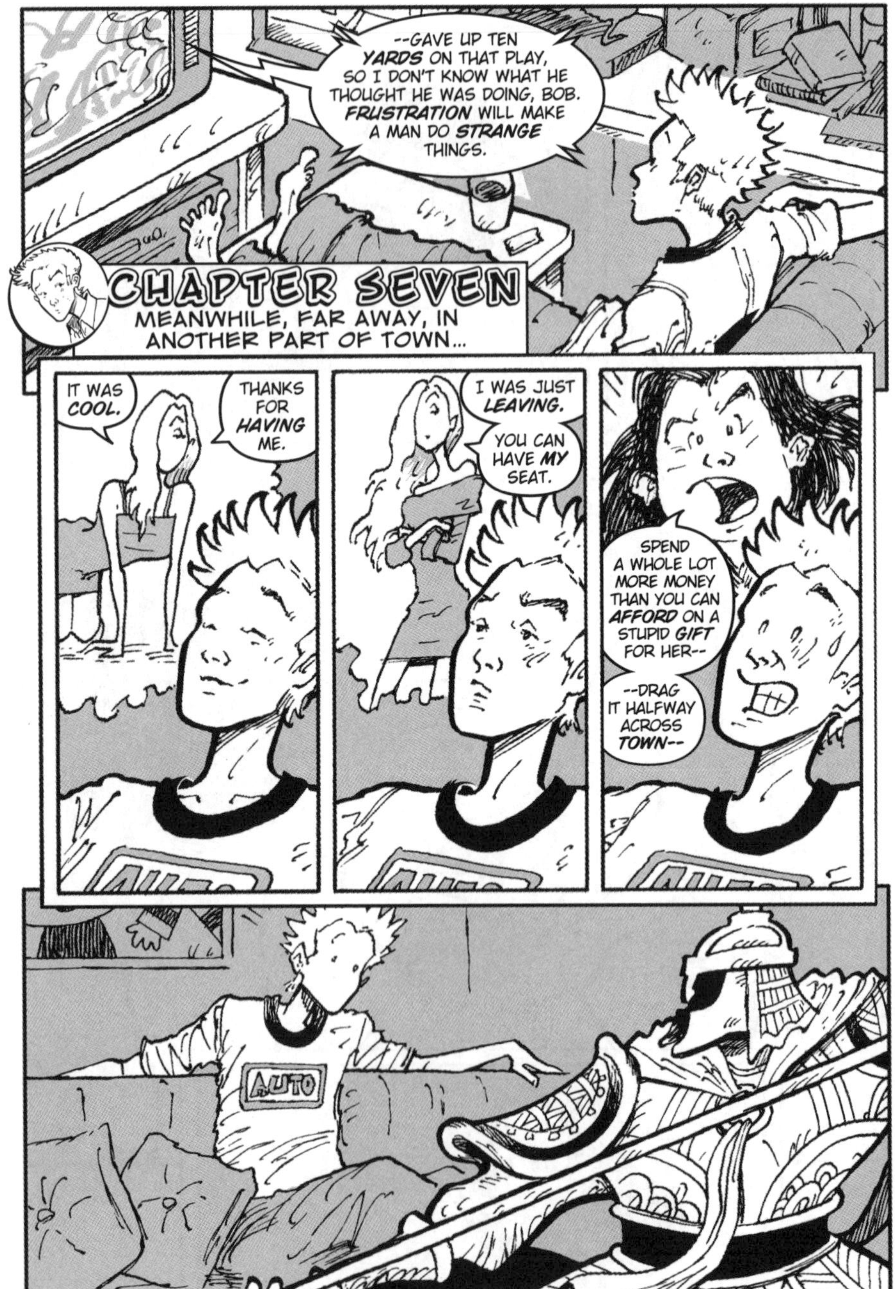
--GAVE UP TEN YARDS ON THAT PLAY, SO I DON'T KNOW WHAT HE THOUGHT HE WAS DOING, BOB. FRUSTRATION WILL MAKE A MAN DO STRANGE THINGS.
CHAPTER SEVEN
MEANWHILE, FAR AWAY, IN ANOTHER PART OF TOWN...
IT WAS COOL.
THANKS FOR HAVING ME.
I WAS JUST LEAVING.
YOU CAN HAVE MY SEAT.
SPEND A WHOLE LOT MORE MONEY THAN YOU CAN AFFORD ON A STUPID GIFT FOR HER--
--DRAG IT HALFWAY ACROSS TOWN--
AUTO

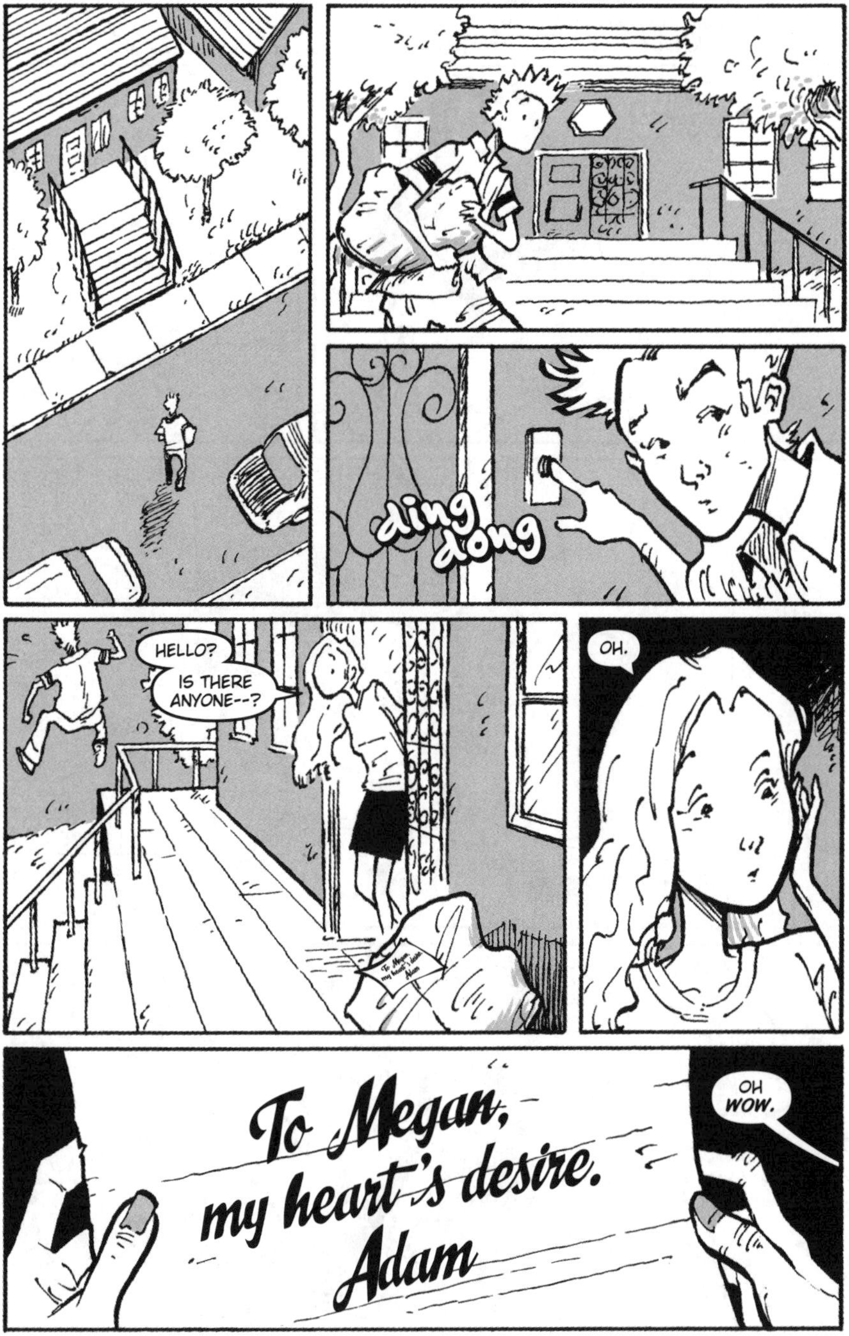
ding dong
HELLO?
IS THERE ANYONE--?
To Megan, my heart's desire. Adam
OH.
To Megan,
my heart's desire.
Adam
OH WOW.

CHAPTER EIGHT

DON'T EVEN READ THIS CHAPTER-- PLEASE! YOU CAN JUST SKIP IT AND READ THE SUMMARY ON PAGE 71.

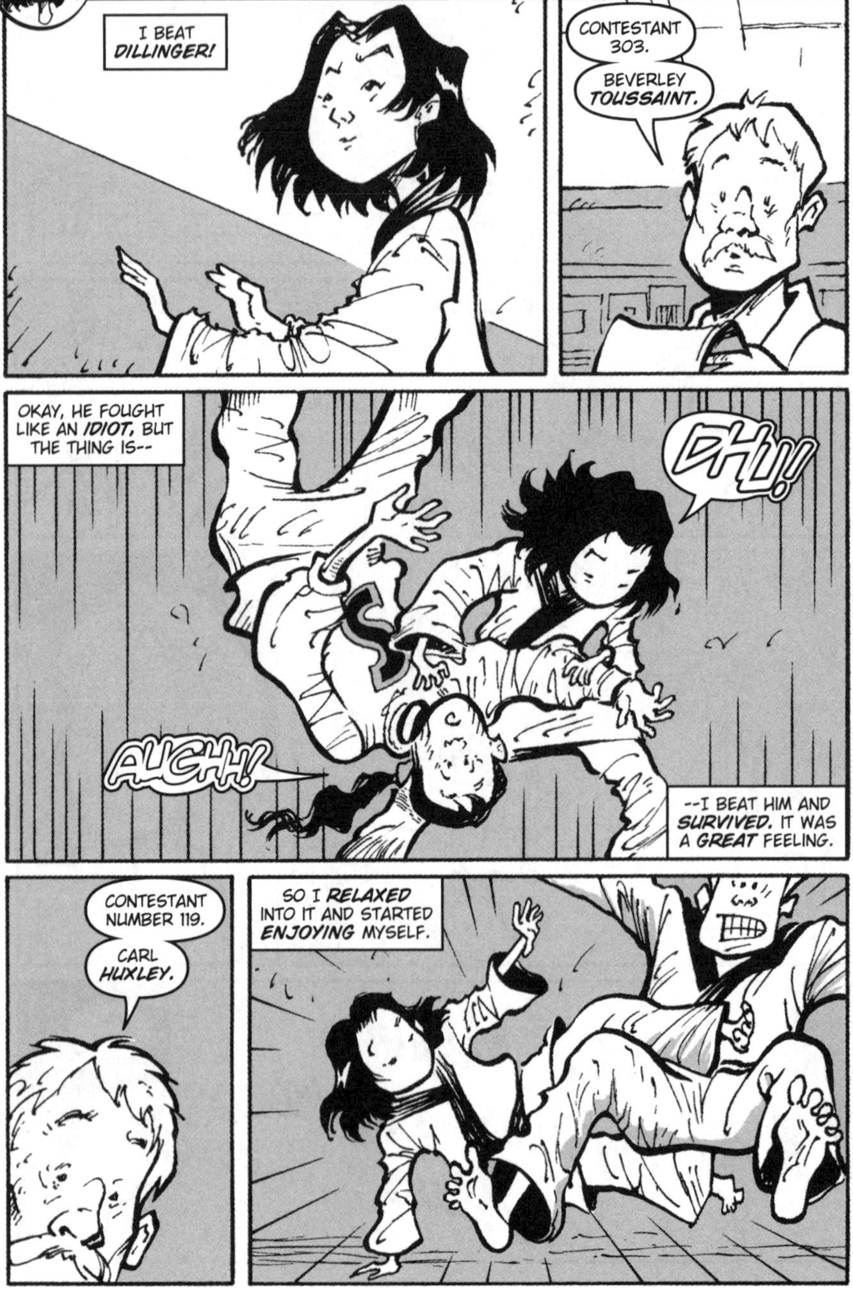

I BEAT *DILLINGER!*
CONTESTANT 303.
BEVERLEY *TOUSSAINT.*
OKAY, HE FOUGHT LIKE AN *IDIOT,* BUT THE THING IS--
DHU!!
AUGH!
--I BEAT HIM AND *SURVIVED.* IT WAS A *GREAT* FEELING.
CONTESTANT NUMBER 119.
CARL *HUXLEY.*
SO I *RELAXED* INTO IT AND STARTED *ENJOYING* MYSELF.

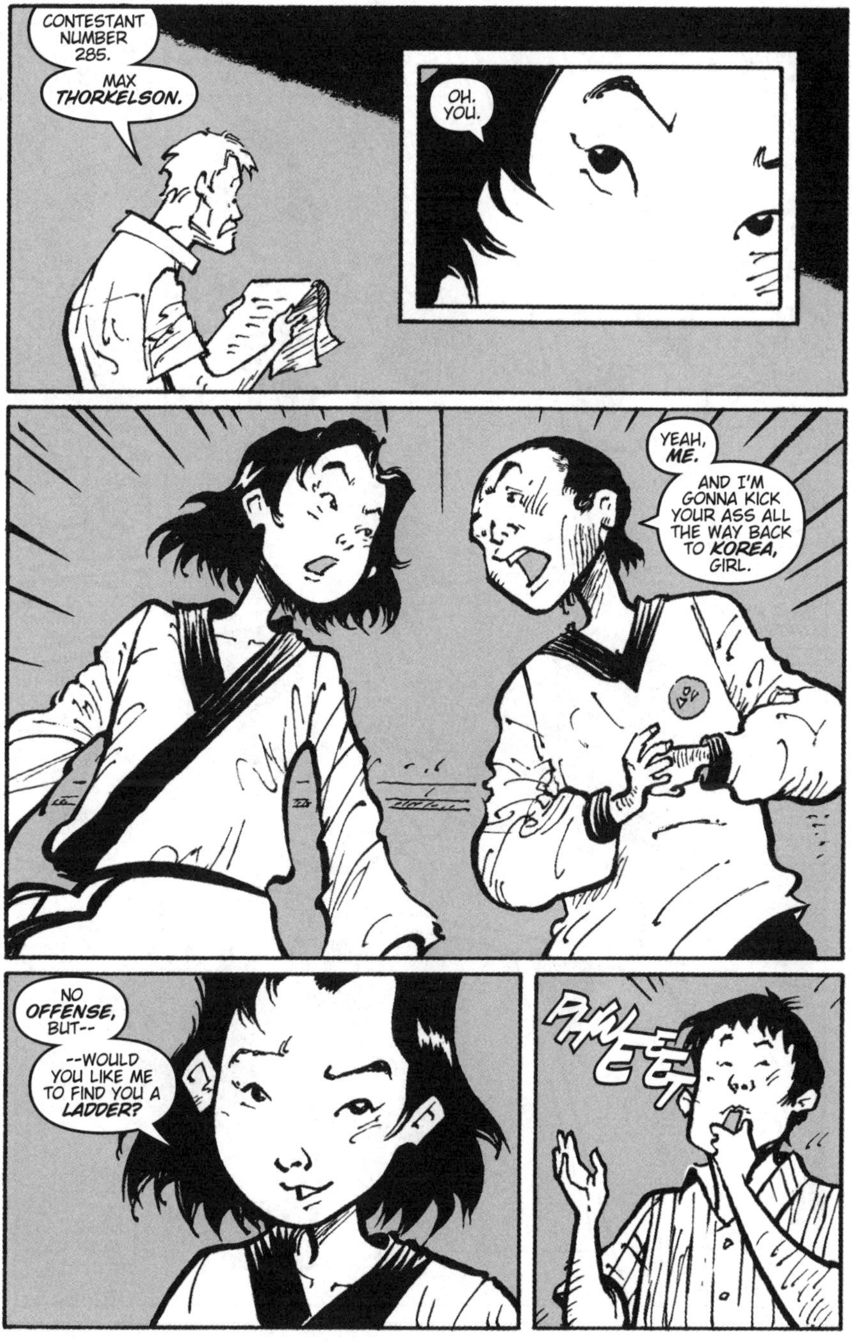
CONTESTANT NUMBER 285.
MAX THORKELSON.
OH. YOU.
YEAH, ME.
AND I'M GONNA KICK YOUR ASS ALL THE WAY BACK TO KOREA, GIRL.
NO OFFENSE, BUT--
--WOULD YOU LIKE ME TO FIND YOU A LADDER?
PHWEEET

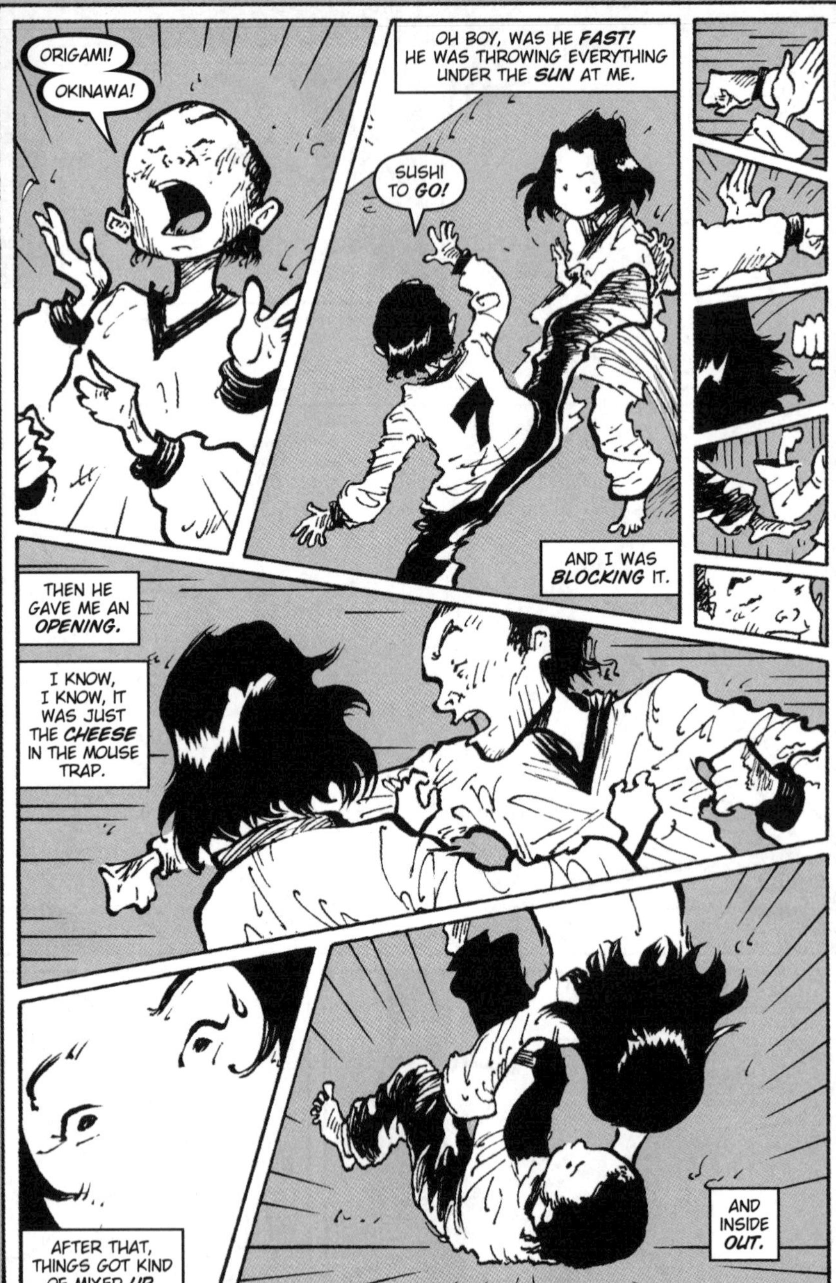
ORIGAMI!
OKINAWA!
OH BOY, WAS HE FAST! HE WAS THROWING EVERYTHING UNDER THE SUN AT ME.
SUSHI TO GO!
AND I WAS BLOCKING IT.
THEN HE GAVE ME AN OPENING.
I KNOW, I KNOW, IT WAS JUST THE CHEESE IN THE MOUSE TRAP.
AFTER THAT, THINGS GOT KIND OF MIXED UP.
AND INSIDE OUT.

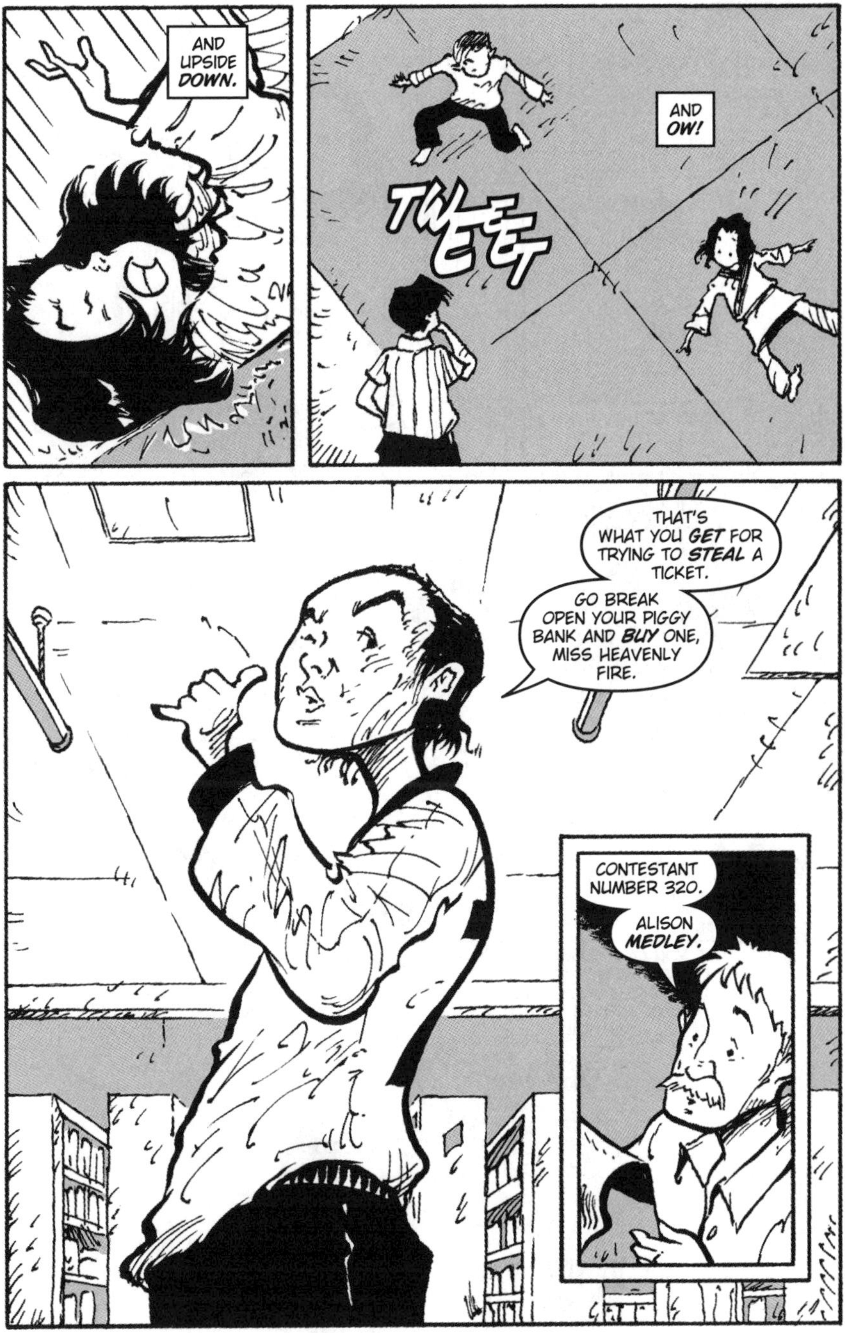
AND UPSIDE DOWN.
AND OW!
TWEET
THAT'S WHAT YOU GET FOR TRYING TO STEAL A TICKET.
GO BREAK OPEN YOUR PIGGY BANK AND BUY ONE, MISS HEAVENLY FIRE.
CONTESTANT NUMBER 320.
ALISON MEDLEY.

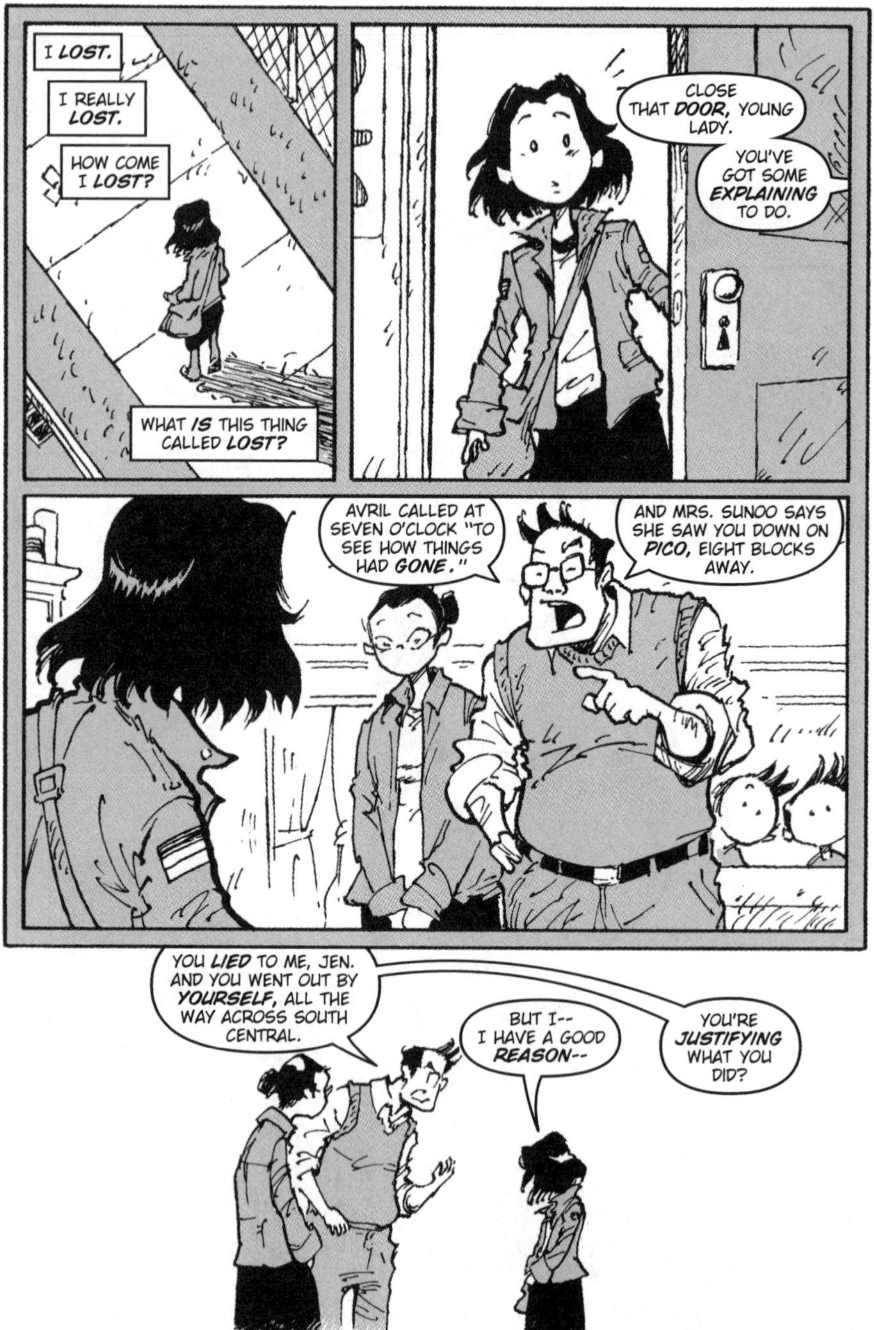
I LOST.
I REALLY LOST.
HOW COME I LOST?
WHAT IS THIS THING CALLED LOST?
CLOSE THAT DOOR, YOUNG LADY.
YOU'VE GOT SOME EXPLAINING TO DO.
AVRIL CALLED AT SEVEN O'CLOCK "TO SEE HOW THINGS HAD GONE."
AND MRS. SUNOO SAYS SHE SAW YOU DOWN ON PICO, EIGHT BLOCKS AWAY.
YOU LIED TO ME, JEN. AND YOU WENT OUT BY YOURSELF, ALL THE WAY ACROSS SOUTH CENTRAL.
BUT I-- I HAVE A GOOD REASON--
YOU'RE JUSTIFYING WHAT YOU DID?

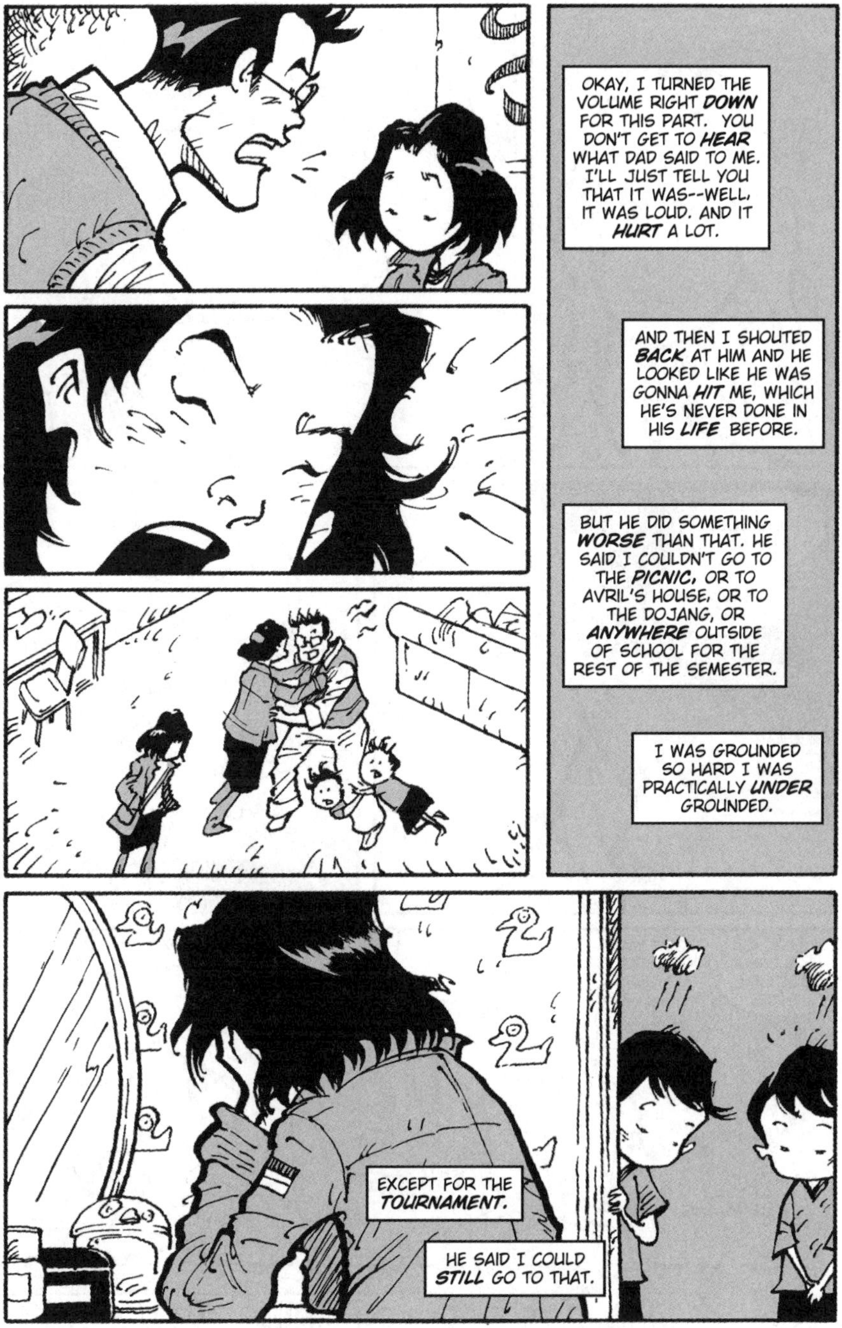
OKAY, I TURNED THE VOLUME RIGHT *DOWN* FOR THIS PART. YOU DON'T GET TO *HEAR* WHAT DAD SAID TO ME. I'LL JUST TELL YOU THAT IT WAS--WELL, IT WAS LOUD. AND IT *HURT* A LOT.
AND THEN I SHOUTED *BACK* AT HIM AND HE LOOKED LIKE HE WAS GONNA *HIT* ME, WHICH HE'S NEVER DONE IN HIS *LIFE* BEFORE.
BUT HE DID SOMETHING *WORSE* THAN THAT. HE SAID I COULDN'T GO TO THE *PICNIC,* OR TO AVRIL'S HOUSE, OR TO THE DOJANG, OR *ANYWHERE* OUTSIDE OF SCHOOL FOR THE REST OF THE SEMESTER.
I WAS GROUNDED SO HARD I WAS PRACTICALLY *UNDER* GROUNDED.
EXCEPT FOR THE *TOURNAMENT.*
HE SAID I COULD *STILL* GO TO THAT.

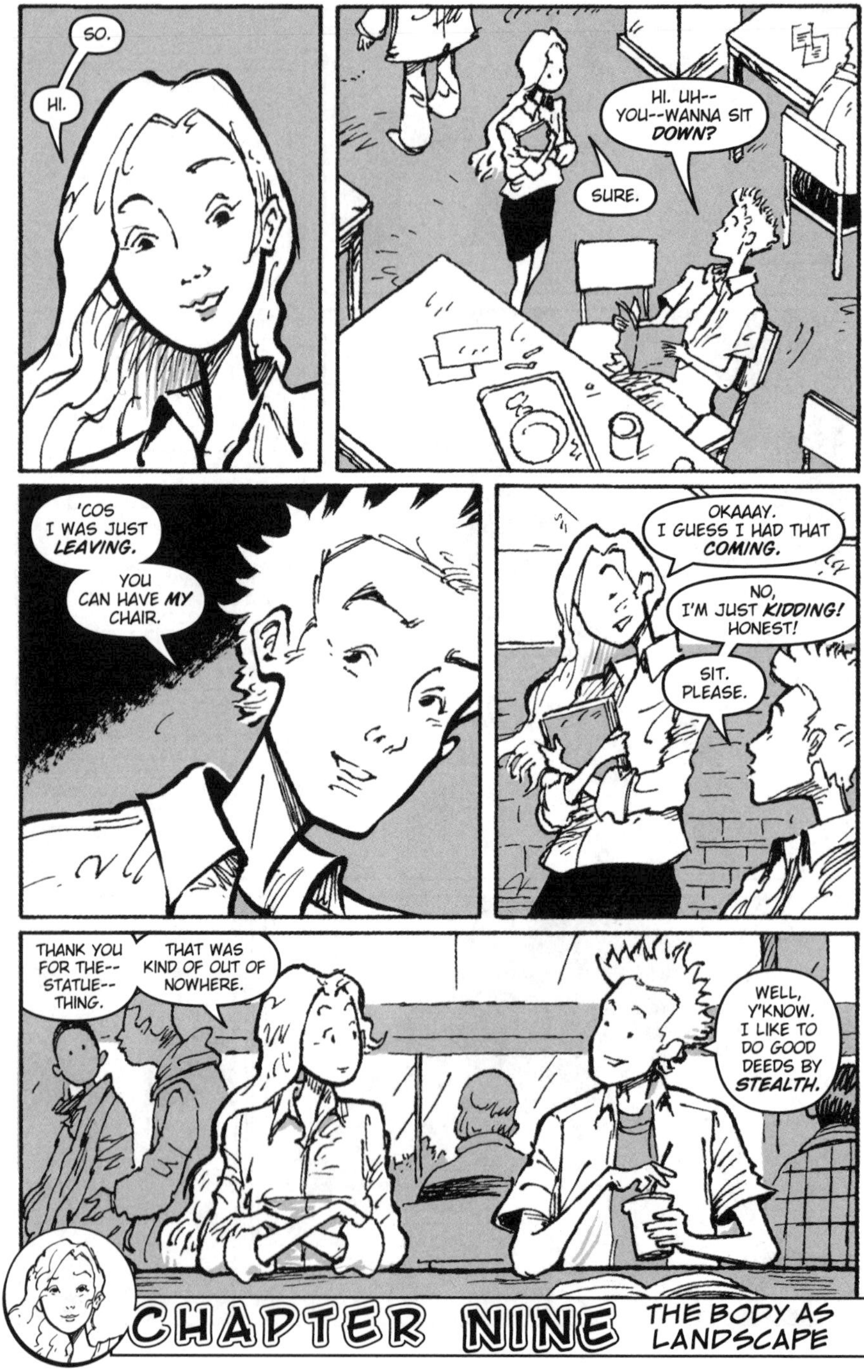
SO.
HI.
HI. UH-- YOU--WANNA SIT DOWN?
SURE.
'COS I WAS JUST LEAVING.
YOU CAN HAVE MY CHAIR.
OKAAAY. I GUESS I HAD THAT COMING.
NO, I'M JUST KIDDING! HONEST!
SIT. PLEASE.
THANK YOU FOR THE-- STATUE-- THING.
THAT WAS KIND OF OUT OF NOWHERE.
WELL, Y'KNOW. I LIKE TO DO GOOD DEEDS BY STEALTH.
CHAPTER NINE
THE BODY AS LANDSCAPE

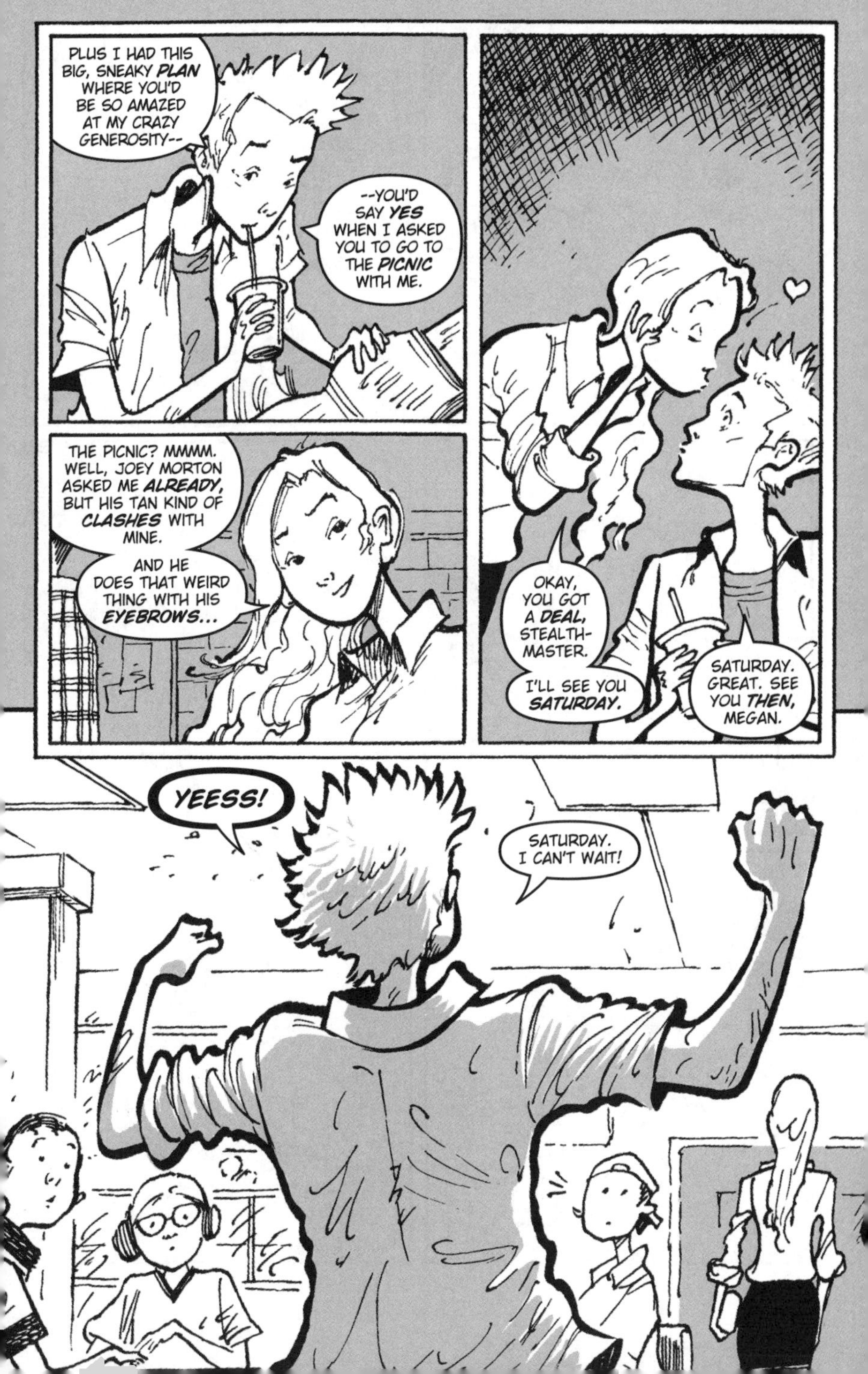
PLUS I HAD THIS BIG, SNEAKY PLAN WHERE YOU'D BE SO AMAZED AT MY CRAZY GENEROSITY--
--YOU'D SAY YES WHEN I ASKED YOU TO GO TO THE PICNIC WITH ME.
THE PICNIC? MMMM. WELL, JOEY MORTON ASKED ME ALREADY, BUT HIS TAN KIND OF CLASHES WITH MINE.
AND HE DOES THAT WEIRD THING WITH HIS EYEBROWS...
OKAY, YOU GOT A DEAL, STEALTH-MASTER.
I'LL SEE YOU SATURDAY.
SATURDAY. GREAT. SEE YOU THEN, MEGAN.
YEESS!
SATURDAY. I CAN'T WAIT!

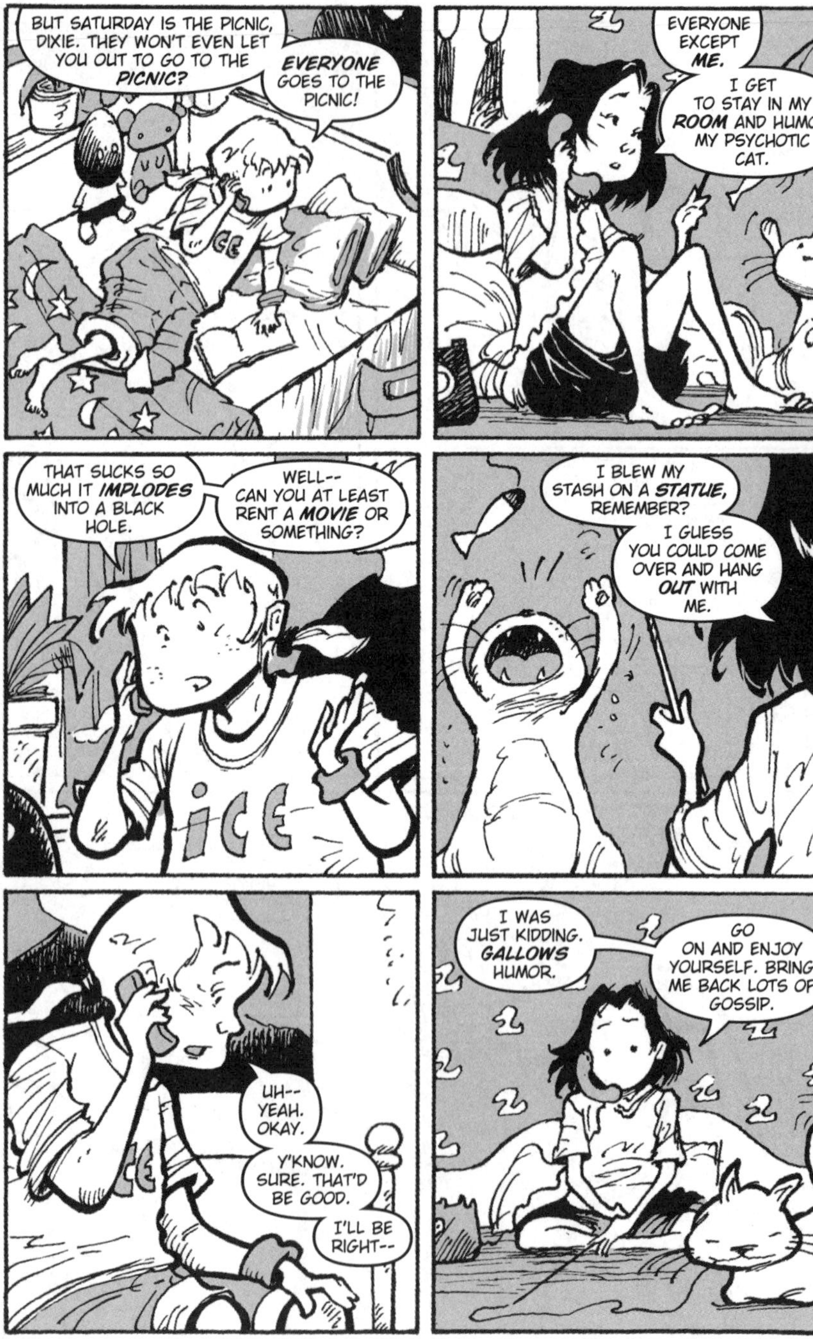
BUT SATURDAY IS THE PICNIC, DIXIE. THEY WON'T EVEN LET YOU OUT TO GO TO THE PICNIC?
EVERYONE GOES TO THE PICNIC!
EVERYONE EXCEPT ME.
I GET TO STAY IN MY ROOM AND HUMOR MY PSYCHOTIC CAT.
THAT SUCKS SO MUCH IT IMPLODES INTO A BLACK HOLE.
WELL-- CAN YOU AT LEAST RENT A MOVIE OR SOMETHING?
I BLEW MY STASH ON A STATUE, REMEMBER?
I GUESS YOU COULD COME OVER AND HANG OUT WITH ME.
UH-- YEAH. OKAY.
Y'KNOW. SURE. THAT'D BE GOOD.
I'LL BE RIGHT--
I WAS JUST KIDDING. GALLOWS HUMOR.
GO ON AND ENJOY YOURSELF. BRING ME BACK LOTS OF GOSSIP.

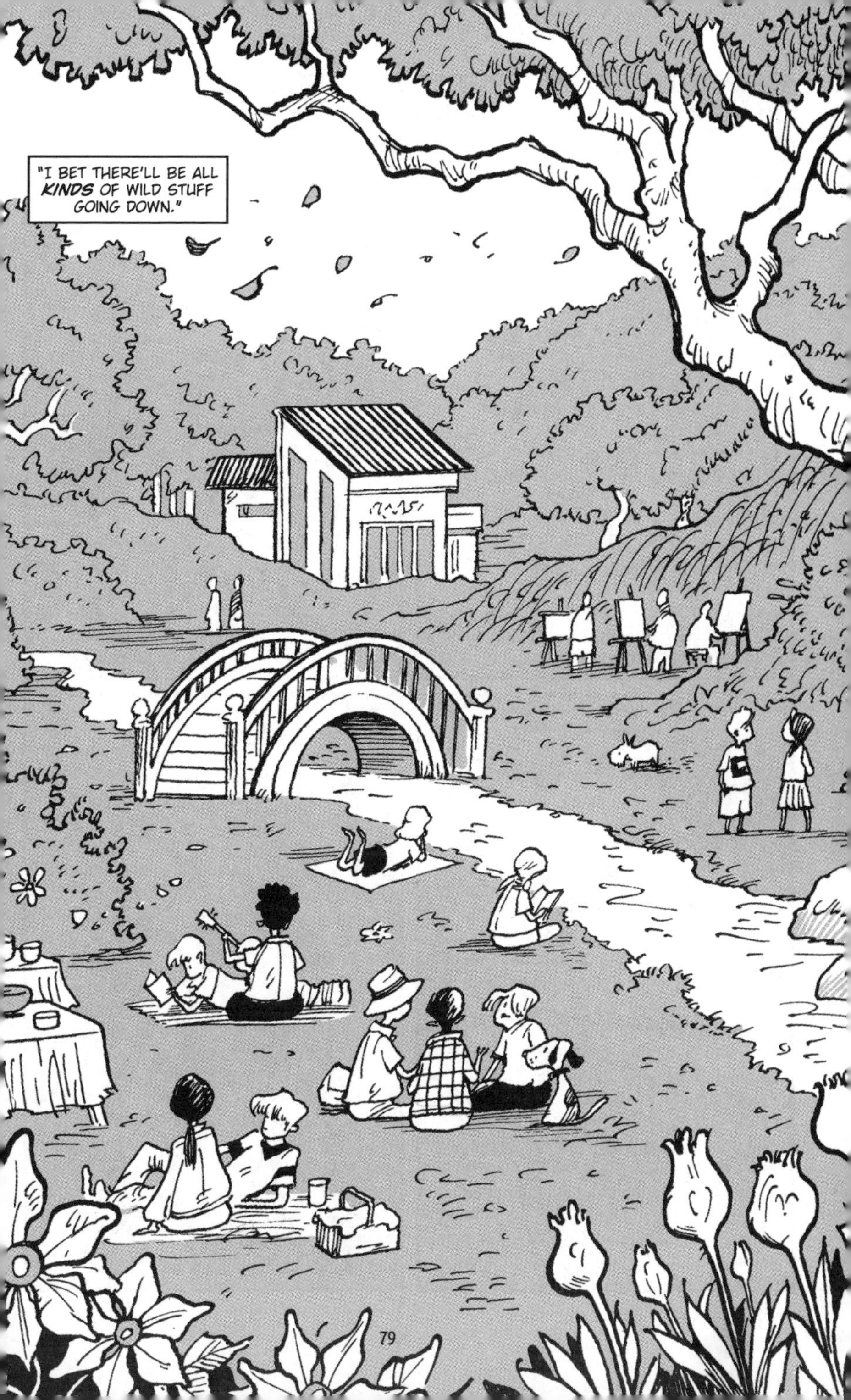
"I BET THERE'LL BE ALL KINDS OF WILD STUFF GOING DOWN."

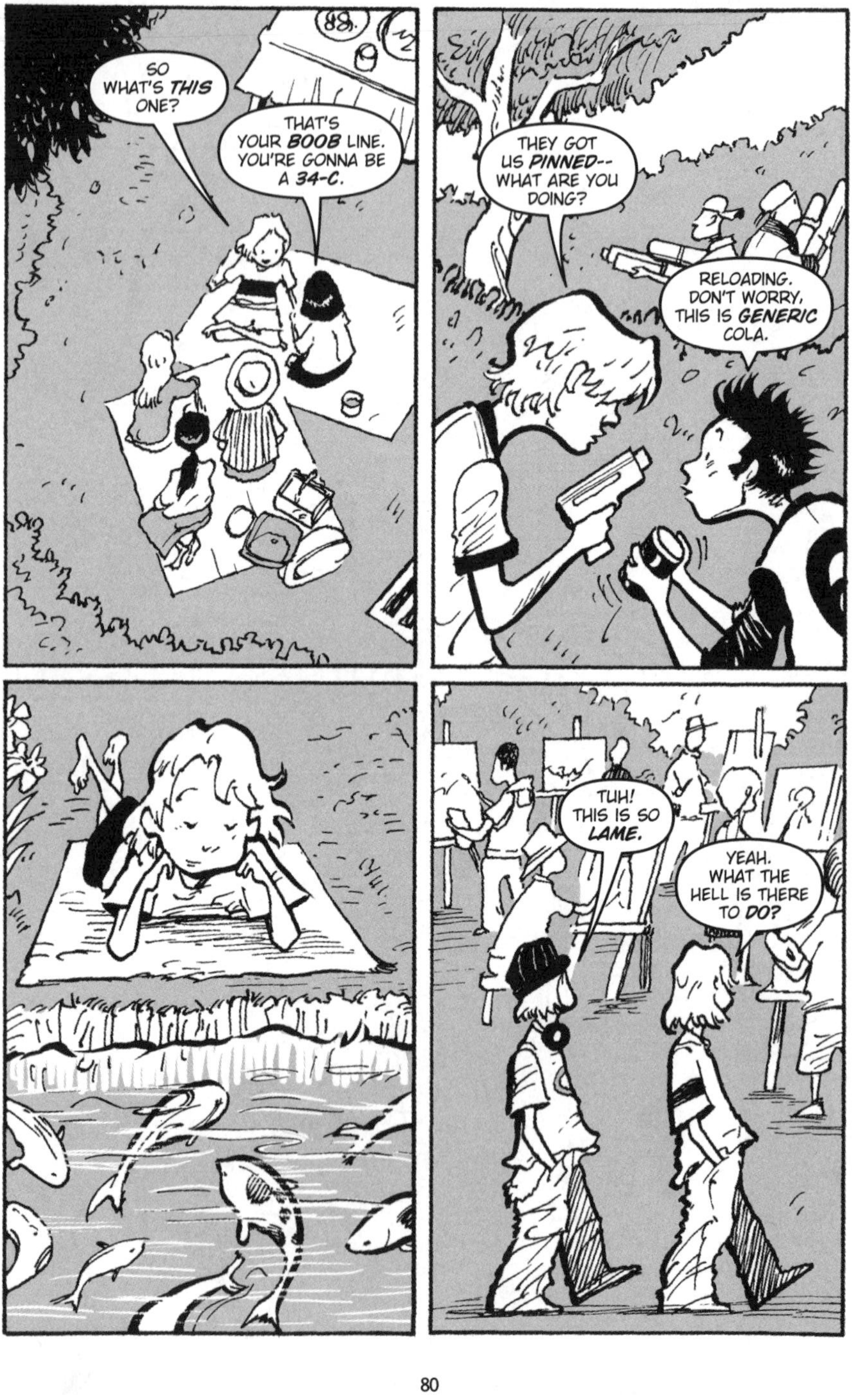
SO WHAT'S THIS ONE?
THAT'S YOUR BOOB LINE. YOU'RE GONNA BE A 34-C.
THEY GOT US PINNED-- WHAT ARE YOU DOING?
RELOADING. DON'T WORRY, THIS IS GENERIC COLA.
TUH! THIS IS SO LAME.
YEAH. WHAT THE HELL IS THERE TO DO?

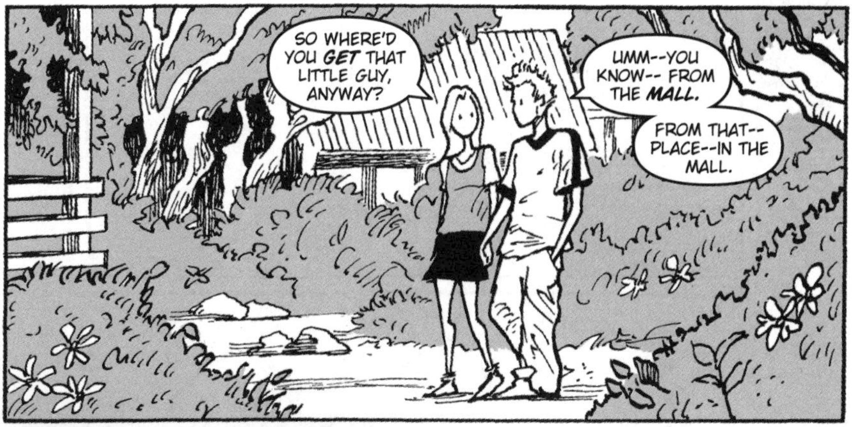
SO WHERE'D YOU GET THAT LITTLE GUY, ANYWAY?
UMM--YOU KNOW-- FROM THE MALL.
FROM THAT--PLACE--IN THE MALL.

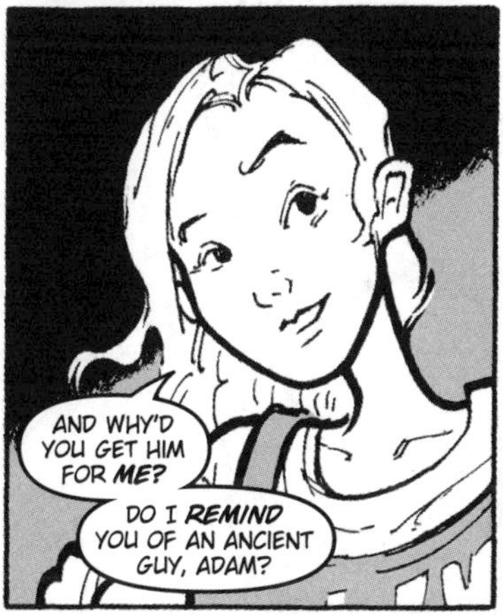
AND WHY'D YOU GET HIM FOR ME?
DO I REMIND YOU OF AN ANCIENT GUY, ADAM?

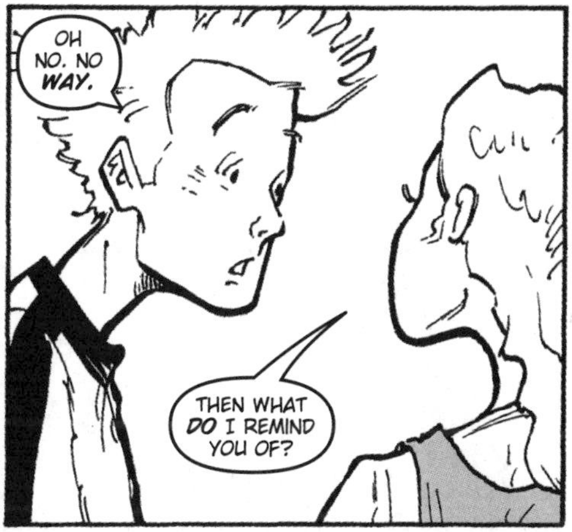
OH NO. NO WAY.
THEN WHAT DO I REMIND YOU OF?

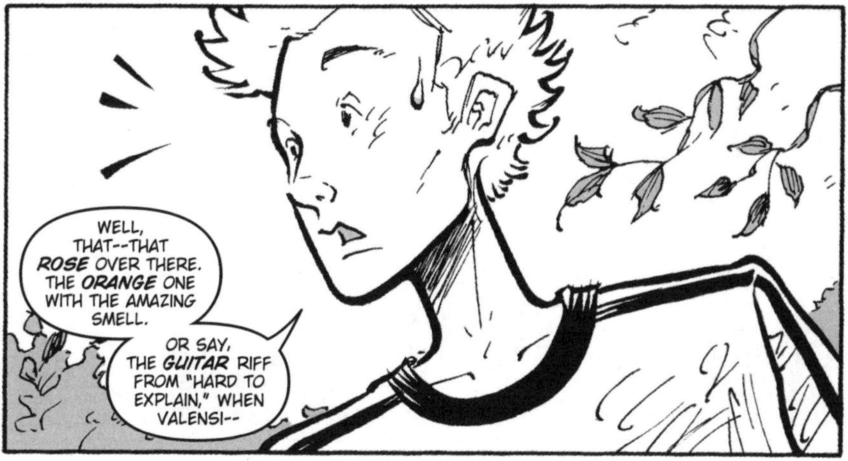
WELL, THAT--THAT ROSE OVER THERE. THE ORANGE ONE WITH THE AMAZING SMELL.
OR SAY, THE GUITAR RIFF FROM "HARD TO EXPLAIN," WHEN VALENSI--

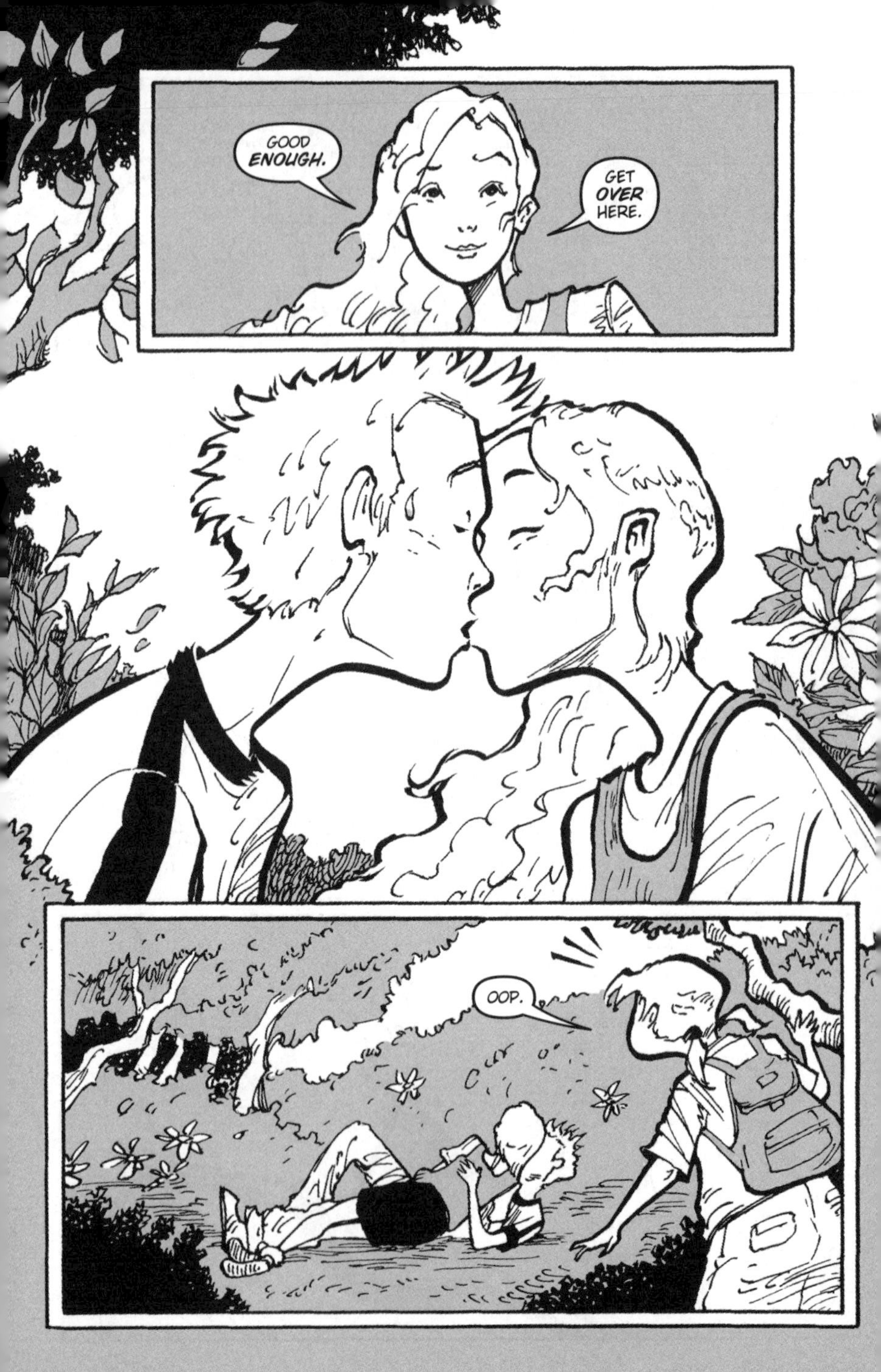
GOOD ENOUGH.
GET OVER HERE.
OOP.

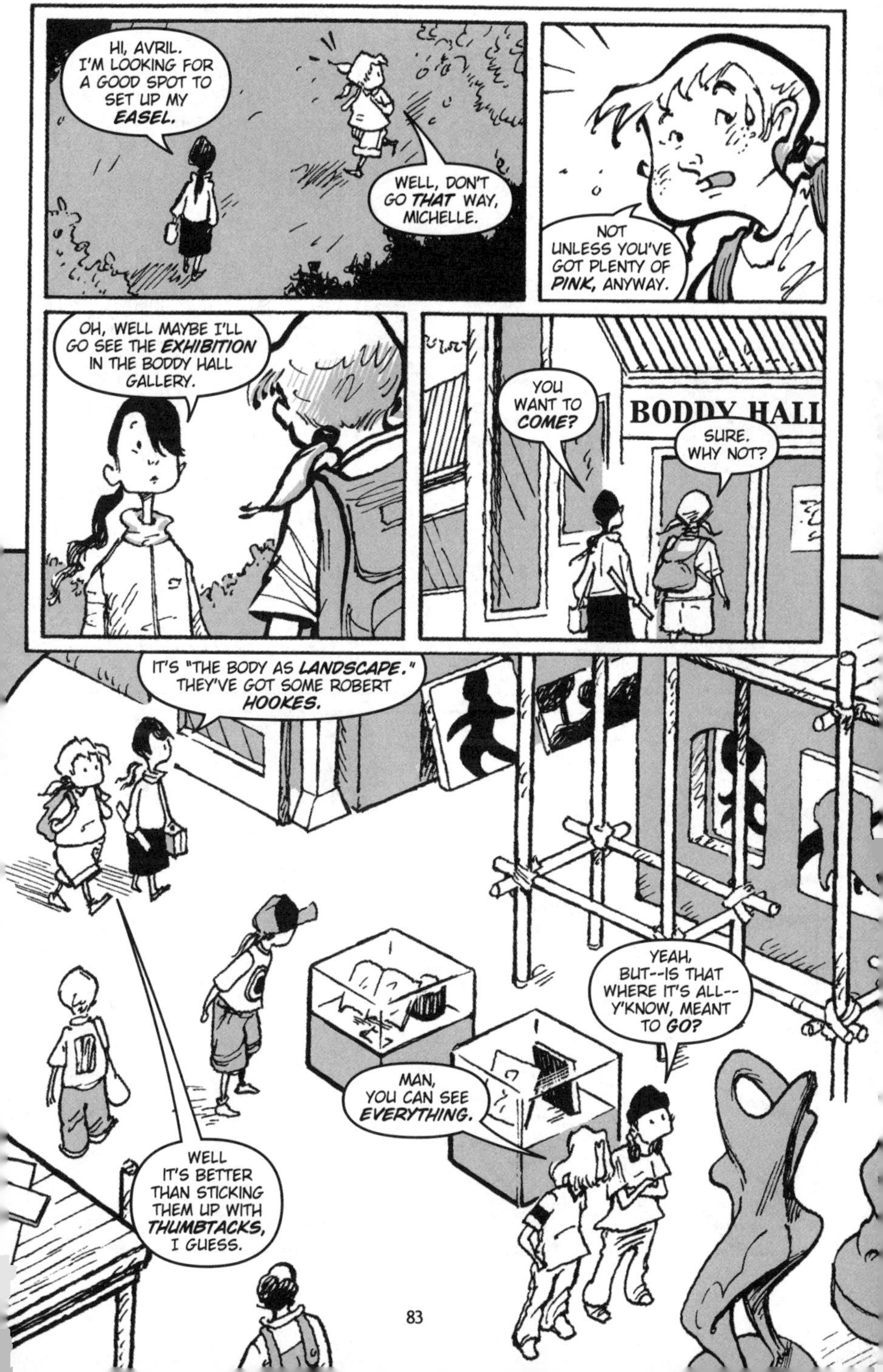
HI, AVRIL. I'M LOOKING FOR A GOOD SPOT TO SET UP MY EASEL.
WELL, DON'T GO THAT WAY, MICHELLE.
NOT UNLESS YOU'VE GOT PLENTY OF PINK, ANYWAY.
OH, WELL MAYBE I'LL GO SEE THE EXHIBITION IN THE BODDY HALL GALLERY.
YOU WANT TO COME?
BODDY HALL
SURE. WHY NOT?
IT'S "THE BODY AS LANDSCAPE." THEY'VE GOT SOME ROBERT HOOKES.
WELL IT'S BETTER THAN STICKING THEM UP WITH THUMBTACKS, I GUESS.
MAN, YOU CAN SEE EVERYTHING.
YEAH, BUT--IS THAT WHERE IT'S ALL-- Y'KNOW, MEANT TO GO?

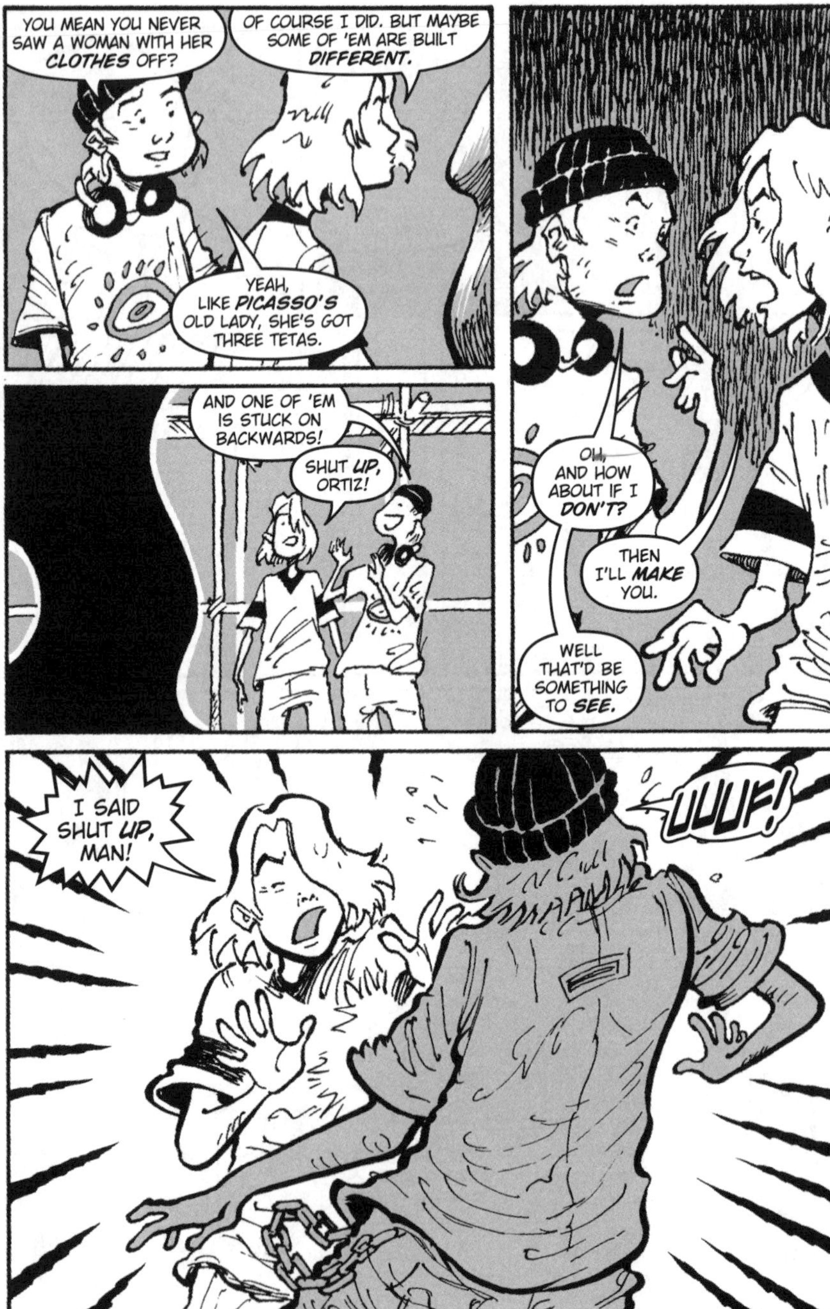

YOU MEAN YOU NEVER SAW A WOMAN WITH HER CLOTHES OFF?
OF COURSE I DID. BUT MAYBE SOME OF 'EM ARE BUILT DIFFERENT.
YEAH, LIKE PICASSO'S OLD LADY, SHE'S GOT THREE TETAS.
AND ONE OF 'EM IS STUCK ON BACKWARDS!
SHUT UP, ORTIZ!
OH, AND HOW ABOUT IF I DON'T?
THEN I'LL MAKE YOU.
WELL THAT'D BE SOMETHING TO SEE.
I SAID SHUT UP, MAN!
UUUF!

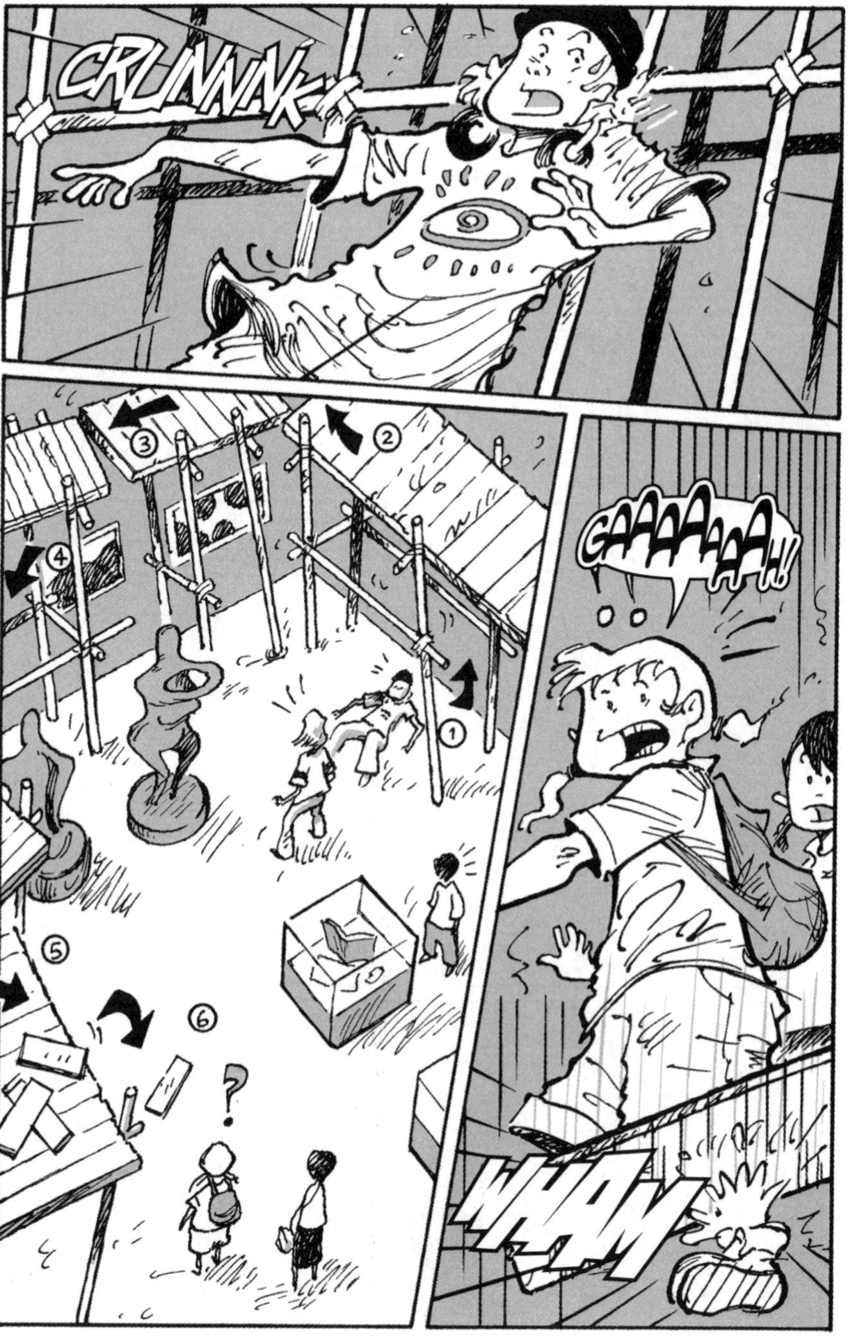
CRUNNNK
GAAAAAAAAH!!
WHAM
?

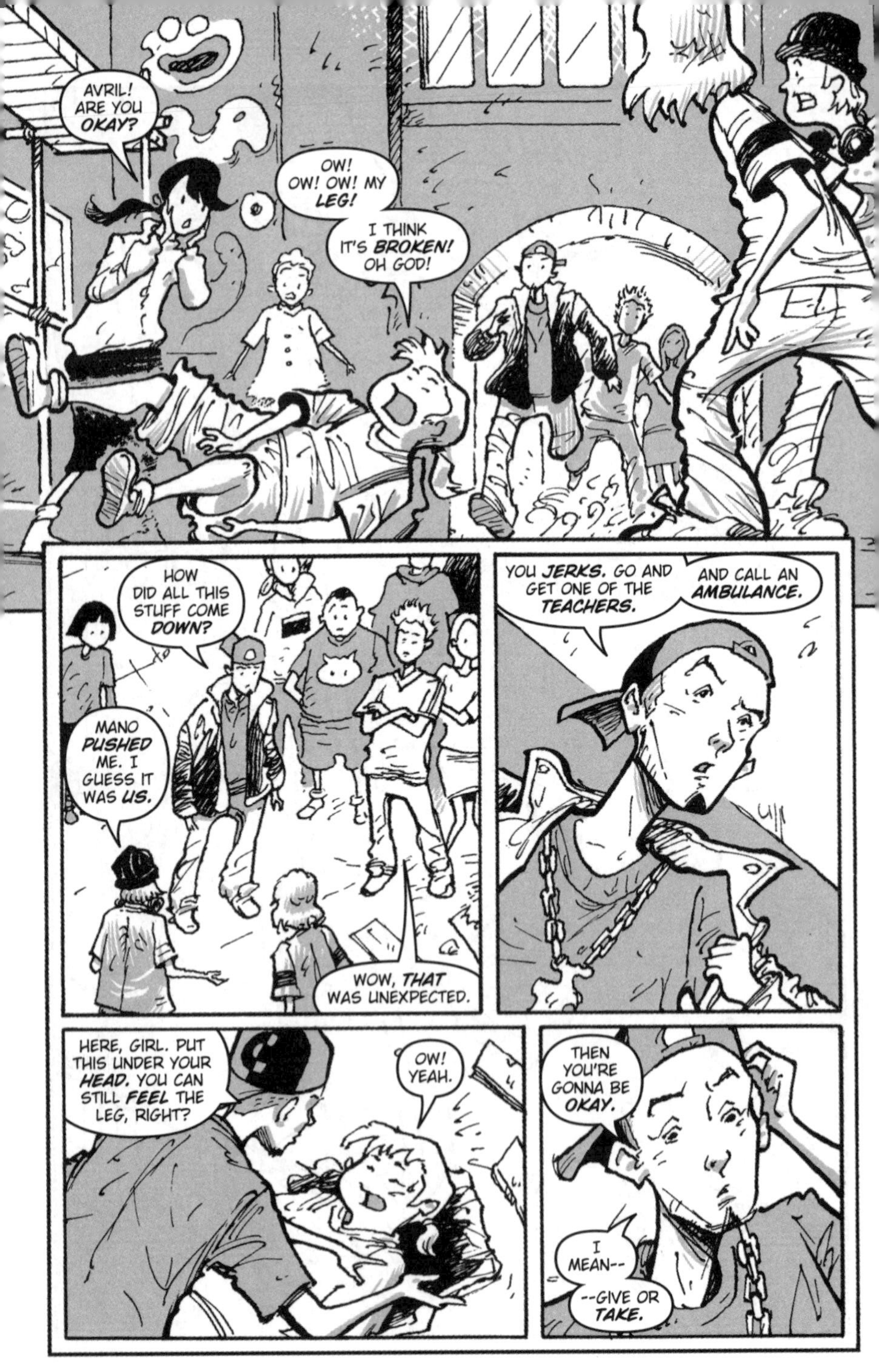
AVRIL! ARE YOU OKAY?
OW! OW! OW! MY LEG!
I THINK IT'S BROKEN! OH GOD!
HOW DID ALL THIS STUFF COME DOWN?
MANO PUSHED ME. I GUESS IT WAS US.
WOW, THAT WAS UNEXPECTED.
YOU JERKS. GO AND GET ONE OF THE TEACHERS.
AND CALL AN AMBULANCE.
HERE, GIRL. PUT THIS UNDER YOUR HEAD. YOU CAN STILL FEEL THE LEG, RIGHT?
OW! YEAH.
THEN YOU'RE GONNA BE OKAY.
I MEAN--
--GIVE OR TAKE.

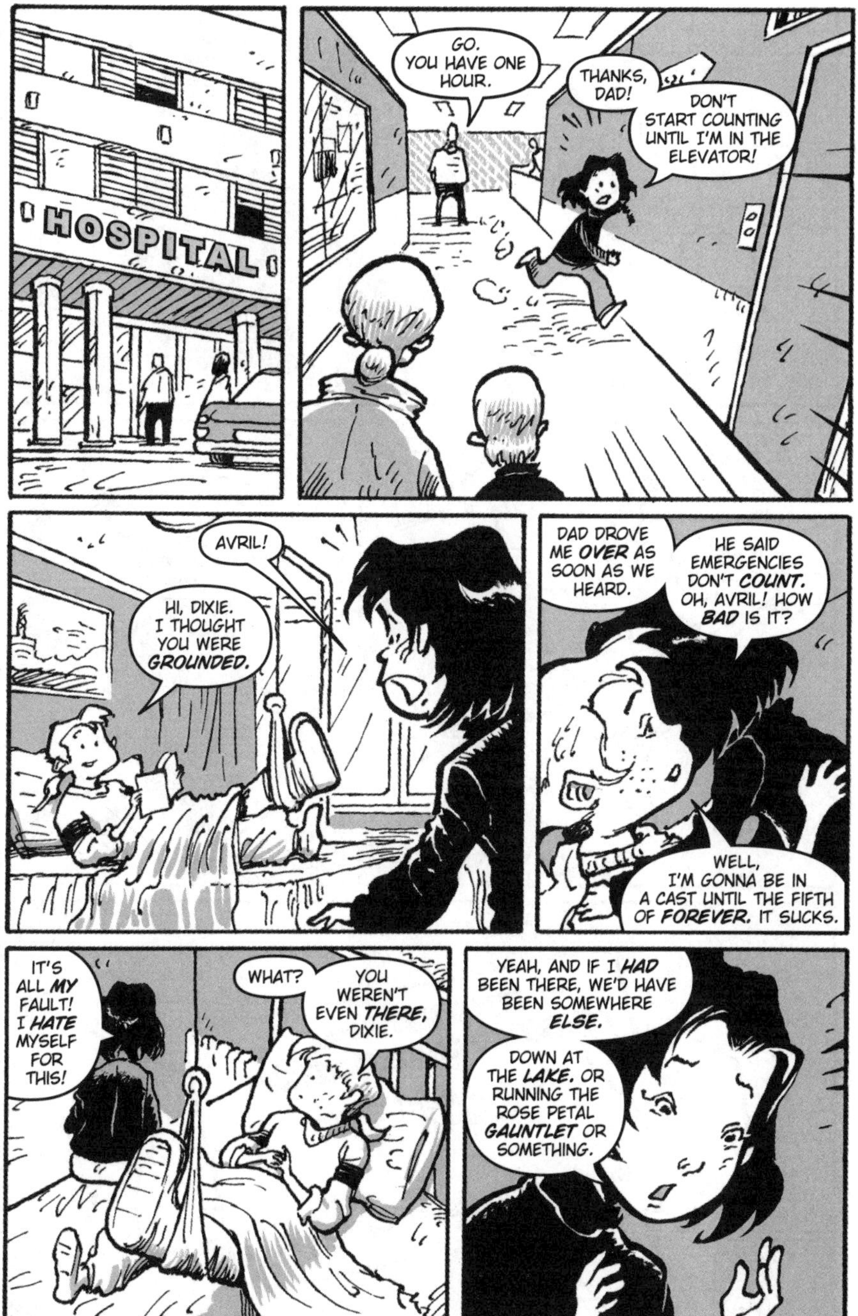
HOSPITAL
GO. YOU HAVE ONE HOUR.
THANKS, DAD!
DON'T START COUNTING UNTIL I'M IN THE ELEVATOR!
AVRIL!
HI, DIXIE. I THOUGHT YOU WERE GROUNDED.
DAD DROVE ME OVER AS SOON AS WE HEARD.
HE SAID EMERGENCIES DON'T COUNT. OH, AVRIL! HOW BAD IS IT?
WELL, I'M GONNA BE IN A CAST UNTIL THE FIFTH OF FOREVER. IT SUCKS.
IT'S ALL MY FAULT! I HATE MYSELF FOR THIS!
WHAT?
YOU WEREN'T EVEN THERE, DIXIE.
YEAH, AND IF I HAD BEEN THERE, WE'D HAVE BEEN SOMEWHERE ELSE.
DOWN AT THE LAKE. OR RUNNING THE ROSE PETAL GAUNTLET OR SOMETHING.

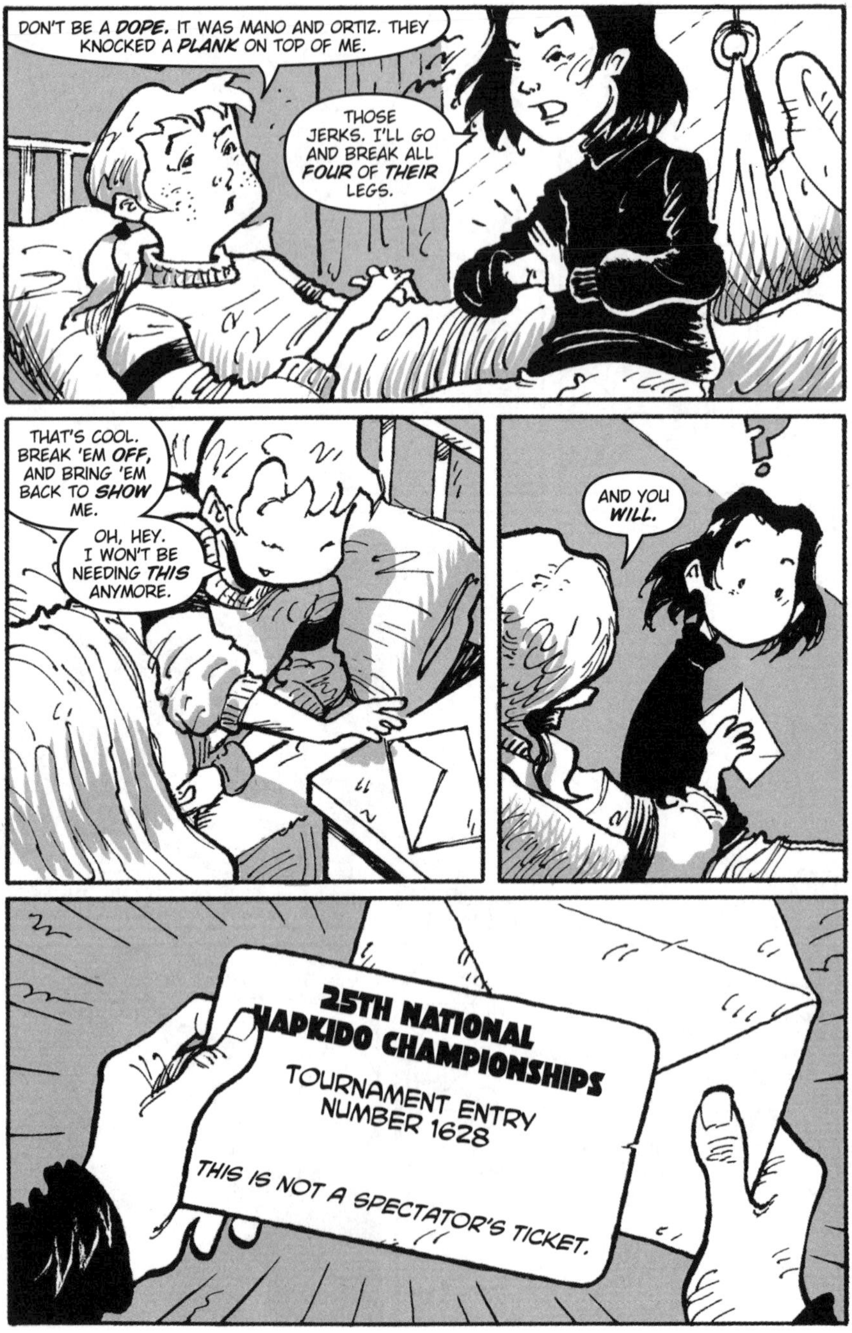
DON'T BE A DOPE. IT WAS MANO AND ORTIZ. THEY KNOCKED A PLANK ON TOP OF ME.
THOSE JERKS. I'LL GO AND BREAK ALL FOUR OF THEIR LEGS.
THAT'S COOL. BREAK 'EM OFF, AND BRING 'EM BACK TO SHOW ME.
OH, HEY. I WON'T BE NEEDING THIS ANYMORE.
AND YOU WILL.
?
25TH NATIONAL HAPKIDO CHAMPIONSHIPS
TOURNAMENT ENTRY NUMBER 1628
THIS IS NOT A SPECTATOR'S TICKET.

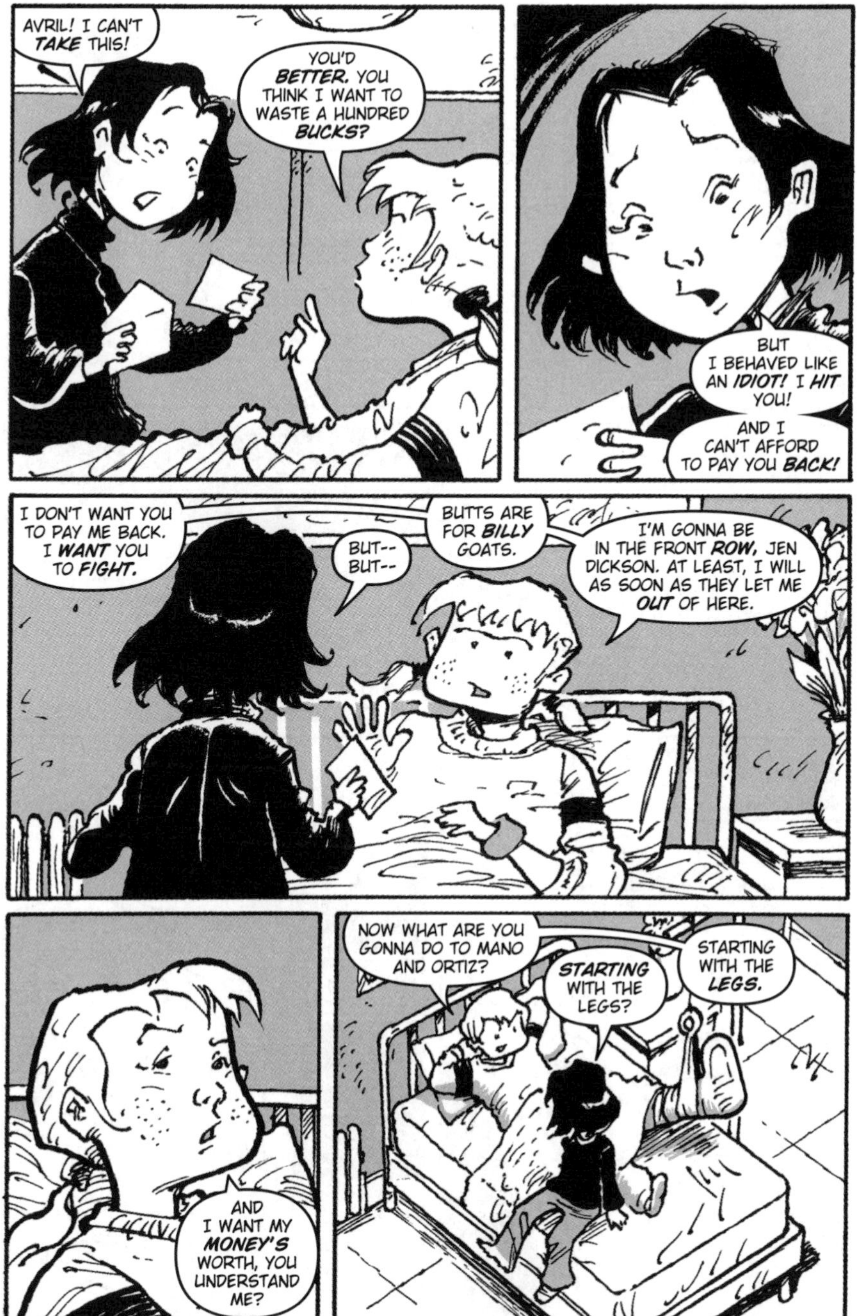
AVRIL! I CAN'T TAKE THIS!
YOU'D BETTER. YOU THINK I WANT TO WASTE A HUNDRED BUCKS?
BUT I BEHAVED LIKE AN IDIOT! I HIT YOU!
AND I CAN'T AFFORD TO PAY YOU BACK!
I DON'T WANT YOU TO PAY ME BACK. I WANT YOU TO FIGHT.
BUT-- BUT--
BUTTS ARE FOR BILLY GOATS.
I'M GONNA BE IN THE FRONT ROW, JEN DICKSON. AT LEAST, I WILL AS SOON AS THEY LET ME OUT OF HERE.
AND I WANT MY MONEY'S WORTH, YOU UNDERSTAND ME?
NOW WHAT ARE YOU GONNA DO TO MANO AND ORTIZ?
STARTING WITH THE LEGS?
STARTING WITH THE LEGS.

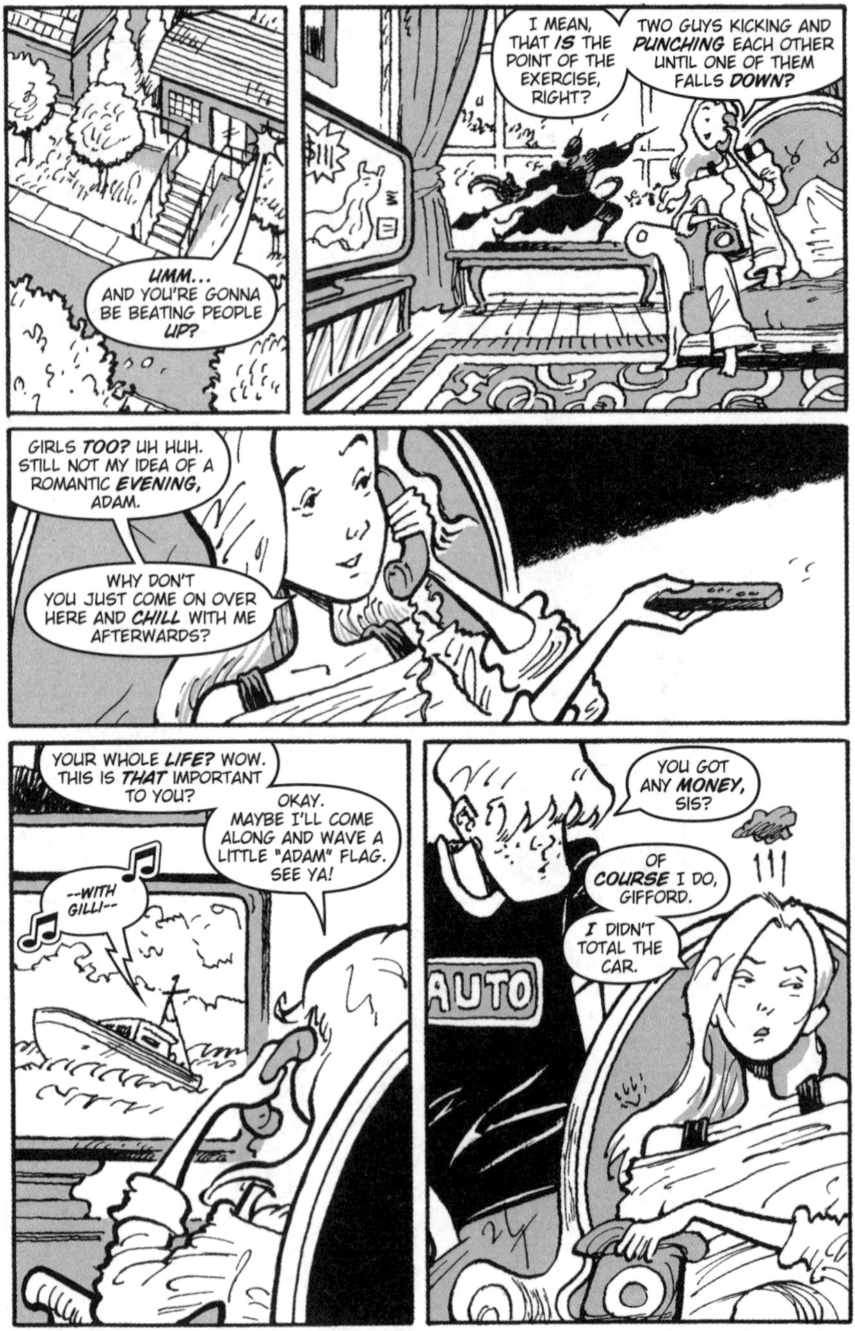
UMM...
AND YOU'RE GONNA
BE BEATING PEOPLE
UP?
I MEAN,
THAT IS THE
POINT OF THE
EXERCISE,
RIGHT?
TWO GUYS KICKING AND
PUNCHING EACH OTHER
UNTIL ONE OF THEM
FALLS DOWN?
GIRLS TOO? UH HUH.
STILL NOT MY IDEA OF A
ROMANTIC EVENING,
ADAM.
WHY DON'T
YOU JUST COME ON OVER
HERE AND CHILL WITH ME
AFTERWARDS?
YOUR WHOLE LIFE? WOW.
THIS IS THAT IMPORTANT
TO YOU?
OKAY.
MAYBE I'LL COME
ALONG AND WAVE A
LITTLE "ADAM" FLAG.
SEE YA!
--WITH
GILLI--
YOU GOT
ANY MONEY,
SIS?
OF
COURSE I DO,
GIFFORD.
I DIDN'T
TOTAL THE
CAR.
AUTO

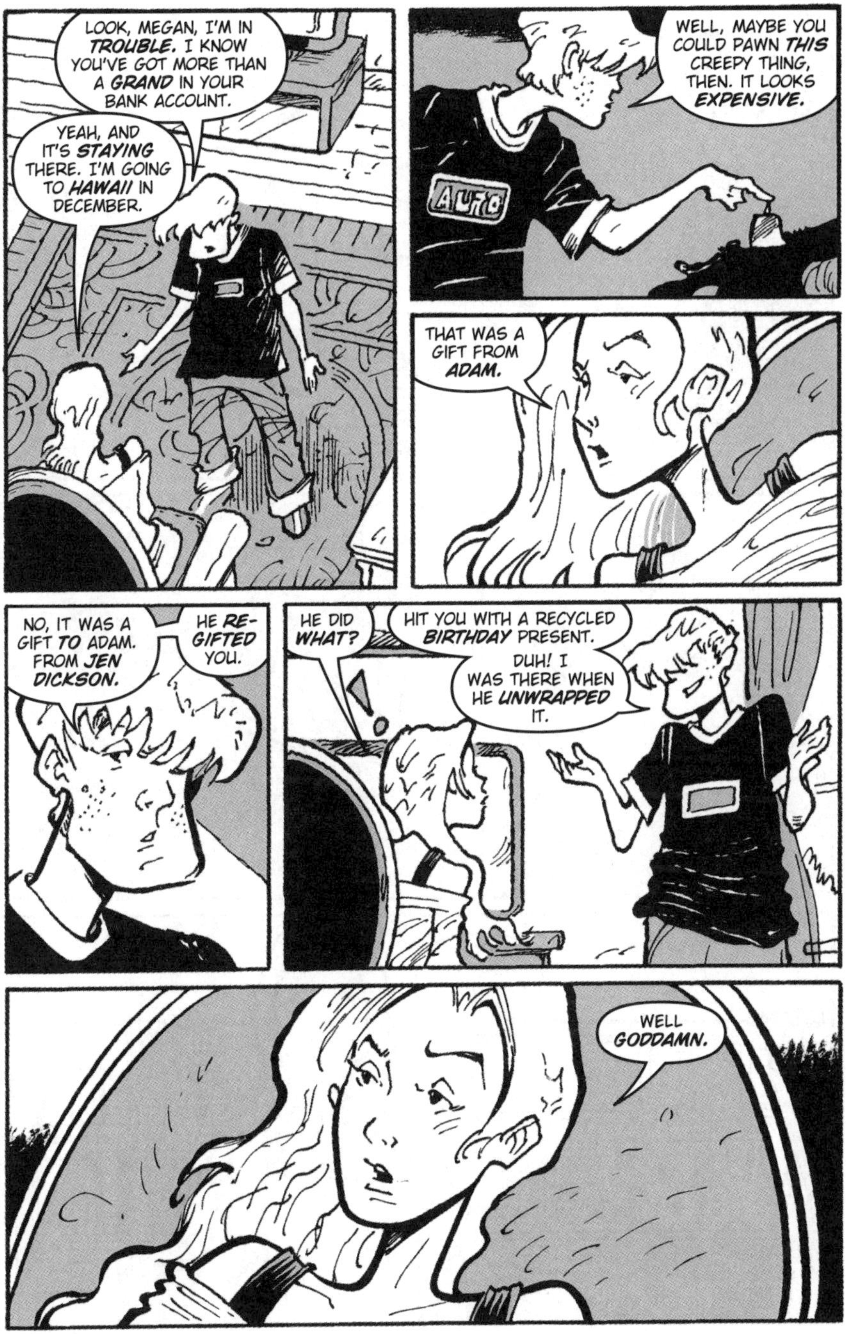
LOOK, MEGAN, I'M IN TROUBLE. I KNOW YOU'VE GOT MORE THAN A GRAND IN YOUR BANK ACCOUNT.
YEAH, AND IT'S STAYING THERE. I'M GOING TO HAWAII IN DECEMBER.
WELL, MAYBE YOU COULD PAWN THIS CREEPY THING, THEN. IT LOOKS EXPENSIVE.
AUFO
THAT WAS A GIFT FROM ADAM.
NO, IT WAS A GIFT TO ADAM. FROM JEN DICKSON.
HE RE-GIFTED YOU.
HE DID WHAT?
HIT YOU WITH A RECYCLED BIRTHDAY PRESENT.
DUH! I WAS THERE WHEN HE UNWRAPPED IT.
WELL GODDAMN.

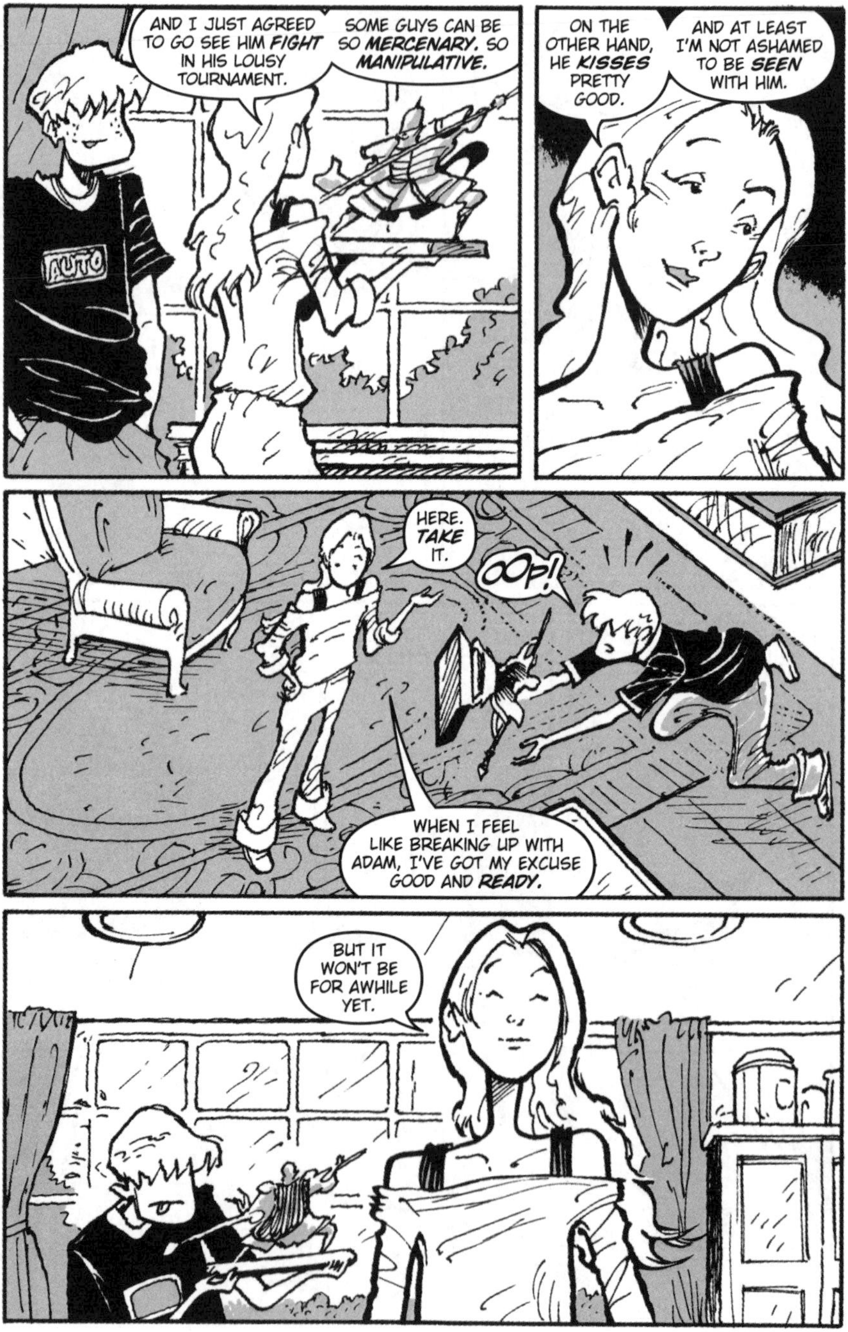
AND I JUST AGREED TO GO SEE HIM FIGHT IN HIS LOUSY TOURNAMENT.
SOME GUYS CAN BE SO MERCENARY. SO MANIPULATIVE.
AUTO
ON THE OTHER HAND, HE KISSES PRETTY GOOD.
AND AT LEAST I'M NOT ASHAMED TO BE SEEN WITH HIM.
HERE. TAKE IT.
OOP!
WHEN I FEEL LIKE BREAKING UP WITH ADAM, I'VE GOT MY EXCUSE GOOD AND READY.
BUT IT WON'T BE FOR AWHILE YET.

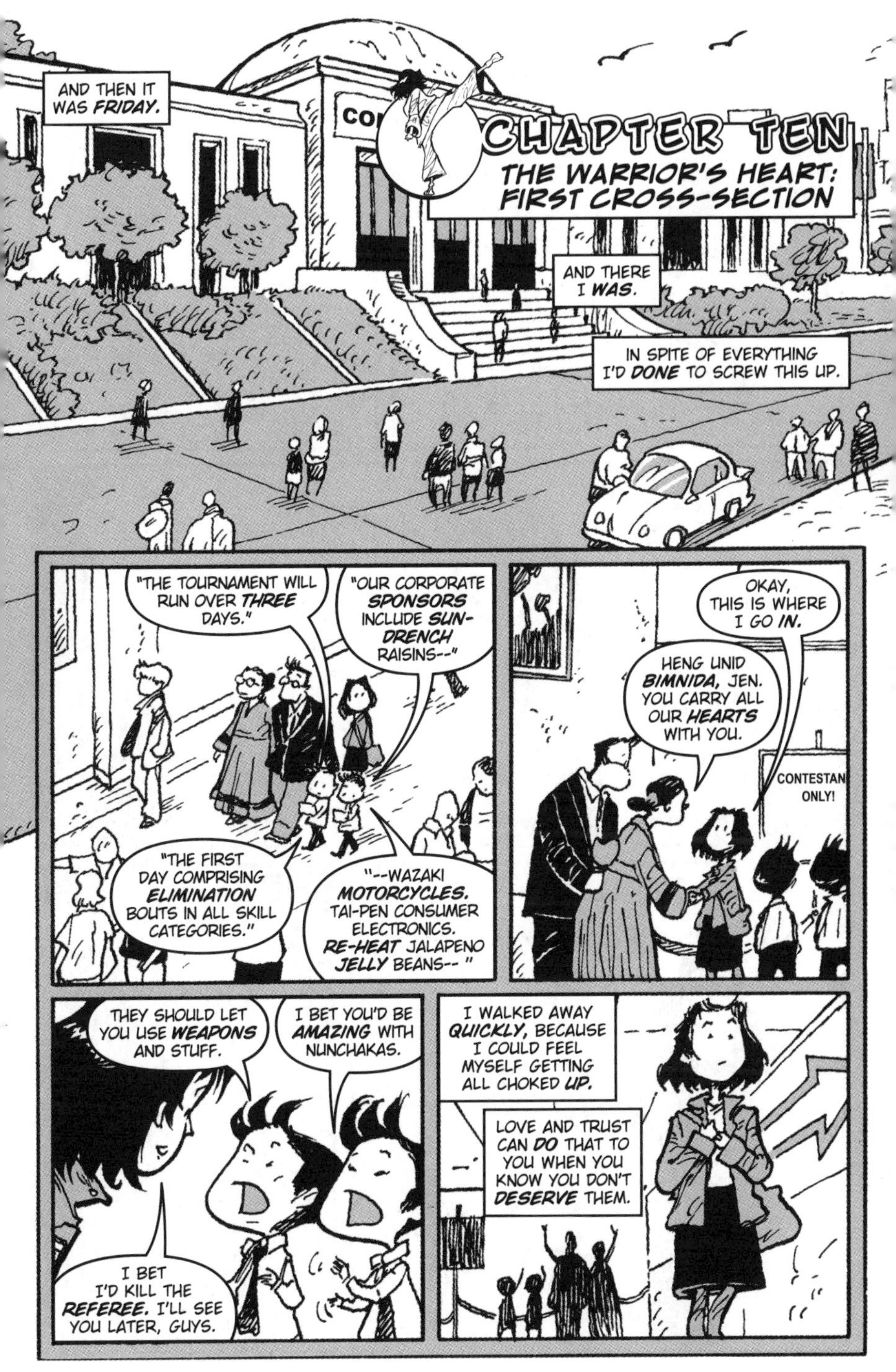
AND THEN IT WAS FRIDAY.
CHAPTER TEN
THE WARRIOR'S HEART: FIRST CROSS-SECTION
AND THERE I WAS.
IN SPITE OF EVERYTHING I'D DONE TO SCREW THIS UP.
"THE TOURNAMENT WILL RUN OVER THREE DAYS."
"OUR CORPORATE SPONSORS INCLUDE SUN-DRENCH RAISINS--"
"THE FIRST DAY COMPRISING ELIMINATION BOUTS IN ALL SKILL CATEGORIES."
"--WAZAKI MOTORCYCLES. TAI-PEN CONSUMER ELECTRONICS. RE-HEAT JALAPENO JELLY BEANS-- "
OKAY, THIS IS WHERE I GO IN.
HENG UNID BIMNIDA, JEN. YOU CARRY ALL OUR HEARTS WITH YOU.
CONTESTAN ONLY!
THEY SHOULD LET YOU USE WEAPONS AND STUFF.
I BET YOU'D BE AMAZING WITH NUNCHAKAS.
I BET I'D KILL THE REFEREE. I'LL SEE YOU LATER, GUYS.
I WALKED AWAY QUICKLY, BECAUSE I COULD FEEL MYSELF GETTING ALL CHOKED UP.
LOVE AND TRUST CAN DO THAT TO YOU WHEN YOU KNOW YOU DON'T DESERVE THEM.

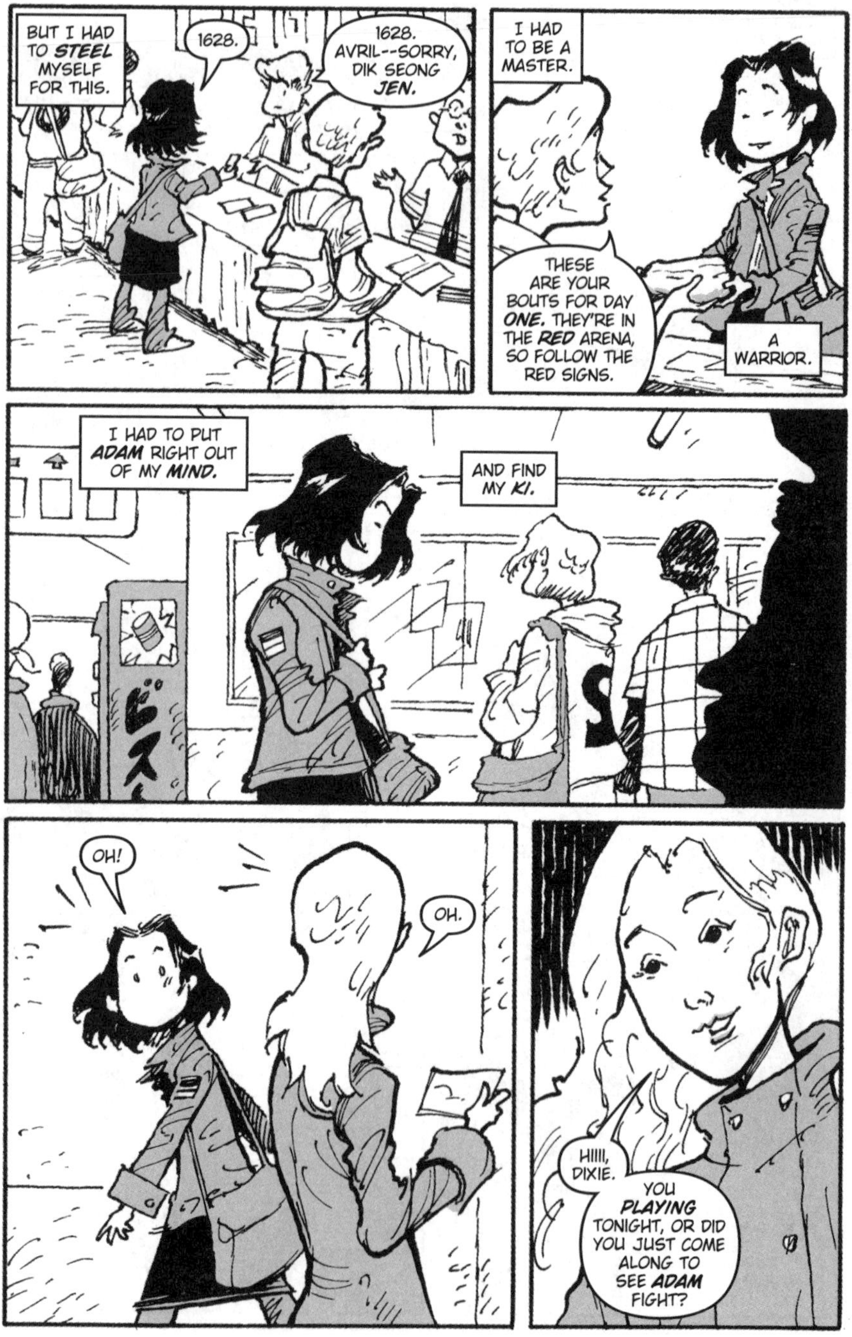
BUT I HAD TO STEEL MYSELF FOR THIS.
1628.
1628. AVRIL--SORRY, DIK SEONG JEN.
I HAD TO BE A MASTER.
THESE ARE YOUR BOUTS FOR DAY ONE. THEY'RE IN THE RED ARENA, SO FOLLOW THE RED SIGNS.
A WARRIOR.
I HAD TO PUT ADAM RIGHT OUT OF MY MIND.
AND FIND MY KI.
OH!
OH.
HIIII, DIXIE.
YOU PLAYING TONIGHT, OR DID YOU JUST COME ALONG TO SEE ADAM FIGHT?

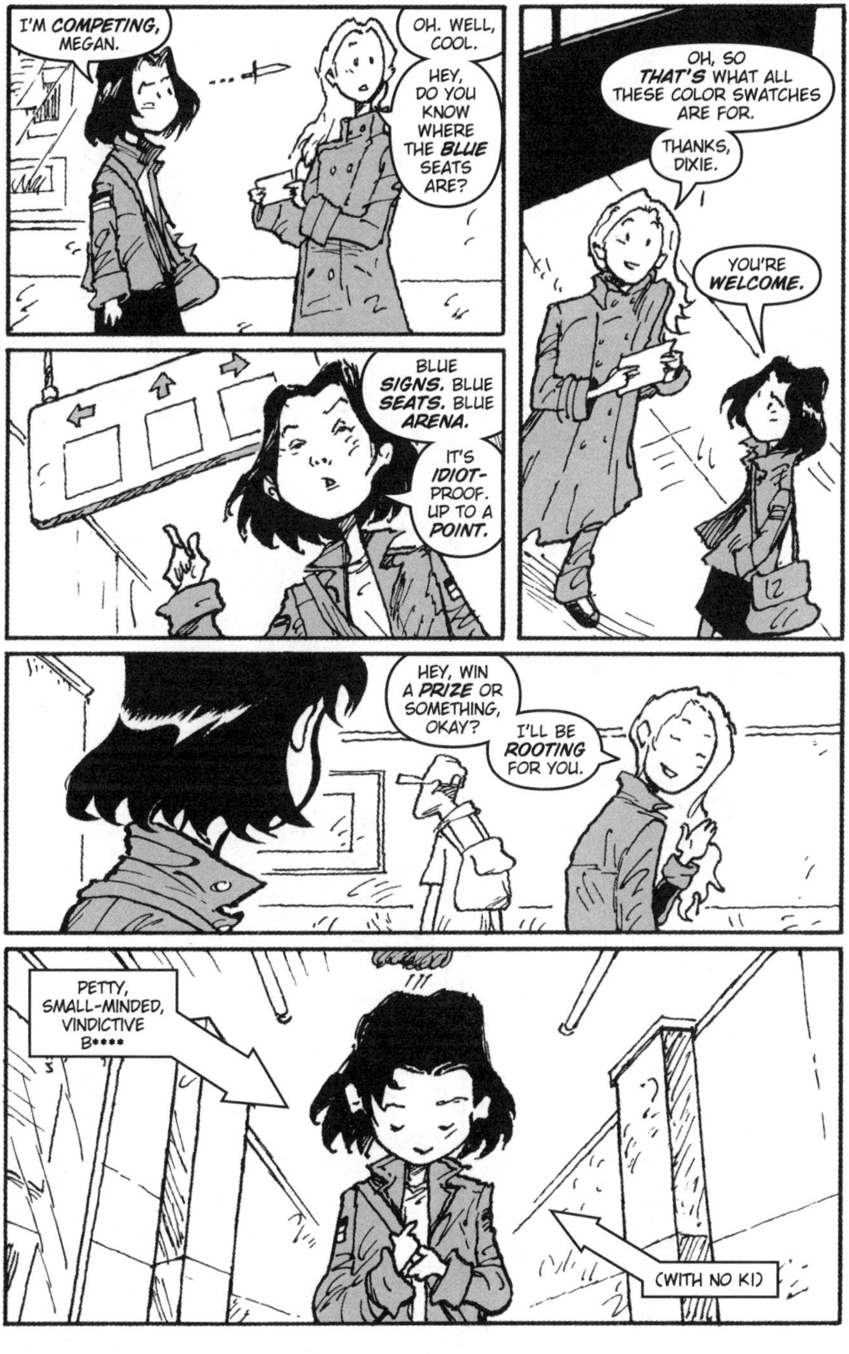

I'M COMPETING, MEGAN.
OH. WELL, COOL.
HEY, DO YOU KNOW WHERE THE BLUE SEATS ARE?
OH, SO THAT'S WHAT ALL THESE COLOR SWATCHES ARE FOR.
THANKS, DIXIE.
YOU'RE WELCOME.
BLUE SIGNS. BLUE SEATS. BLUE ARENA.
IT'S IDIOT-PROOF. UP TO A POINT.
HEY, WIN A PRIZE OR SOMETHING, OKAY?
I'LL BE ROOTING FOR YOU.
PETTY, SMALL-MINDED, VINDICTIVE B****
(WITH NO KI)

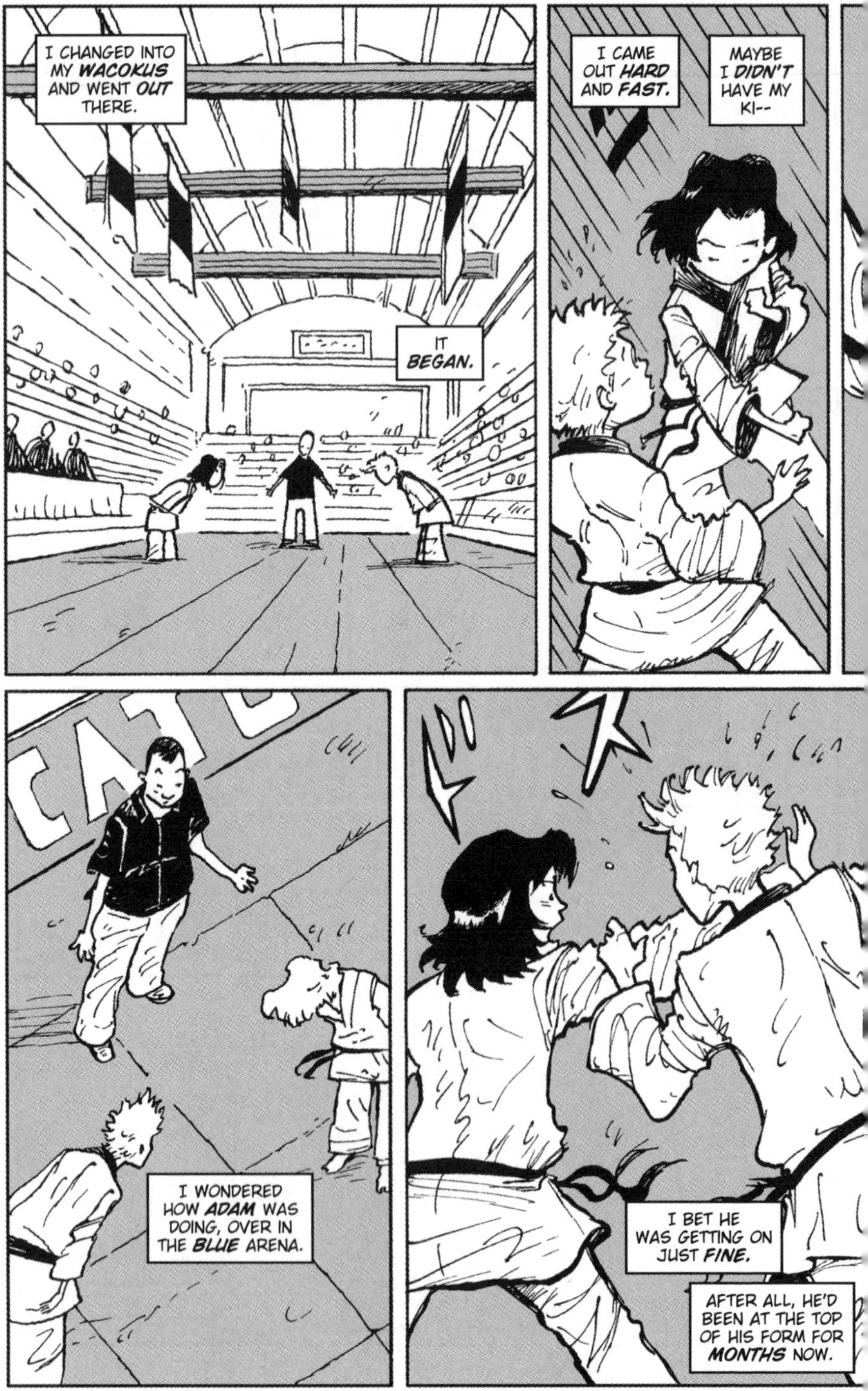
I CHANGED INTO MY WACOKUS AND WENT OUT THERE.
IT BEGAN.
I CAME OUT HARD AND FAST.
MAYBE I DIDN'T HAVE MY KI--
I WONDERED HOW ADAM WAS DOING, OVER IN THE BLUE ARENA.
I BET HE WAS GETTING ON JUST FINE.
AFTER ALL, HE'D BEEN AT THE TOP OF HIS FORM FOR MONTHS NOW.

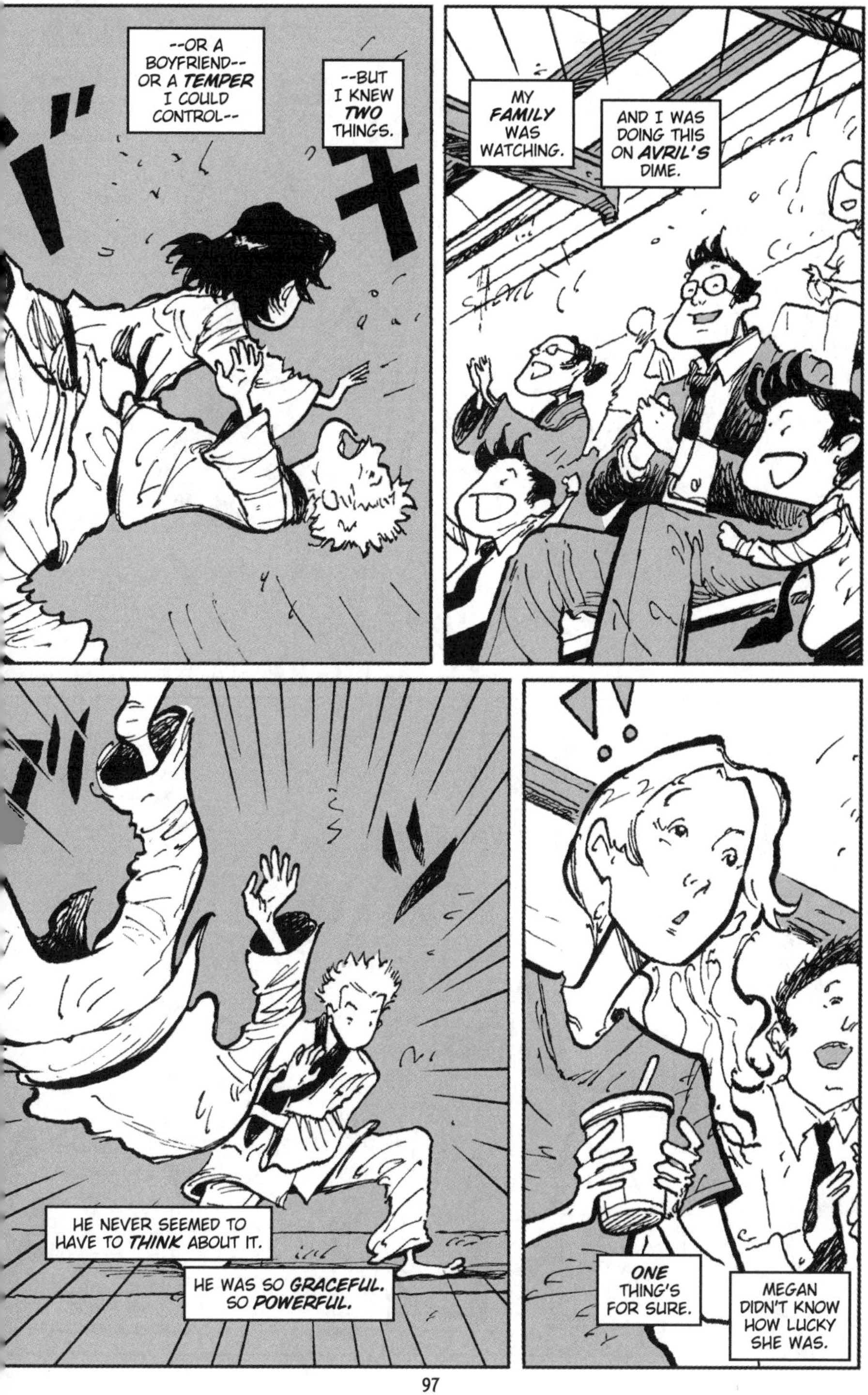

--OR A BOYFRIEND-- OR A TEMPER I COULD CONTROL--
--BUT I KNEW TWO THINGS.
MY FAMILY WAS WATCHING.
AND I WAS DOING THIS ON AVRIL'S DIME.
HE NEVER SEEMED TO HAVE TO THINK ABOUT IT.
HE WAS SO GRACEFUL. SO POWERFUL.
ONE THING'S FOR SURE.
MEGAN DIDN'T KNOW HOW LUCKY SHE WAS.

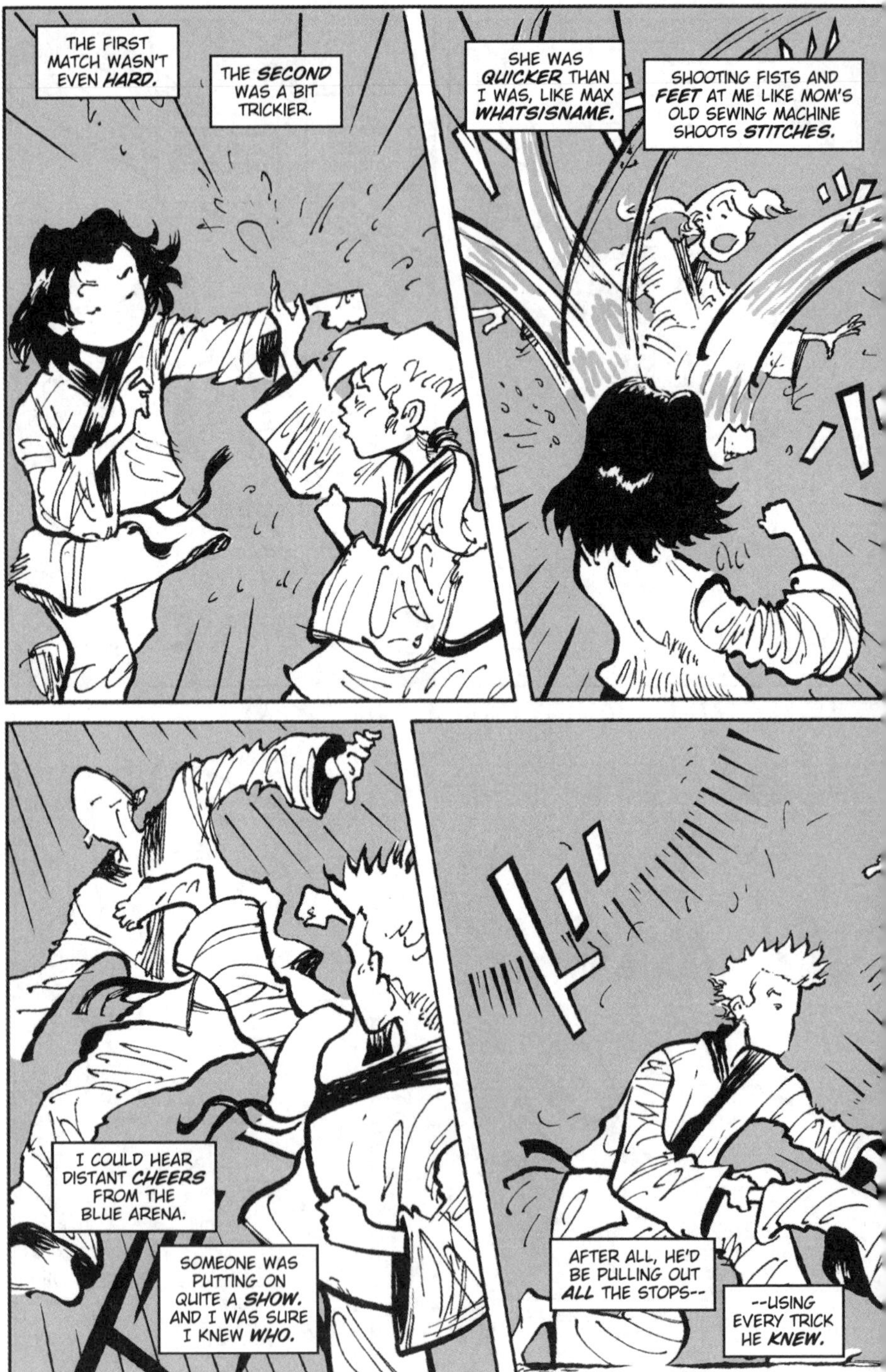
THE FIRST MATCH WASN'T EVEN HARD.
THE SECOND WAS A BIT TRICKIER.
SHE WAS QUICKER THAN I WAS, LIKE MAX WHATSISNAME.
SHOOTING FISTS AND FEET AT ME LIKE MOM'S OLD SEWING MACHINE SHOOTS STITCHES.
I COULD HEAR DISTANT CHEERS FROM THE BLUE ARENA.
SOMEONE WAS PUTTING ON QUITE A SHOW. AND I WAS SURE I KNEW WHO.
AFTER ALL, HE'D BE PULLING OUT ALL THE STOPS--
--USING EVERY TRICK HE KNEW.

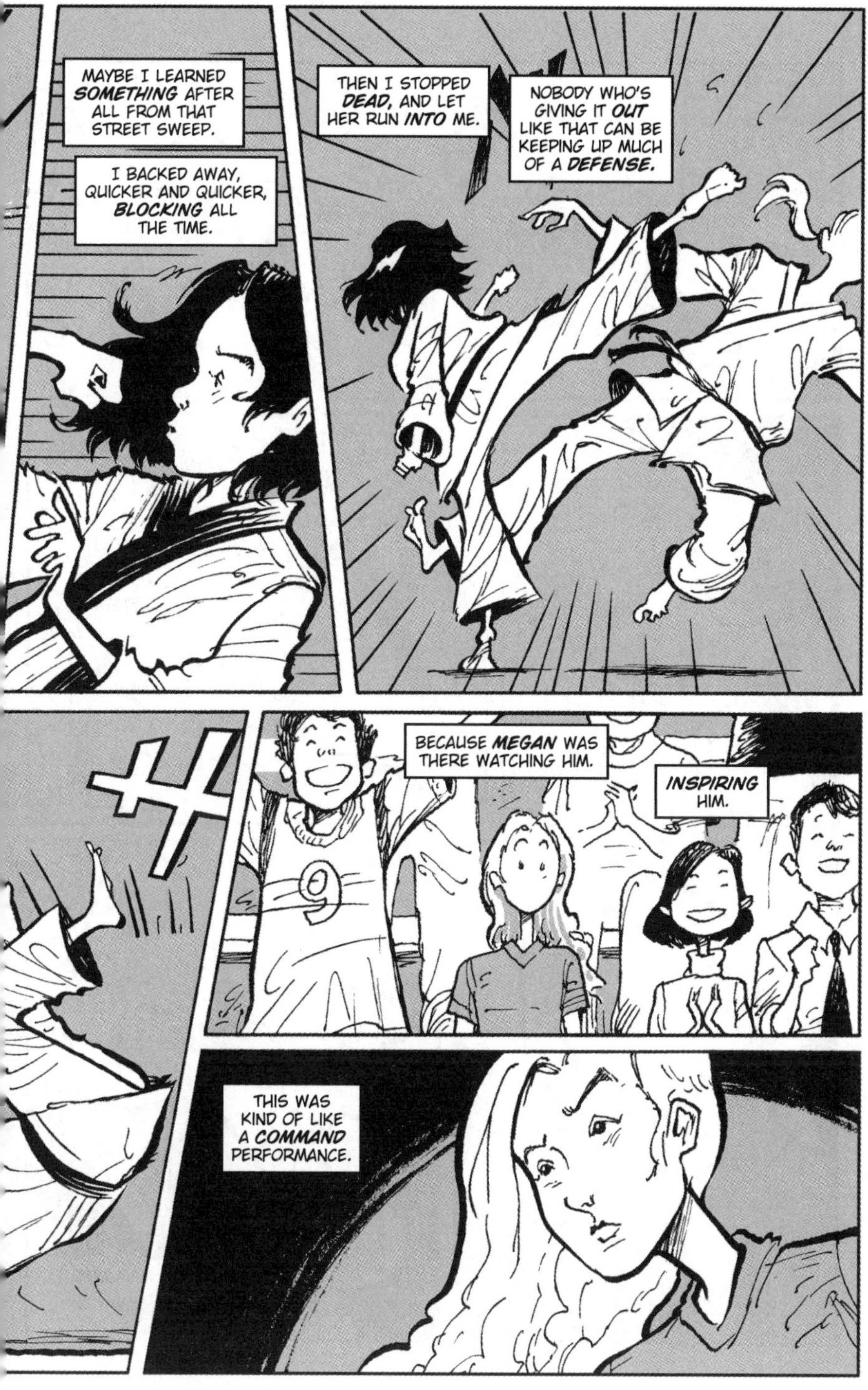
MAYBE I LEARNED SOMETHING AFTER ALL FROM THAT STREET SWEEP.
I BACKED AWAY, QUICKER AND QUICKER, BLOCKING ALL THE TIME.
THEN I STOPPED DEAD, AND LET HER RUN INTO ME.
NOBODY WHO'S GIVING IT OUT LIKE THAT CAN BE KEEPING UP MUCH OF A DEFENSE.
BECAUSE MEGAN WAS THERE WATCHING HIM.
INSPIRING HIM.
THIS WAS KIND OF LIKE A COMMAND PERFORMANCE.

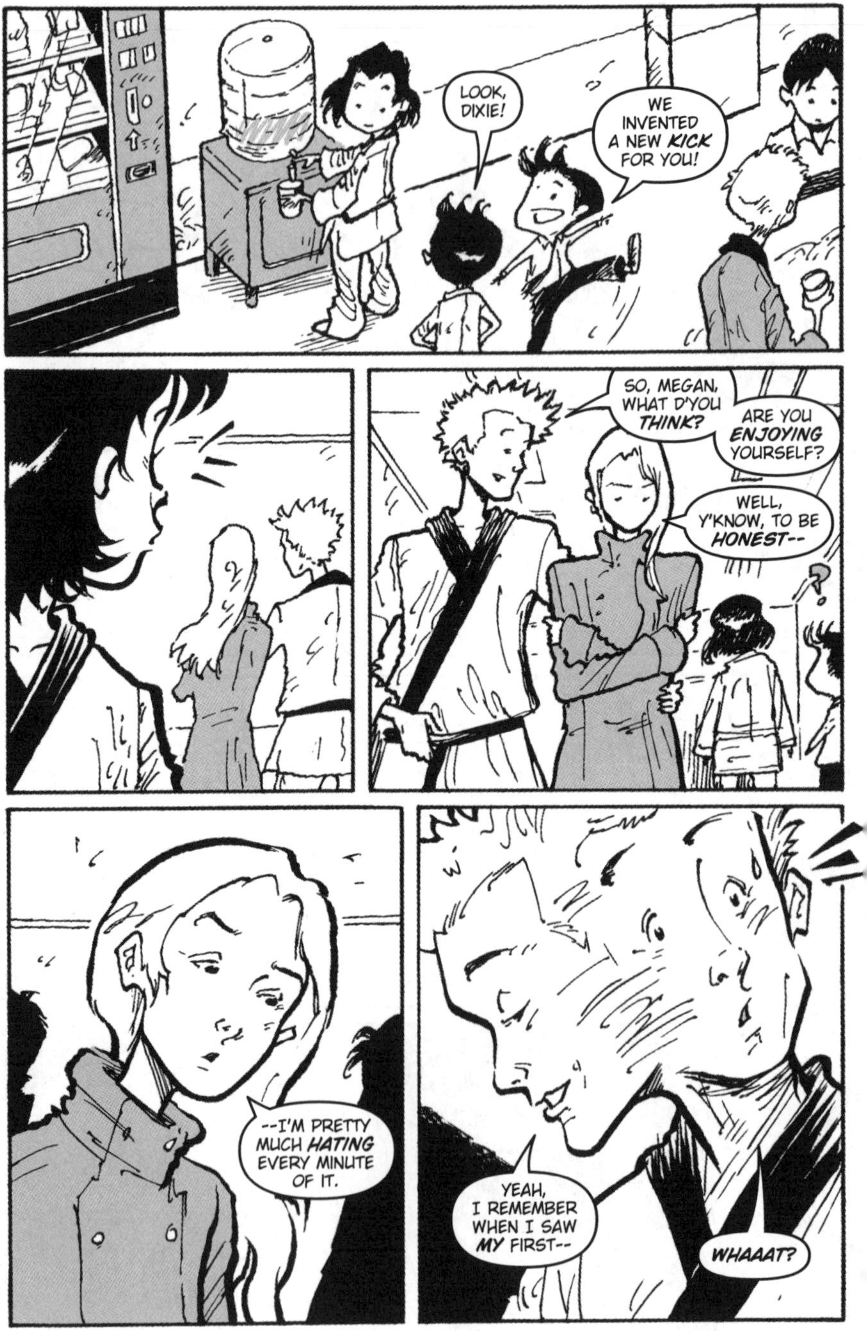
LOOK, DIXIE!
WE INVENTED A NEW KICK FOR YOU!
SO, MEGAN, WHAT D'YOU THINK?
ARE YOU ENJOYING YOURSELF?
WELL, Y'KNOW, TO BE HONEST--
--I'M PRETTY MUCH HATING EVERY MINUTE OF IT.
YEAH, I REMEMBER WHEN I SAW MY FIRST--
WHAAAT?

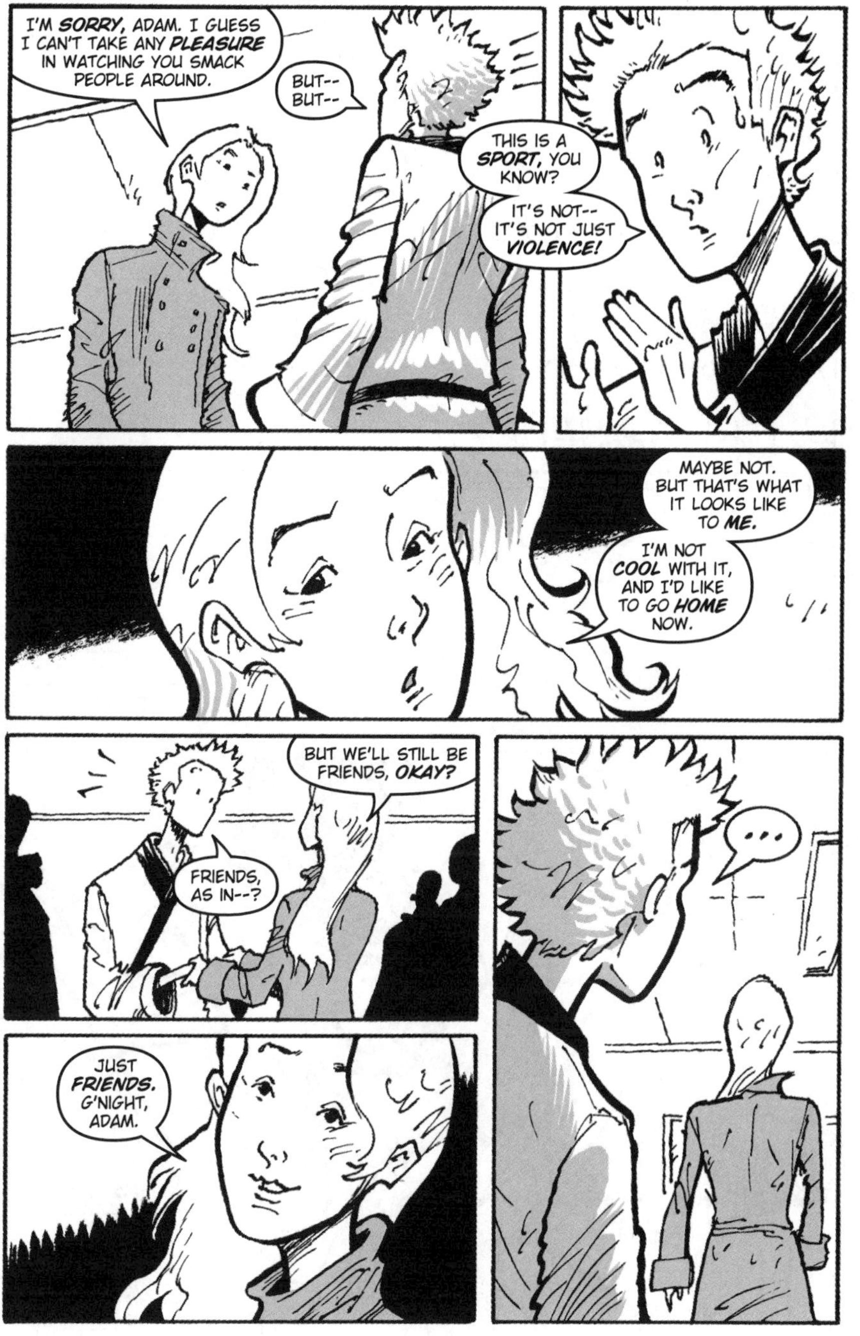
I'M SORRY, ADAM. I GUESS I CAN'T TAKE ANY PLEASURE IN WATCHING YOU SMACK PEOPLE AROUND.
BUT-- BUT--
THIS IS A SPORT, YOU KNOW?
IT'S NOT-- IT'S NOT JUST VIOLENCE!
MAYBE NOT. BUT THAT'S WHAT IT LOOKS LIKE TO ME.
I'M NOT COOL WITH IT, AND I'D LIKE TO GO HOME NOW.
BUT WE'LL STILL BE FRIENDS, OKAY?
FRIENDS, AS IN--?
JUST FRIENDS. G'NIGHT, ADAM.
...

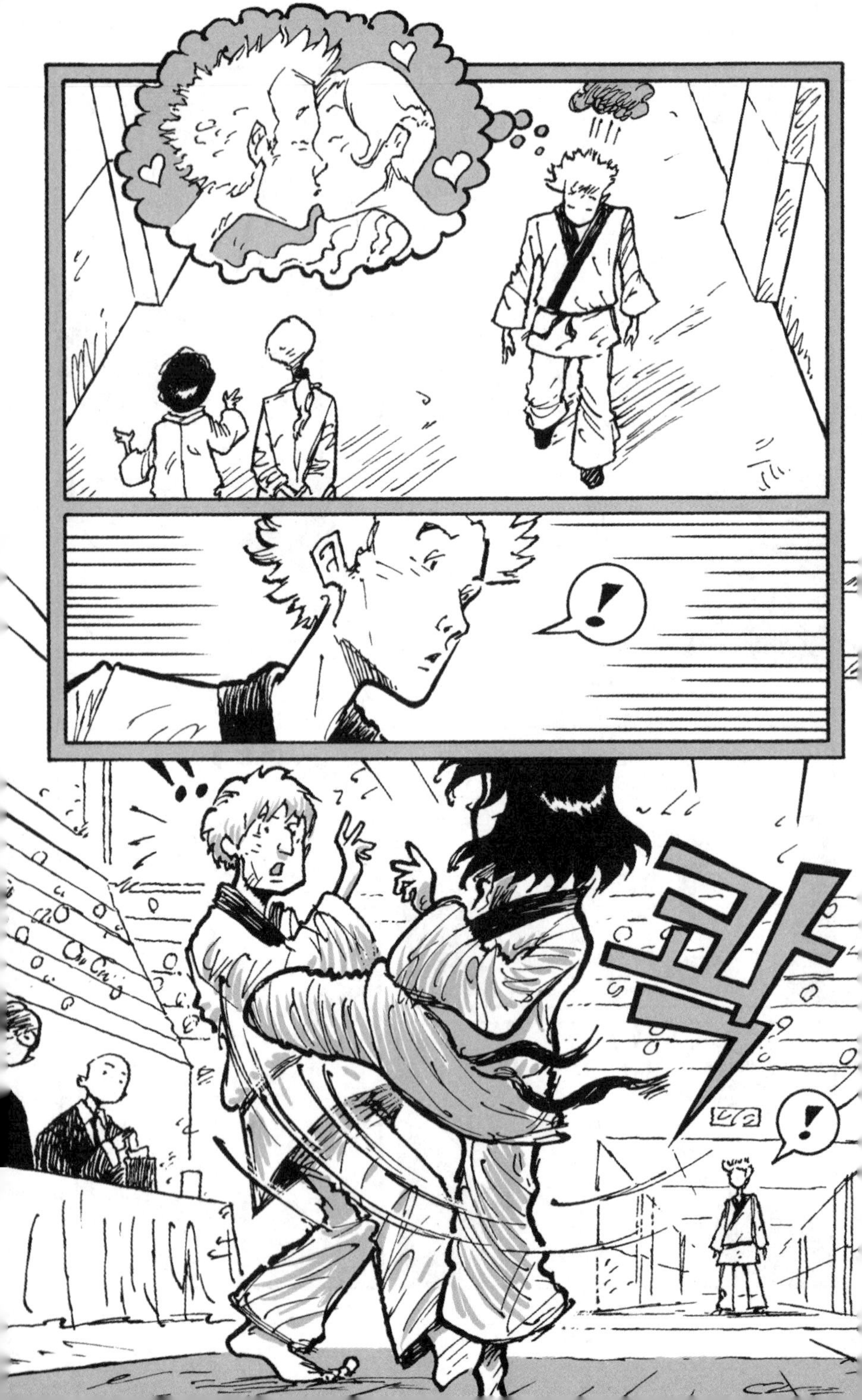
!
!!
!

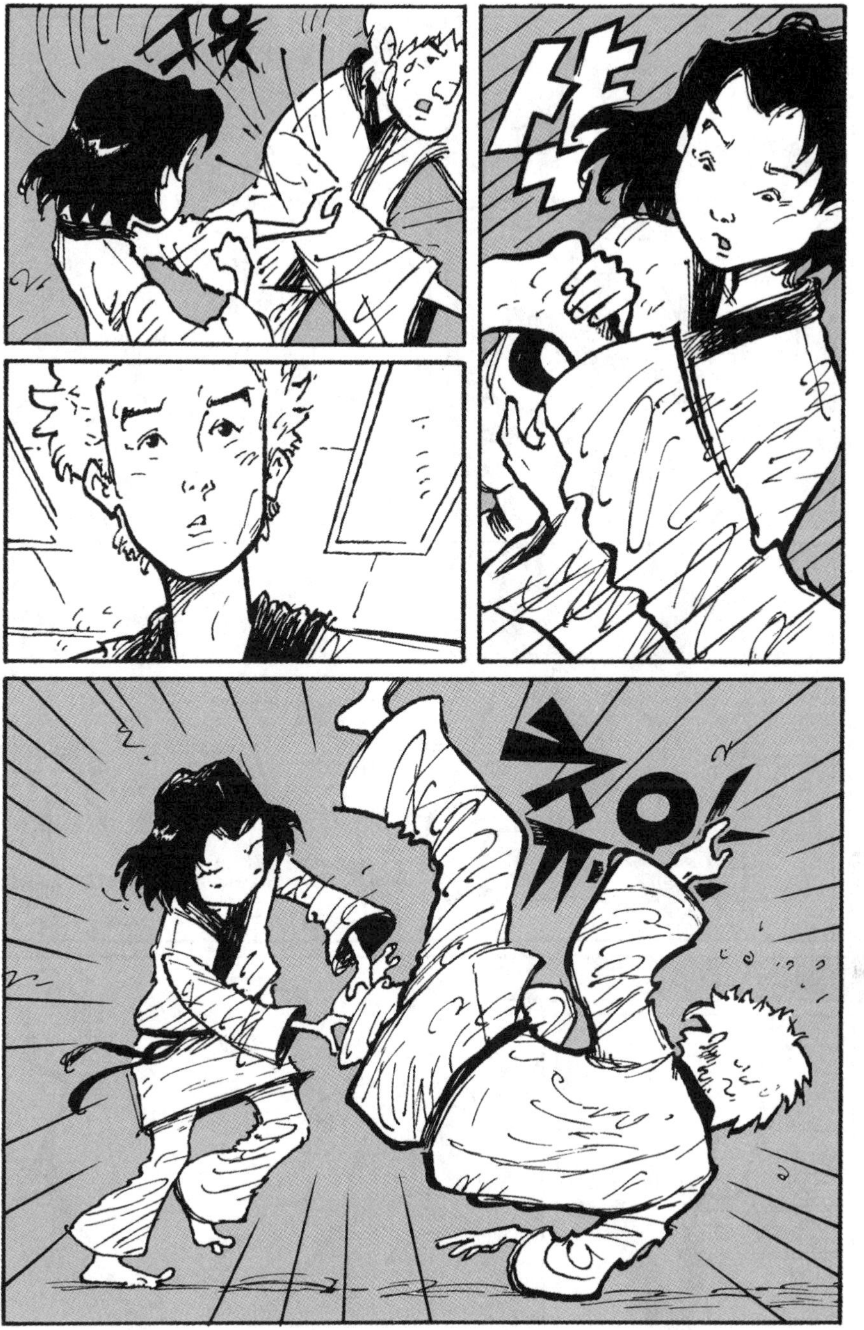

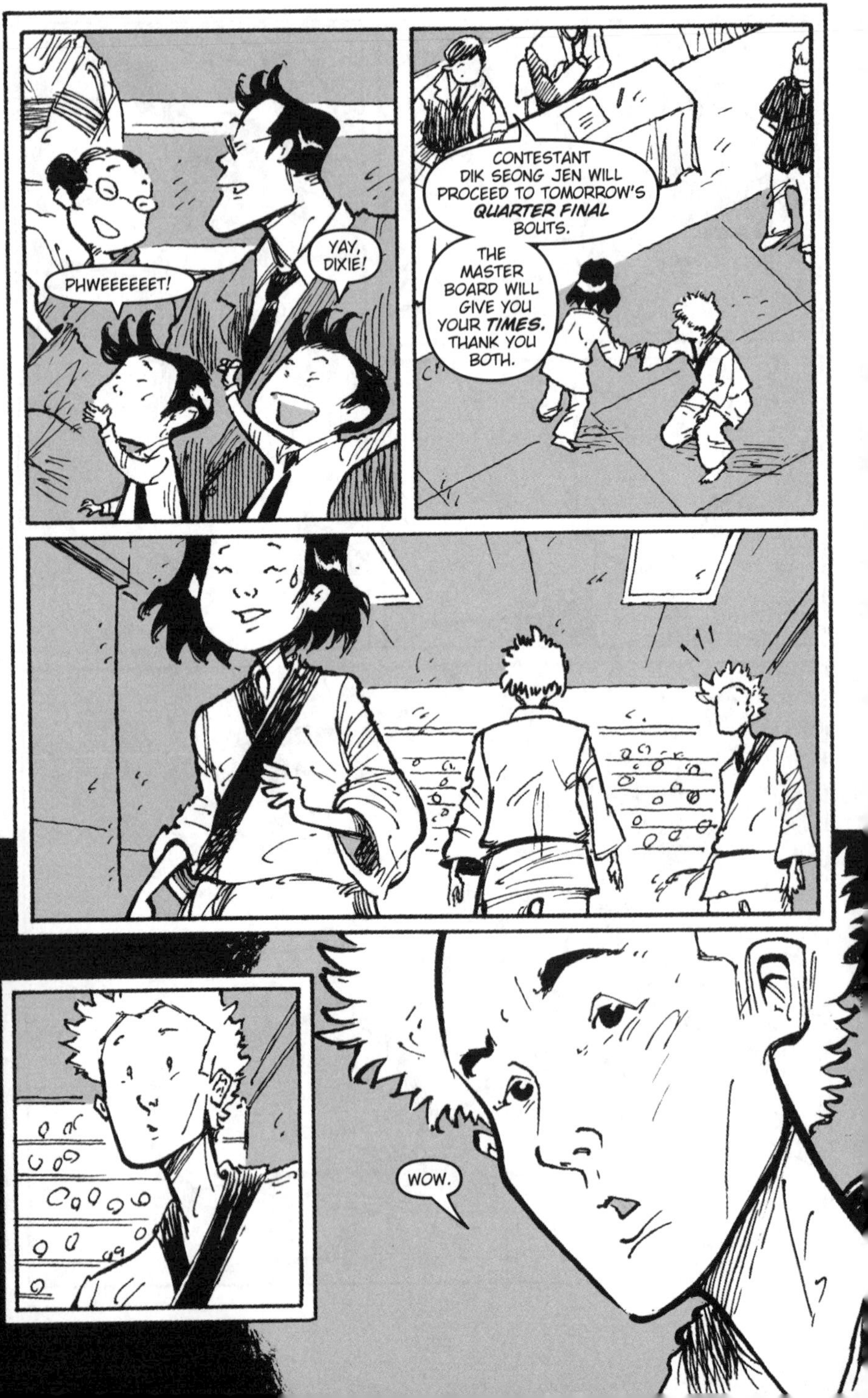
PHWEEEEEET!
YAY, DIXIE!
CONTESTANT DIK SEONG JEN WILL PROCEED TO TOMORROW'S ***QUARTER FINAL*** BOUTS.
THE MASTER BOARD WILL GIVE YOU YOUR ***TIMES.*** THANK YOU BOTH.
WOW.

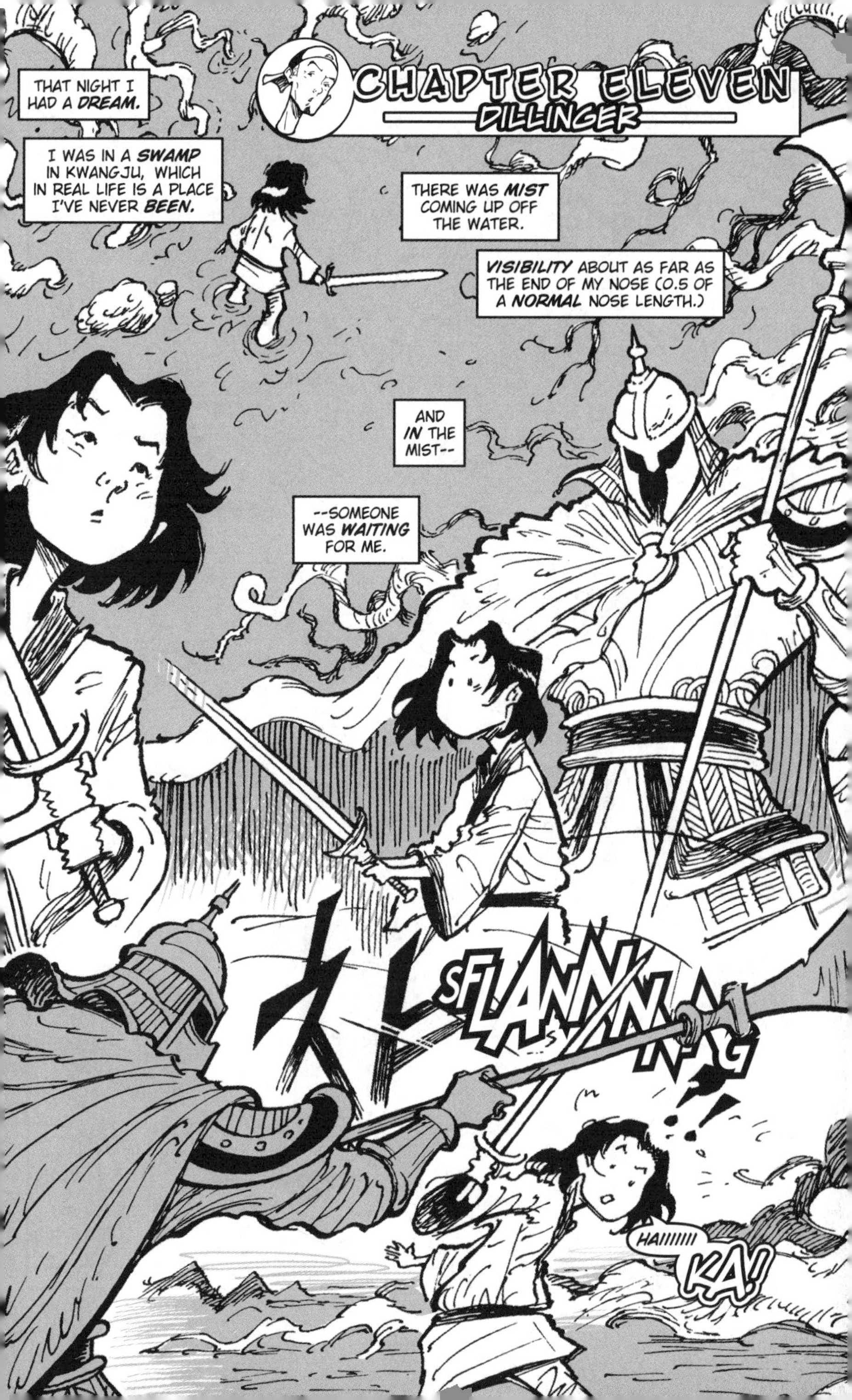

CHAPTER ELEVEN
DILLINGER
THAT NIGHT I HAD A DREAM.
I WAS IN A SWAMP IN KWANGJU, WHICH IN REAL LIFE IS A PLACE I'VE NEVER BEEN.
THERE WAS MIST COMING UP OFF THE WATER.
VISIBILITY ABOUT AS FAR AS THE END OF MY NOSE (0.5 OF A NORMAL NOSE LENGTH.)
AND IN THE MIST--
--SOMEONE WAS WAITING FOR ME.
SFLANNNNNG
HAIIIIIII KA!

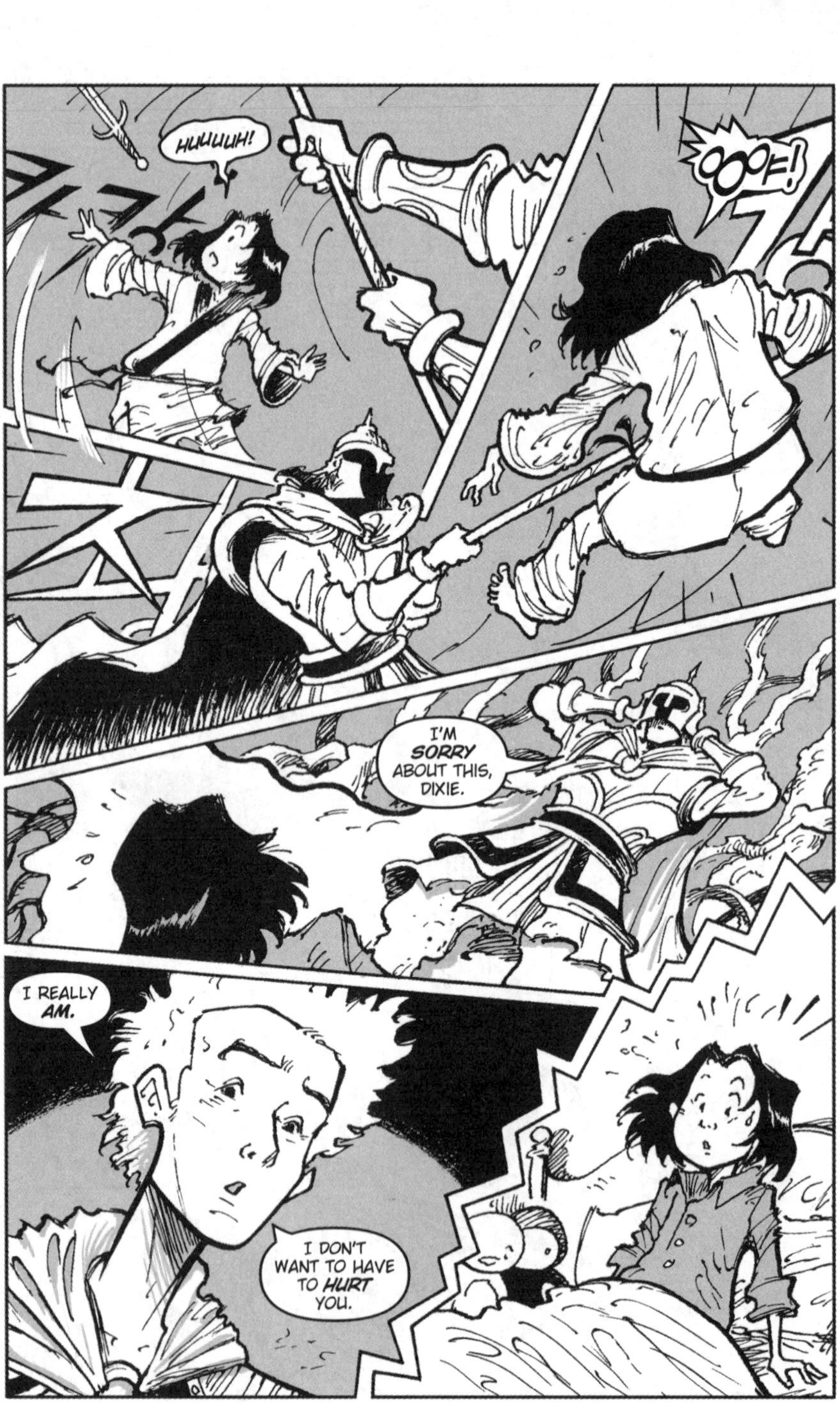
HUUUUH!
OOOF!
I'M SORRY ABOUT THIS, DIXIE.
I REALLY AM.
I DON'T WANT TO HAVE TO HURT YOU.

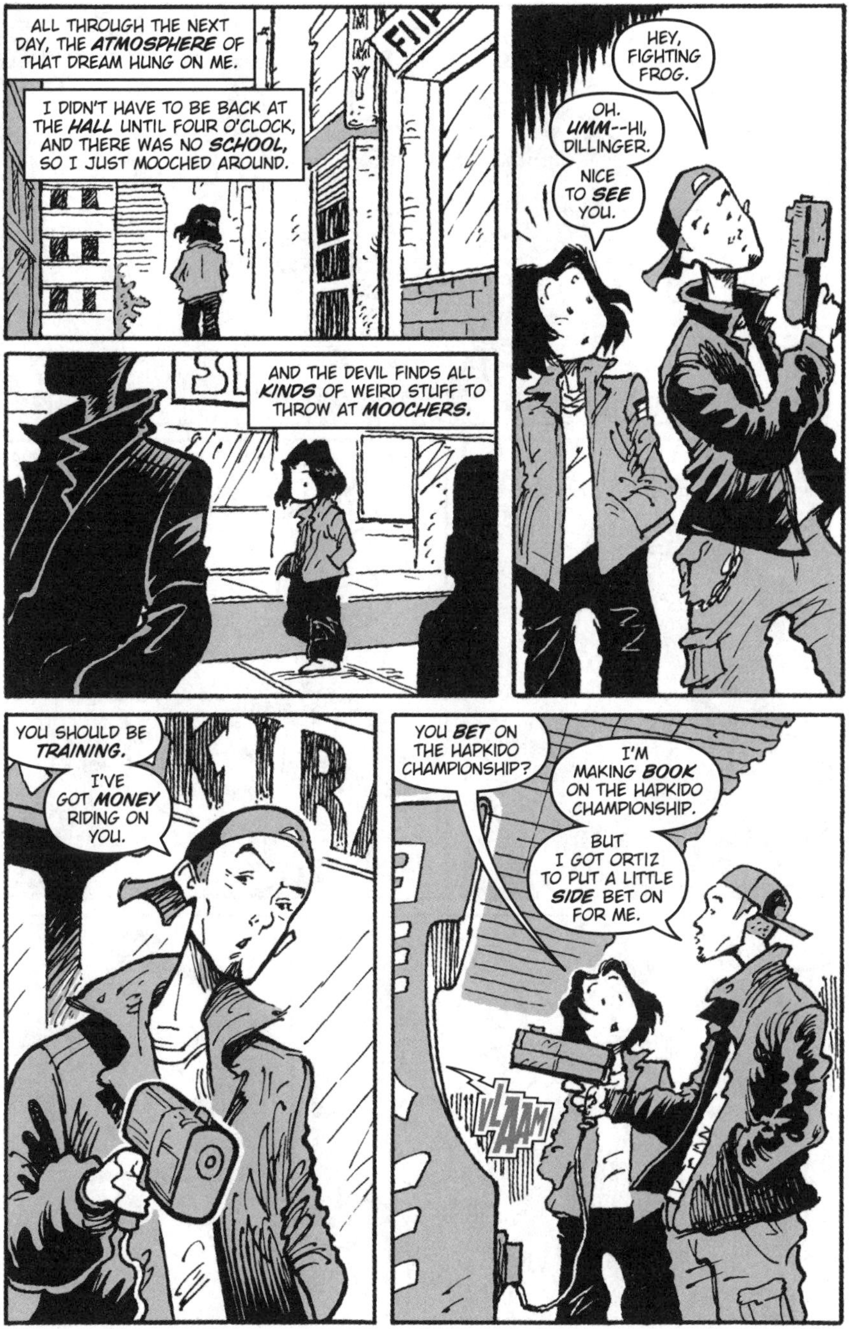

ALL THROUGH THE NEXT DAY, THE ATMOSPHERE OF THAT DREAM HUNG ON ME.
I DIDN'T HAVE TO BE BACK AT THE HALL UNTIL FOUR O'CLOCK, AND THERE WAS NO SCHOOL, SO I JUST MOOCHED AROUND.
AND THE DEVIL FINDS ALL KINDS OF WEIRD STUFF TO THROW AT MOOCHERS.
HEY, FIGHTING FROG.
OH. UMM--HI, DILLINGER.
NICE TO SEE YOU.
YOU SHOULD BE TRAINING.
I'VE GOT MONEY RIDING ON YOU.
YOU BET ON THE HAPKIDO CHAMPIONSHIP?
I'M MAKING BOOK ON THE HAPKIDO CHAMPIONSHIP.
BUT I GOT ORTIZ TO PUT A LITTLE SIDE BET ON FOR ME.
VLAAM

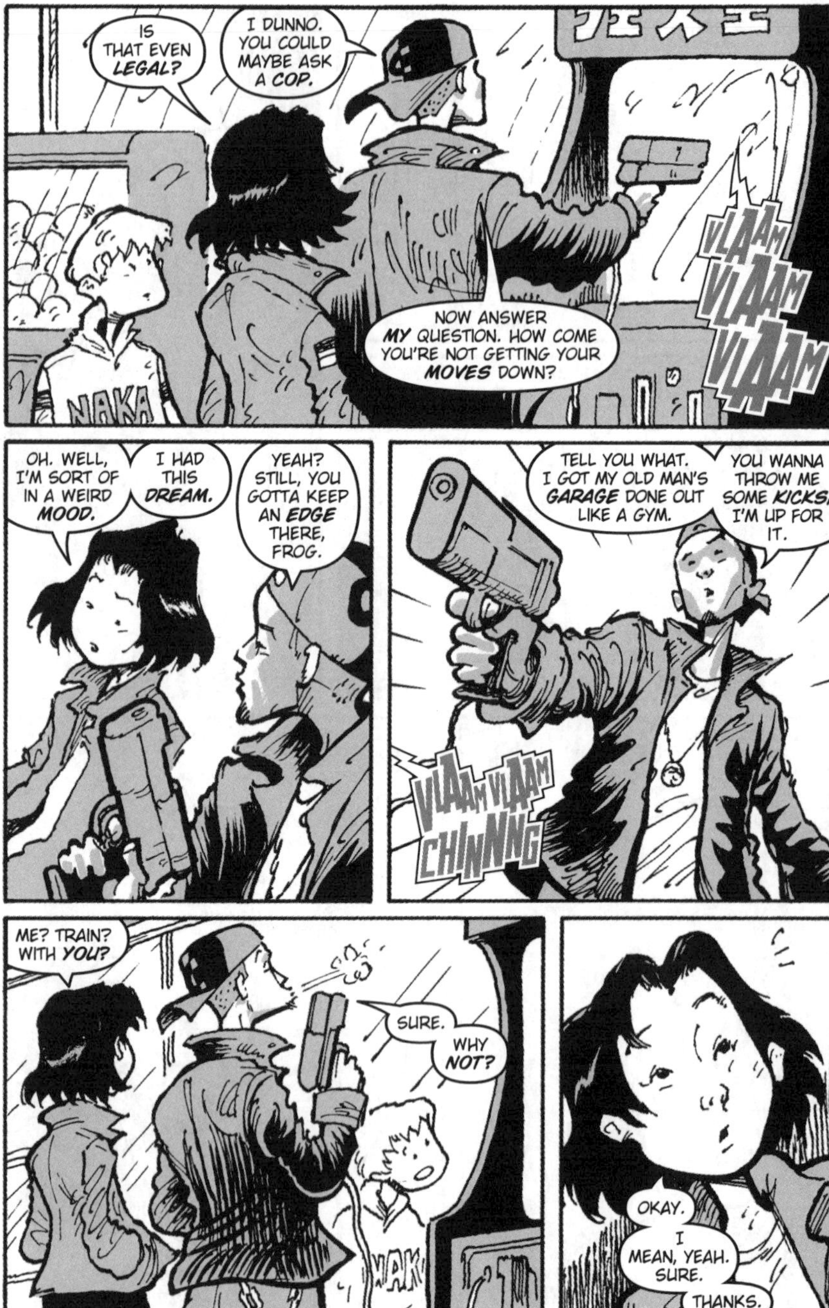
IS THAT EVEN LEGAL?
I DUNNO. YOU COULD MAYBE ASK A COP.
NOW ANSWER MY QUESTION. HOW COME YOU'RE NOT GETTING YOUR MOVES DOWN?
VLAAM VLAAM VLAAM
NAKA
OH. WELL, I'M SORT OF IN A WEIRD MOOD.
I HAD THIS DREAM.
YEAH? STILL, YOU GOTTA KEEP AN EDGE THERE, FROG.
TELL YOU WHAT. I GOT MY OLD MAN'S GARAGE DONE OUT LIKE A GYM.
YOU WANNA THROW ME SOME KICKS, I'M UP FOR IT.
VLAAM VLAAM CHINNNG
ME? TRAIN? WITH YOU?
SURE.
WHY NOT?
OKAY.
I MEAN, YEAH. SURE.
THANKS.

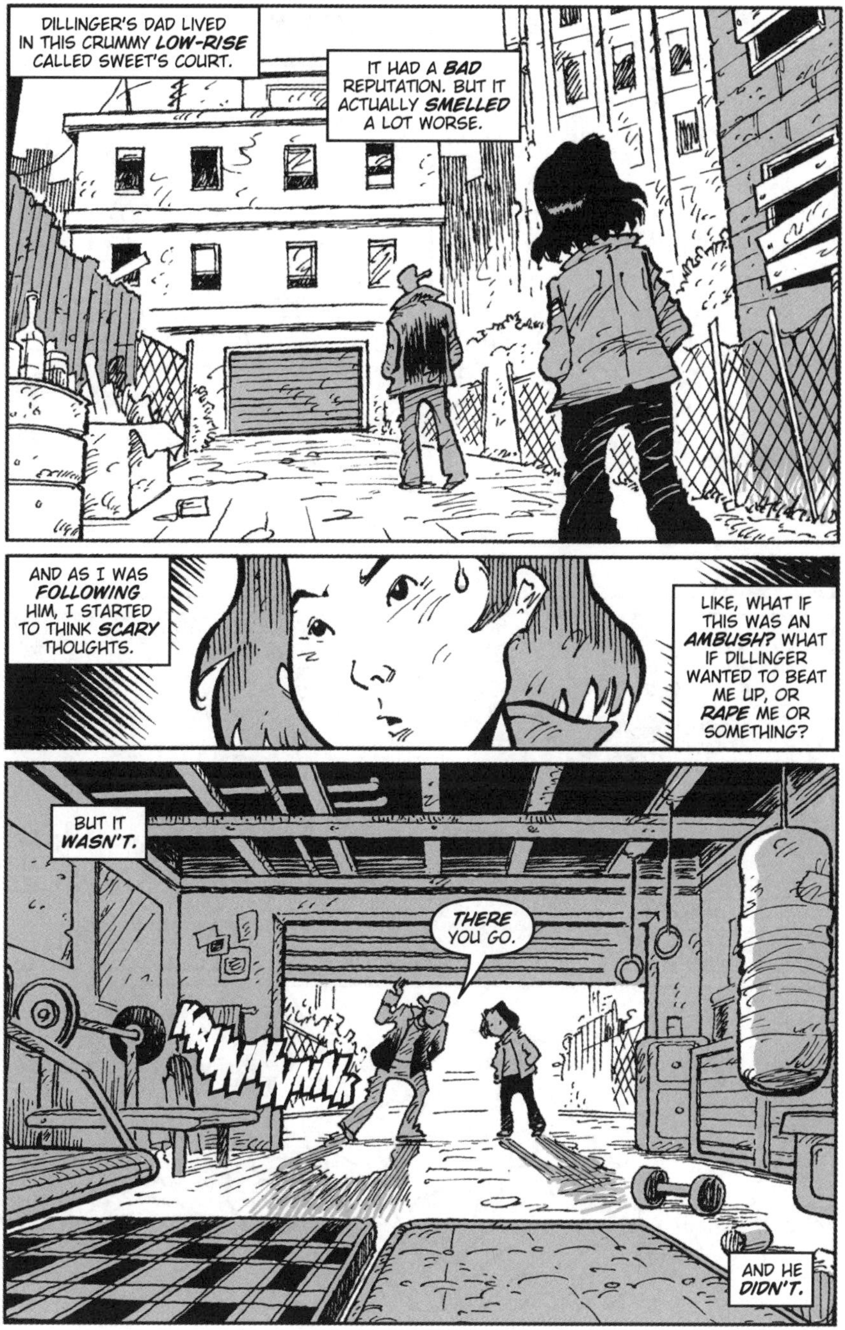

DILLINGER'S DAD LIVED IN THIS CRUMMY LOW-RISE CALLED SWEET'S COURT.
IT HAD A BAD REPUTATION. BUT IT ACTUALLY SMELLED A LOT WORSE.
AND AS I WAS FOLLOWING HIM, I STARTED TO THINK SCARY THOUGHTS.
LIKE, WHAT IF THIS WAS AN AMBUSH? WHAT IF DILLINGER WANTED TO BEAT ME UP, OR RAPE ME OR SOMETHING?
BUT IT WASN'T.
THERE YOU GO.
KRUNNNNNNK
AND HE DIDN'T.

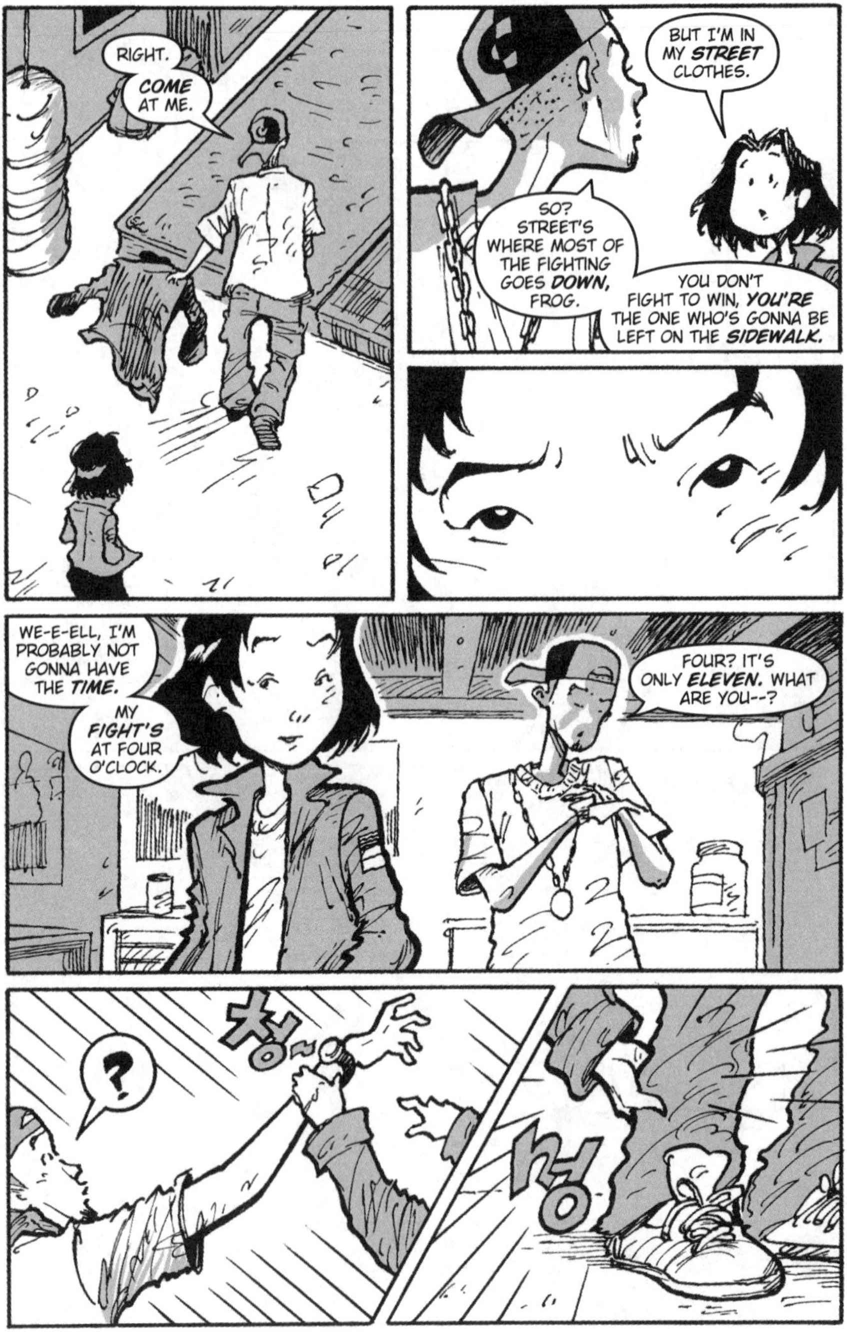
RIGHT.
COME AT ME.
BUT I'M IN MY STREET CLOTHES.
SO? STREET'S WHERE MOST OF THE FIGHTING GOES DOWN, FROG.
YOU DON'T FIGHT TO WIN, YOU'RE THE ONE WHO'S GONNA BE LEFT ON THE SIDEWALK.
WE-E-ELL, I'M PROBABLY NOT GONNA HAVE THE TIME.
MY FIGHT'S AT FOUR O'CLOCK.
FOUR? IT'S ONLY ELEVEN. WHAT ARE YOU--?
?

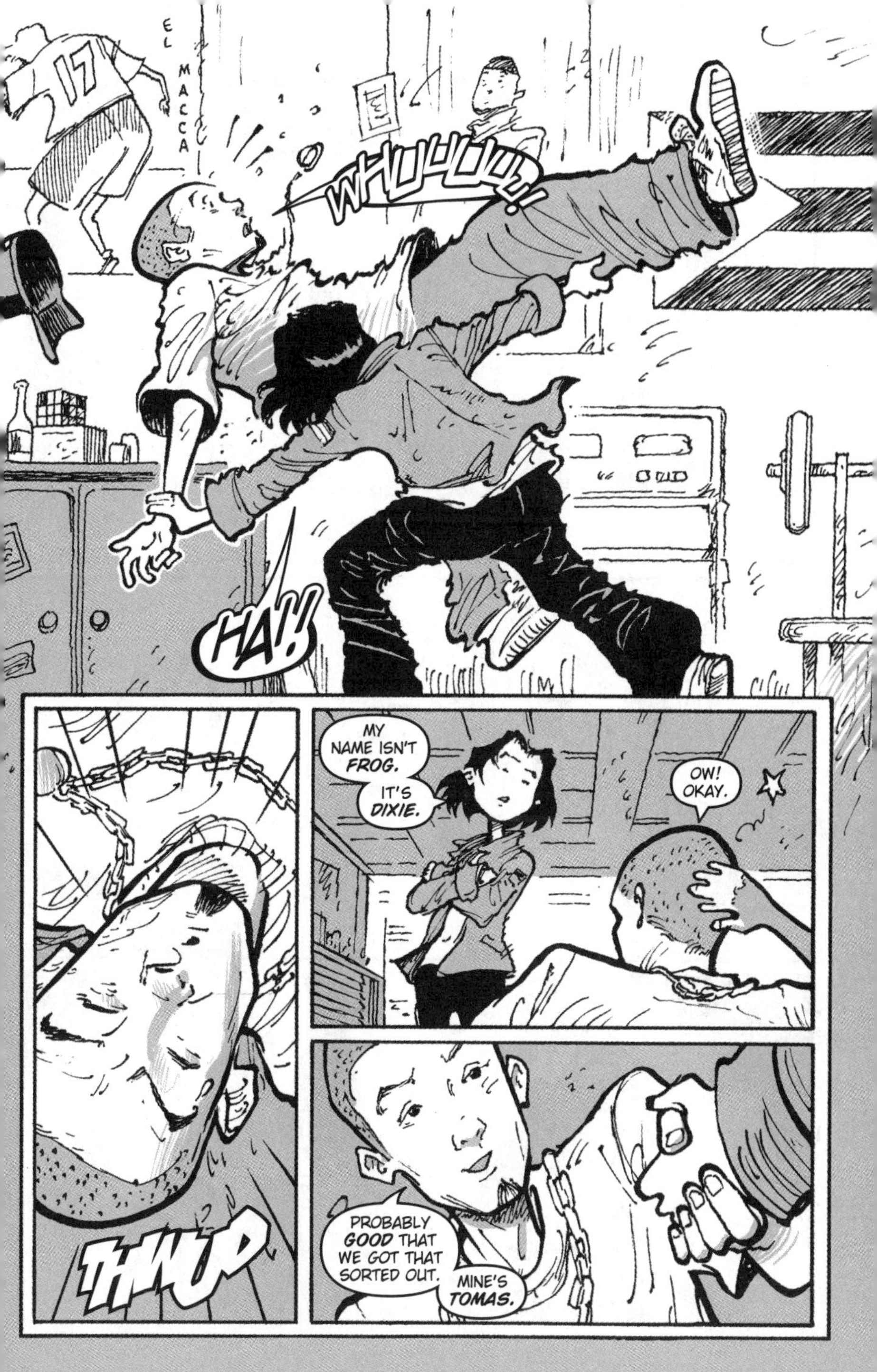
EL MACCA
WHUUUUU!!
HA!!
THWUD
MY NAME ISN'T FROG.
IT'S DIXIE.
OW! OKAY.
PROBABLY GOOD THAT WE GOT THAT SORTED OUT.
MINE'S TOMAS.

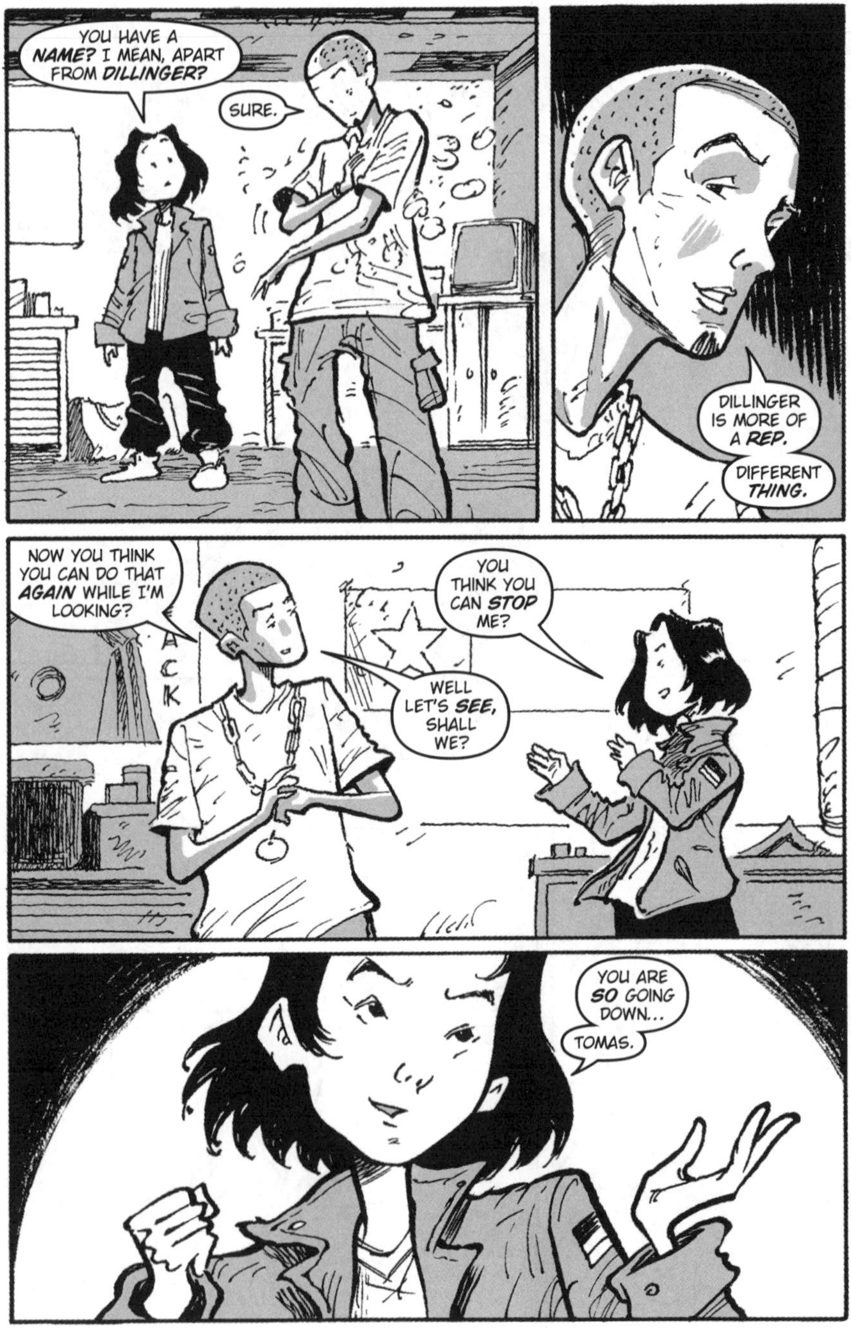

YOU HAVE A NAME? I MEAN, APART FROM DILLINGER?
SURE.
DILLINGER IS MORE OF A REP.
DIFFERENT THING.
NOW YOU THINK YOU CAN DO THAT AGAIN WHILE I'M LOOKING?
YOU THINK YOU CAN STOP ME?
WELL LET'S SEE, SHALL WE?
YOU ARE SO GOING DOWN...
TOMAS.

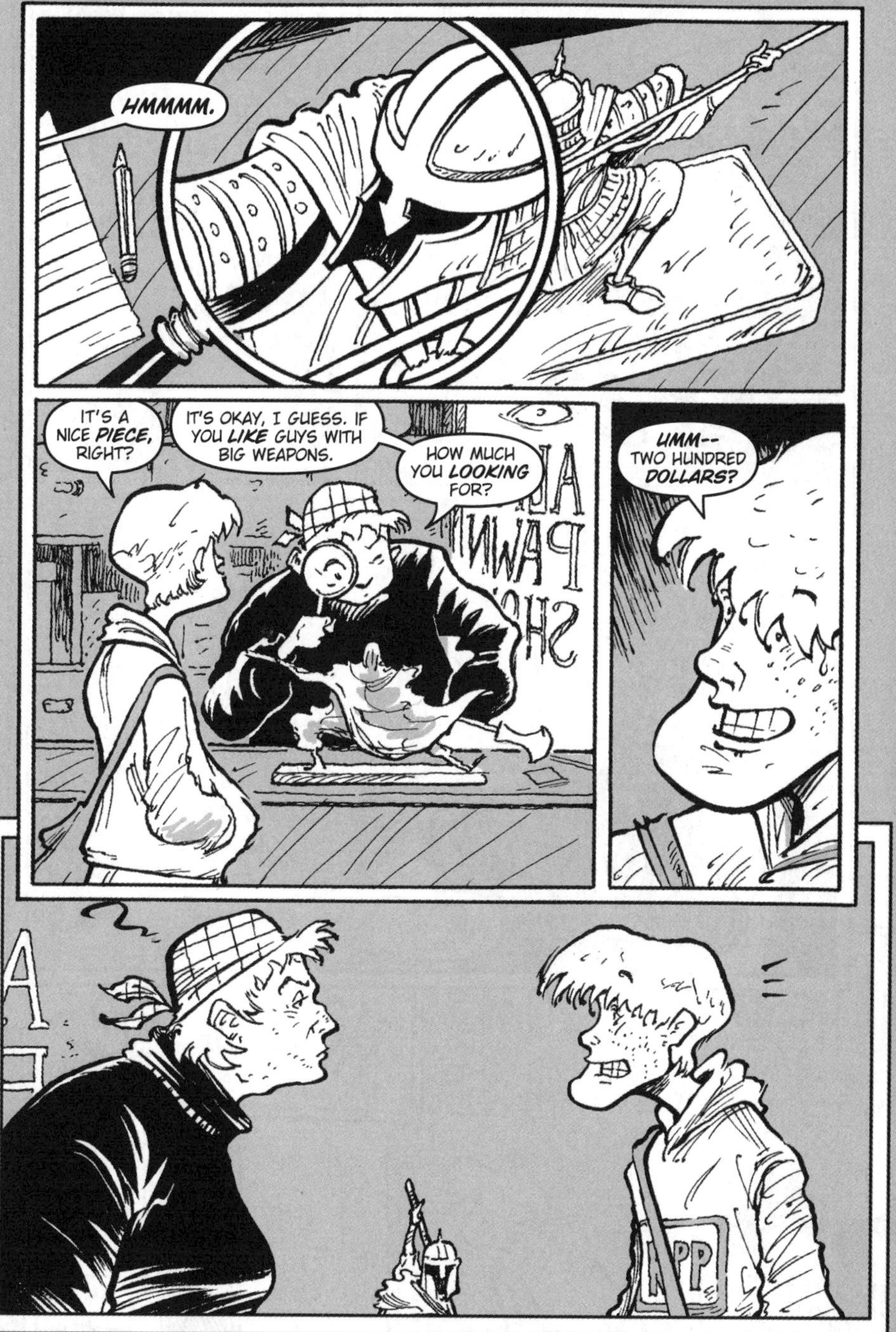
HMMMM.
IT'S A NICE PIECE, RIGHT?
IT'S OKAY, I GUESS. IF YOU LIKE GUYS WITH BIG WEAPONS.
HOW MUCH YOU LOOKING FOR?
UMM-- TWO HUNDRED DOLLARS?

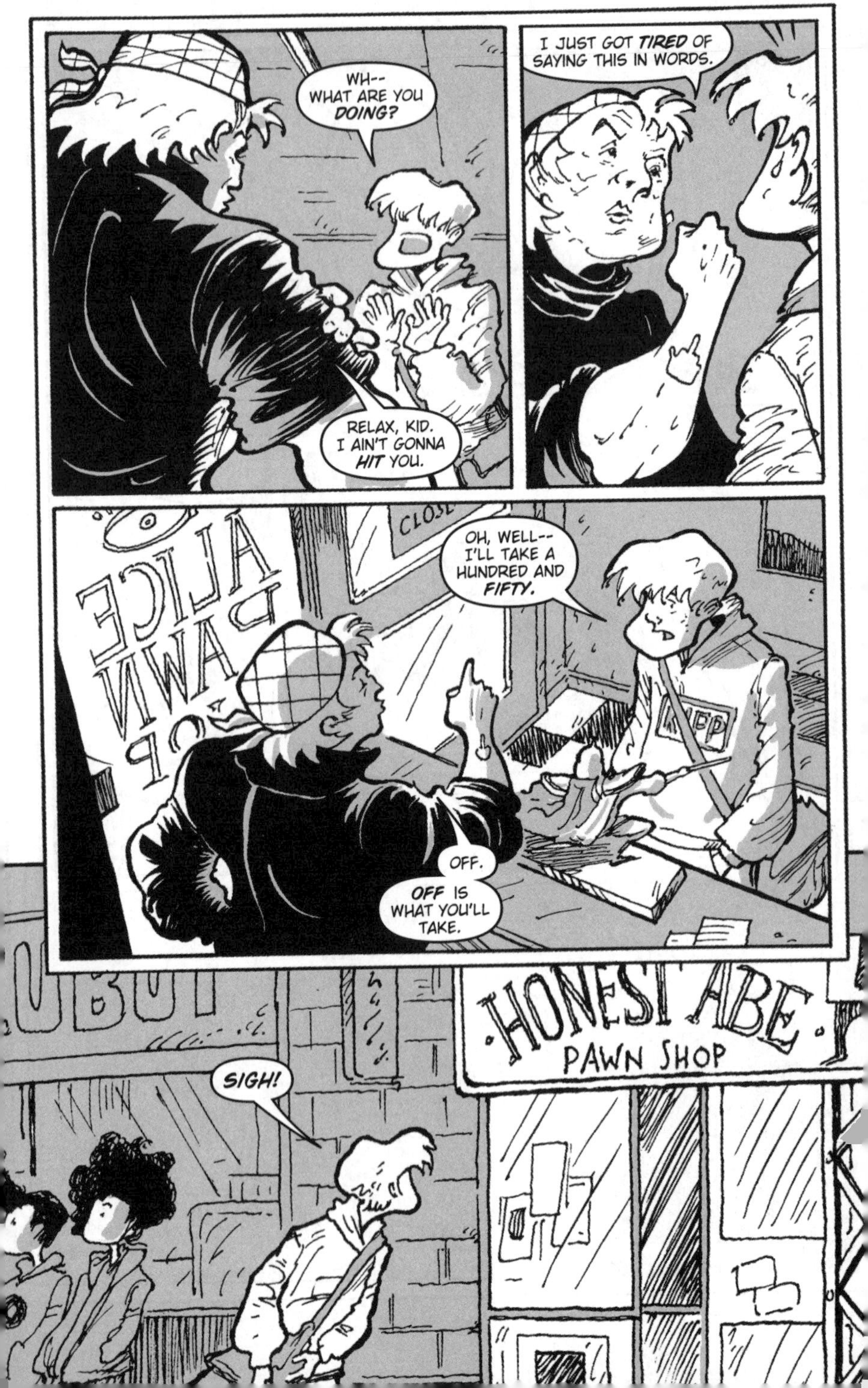
WH--
WHAT ARE YOU
DOING?
RELAX, KID.
I AIN'T GONNA
HIT YOU.
I JUST GOT TIRED OF
SAYING THIS IN WORDS.
ALICE
PAWN
SHOP
CLOSE
OH, WELL--
I'LL TAKE A
HUNDRED AND
FIFTY.
OFF.
OFF IS
WHAT YOU'LL
TAKE.
HONEST ABE
PAWN SHOP
SIGH!

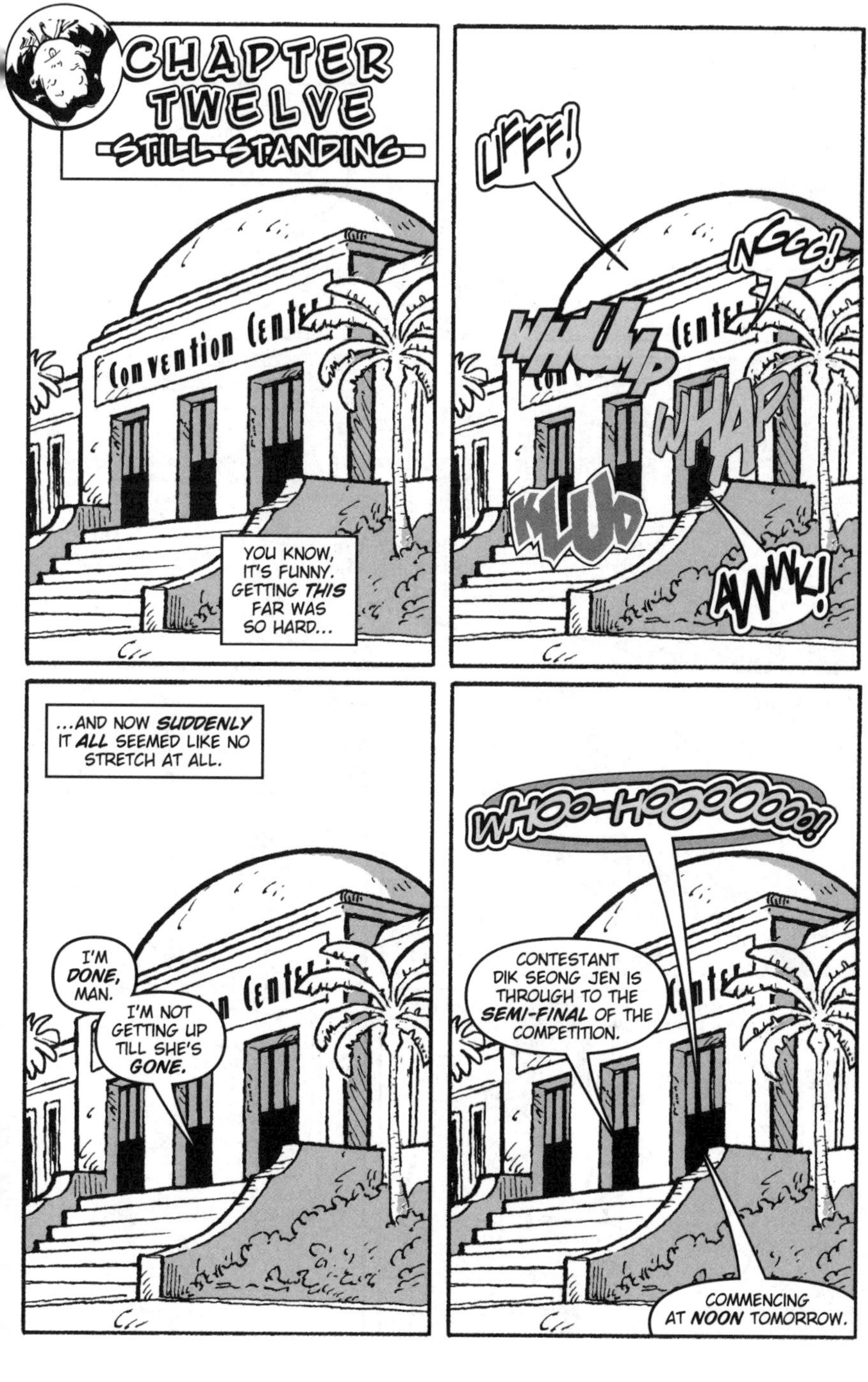
CHAPTER TWELVE
-STILL STANDING-
Convention Center
YOU KNOW, IT'S FUNNY. GETTING *THIS* FAR WAS SO HARD...
UFFF!
NGGG!
WHUMP
WHAP
KLUD
AWWK!
...AND NOW *SUDDENLY* IT *ALL* SEEMED LIKE NO STRETCH AT ALL.
I'M *DONE,* MAN.
I'M NOT GETTING UP TILL SHE'S *GONE.*
WHOO-HOOOOOOO!
CONTESTANT DIK SEONG JEN IS THROUGH TO THE *SEMI-FINAL* OF THE COMPETITION.
COMMENCING AT *NOON* TOMORROW.

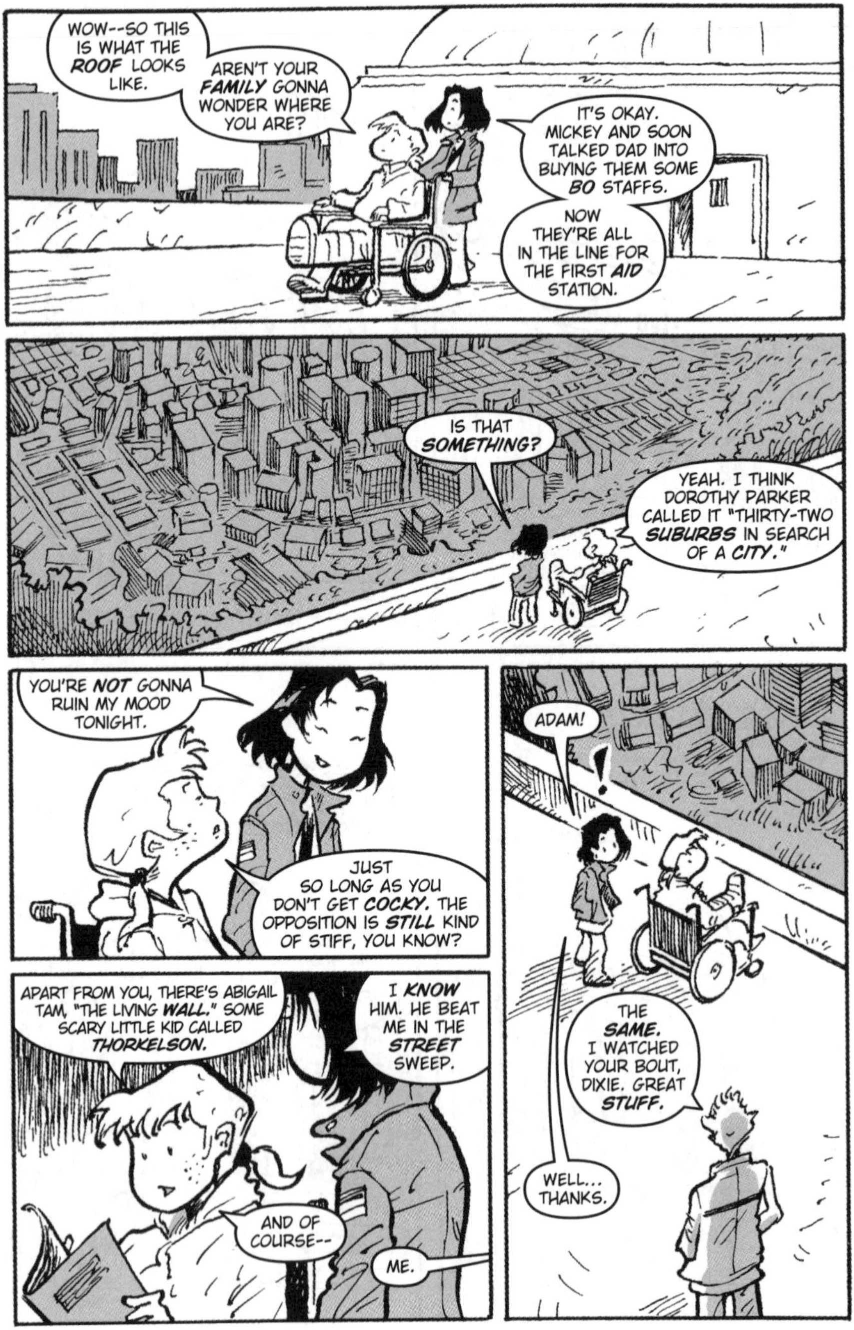
WOW--SO THIS IS WHAT THE ROOF LOOKS LIKE.
AREN'T YOUR FAMILY GONNA WONDER WHERE YOU ARE?
IT'S OKAY. MICKEY AND SOON TALKED DAD INTO BUYING THEM SOME BO STAFFS.
NOW THEY'RE ALL IN THE LINE FOR THE FIRST AID STATION.
IS THAT SOMETHING?
YEAH. I THINK DOROTHY PARKER CALLED IT "THIRTY-TWO SUBURBS IN SEARCH OF A CITY."
YOU'RE NOT GONNA RUIN MY MOOD TONIGHT.
JUST SO LONG AS YOU DON'T GET COCKY. THE OPPOSITION IS STILL KIND OF STIFF, YOU KNOW?
APART FROM YOU, THERE'S ABIGAIL TAM, "THE LIVING WALL." SOME SCARY LITTLE KID CALLED THORKELSON.
I KNOW HIM. HE BEAT ME IN THE STREET SWEEP.
AND OF COURSE--
ME.
ADAM!
!
THE SAME. I WATCHED YOUR BOUT, DIXIE. GREAT STUFF.
WELL... THANKS.

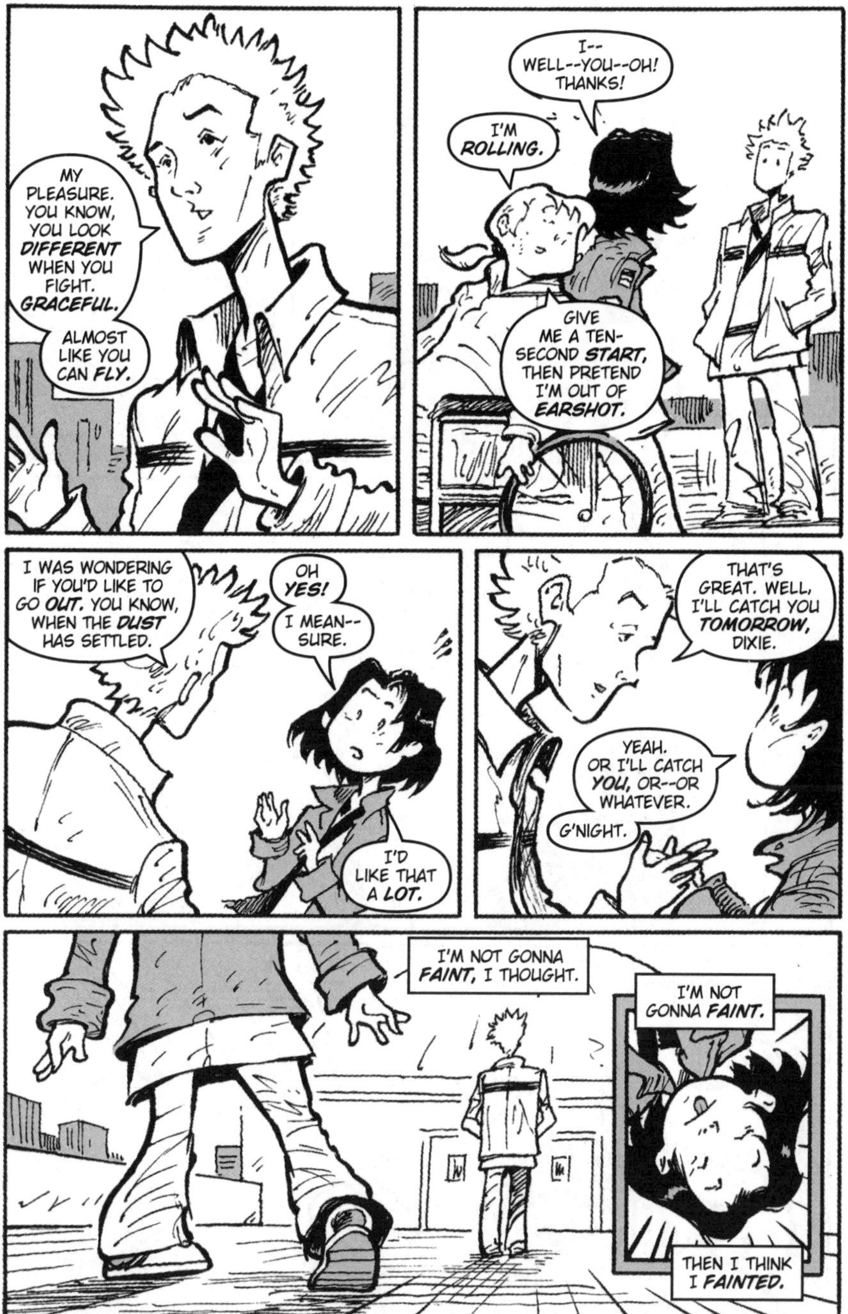
MY PLEASURE. YOU KNOW, YOU LOOK DIFFERENT WHEN YOU FIGHT. GRACEFUL.
ALMOST LIKE YOU CAN FLY.
I-- WELL--YOU--OH! THANKS!
I'M ROLLING.
GIVE ME A TEN-SECOND START, THEN PRETEND I'M OUT OF EARSHOT.
I WAS WONDERING IF YOU'D LIKE TO GO OUT. YOU KNOW, WHEN THE DUST HAS SETTLED.
OH YES!
I MEAN-- SURE.
I'D LIKE THAT A LOT.
THAT'S GREAT. WELL, I'LL CATCH YOU TOMORROW, DIXIE.
YEAH. OR I'LL CATCH YOU, OR--OR WHATEVER.
G'NIGHT.
I'M NOT GONNA FAINT, I THOUGHT.
I'M NOT GONNA FAINT.
THEN I THINK I FAINTED.

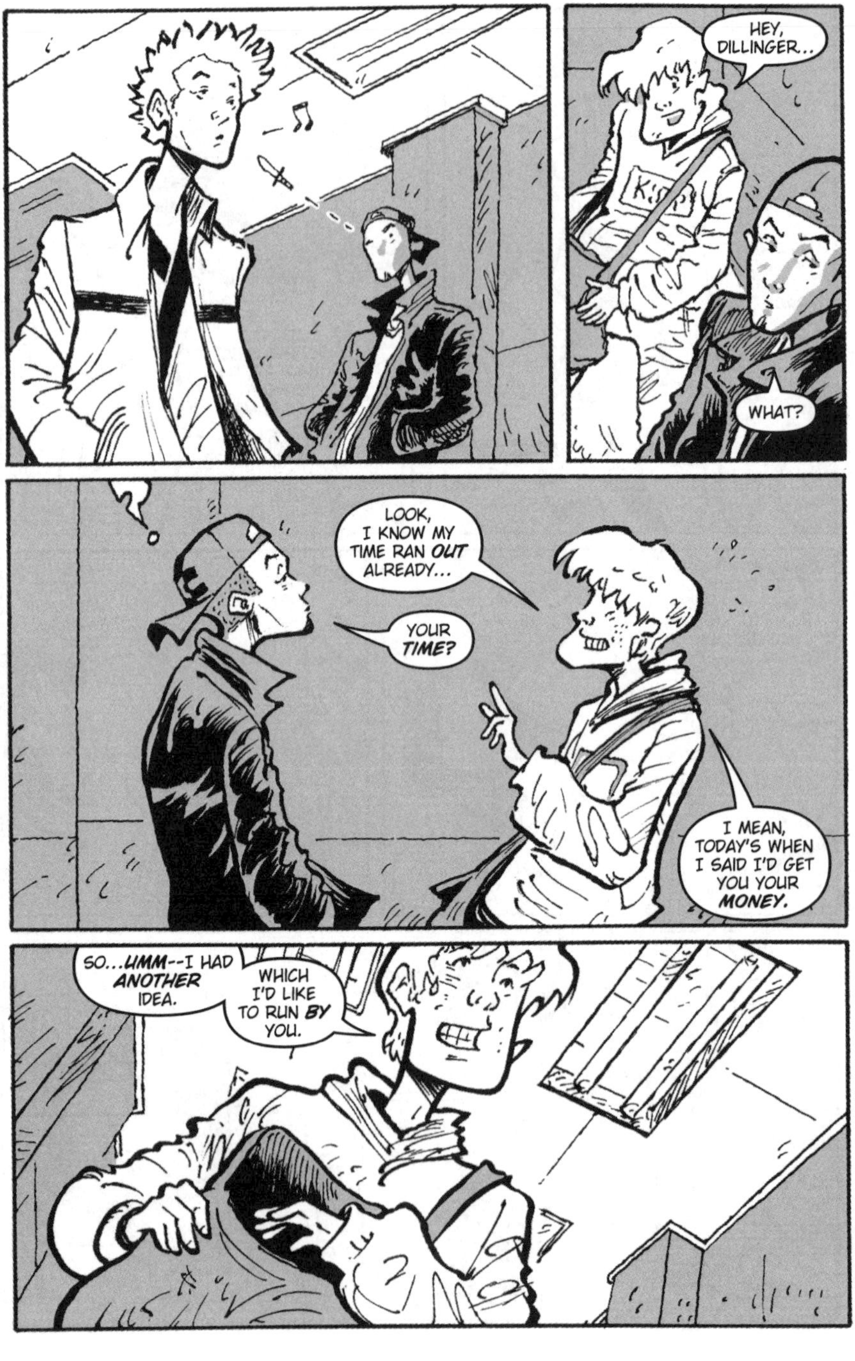
HEY, DILLINGER...
WHAT?
LOOK, I KNOW MY TIME RAN OUT ALREADY...
YOUR TIME?
I MEAN, TODAY'S WHEN I SAID I'D GET YOU YOUR MONEY.
SO...UMM--I HAD ANOTHER IDEA.
WHICH I'D LIKE TO RUN BY YOU.

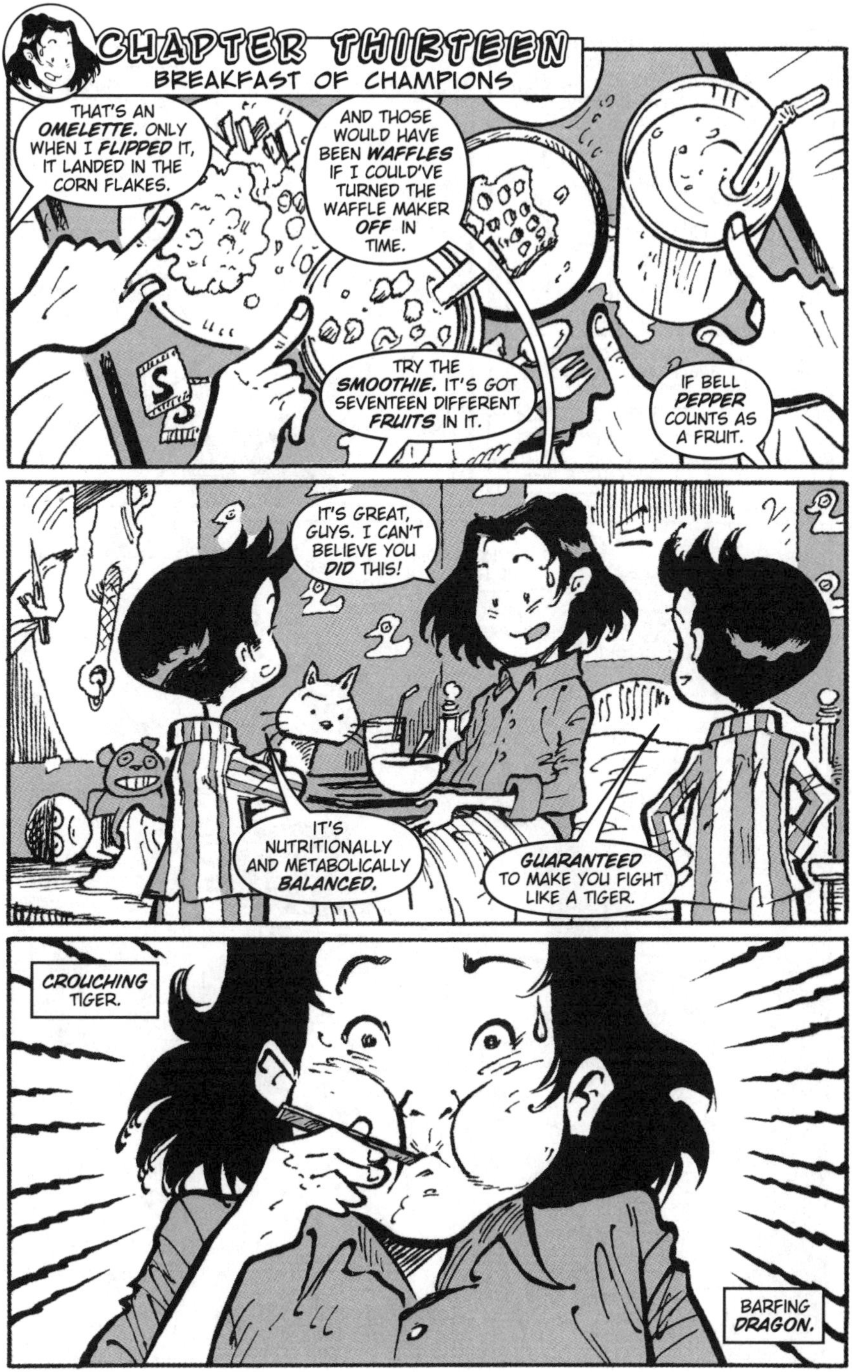
CHAPTER THIRTEEN
BREAKFAST OF CHAMPIONS
THAT'S AN OMELETTE. ONLY WHEN I FLIPPED IT, IT LANDED IN THE CORN FLAKES.
AND THOSE WOULD HAVE BEEN WAFFLES IF I COULD'VE TURNED THE WAFFLE MAKER OFF IN TIME.
TRY THE SMOOTHIE. IT'S GOT SEVENTEEN DIFFERENT FRUITS IN IT.
IF BELL PEPPER COUNTS AS A FRUIT.
IT'S GREAT, GUYS. I CAN'T BELIEVE YOU DID THIS!
IT'S NUTRITIONALLY AND METABOLICALLY BALANCED.
GUARANTEED TO MAKE YOU FIGHT LIKE A TIGER.
CROUCHING TIGER.
BARFING DRAGON.

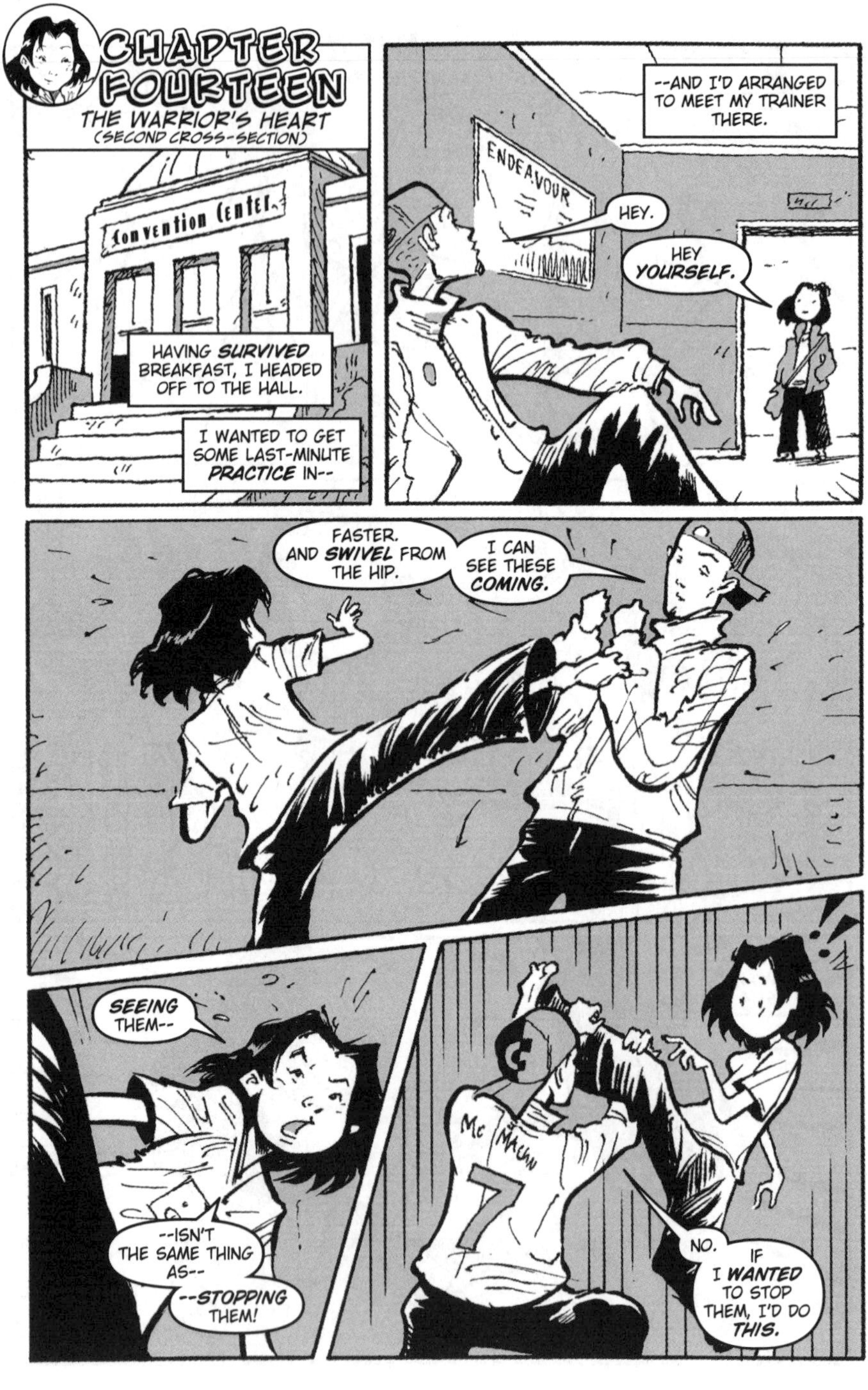
CHAPTER FOURTEEN
THE WARRIOR'S HEART
(SECOND CROSS-SECTION)
Convention Center
HAVING SURVIVED BREAKFAST, I HEADED OFF TO THE HALL.
I WANTED TO GET SOME LAST-MINUTE PRACTICE IN--
--AND I'D ARRANGED TO MEET MY TRAINER THERE.
ENDEAVOUR
HEY.
HEY YOURSELF.
FASTER. AND SWIVEL FROM THE HIP.
I CAN SEE THESE COMING.
SEEING THEM--
--ISN'T THE SAME THING AS--
--STOPPING THEM!
NO.
IF I WANTED TO STOP THEM, I'D DO THIS.
McMAHON
7

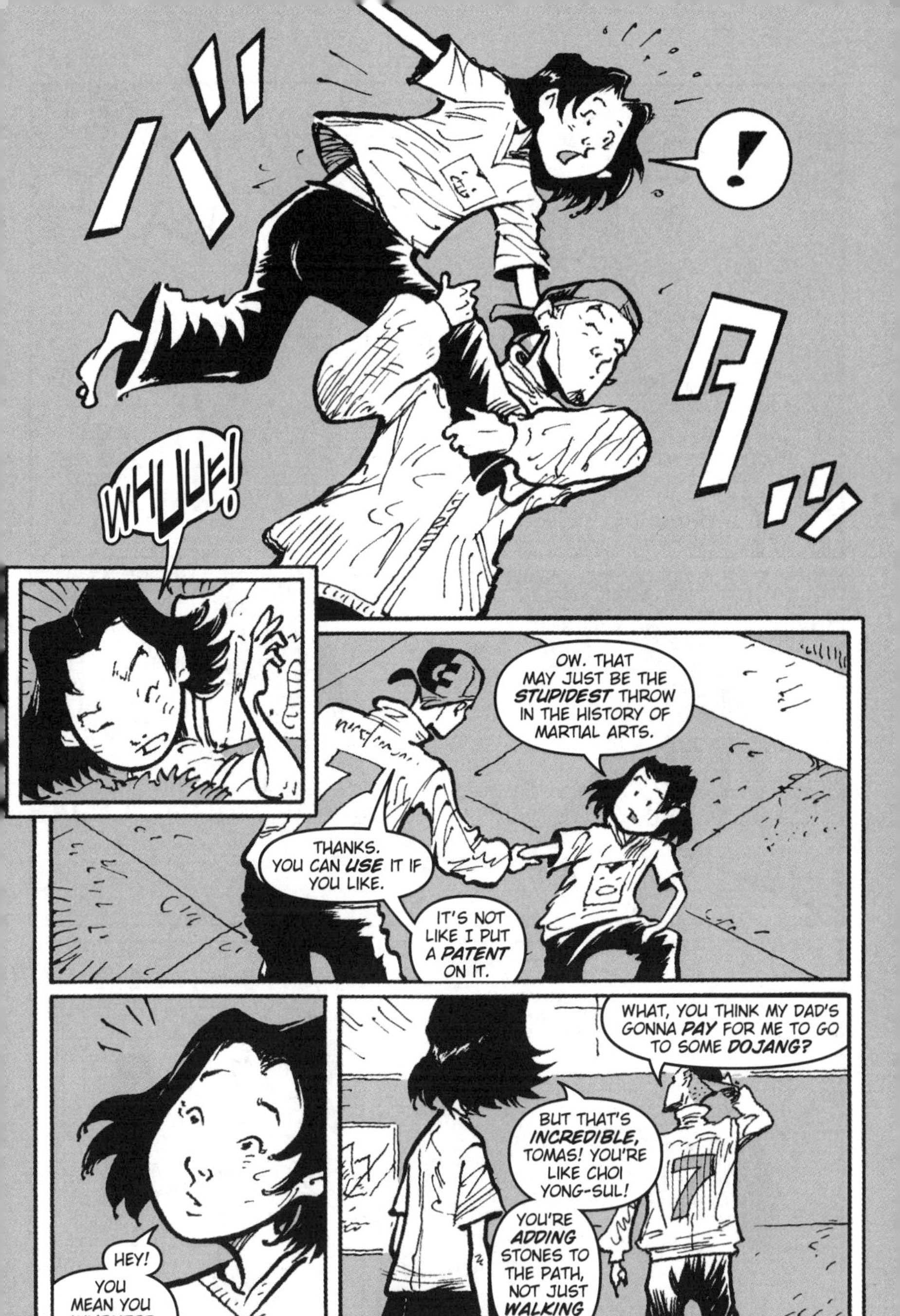
バ
!
タッ
WHUUF!
OW. THAT MAY JUST BE THE STUPIDEST THROW IN THE HISTORY OF MARTIAL ARTS.
THANKS. YOU CAN USE IT IF YOU LIKE.
IT'S NOT LIKE I PUT A PATENT ON IT.
HEY! YOU MEAN YOU INVENTED THAT MOVE?
WHAT, YOU THINK MY DAD'S GONNA PAY FOR ME TO GO TO SOME DOJANG?
BUT THAT'S INCREDIBLE, TOMAS! YOU'RE LIKE CHOI YONG-SUL!
YOU'RE ADDING STONES TO THE PATH, NOT JUST WALKING ON IT.

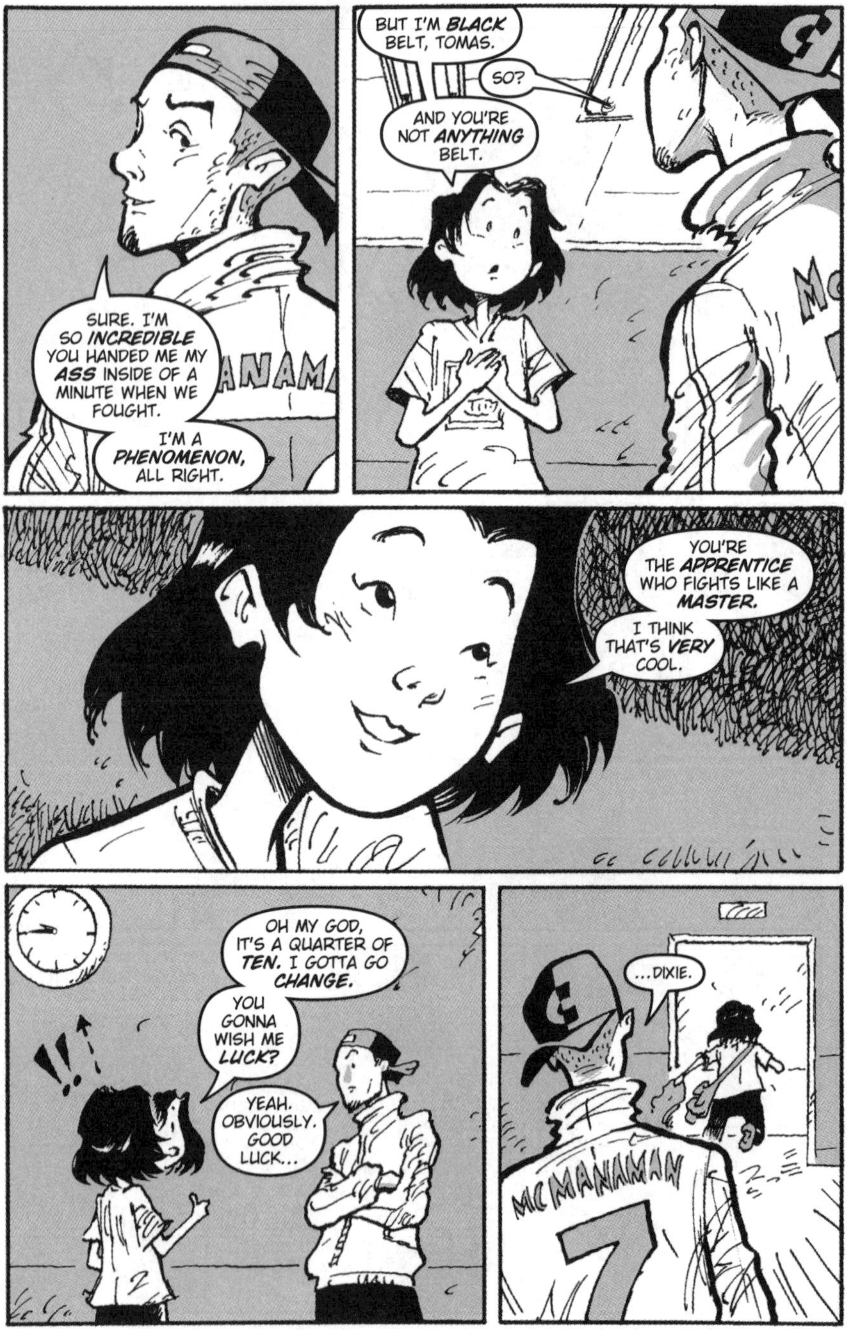
SURE. I'M SO INCREDIBLE YOU HANDED ME MY ASS INSIDE OF A MINUTE WHEN WE FOUGHT.
I'M A PHENOMENON, ALL RIGHT.
BUT I'M BLACK BELT, TOMAS.
SO?
AND YOU'RE NOT ANYTHING BELT.
YOU'RE THE APPRENTICE WHO FIGHTS LIKE A MASTER.
I THINK THAT'S VERY COOL.
OH MY GOD, IT'S A QUARTER OF TEN. I GOTTA GO CHANGE.
YOU GONNA WISH ME LUCK?
YEAH. OBVIOUSLY. GOOD LUCK...
!!
...DIXIE.
MCMANAMAN
7

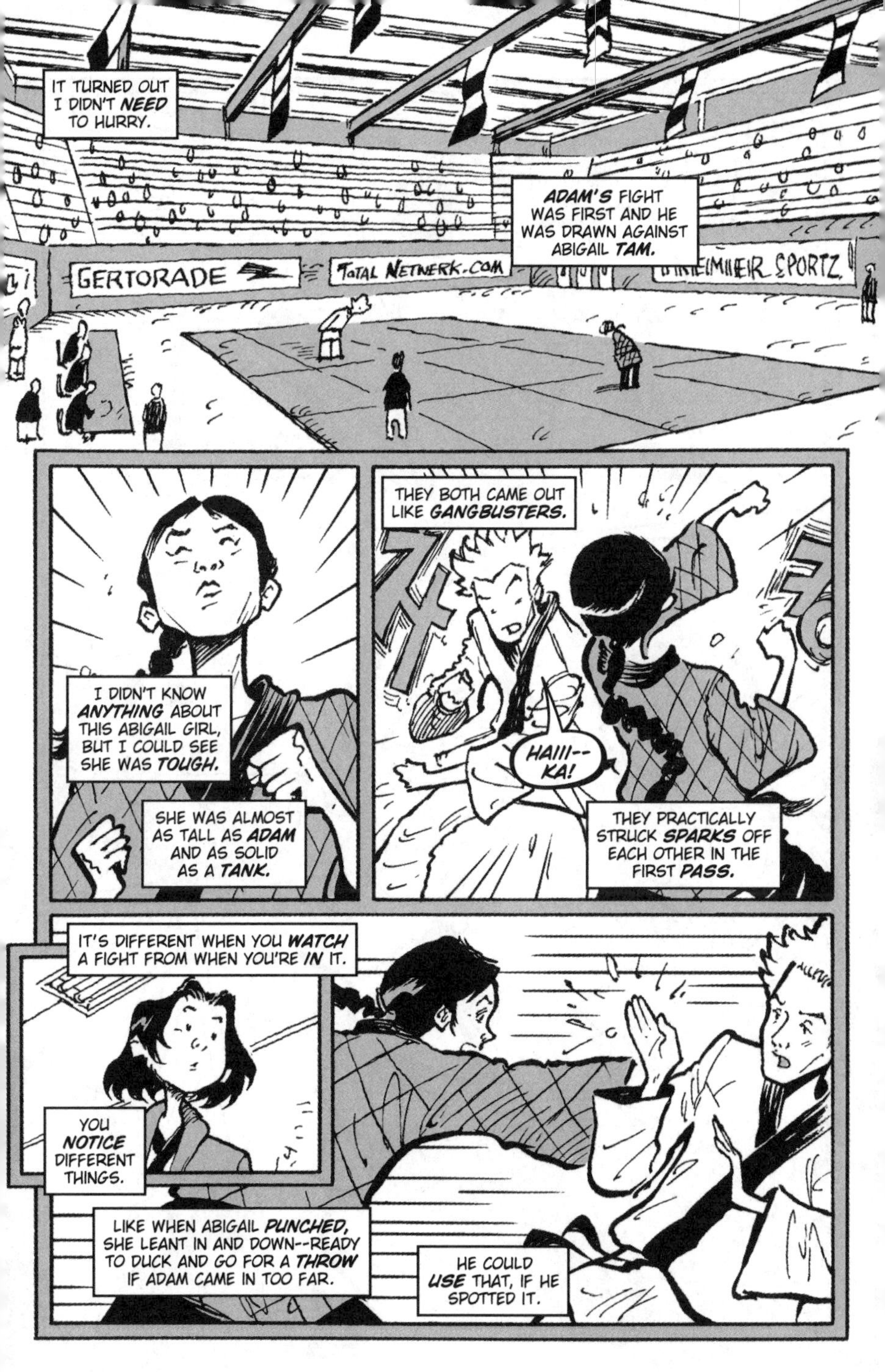
IT TURNED OUT I DIDN'T NEED TO HURRY.
ADAM'S FIGHT WAS FIRST AND HE WAS DRAWN AGAINST ABIGAIL TAM.
GERTORADE
TOTAL NETWERK.COM
PREMIER SPORTZ
I DIDN'T KNOW ANYTHING ABOUT THIS ABIGAIL GIRL, BUT I COULD SEE SHE WAS TOUGH.
SHE WAS ALMOST AS TALL AS ADAM AND AS SOLID AS A TANK.
THEY BOTH CAME OUT LIKE GANGBUSTERS.
HAIII--KA!
THEY PRACTICALLY STRUCK SPARKS OFF EACH OTHER IN THE FIRST PASS.
IT'S DIFFERENT WHEN YOU WATCH A FIGHT FROM WHEN YOU'RE IN IT.
YOU NOTICE DIFFERENT THINGS.
LIKE WHEN ABIGAIL PUNCHED, SHE LEANT IN AND DOWN--READY TO DUCK AND GO FOR A THROW IF ADAM CAME IN TOO FAR.
HE COULD USE THAT, IF HE SPOTTED IT.

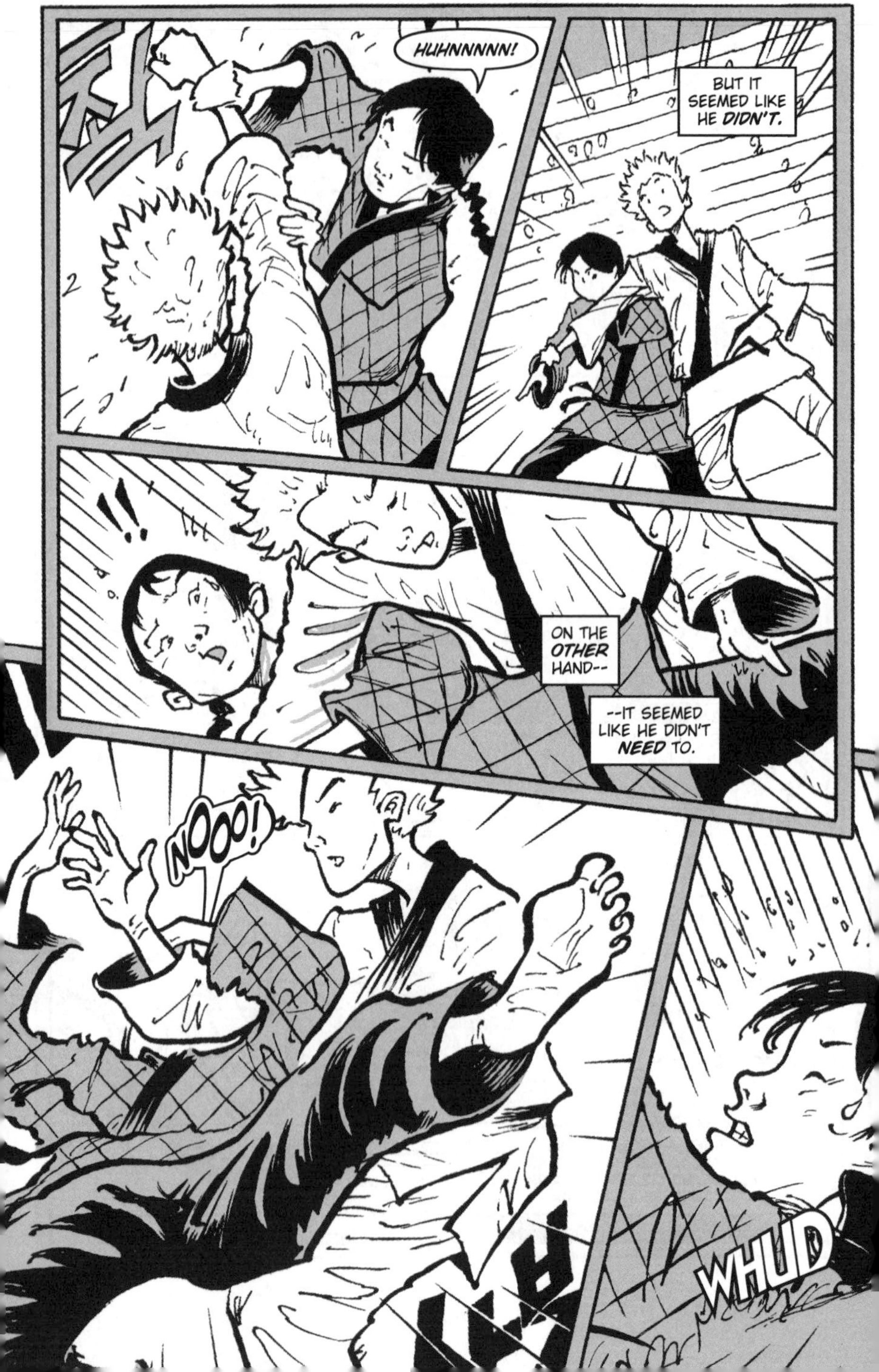

HUHNNNNN!
BUT IT SEEMED LIKE HE DIDN'T.
ON THE OTHER HAND--
--IT SEEMED LIKE HE DIDN'T NEED TO.
NOOO!
WHUD

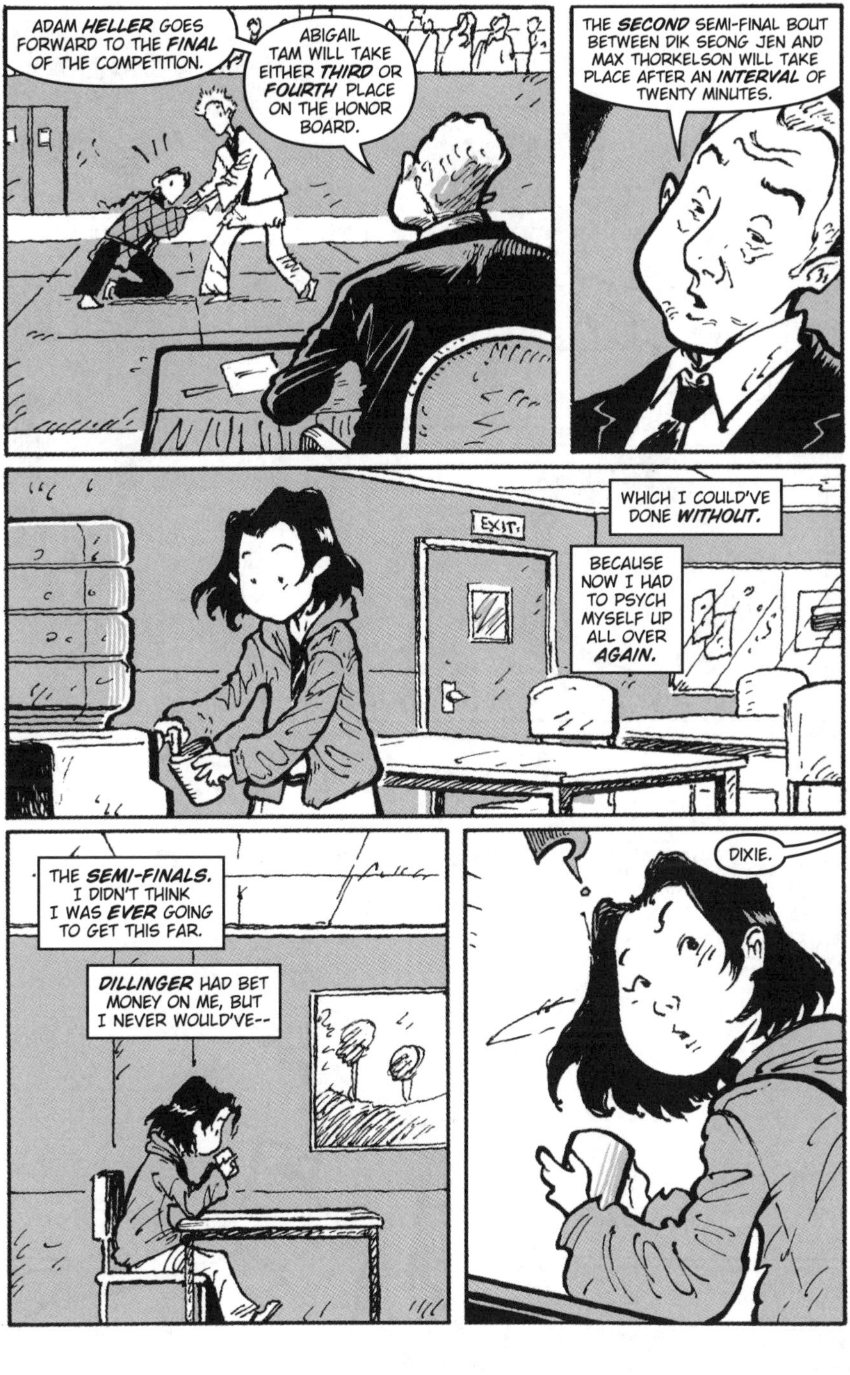
ADAM HELLER GOES FORWARD TO THE FINAL OF THE COMPETITION.
ABIGAIL TAM WILL TAKE EITHER THIRD OR FOURTH PLACE ON THE HONOR BOARD.
THE SECOND SEMI-FINAL BOUT BETWEEN DIK SEONG JEN AND MAX THORKELSON WILL TAKE PLACE AFTER AN INTERVAL OF TWENTY MINUTES.
EXIT
WHICH I COULD'VE DONE WITHOUT.
BECAUSE NOW I HAD TO PSYCH MYSELF UP ALL OVER AGAIN.
THE SEMI-FINALS. I DIDN'T THINK I WAS EVER GOING TO GET THIS FAR.
DILLINGER HAD BET MONEY ON ME, BUT I NEVER WOULD'VE--
DIXIE.

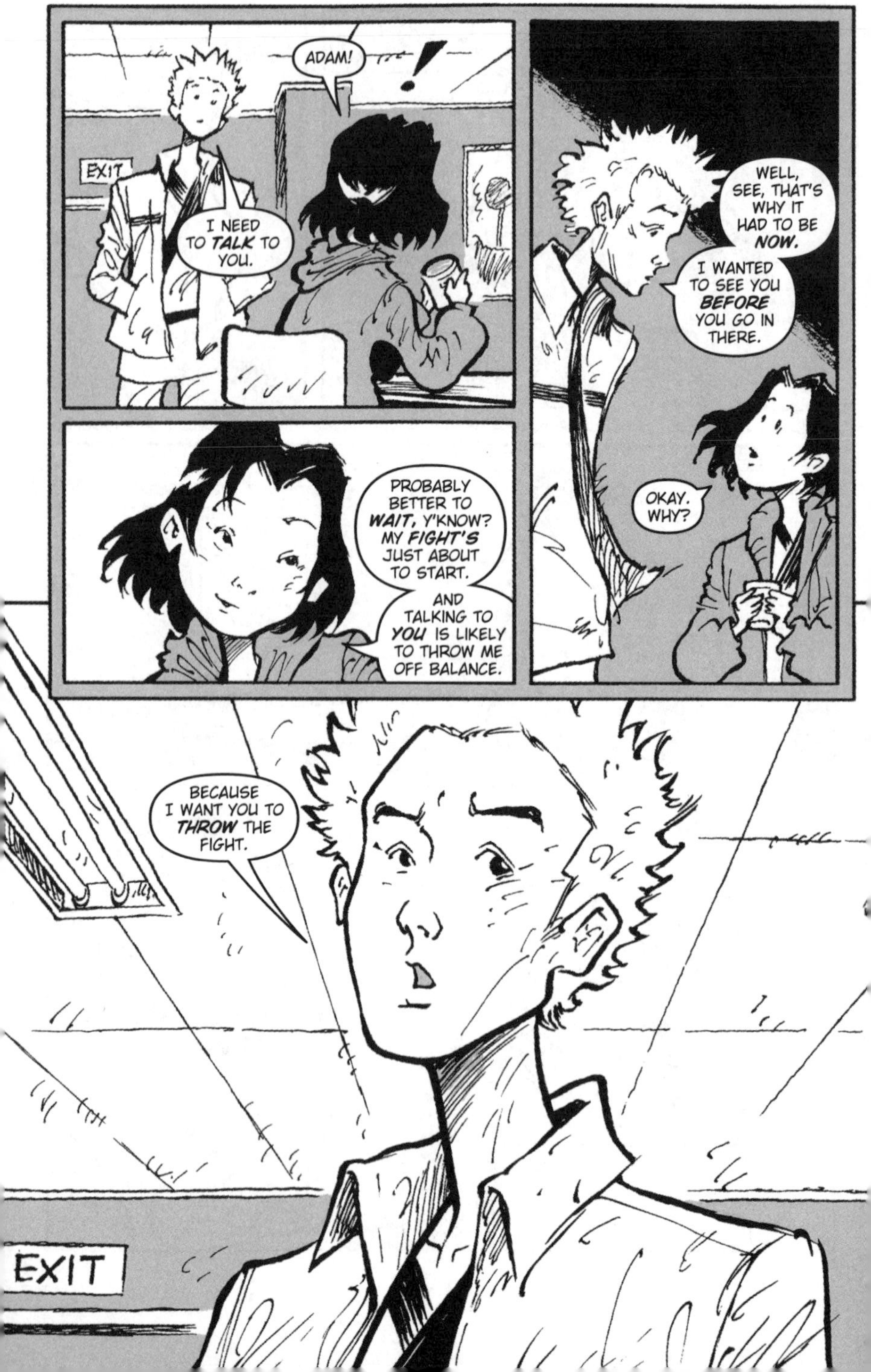
ADAM!
!
EXIT
I NEED TO TALK TO YOU.
WELL, SEE, THAT'S WHY IT HAD TO BE NOW.
I WANTED TO SEE YOU BEFORE YOU GO IN THERE.
OKAY. WHY?
PROBABLY BETTER TO WAIT, Y'KNOW? MY FIGHT'S JUST ABOUT TO START.
AND TALKING TO YOU IS LIKELY TO THROW ME OFF BALANCE.
BECAUSE I WANT YOU TO THROW THE FIGHT.
EXIT

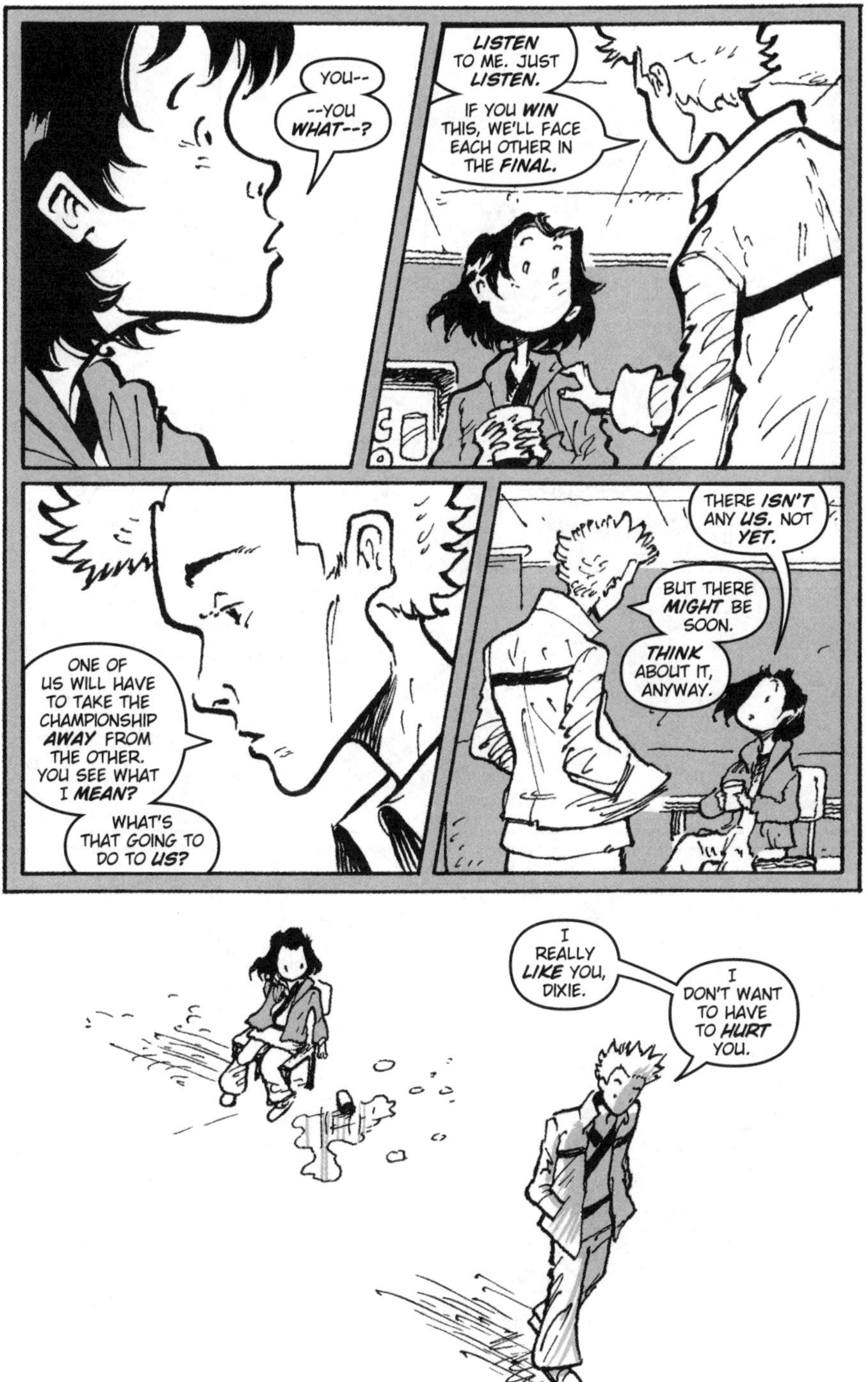
YOU--
--YOU WHAT--?
LISTEN TO ME. JUST LISTEN.
IF YOU WIN THIS, WE'LL FACE EACH OTHER IN THE FINAL.
ONE OF US WILL HAVE TO TAKE THE CHAMPIONSHIP AWAY FROM THE OTHER. YOU SEE WHAT I MEAN?
WHAT'S THAT GOING TO DO TO US?
THERE ISN'T ANY US. NOT YET.
BUT THERE MIGHT BE SOON.
THINK ABOUT IT, ANYWAY.
I REALLY LIKE YOU, DIXIE.
I DON'T WANT TO HAVE TO HURT YOU.

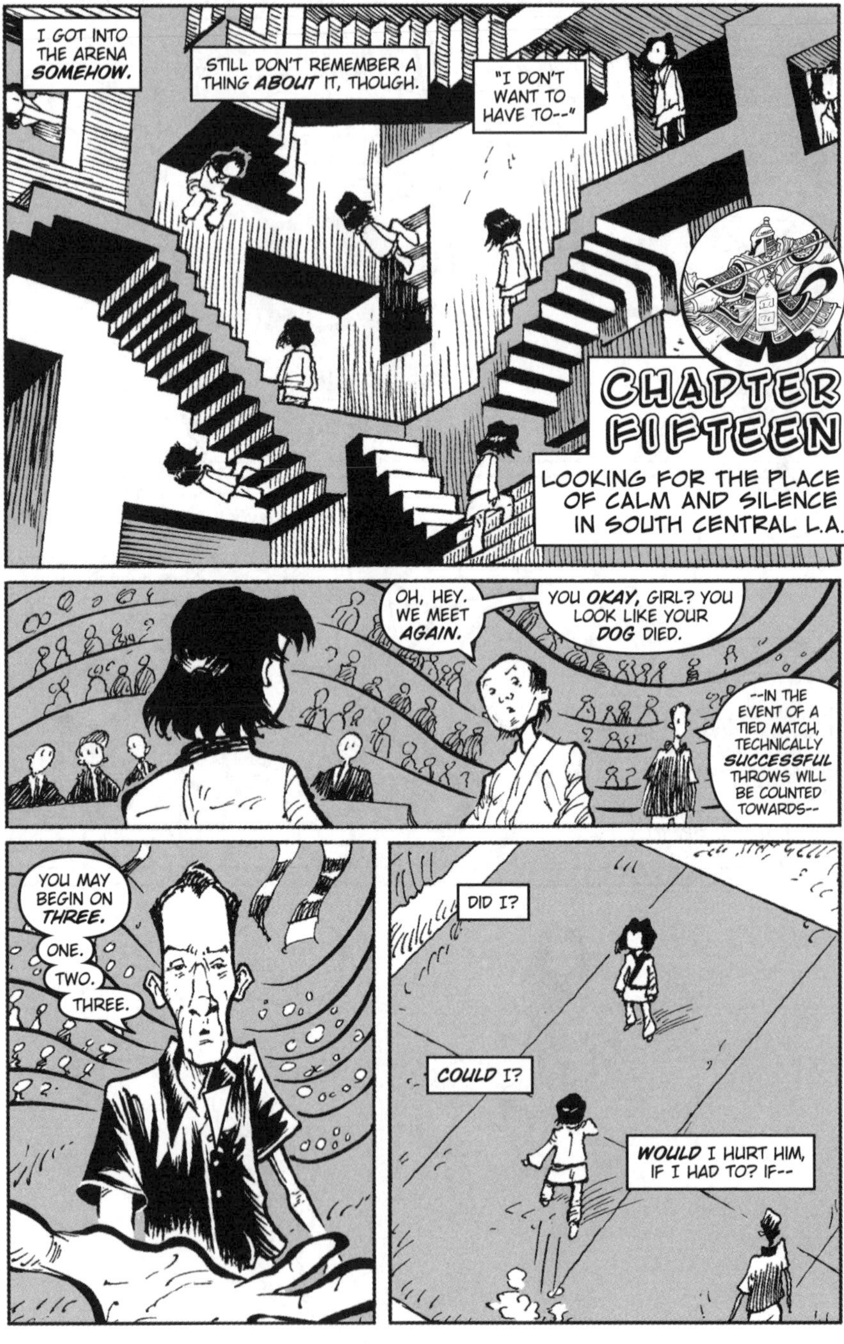
I GOT INTO THE ARENA SOMEHOW.
STILL DON'T REMEMBER A THING ABOUT IT, THOUGH.
"I DON'T WANT TO HAVE TO--"
CHAPTER FIFTEEN
LOOKING FOR THE PLACE OF CALM AND SILENCE IN SOUTH CENTRAL L.A.
OH, HEY. WE MEET AGAIN.
YOU OKAY, GIRL? YOU LOOK LIKE YOUR DOG DIED.
--IN THE EVENT OF A TIED MATCH, TECHNICALLY SUCCESSFUL THROWS WILL BE COUNTED TOWARDS--
YOU MAY BEGIN ON THREE.
ONE.
TWO.
THREE.
DID I?
COULD I?
WOULD I HURT HIM, IF I HAD TO? IF--

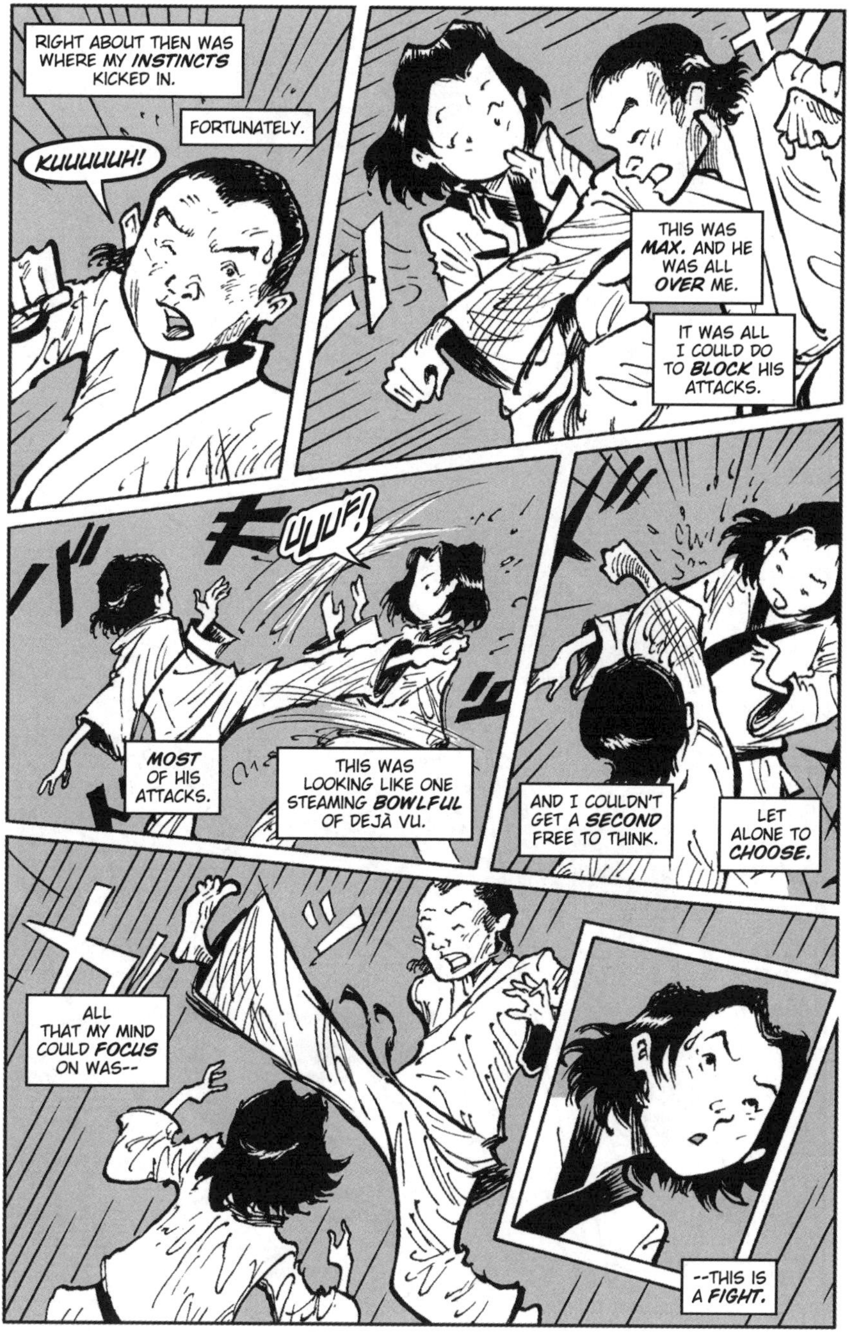
RIGHT ABOUT THEN WAS WHERE MY INSTINCTS KICKED IN.
FORTUNATELY.
KUUUUUH!
THIS WAS MAX. AND HE WAS ALL OVER ME.
IT WAS ALL I COULD DO TO BLOCK HIS ATTACKS.
UUUF!
MOST OF HIS ATTACKS.
THIS WAS LOOKING LIKE ONE STEAMING BOWLFUL OF DEJÀ VU.
AND I COULDN'T GET A SECOND FREE TO THINK.
LET ALONE TO CHOOSE.
ALL THAT MY MIND COULD FOCUS ON WAS--
--THIS IS A FIGHT.

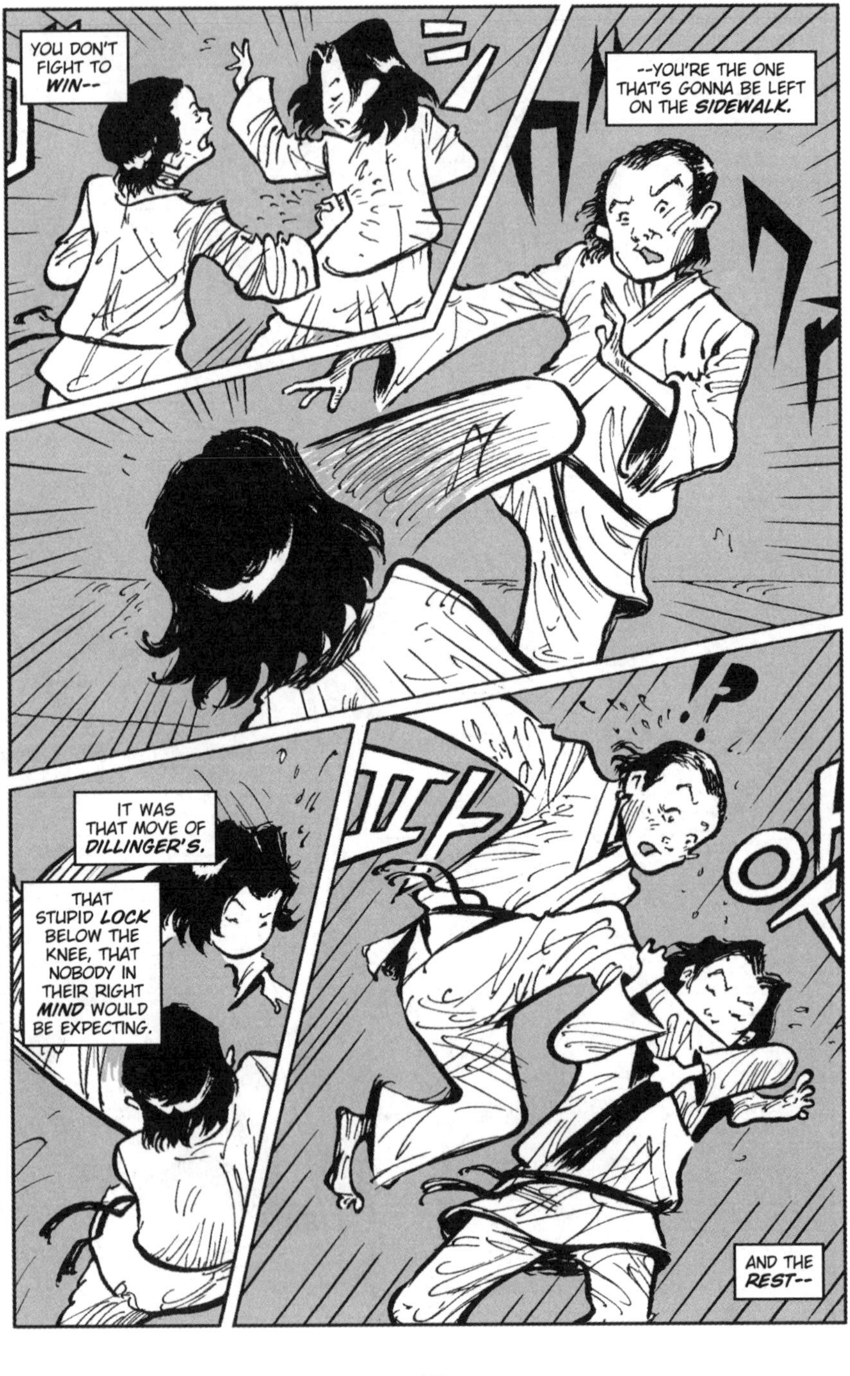
YOU DON'T FIGHT TO WIN--
--YOU'RE THE ONE THAT'S GONNA BE LEFT ON THE SIDEWALK.
IT WAS THAT MOVE OF DILLINGER'S.
THAT STUPID LOCK BELOW THE KNEE, THAT NOBODY IN THEIR RIGHT MIND WOULD BE EXPECTING.
AND THE REST--

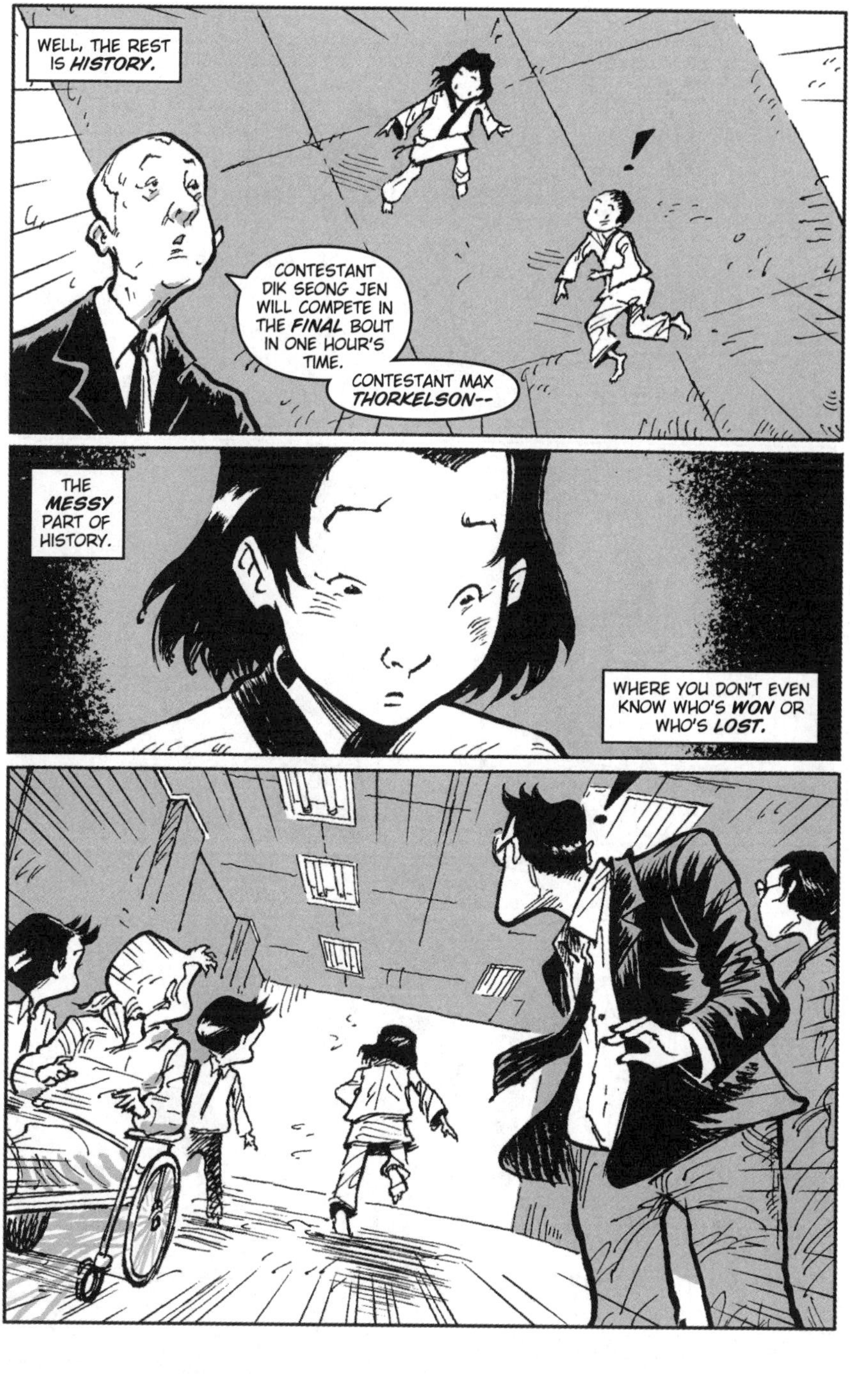
WELL, THE REST IS *HISTORY.*
!
CONTESTANT DIK SEONG JEN WILL COMPETE IN THE *FINAL* BOUT IN ONE HOUR'S TIME.
CONTESTANT MAX *THORKELSON--*
THE *MESSY* PART OF HISTORY.
WHERE YOU DON'T EVEN KNOW WHO'S *WON* OR WHO'S *LOST.*
!

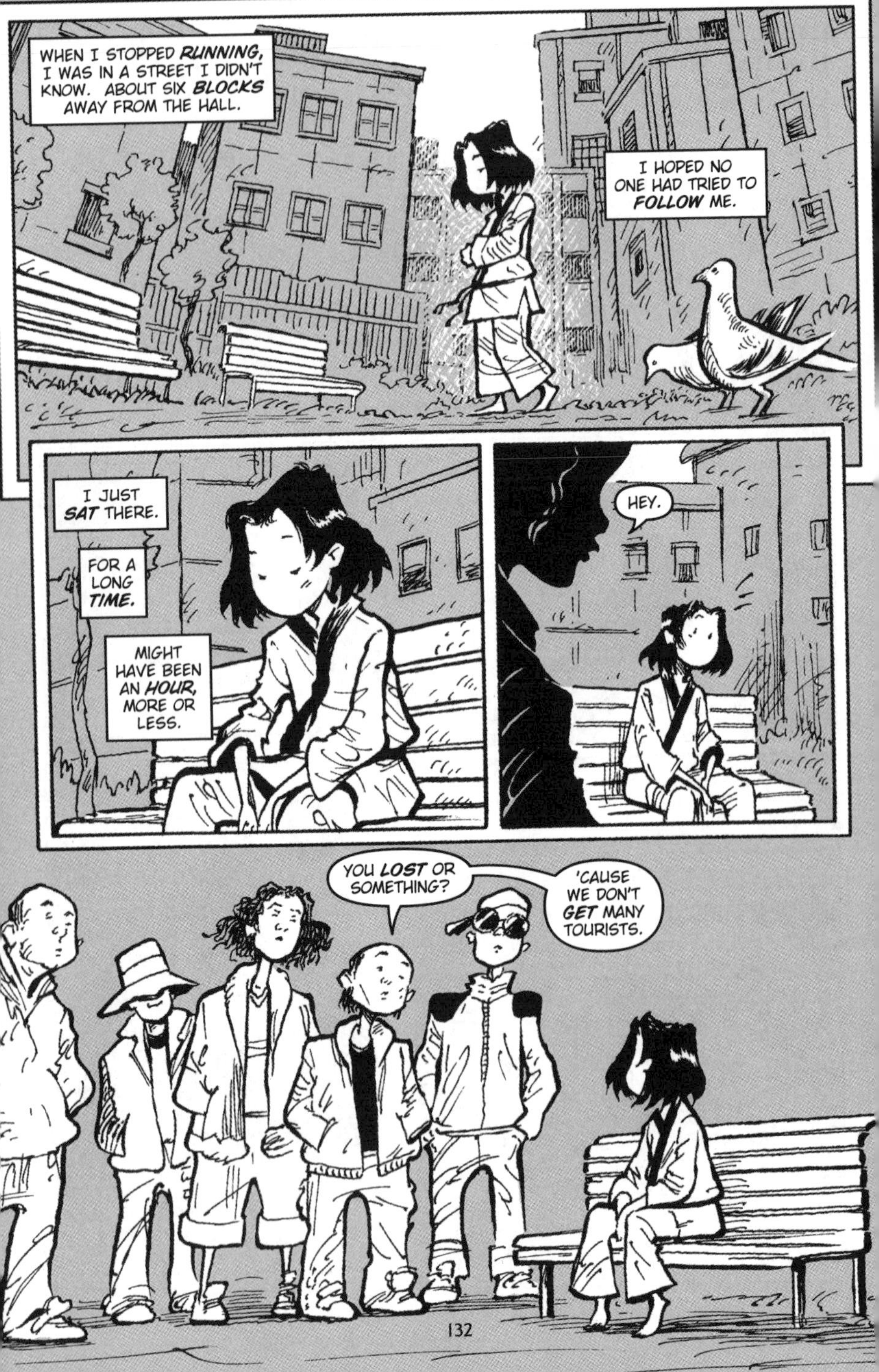
WHEN I STOPPED RUNNING, I WAS IN A STREET I DIDN'T KNOW. ABOUT SIX BLOCKS AWAY FROM THE HALL.
I HOPED NO ONE HAD TRIED TO FOLLOW ME.
I JUST SAT THERE.
FOR A LONG TIME.
MIGHT HAVE BEEN AN HOUR, MORE OR LESS.
HEY.
YOU LOST OR SOMETHING?
'CAUSE WE DON'T GET MANY TOURISTS.

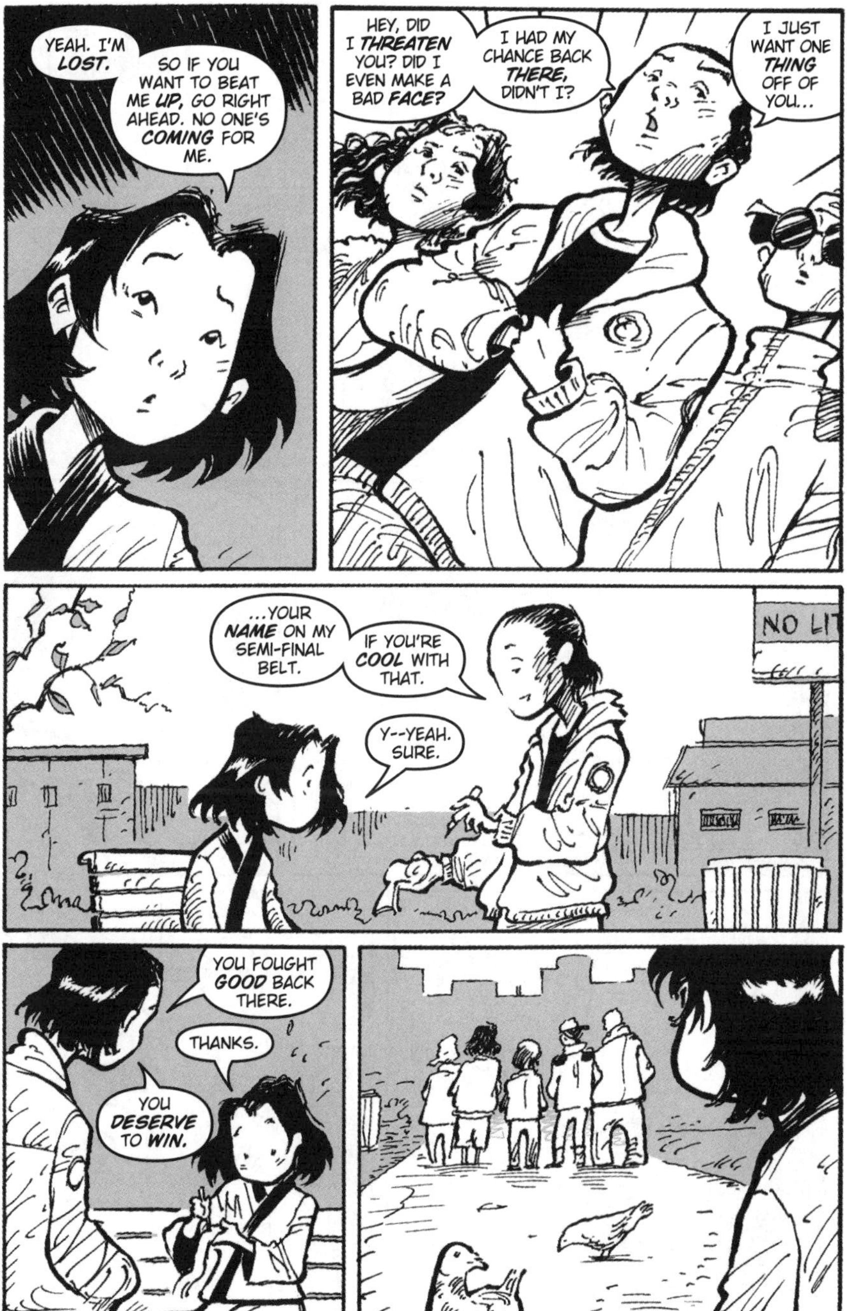
YEAH. I'M LOST.
SO IF YOU WANT TO BEAT ME UP, GO RIGHT AHEAD. NO ONE'S COMING FOR ME.
HEY, DID I THREATEN YOU? DID I EVEN MAKE A BAD FACE?
I HAD MY CHANCE BACK THERE, DIDN'T I?
I JUST WANT ONE THING OFF OF YOU...
...YOUR NAME ON MY SEMI-FINAL BELT.
IF YOU'RE COOL WITH THAT.
NO LI
Y--YEAH. SURE.
YOU FOUGHT GOOD BACK THERE.
THANKS.
YOU DESERVE TO WIN.

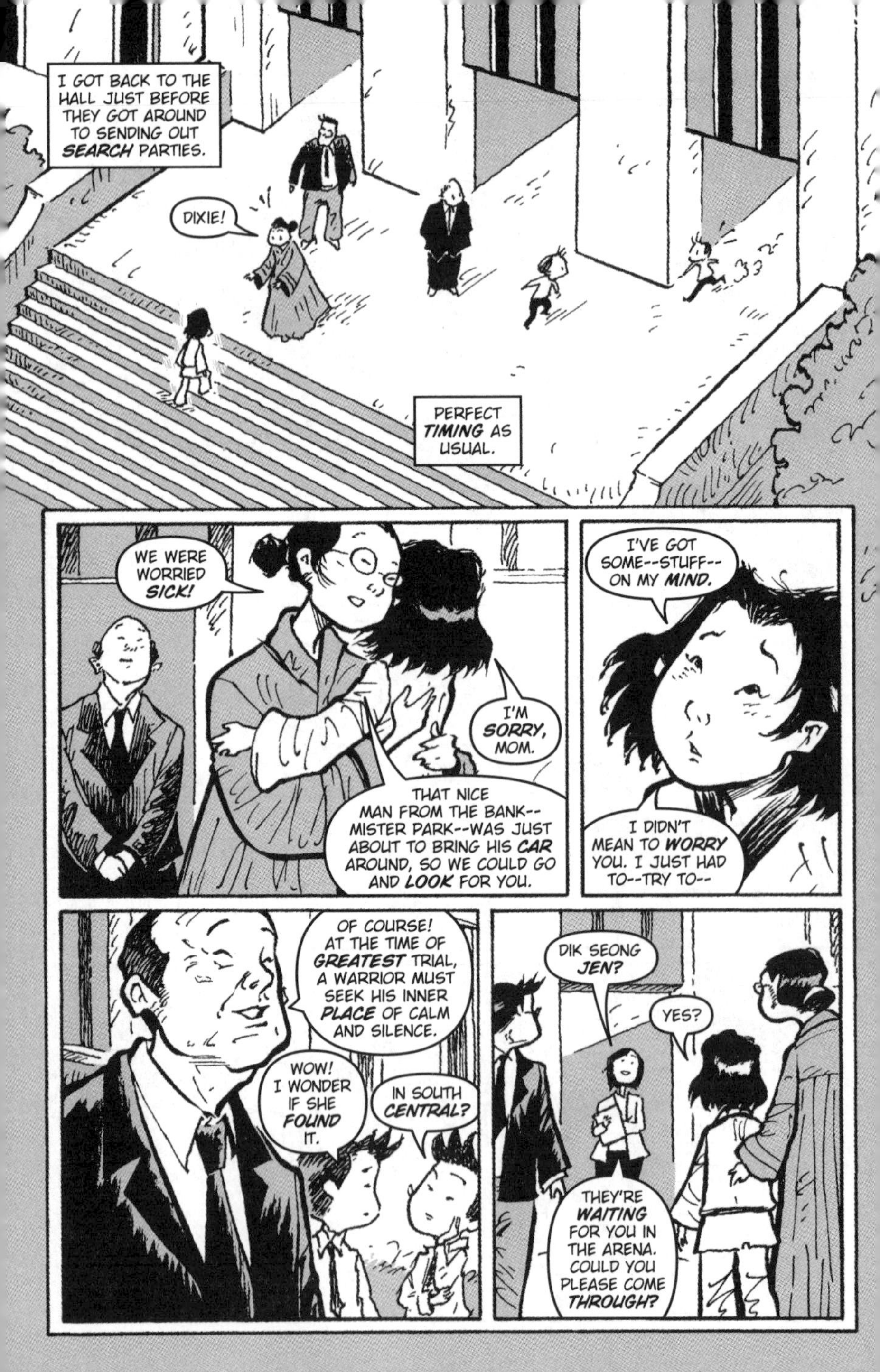
I GOT BACK TO THE HALL JUST BEFORE THEY GOT AROUND TO SENDING OUT SEARCH PARTIES.
DIXIE!
PERFECT TIMING AS USUAL.
WE WERE WORRIED SICK!
I'M SORRY, MOM.
THAT NICE MAN FROM THE BANK--MISTER PARK--WAS JUST ABOUT TO BRING HIS CAR AROUND, SO WE COULD GO AND LOOK FOR YOU.
I'VE GOT SOME--STUFF--ON MY MIND.
I DIDN'T MEAN TO WORRY YOU. I JUST HAD TO--TRY TO--
OF COURSE! AT THE TIME OF GREATEST TRIAL, A WARRIOR MUST SEEK HIS INNER PLACE OF CALM AND SILENCE.
WOW! I WONDER IF SHE FOUND IT.
IN SOUTH CENTRAL?
DIK SEONG JEN?
YES?
THEY'RE WAITING FOR YOU IN THE ARENA. COULD YOU PLEASE COME THROUGH?

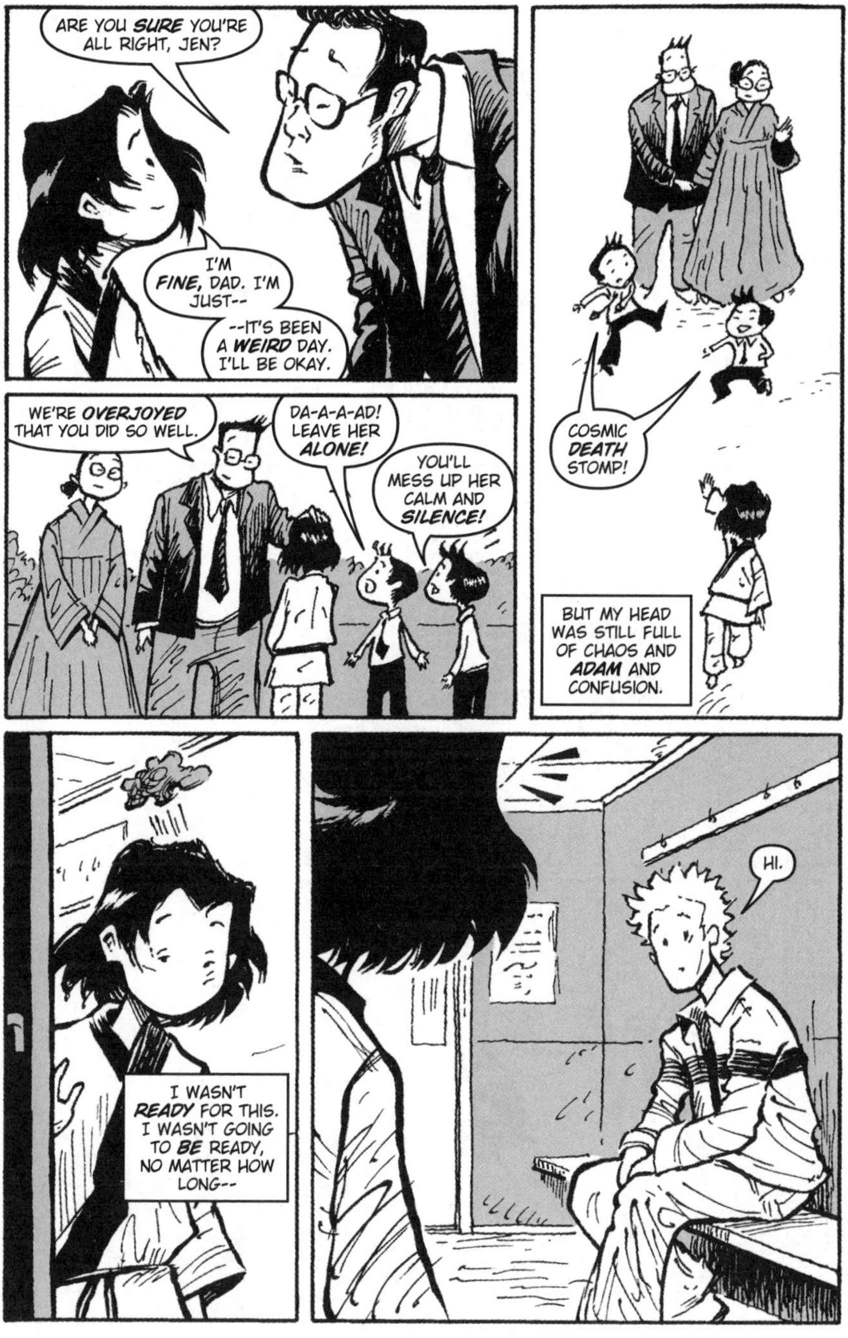
ARE YOU SURE YOU'RE ALL RIGHT, JEN?
I'M FINE, DAD. I'M JUST--
--IT'S BEEN A WEIRD DAY. I'LL BE OKAY.
COSMIC DEATH STOMP!
WE'RE OVERJOYED THAT YOU DID SO WELL.
DA-A-A-AD! LEAVE HER ALONE!
YOU'LL MESS UP HER CALM AND SILENCE!
BUT MY HEAD WAS STILL FULL OF CHAOS AND ADAM AND CONFUSION.
I WASN'T READY FOR THIS. I WASN'T GOING TO BE READY, NO MATTER HOW LONG--
HI.

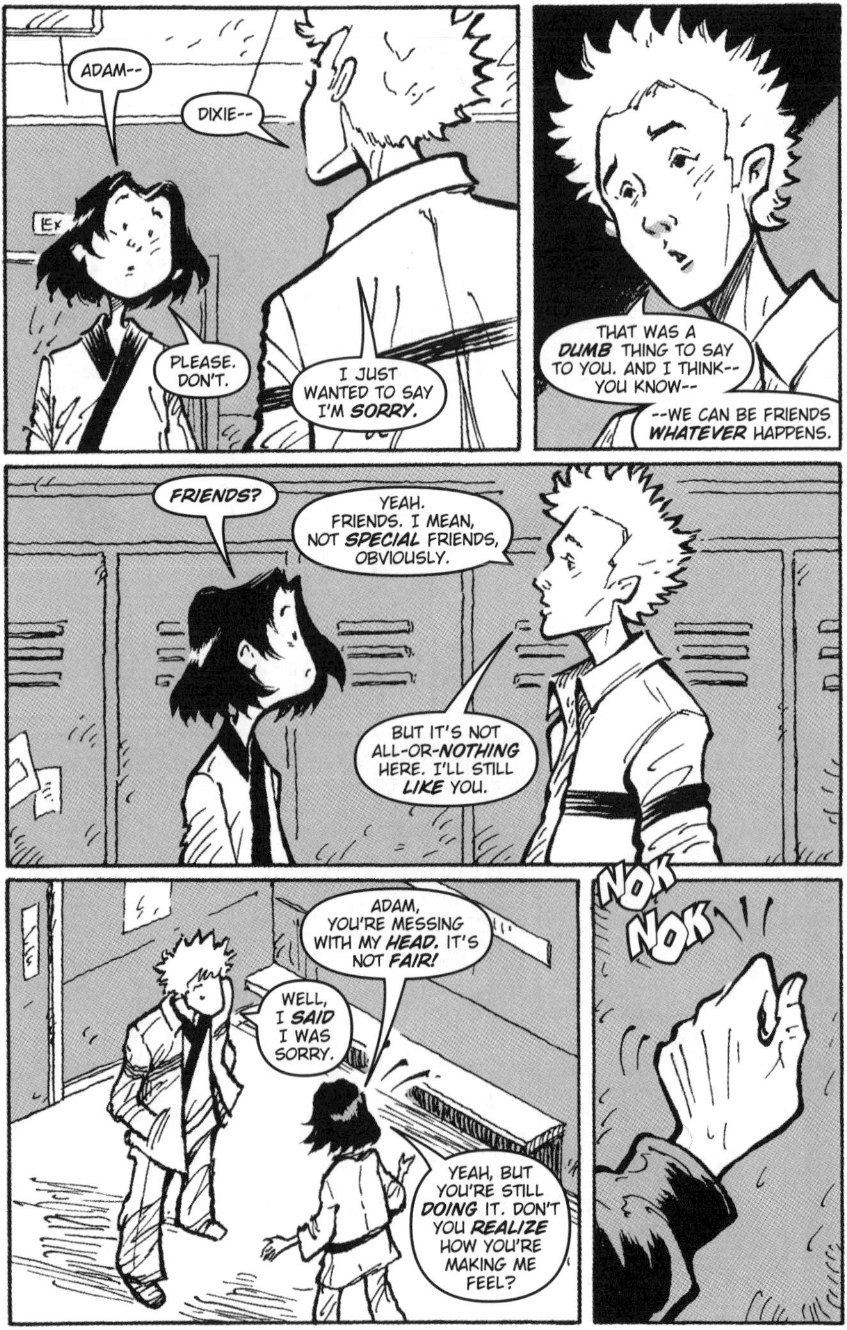
ADAM--
DIXIE--
PLEASE. DON'T.
I JUST WANTED TO SAY I'M *SORRY.*
THAT WAS A *DUMB* THING TO SAY TO YOU. AND I THINK-- YOU KNOW--
--WE CAN BE FRIENDS *WHATEVER* HAPPENS.
FRIENDS?
YEAH. FRIENDS. I MEAN, NOT *SPECIAL* FRIENDS, OBVIOUSLY.
BUT IT'S NOT ALL-OR-*NOTHING* HERE. I'LL STILL *LIKE* YOU.
ADAM, YOU'RE MESSING WITH MY *HEAD.* IT'S NOT *FAIR!*
WELL, I *SAID* I WAS SORRY.
YEAH, BUT YOU'RE STILL *DOING* IT. DON'T YOU *REALIZE* HOW YOU'RE MAKING ME FEEL?
NOK
NOK

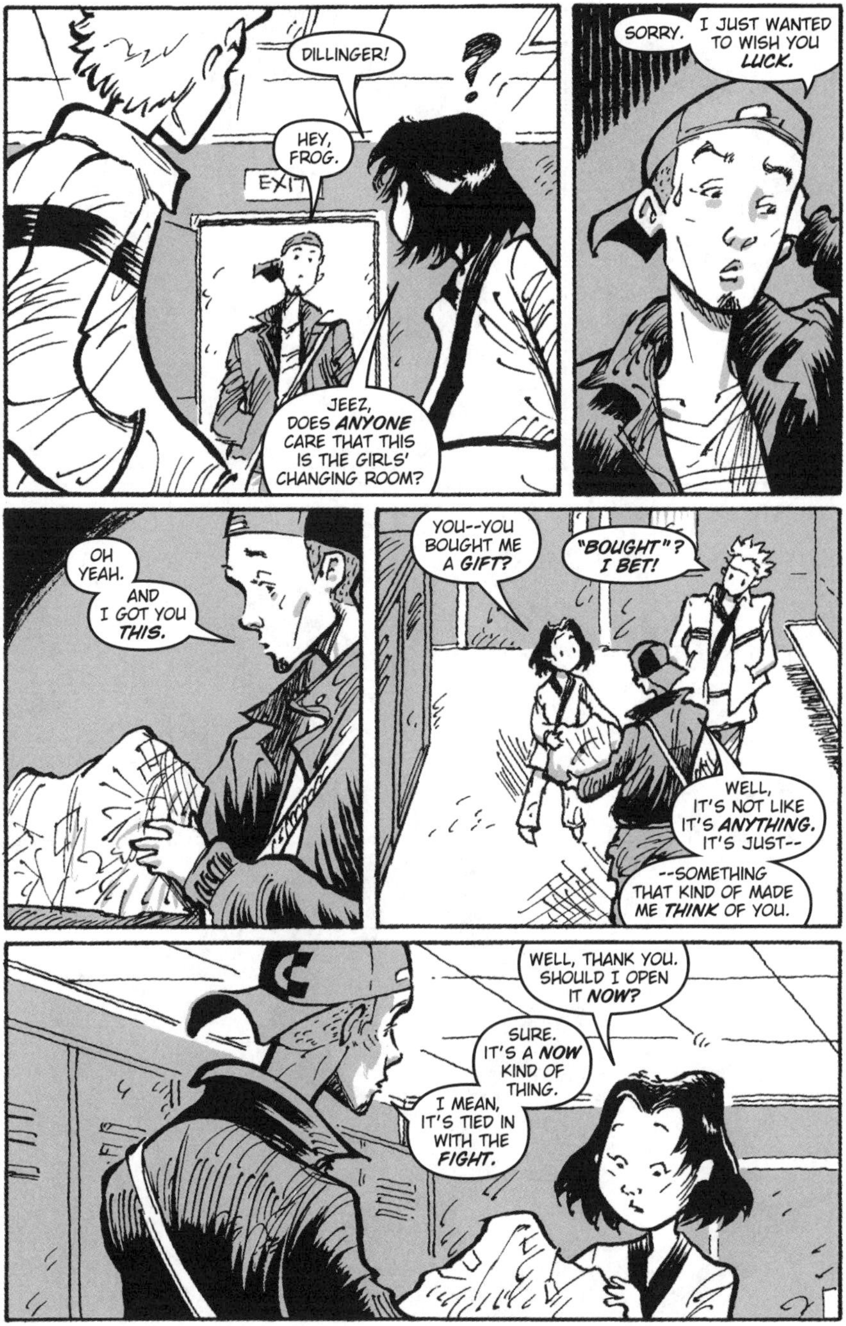
DILLINGER!
HEY, FROG.
EXIT
JEEZ, DOES ANYONE CARE THAT THIS IS THE GIRLS' CHANGING ROOM?
SORRY.
I JUST WANTED TO WISH YOU LUCK.
OH YEAH.
AND I GOT YOU THIS.
YOU--YOU BOUGHT ME A GIFT?
"BOUGHT"? I BET!
WELL, IT'S NOT LIKE IT'S ANYTHING. IT'S JUST--
--SOMETHING THAT KIND OF MADE ME THINK OF YOU.
WELL, THANK YOU. SHOULD I OPEN IT NOW?
SURE. IT'S A NOW KIND OF THING.
I MEAN, IT'S TIED IN WITH THE FIGHT.

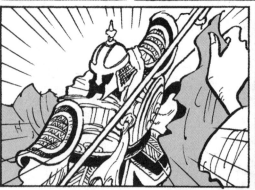

D'YOU *LIKE* IT?

I MEAN, IF YOU *DON'T,* IT DON'T MATTER. I'LL JUST-- TOSS IT IN THE *TRASH.*

AND THIS IS *MINE?*

I CAN DO WHATEVER I *LIKE* WITH IT?

DIXIE, I KNOW HOW THIS--

YEAH. SURE.

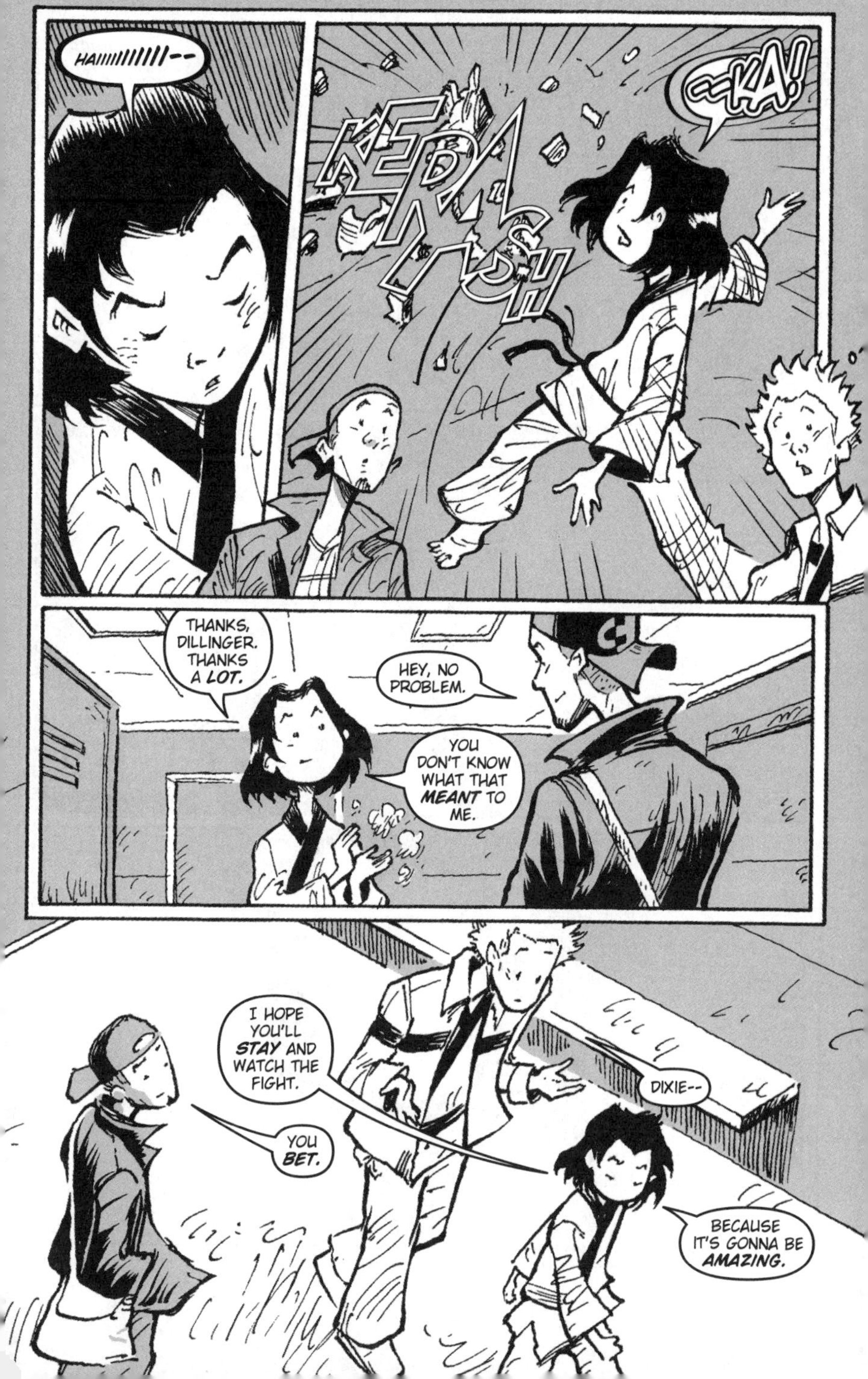
HAIIIIIIIIII--
KERRASH
--KA!
THANKS, DILLINGER. THANKS A LOT.
HEY, NO PROBLEM.
YOU DON'T KNOW WHAT THAT MEANT TO ME.
I HOPE YOU'LL STAY AND WATCH THE FIGHT.
YOU BET.
DIXIE--
BECAUSE IT'S GONNA BE AMAZING.

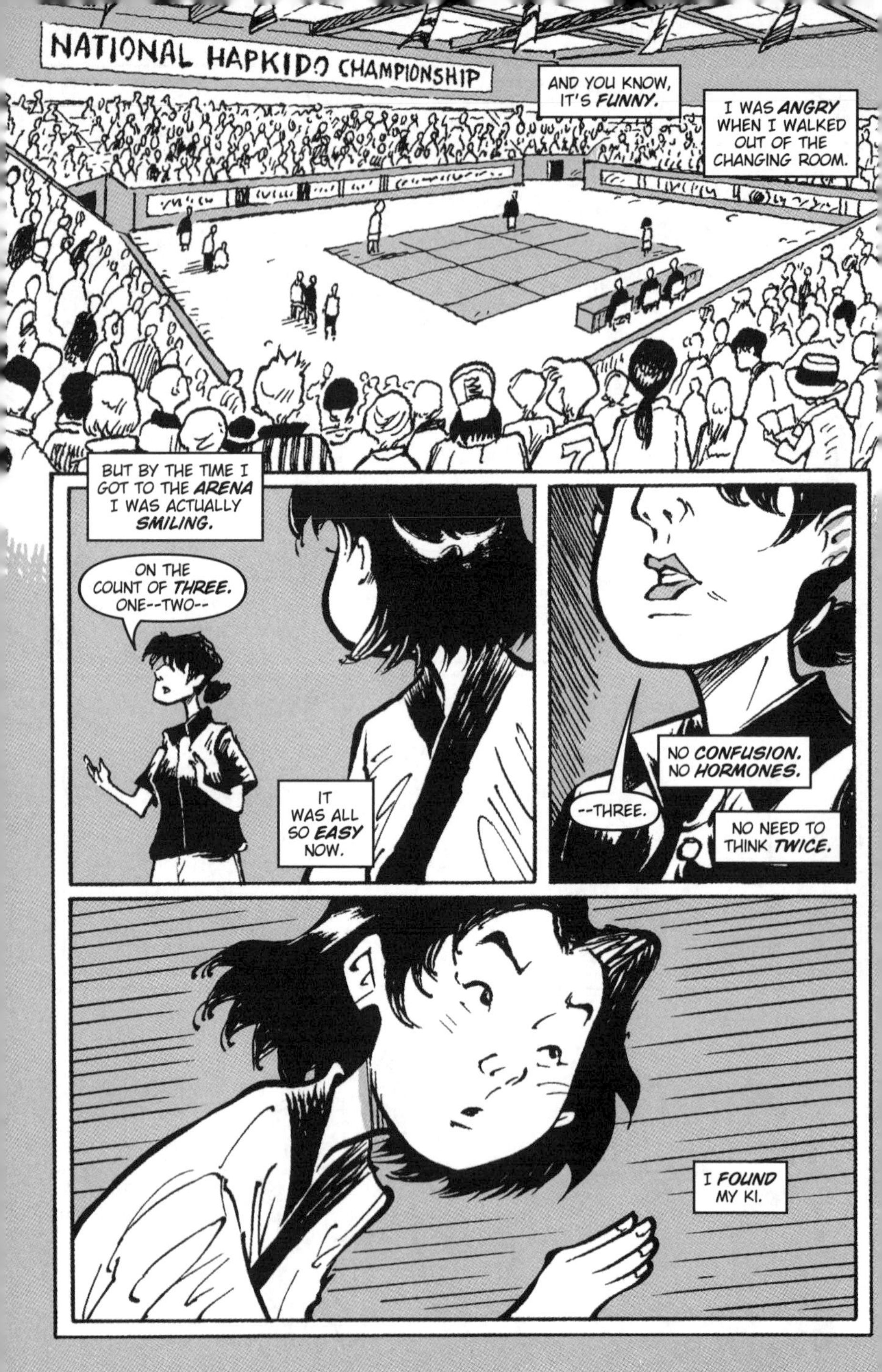

NATIONAL HAPKIDO CHAMPIONSHIP
AND YOU KNOW, IT'S FUNNY.
I WAS ANGRY WHEN I WALKED OUT OF THE CHANGING ROOM.
BUT BY THE TIME I GOT TO THE ARENA I WAS ACTUALLY SMILING.
ON THE COUNT OF THREE. ONE--TWO--
IT WAS ALL SO EASY NOW.
NO CONFUSION. NO HORMONES.
--THREE.
NO NEED TO THINK TWICE.
I FOUND MY KI.

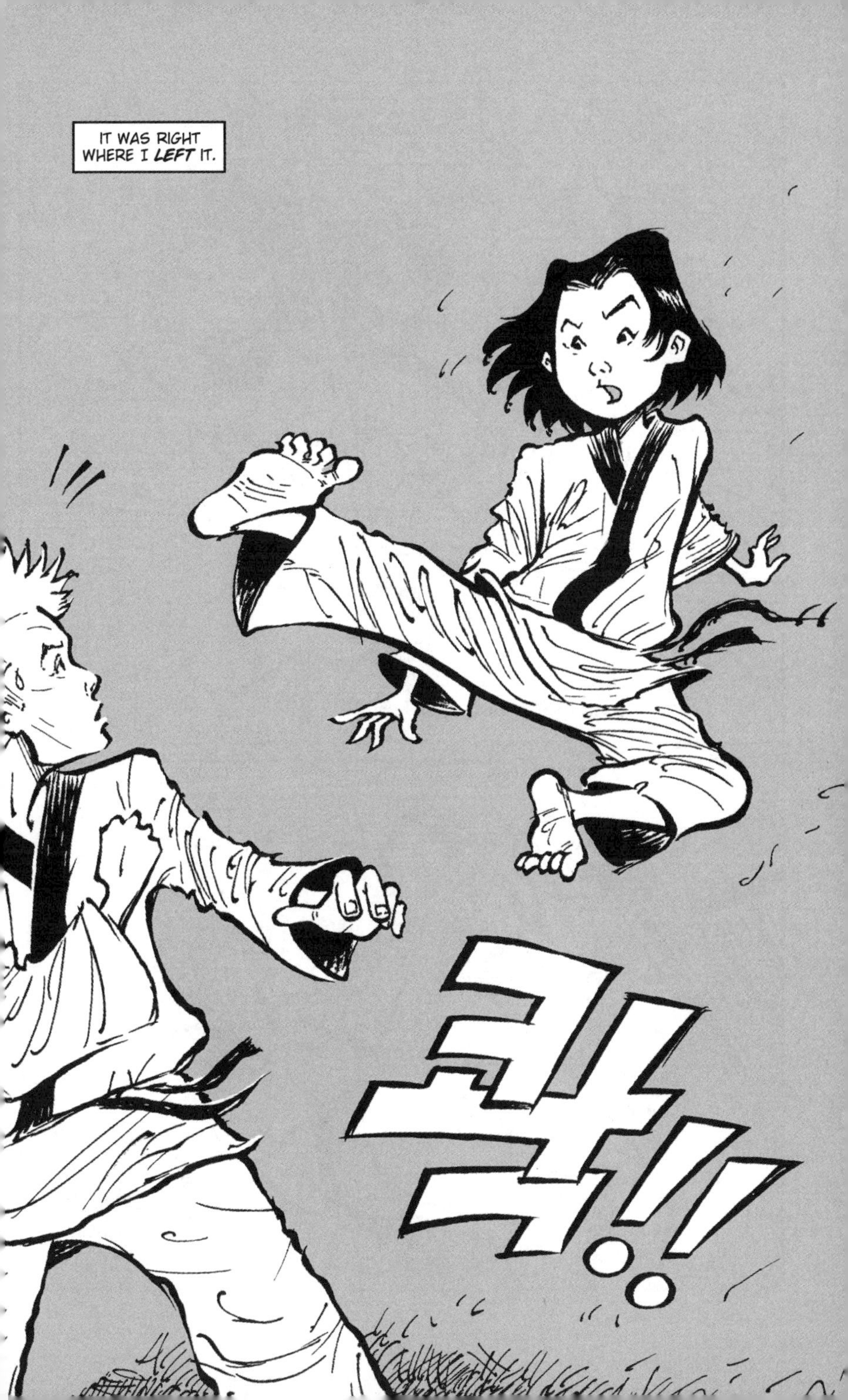
IT WAS RIGHT WHERE I LEFT IT.

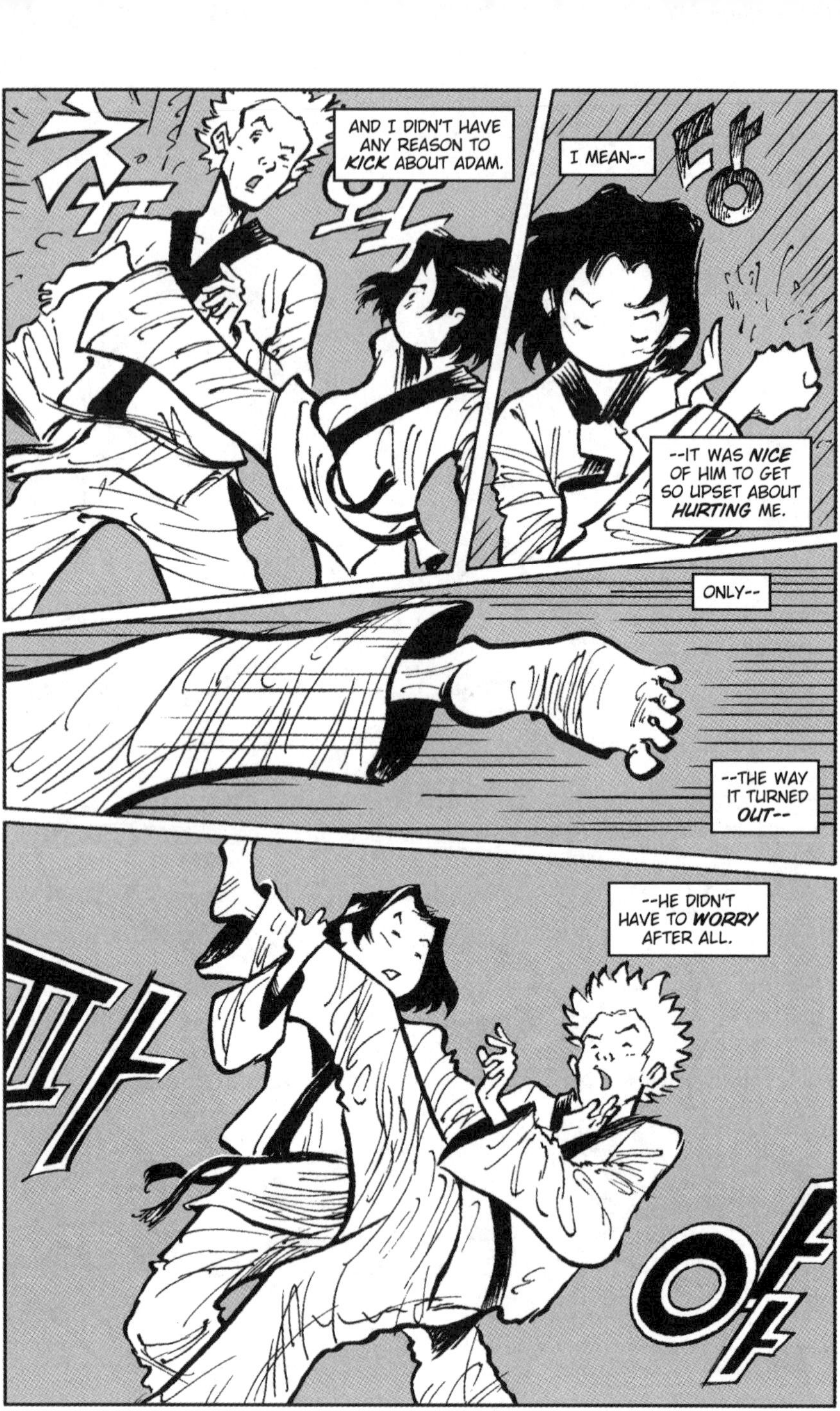
AND I DIDN'T HAVE ANY REASON TO KICK ABOUT ADAM.
I MEAN--
--IT WAS NICE OF HIM TO GET SO UPSET ABOUT HURTING ME.
ONLY--
--THE WAY IT TURNED OUT--
--HE DIDN'T HAVE TO WORRY AFTER ALL.

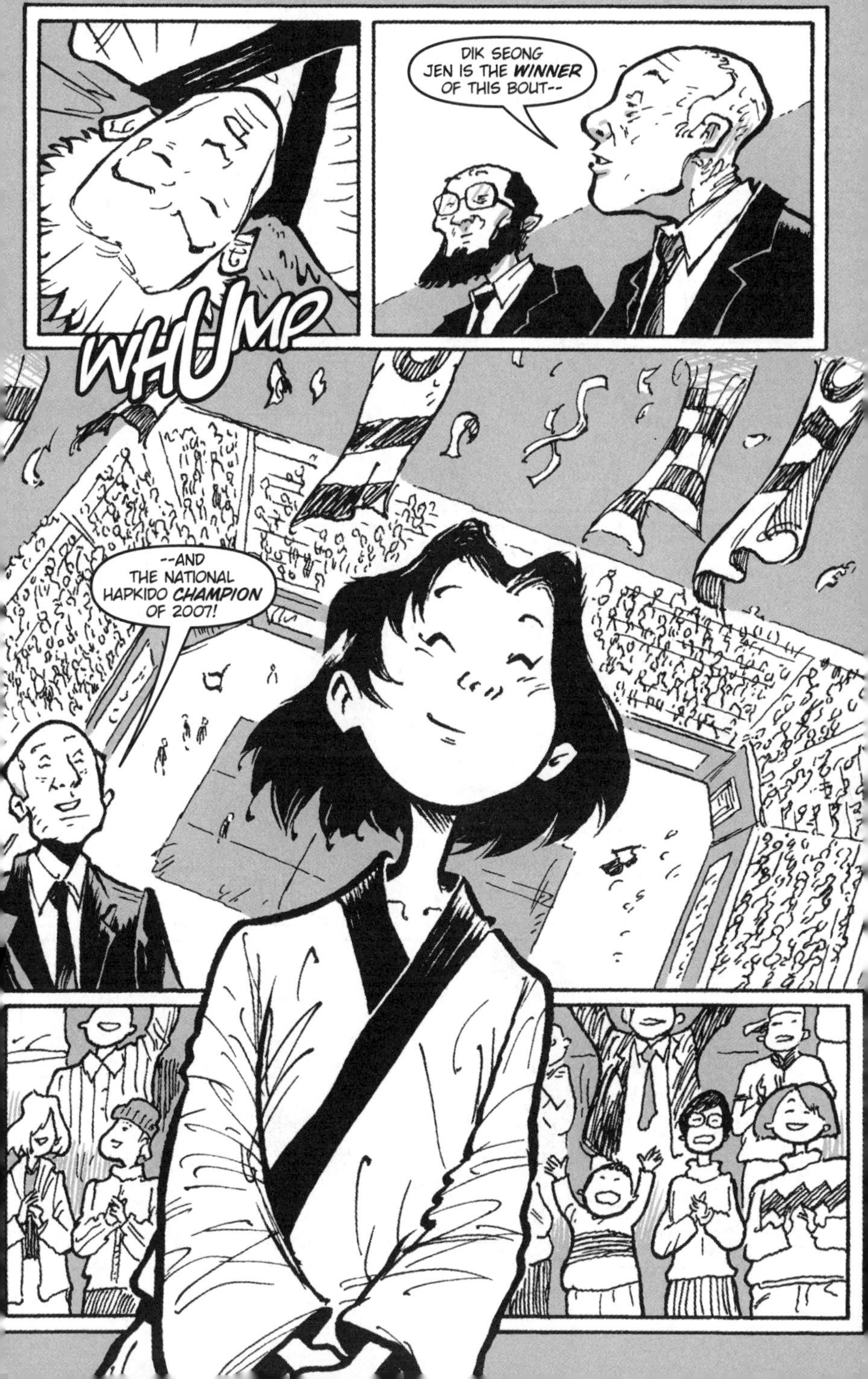
WHUMP
DIK SEONG JEN IS THE WINNER OF THIS BOUT--
--AND THE NATIONAL HAPKIDO CHAMPION OF 2007!

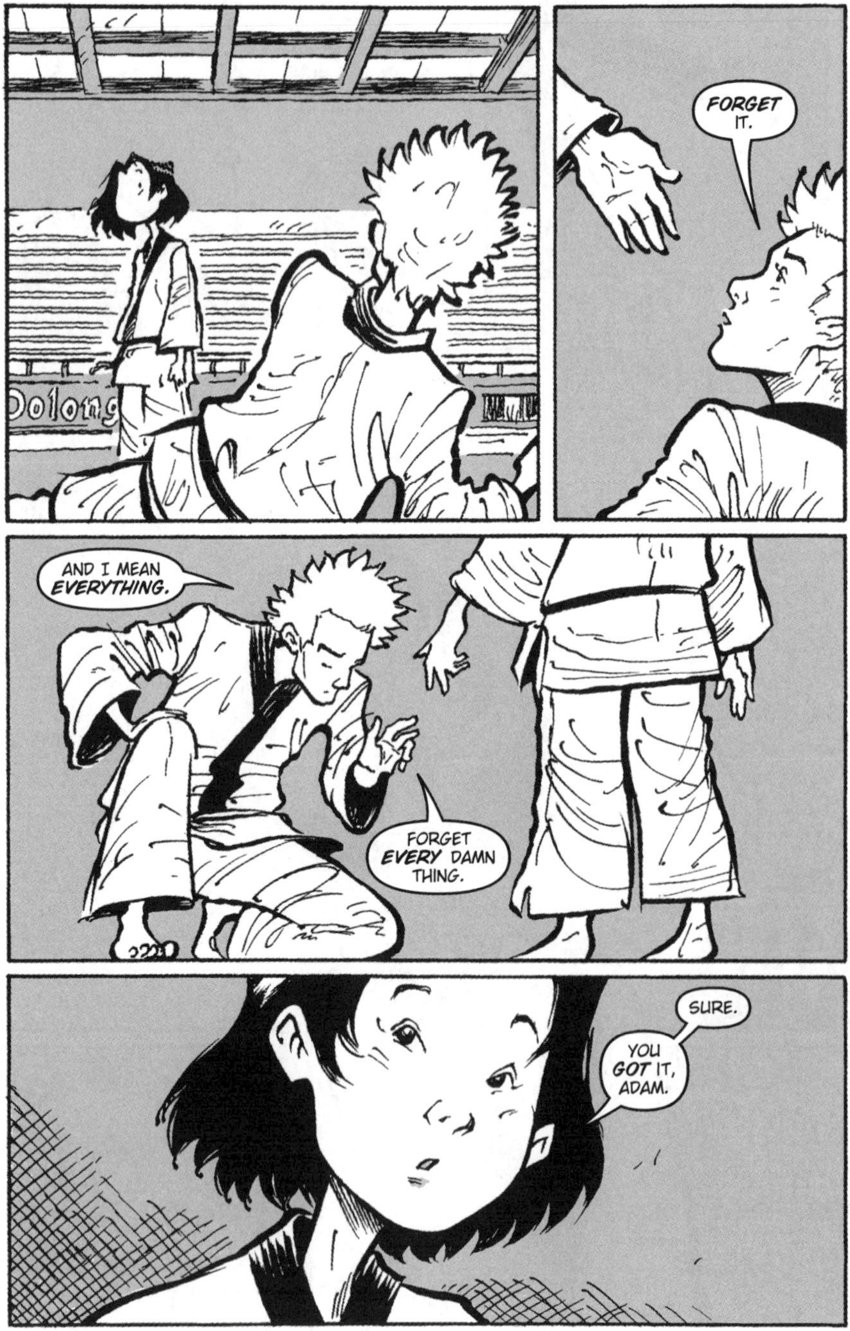
Oolong
FORGET IT.
AND I MEAN EVERYTHING.
FORGET EVERY DAMN THING.
SURE.
YOU GOT IT, ADAM.

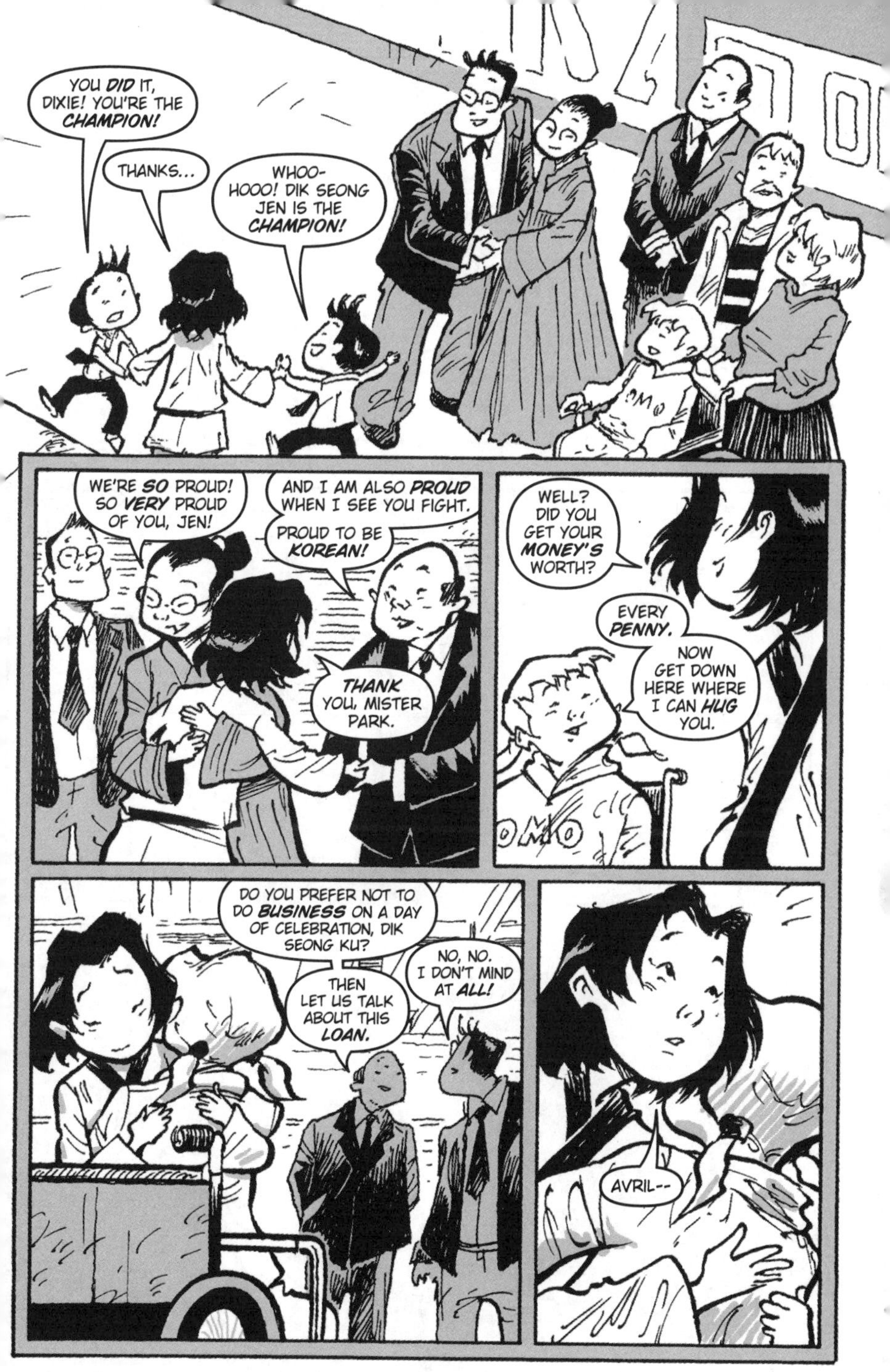
YOU DID IT, DIXIE! YOU'RE THE CHAMPION!
THANKS...
WHOO-HOOO! DIK SEONG JEN IS THE CHAMPION!
WE'RE SO PROUD! SO VERY PROUD OF YOU, JEN!
AND I AM ALSO PROUD WHEN I SEE YOU FIGHT.
PROUD TO BE KOREAN!
THANK YOU, MISTER PARK.
WELL? DID YOU GET YOUR MONEY'S WORTH?
EVERY PENNY.
NOW GET DOWN HERE WHERE I CAN HUG YOU.
DO YOU PREFER NOT TO DO BUSINESS ON A DAY OF CELEBRATION, DIK SEONG KU?
NO, NO. I DON'T MIND AT ALL!
THEN LET US TALK ABOUT THIS LOAN.
AVRIL--

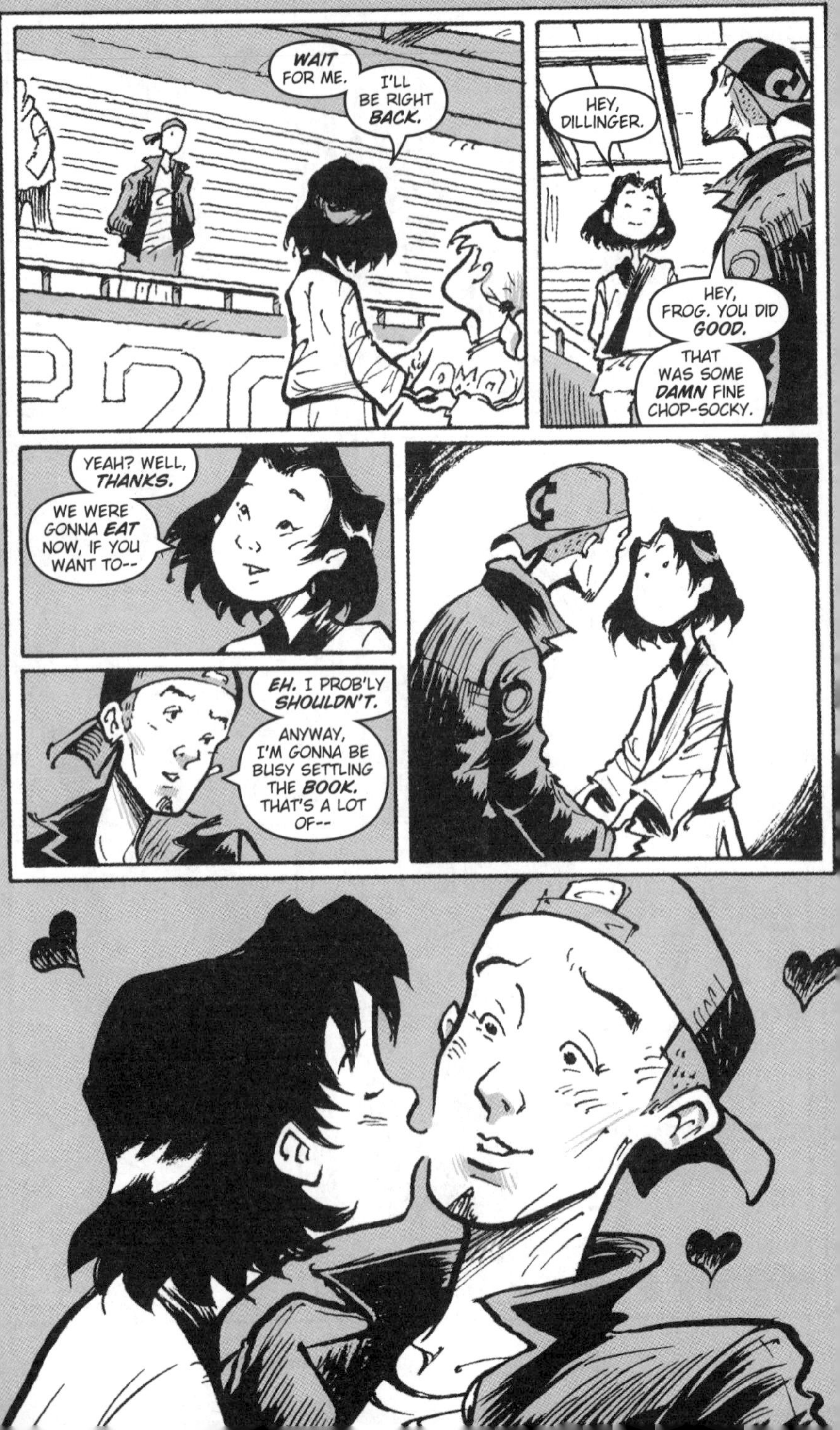
WAIT FOR ME.
I'LL BE RIGHT BACK.
HEY, DILLINGER.
HEY, FROG. YOU DID GOOD.
THAT WAS SOME DAMN FINE CHOP-SOCKY.
YEAH? WELL, THANKS.
WE WERE GONNA EAT NOW, IF YOU WANT TO--
EH. I PROB'LY SHOULDN'T.
ANYWAY, I'M GONNA BE BUSY SETTLING THE BOOK. THAT'S A LOT OF--

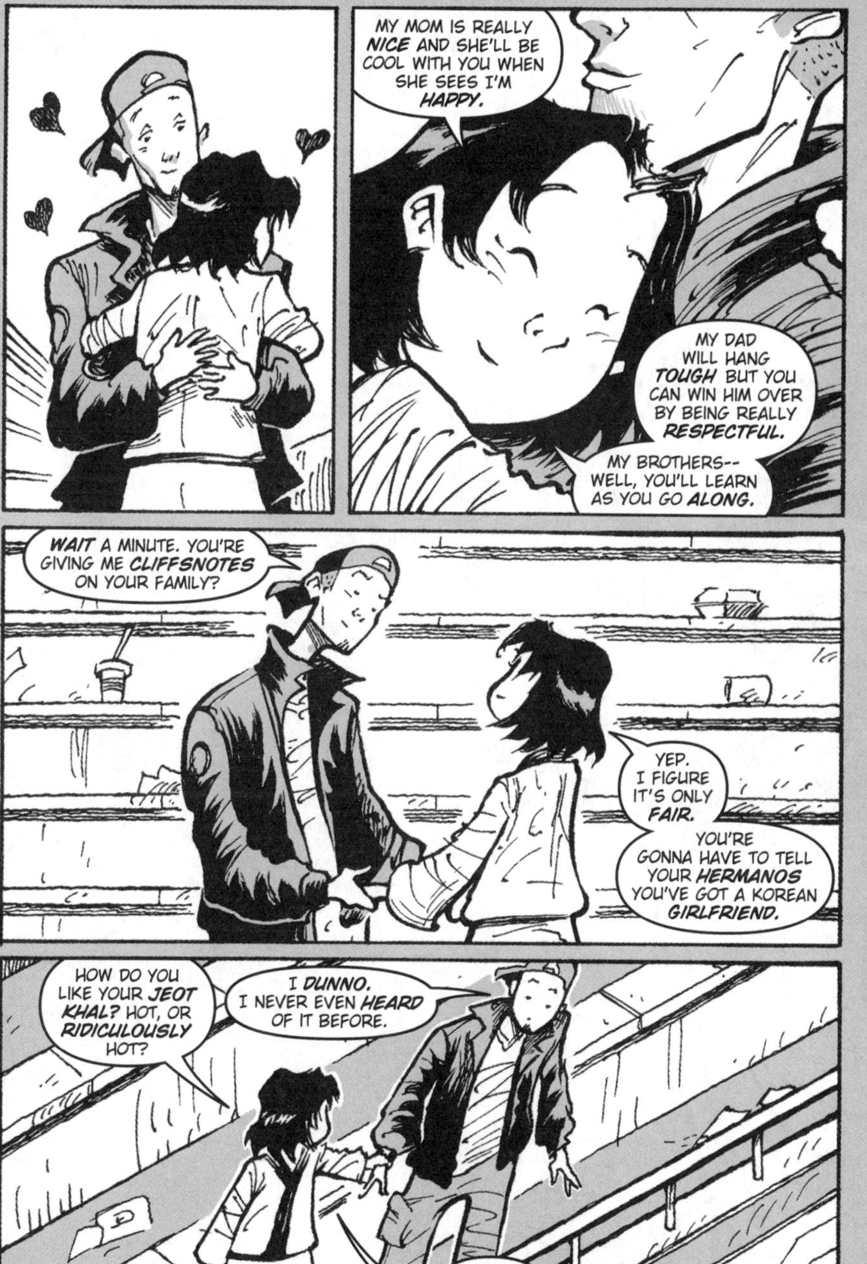
MY MOM IS REALLY NICE AND SHE'LL BE COOL WITH YOU WHEN SHE SEES I'M HAPPY.
MY DAD WILL HANG TOUGH BUT YOU CAN WIN HIM OVER BY BEING REALLY RESPECTFUL.
MY BROTHERS-- WELL, YOU'LL LEARN AS YOU GO ALONG.
WAIT A MINUTE. YOU'RE GIVING ME CLIFFSNOTES ON YOUR FAMILY?
YEP. I FIGURE IT'S ONLY FAIR.
YOU'RE GONNA HAVE TO TELL YOUR HERMANOS YOU'VE GOT A KOREAN GIRLFRIEND.
HOW DO YOU LIKE YOUR JEOT KHAL? HOT, OR RIDICULOUSLY HOT?
I DUNNO. I NEVER EVEN HEARD OF IT BEFORE.
THEN COME AND FIND OUT...

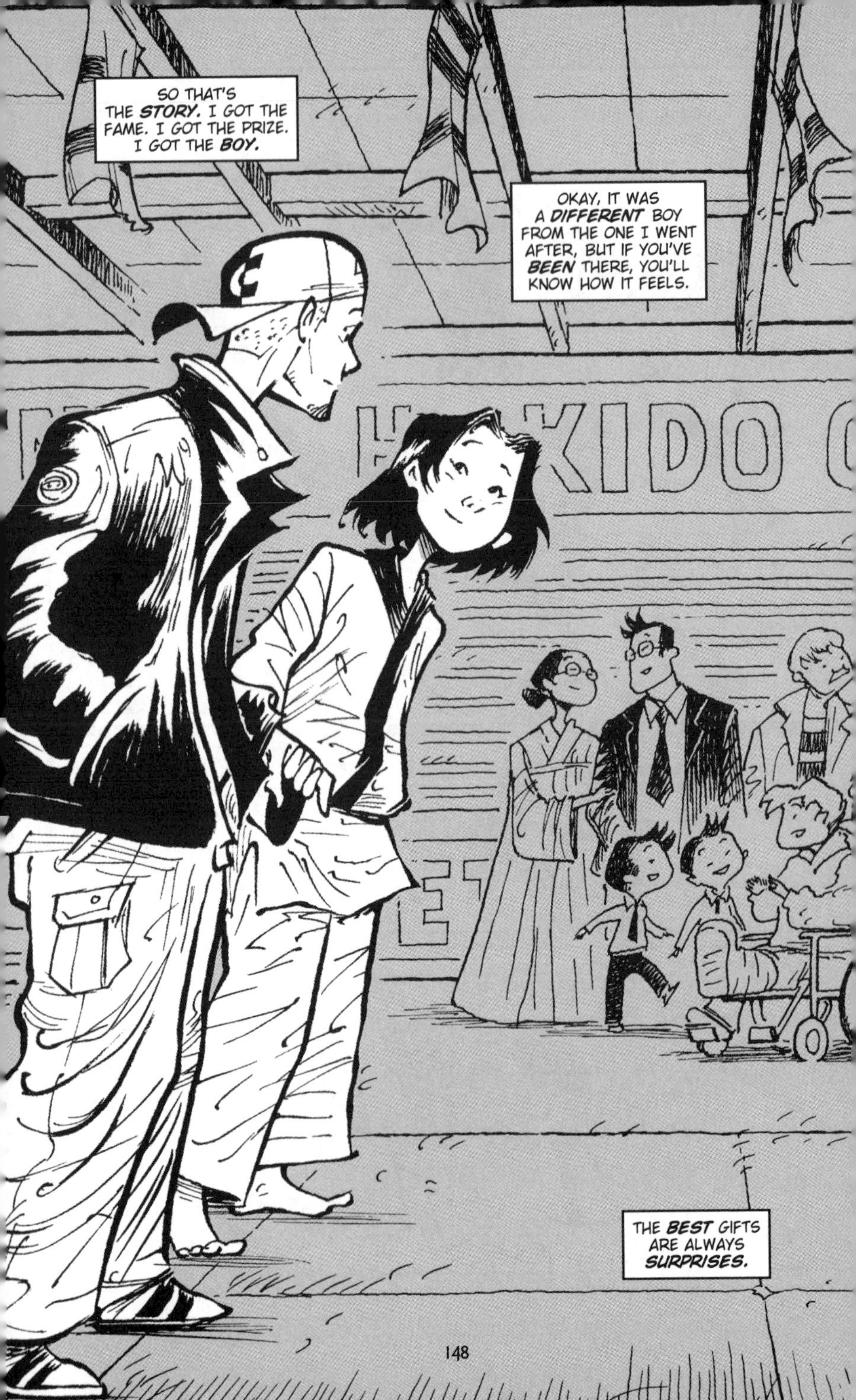
SO THAT'S THE STORY. I GOT THE FAME. I GOT THE PRIZE. I GOT THE BOY.
OKAY, IT WAS A DIFFERENT BOY FROM THE ONE I WENT AFTER, BUT IF YOU'VE BEEN THERE, YOU'LL KNOW HOW IT FEELS.
THE BEST GIFTS ARE ALWAYS SURPRISES.

The End.

MIKE CAREY

Mike is a comics writer, novelist and screenwriter who lives and works in London and is best known for his VERTIGO work on the multiple Eisner-nominated LUCIFER series and MY FAITH IN FRANKIE. His screenplay *Frost Flowers* will be a feature film starring Holly Hunter and James McEvoy. He wants it known that the human body has 206 bones. In researching the hapkido moves in RE-GIFTERS, Mike broke all but three of them. Next Up: Co-writing the MINX book CONFESSIONS OF A BLABBERMOUTH with his daughter, Louise — should he survive the experience.

SONNY LIEW

Sonny is an illustrator currently residing in Singapore. His work includes MY FAITH IN FRANKIE, *Malinky Robot* and contributions to the *Flight* and *24Seven* anthologies. Currently working on the series *Wonderland* for Slave Labor Graphics and Disney, Sonny has been nominated for an Eisner Award and can been reached at sonnyliew.com.

MARC HEMPEL

Originally from Chicago, Marc now lives in Baltimore, Maryland, where he enjoys relative fame as "America's Most Beloved Semi-Obscure Cartoonist." He is best known for his collaboration with Neil Gaiman on THE SANDMAN: THE KINDLY ONES and is a regular contributor to MAD Magazine.

S P E C I A L   B A C K S T A G E   P A S S :

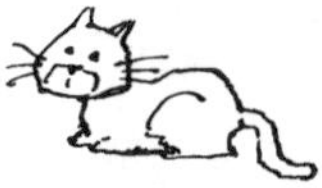

If you liked the story you've just read, fear not: Other MINX books will be available in the months to come. MINX is a line of books that's designed especially for you — someone who's a bit bored with straight fiction and ready for stories that are visually exciting beyond words — literally. In fact, we thought you might like to get in on a secret, behind-the-scenes look at a few of the new MINX titles that will aid in your escape to cool places during the long, hot summer. So hurry up and turn the page already!

And be sure to check out other exclusive material at

www.titanbooks.com

By the highly acclaimed author of *Boy Proof* and *The Queen of Cool*

THE PLAIN JANES

CECIL CASTELLUCCI
and JIM RUGG

Four girls named Jane are anything but ordinary once they form a

secret art gang and take on Suburbia by painting the town P.L.A.I.N. —

People Loving Art In Neighborhoods.

OUT NOW!

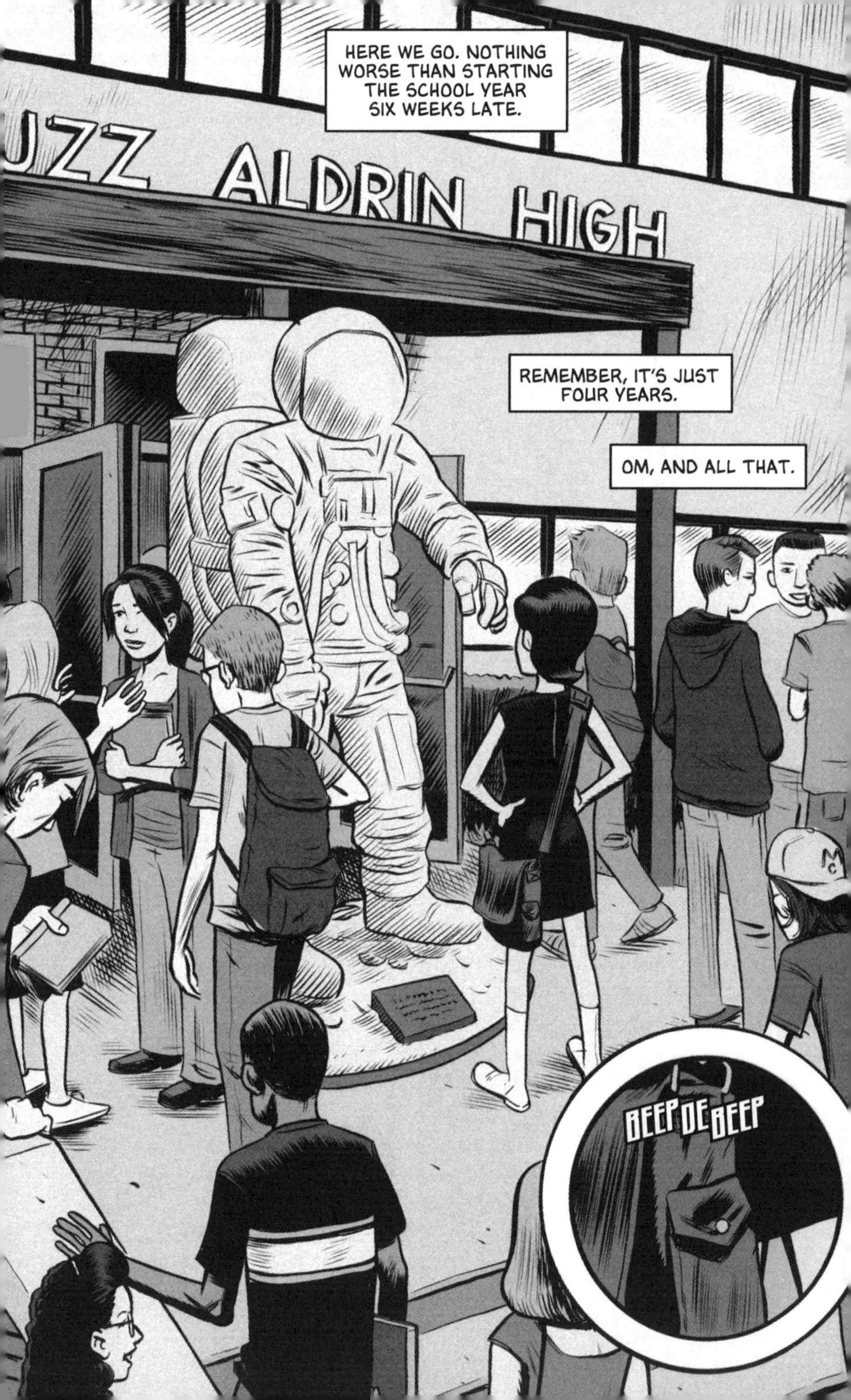
HERE WE GO. NOTHING WORSE THAN STARTING THE SCHOOL YEAR SIX WEEKS LATE.
UZZ ALDRIN HIGH
REMEMBER, IT'S JUST FOUR YEARS.
OM, AND ALL THAT.
BEEP DE BEEP

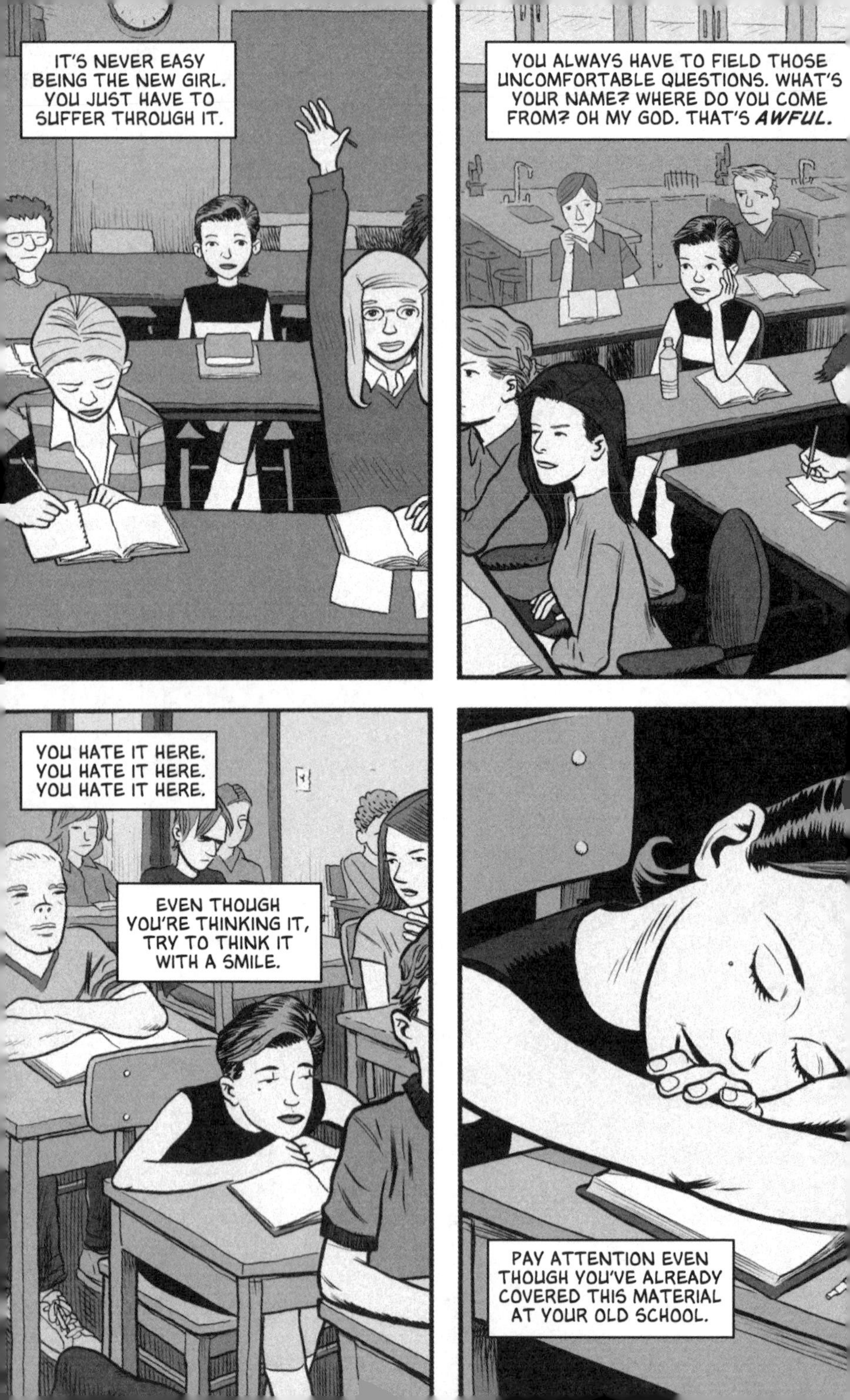
IT'S NEVER EASY BEING THE NEW GIRL. YOU JUST HAVE TO SUFFER THROUGH IT.
YOU ALWAYS HAVE TO FIELD THOSE UNCOMFORTABLE QUESTIONS. WHAT'S YOUR NAME? WHERE DO YOU COME FROM? OH MY GOD. THAT'S AWFUL.
YOU HATE IT HERE. YOU HATE IT HERE. YOU HATE IT HERE.
EVEN THOUGH YOU'RE THINKING IT, TRY TO THINK IT WITH A SMILE.
PAY ATTENTION EVEN THOUGH YOU'VE ALREADY COVERED THIS MATERIAL AT YOUR OLD SCHOOL.

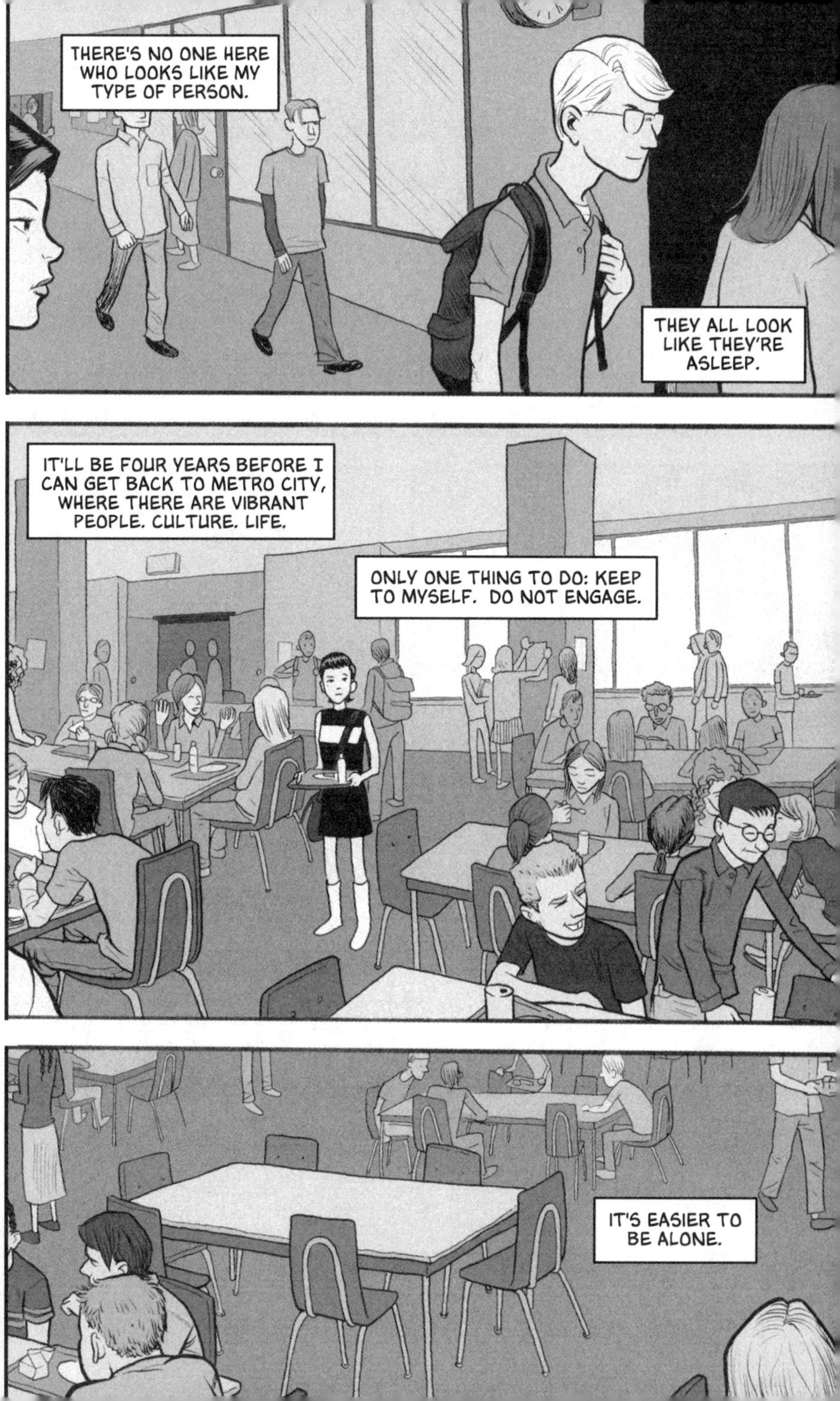
THERE'S NO ONE HERE WHO LOOKS LIKE MY TYPE OF PERSON.
THEY ALL LOOK LIKE THEY'RE ASLEEP.
IT'LL BE FOUR YEARS BEFORE I CAN GET BACK TO METRO CITY, WHERE THERE ARE VIBRANT PEOPLE. CULTURE. LIFE.
ONLY ONE THING TO DO: KEEP TO MYSELF. DO NOT ENGAGE.
IT'S EASIER TO BE ALONE.

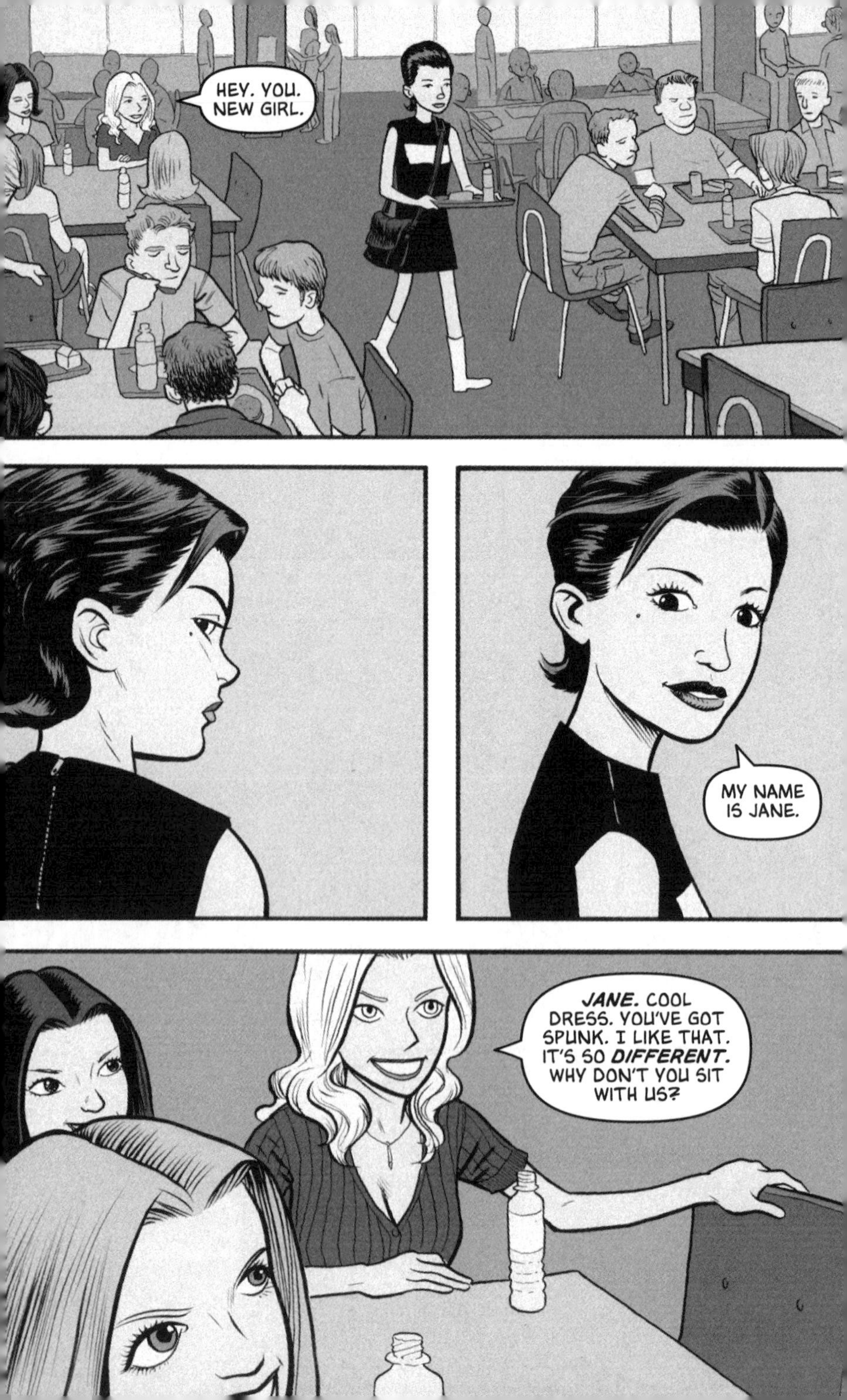
HEY. YOU. NEW GIRL.
MY NAME IS JANE.
JANE. COOL DRESS. YOU'VE GOT SPUNK. I LIKE THAT. IT'S SO DIFFERENT. WHY DON'T YOU SIT WITH US?

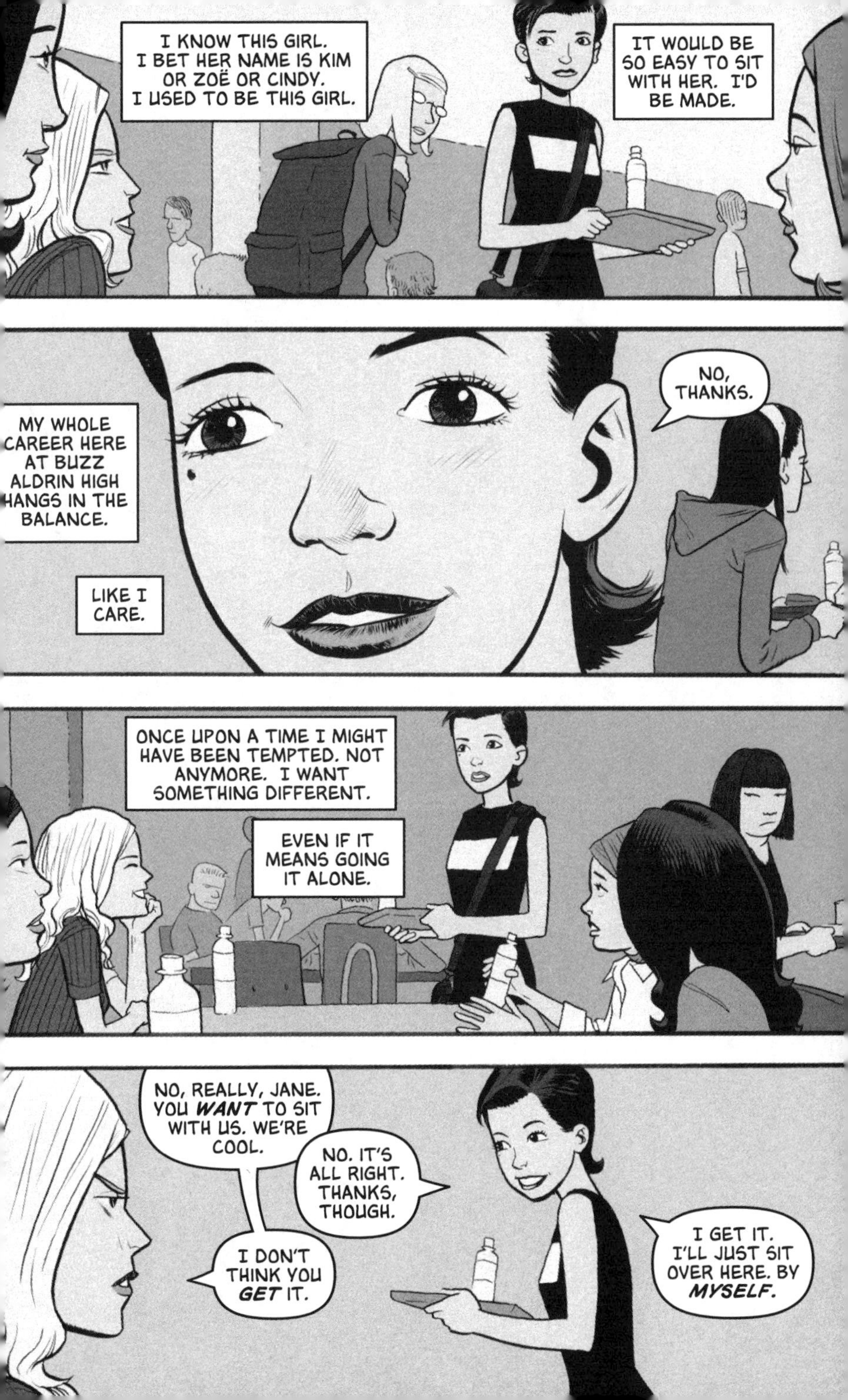
I KNOW THIS GIRL. I BET HER NAME IS KIM OR ZOË OR CINDY. I USED TO BE THIS GIRL.
IT WOULD BE SO EASY TO SIT WITH HER. I'D BE MADE.
MY WHOLE CAREER HERE AT BUZZ ALDRIN HIGH HANGS IN THE BALANCE.
NO, THANKS.
LIKE I CARE.
ONCE UPON A TIME I MIGHT HAVE BEEN TEMPTED. NOT ANYMORE. I WANT SOMETHING DIFFERENT.
EVEN IF IT MEANS GOING IT ALONE.
NO, REALLY, JANE. YOU *WANT* TO SIT WITH US. WE'RE COOL.
NO. IT'S ALL RIGHT. THANKS, THOUGH.
I DON'T THINK YOU *GET* IT.
I GET IT. I'LL JUST SIT OVER HERE. BY *MYSELF*.

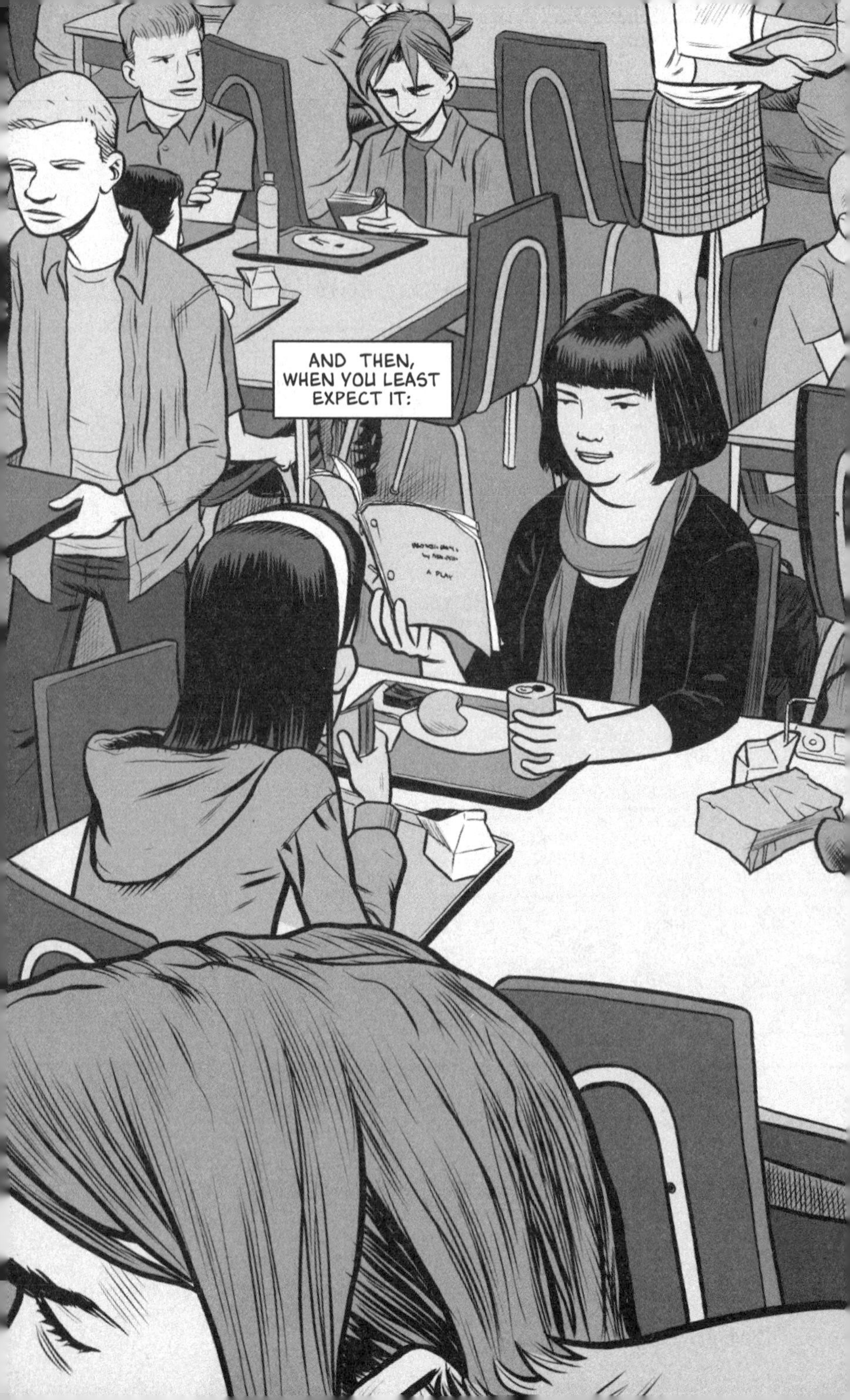
AND THEN, WHEN YOU LEAST EXPECT IT:

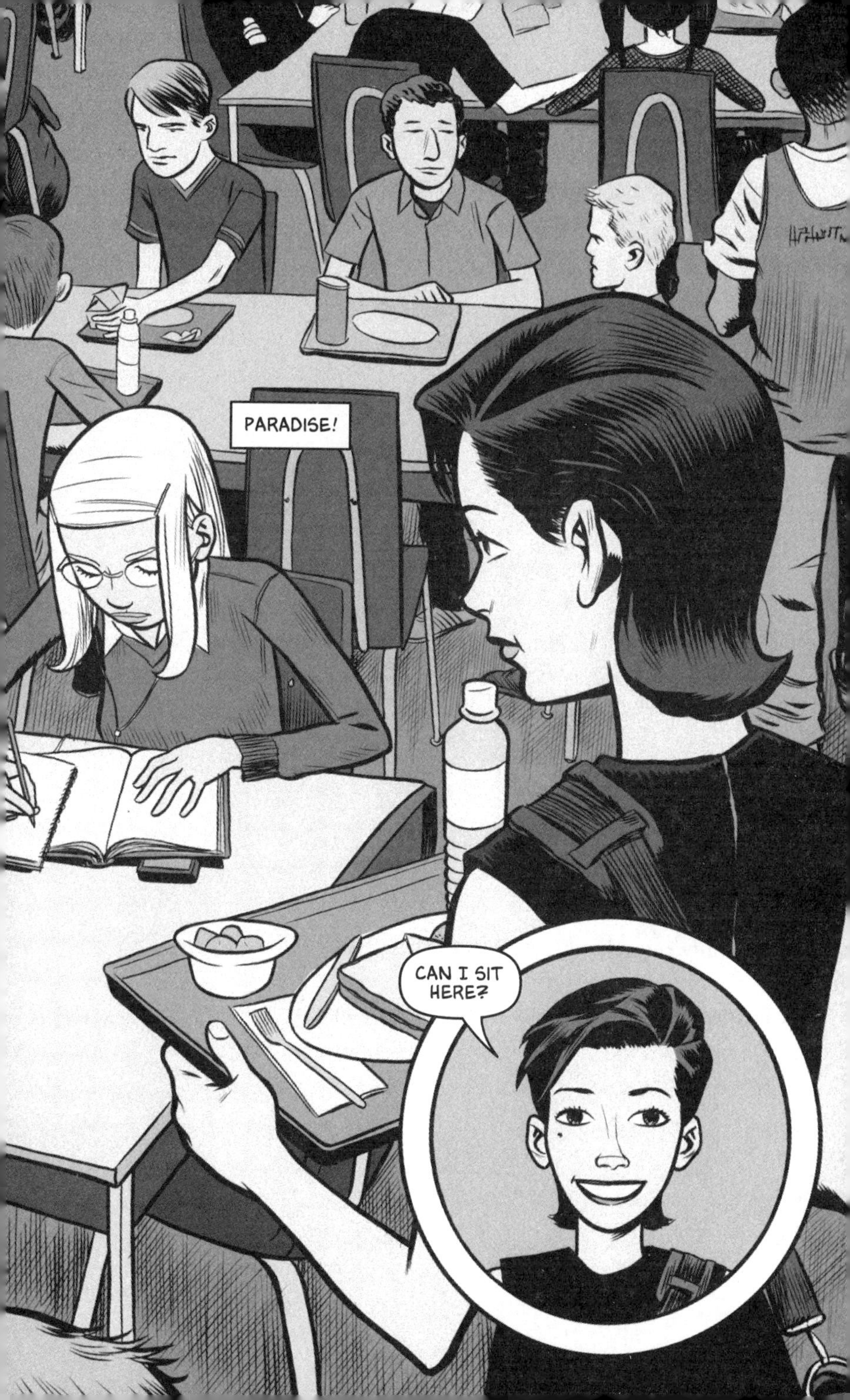
PARADISE!
CAN I SIT HERE?

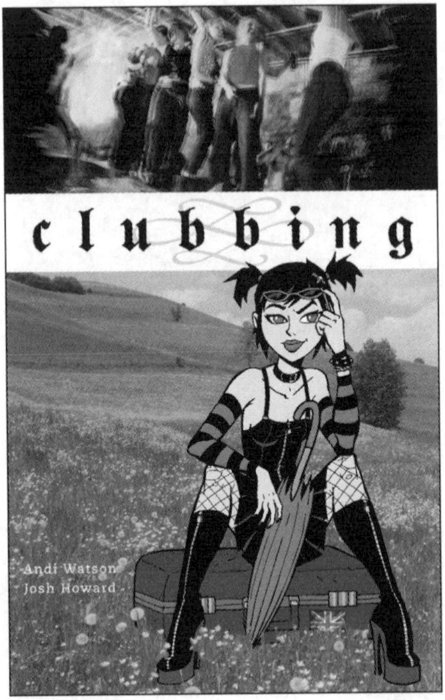
clubbing
Andi Watson
Josh Howard

A spoiled, rebellious London teenager conquers the stuffy English countryside when she solves a murder mystery on the 19th hole of her grandparents' golf course.

COMING IN AUGUST 2007 ■ Read on.

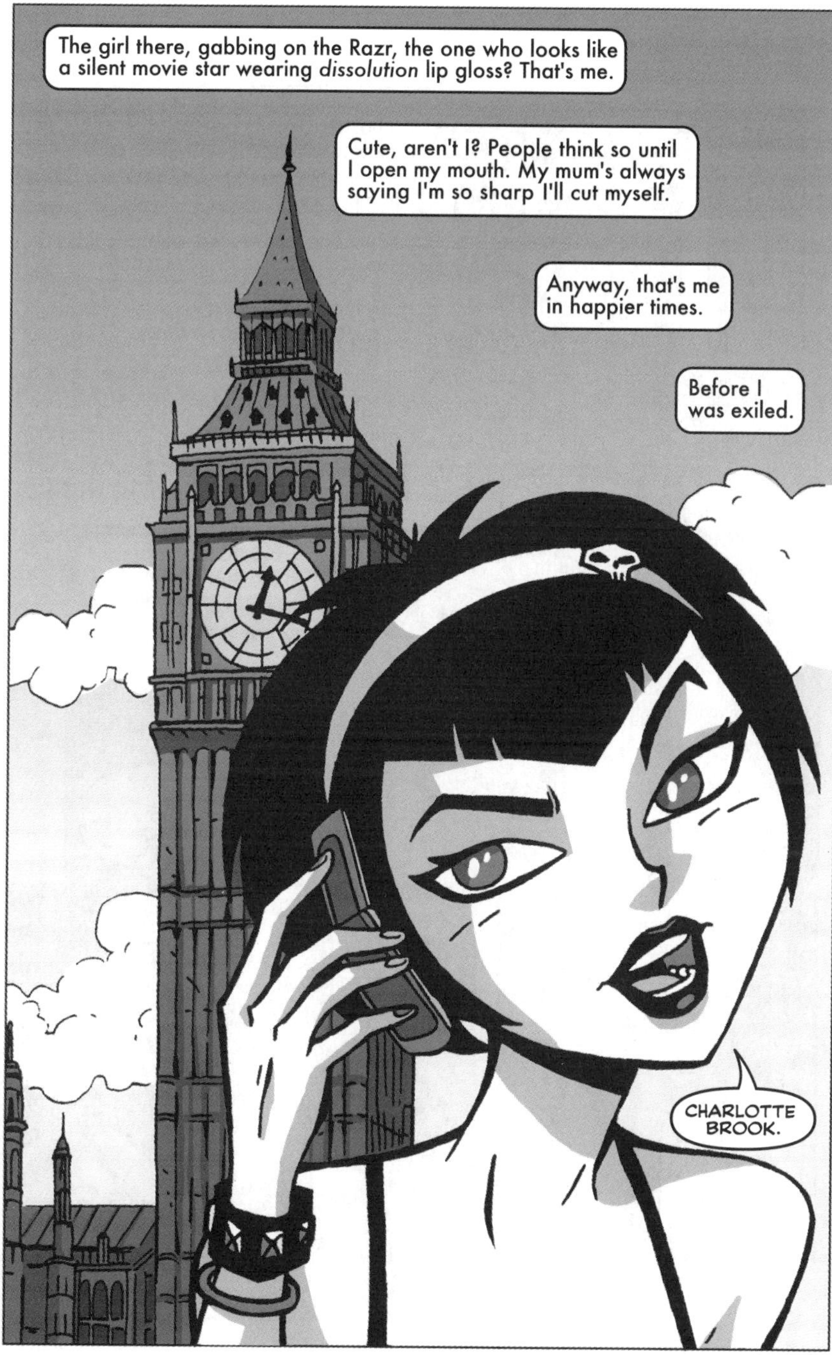
The girl there, gabbing on the Razr, the one who looks like a silent movie star wearing *dissolution* lip gloss? That's me.
Cute, aren't I? People think so until I open my mouth. My mum's always saying I'm so sharp I'll cut myself.
Anyway, that's me in happier times.
Before I was exiled.
CHARLOTTE BROOK.

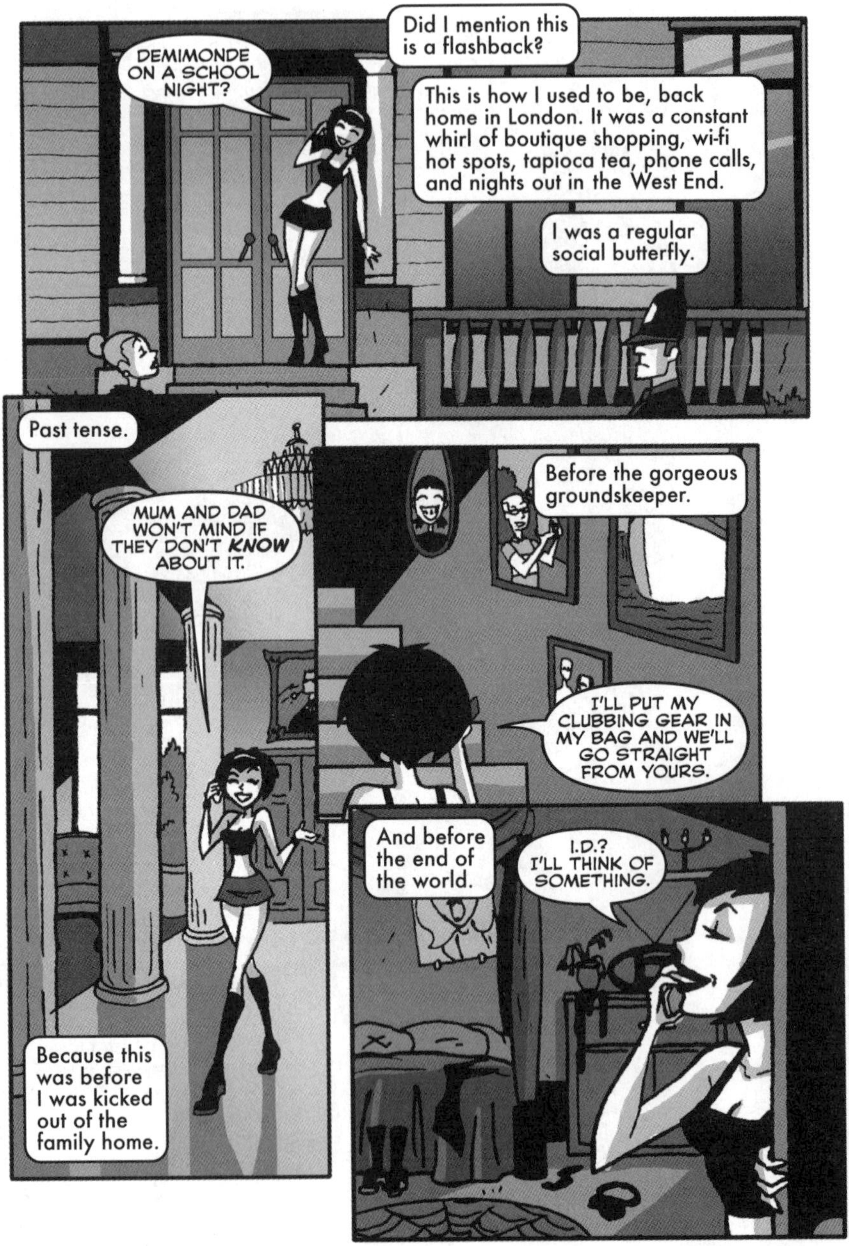
DEMIMONDE ON A SCHOOL NIGHT?
Did I mention this is a flashback?
This is how I used to be, back home in London. It was a constant whirl of boutique shopping, wi-fi hot spots, tapioca tea, phone calls, and nights out in the West End.
I was a regular social butterfly.
Past tense.
MUM AND DAD WON'T MIND IF THEY DON'T KNOW ABOUT IT.
Because this was before I was kicked out of the family home.
Before the gorgeous groundskeeper.
I'LL PUT MY CLUBBING GEAR IN MY BAG AND WE'LL GO STRAIGHT FROM YOURS.
And before the end of the world.
I.D.? I'LL THINK OF SOMETHING.

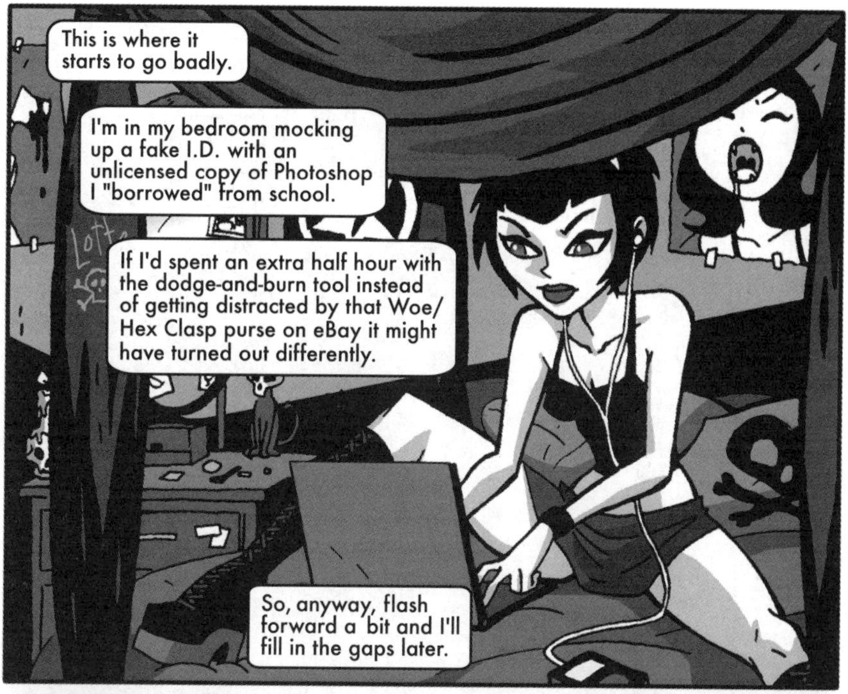
This is where it starts to go badly.
I'm in my bedroom mocking up a fake I.D. with an unlicensed copy of Photoshop I "borrowed" from school.
If I'd spent an extra half hour with the dodge-and-burn tool instead of getting distracted by that Woe/Hex Clasp purse on eBay it might have turned out differently.
So, anyway, flash forward a bit and I'll fill in the gaps later.

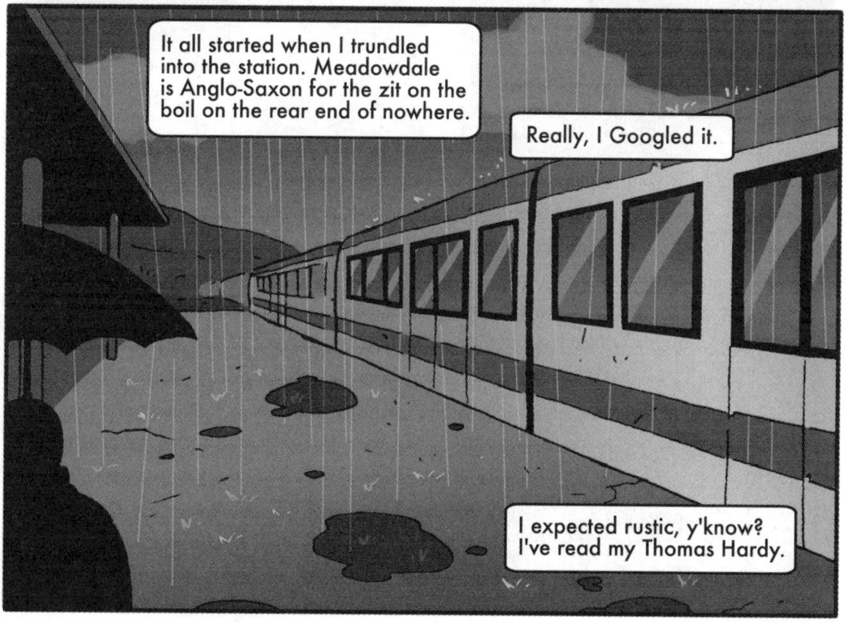
It all started when I trundled into the station. Meadowdale is Anglo-Saxon for the zit on the boil on the rear end of nowhere.
Really, I Googled it.
I expected rustic, y'know? I've read my Thomas Hardy.

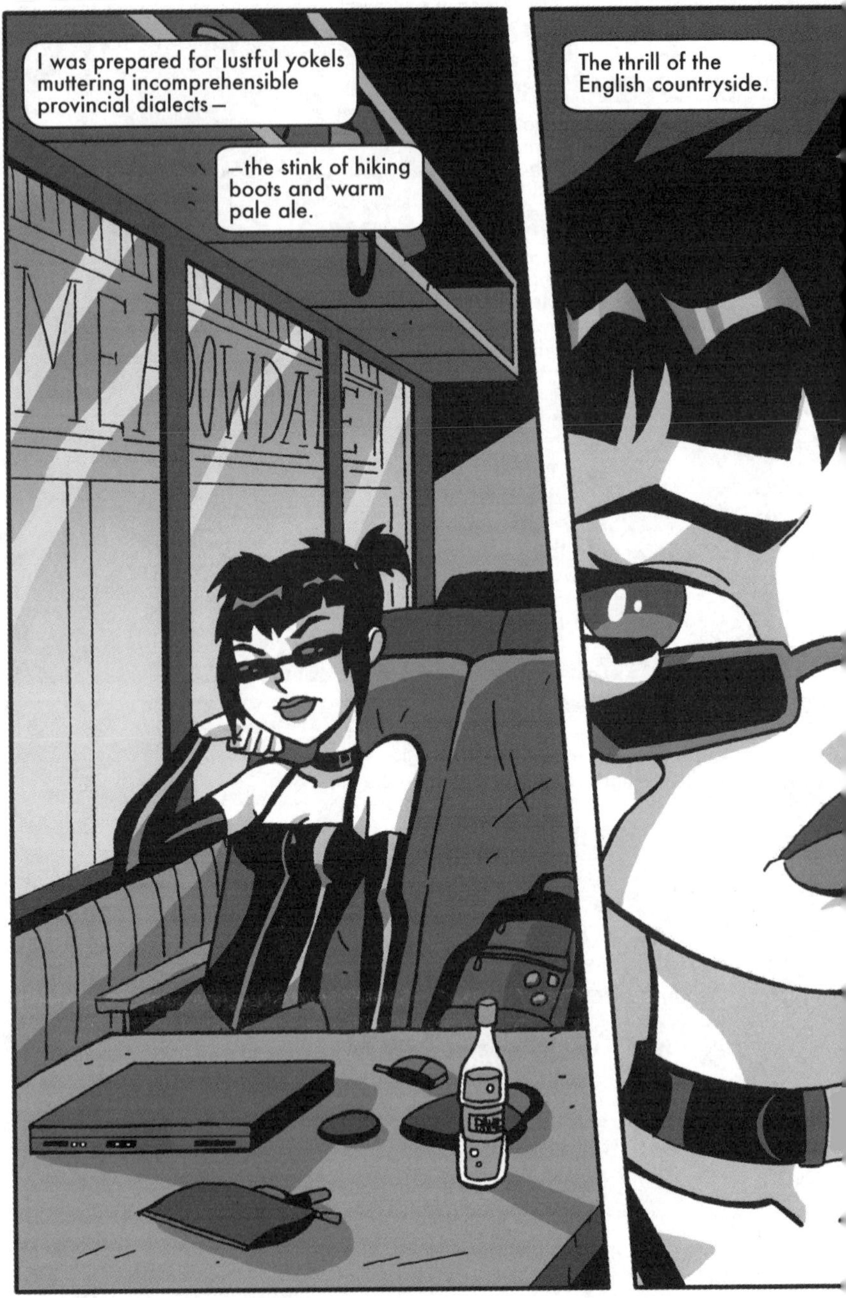
I was prepared for lustful yokels muttering incomprehensible provincial dialects—
—the stink of hiking boots and warm pale ale.
The thrill of the English countryside.

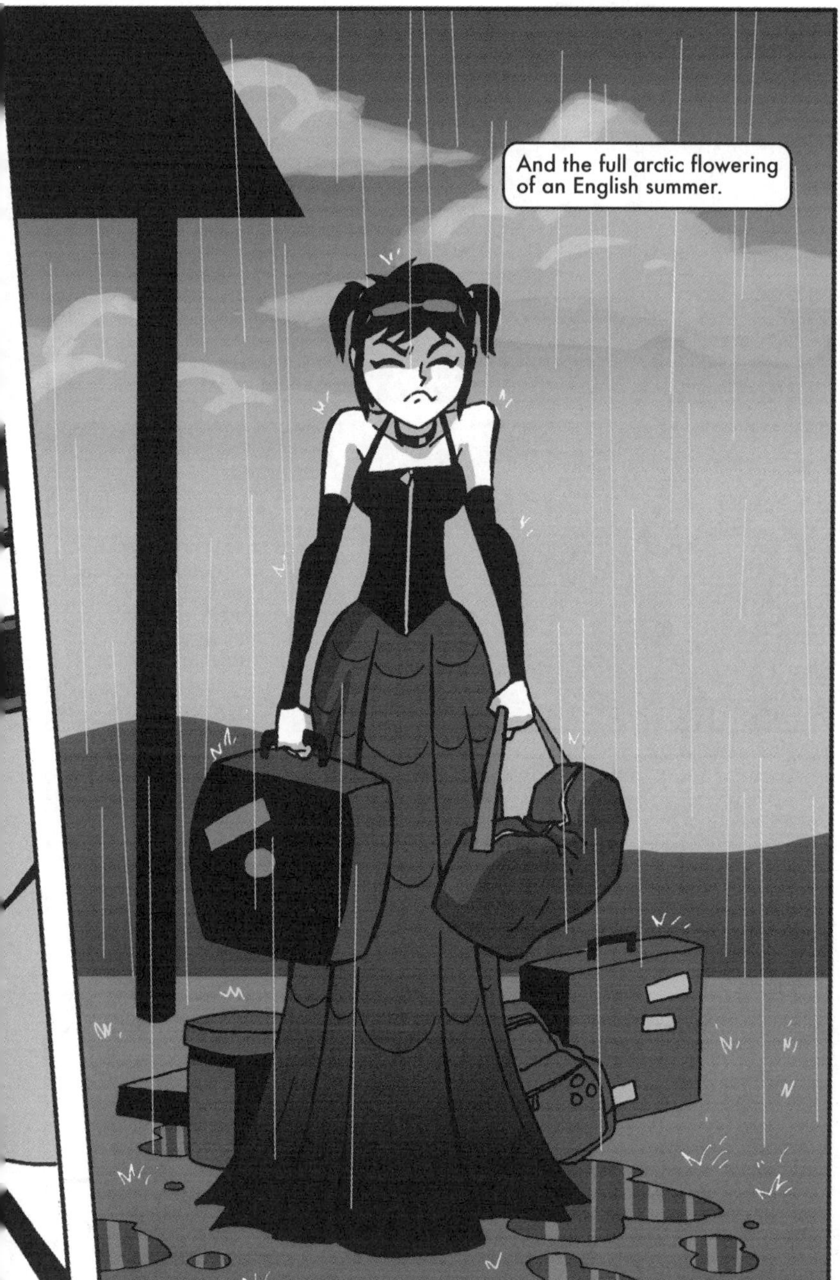
And the full arctic flowering of an English summer.

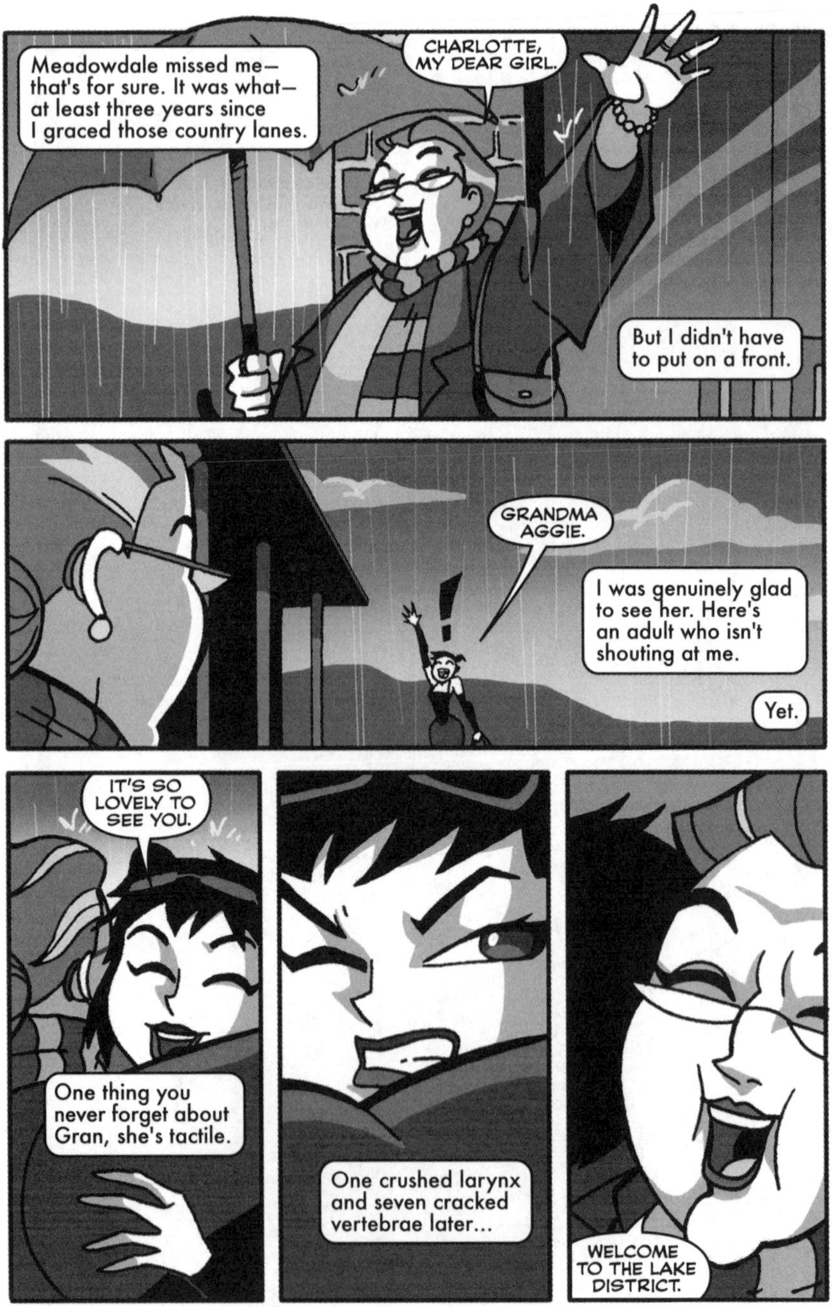
Meadowdale missed me—that's for sure. It was what—at least three years since I graced those country lanes.
CHARLOTTE, MY DEAR GIRL.
But I didn't have to put on a front.
GRANDMA AGGIE.
I was genuinely glad to see her. Here's an adult who isn't shouting at me.
Yet.
IT'S SO LOVELY TO SEE YOU.
One thing you never forget about Gran, she's tactile.
One crushed larynx and seven cracked vertebrae later...
WELCOME TO THE LAKE DISTRICT.

Derek Kirk Kim & Jesse Hamm

Good As Lily

What would you do if versions of yourself at ages 6, 29 and 70

suddenly became part of your already complicated high school life?

COMING IN SEPTEMBER 2007 ■ Read on,
but please note: the following pages are not sequential.

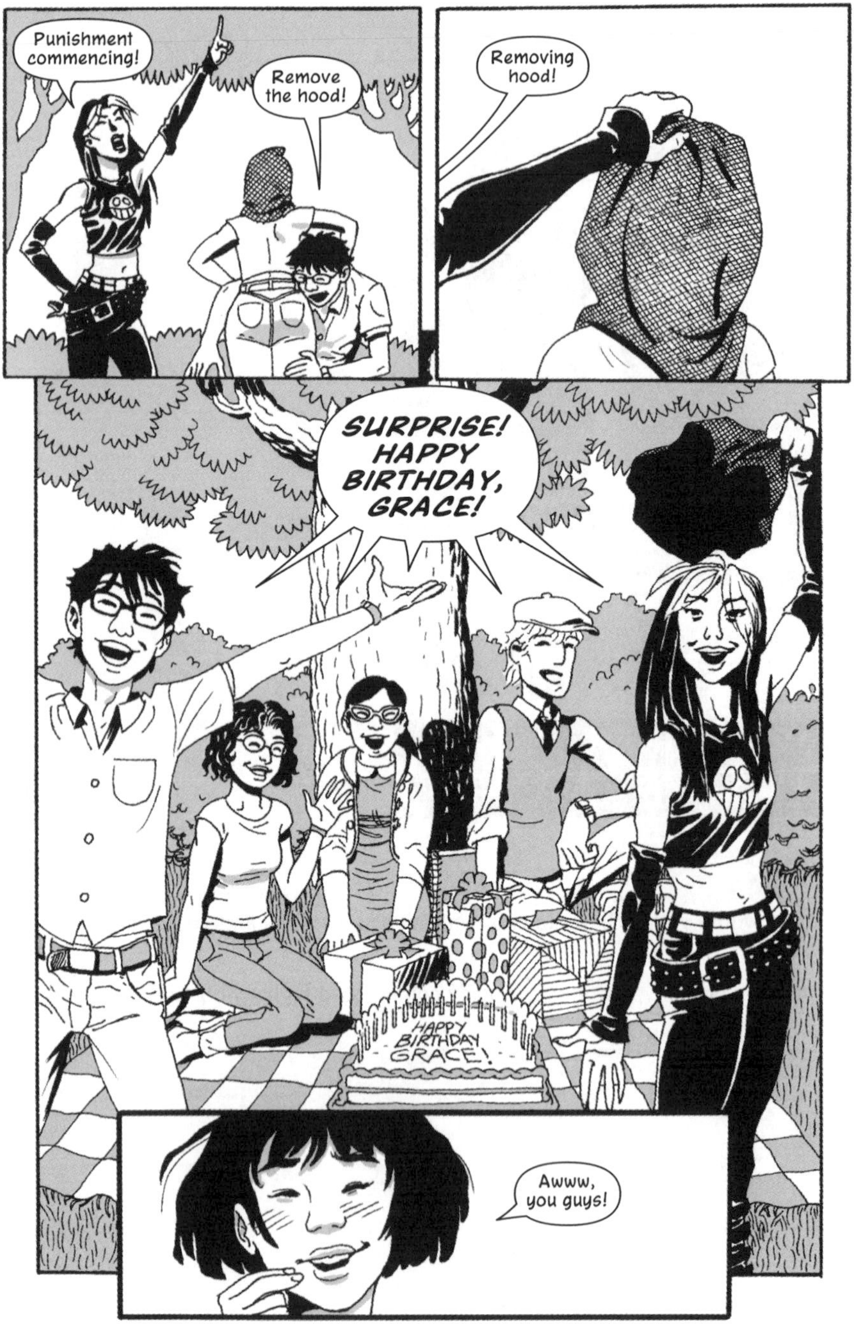
Punishment commencing!
Remove the hood!
Removing hood!
SURPRISE! HAPPY BIRTHDAY, GRACE!
HAPPY BIRTHDAY GRACE!
Awww, you guys!

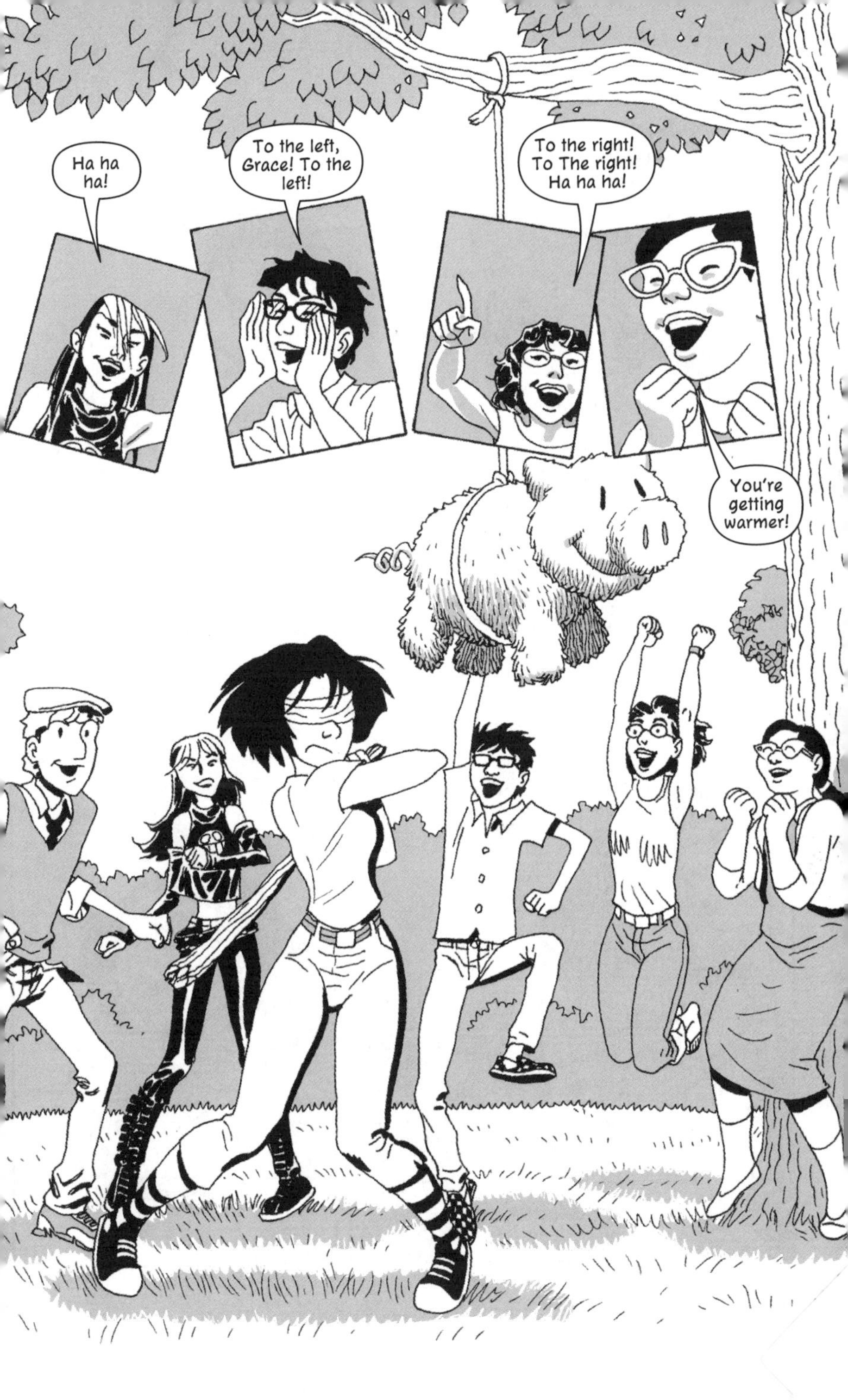
Ha ha ha!
To the left, Grace! To the left!
To the right! To The right! Ha ha ha!
You're getting warmer!

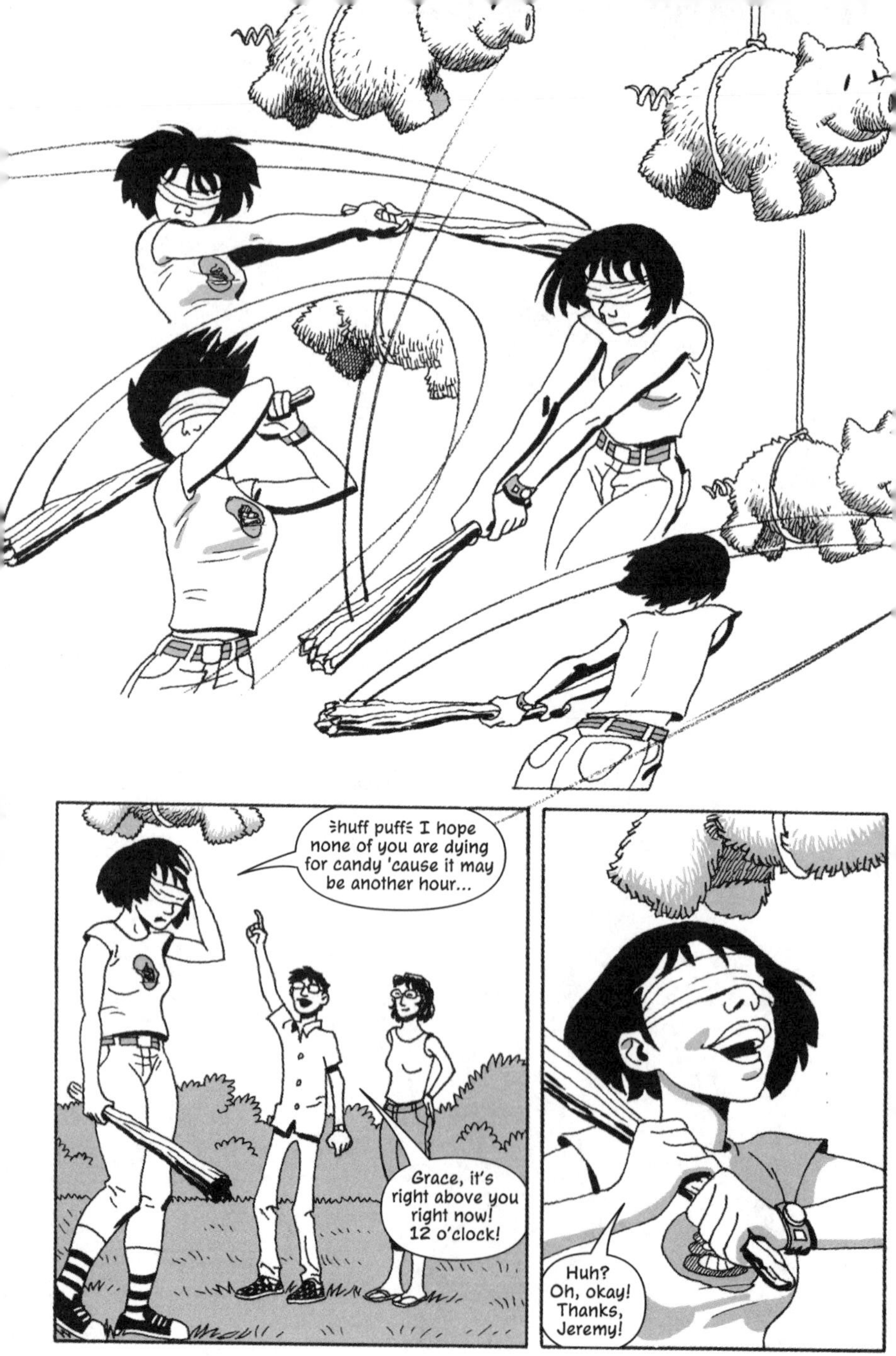

⸗huff puff⸗ I hope none of you are dying for candy 'cause it may be another hour...
Grace, it's right above you right now! 12 o'clock!
Huh? Oh, okay! Thanks, Jeremy!

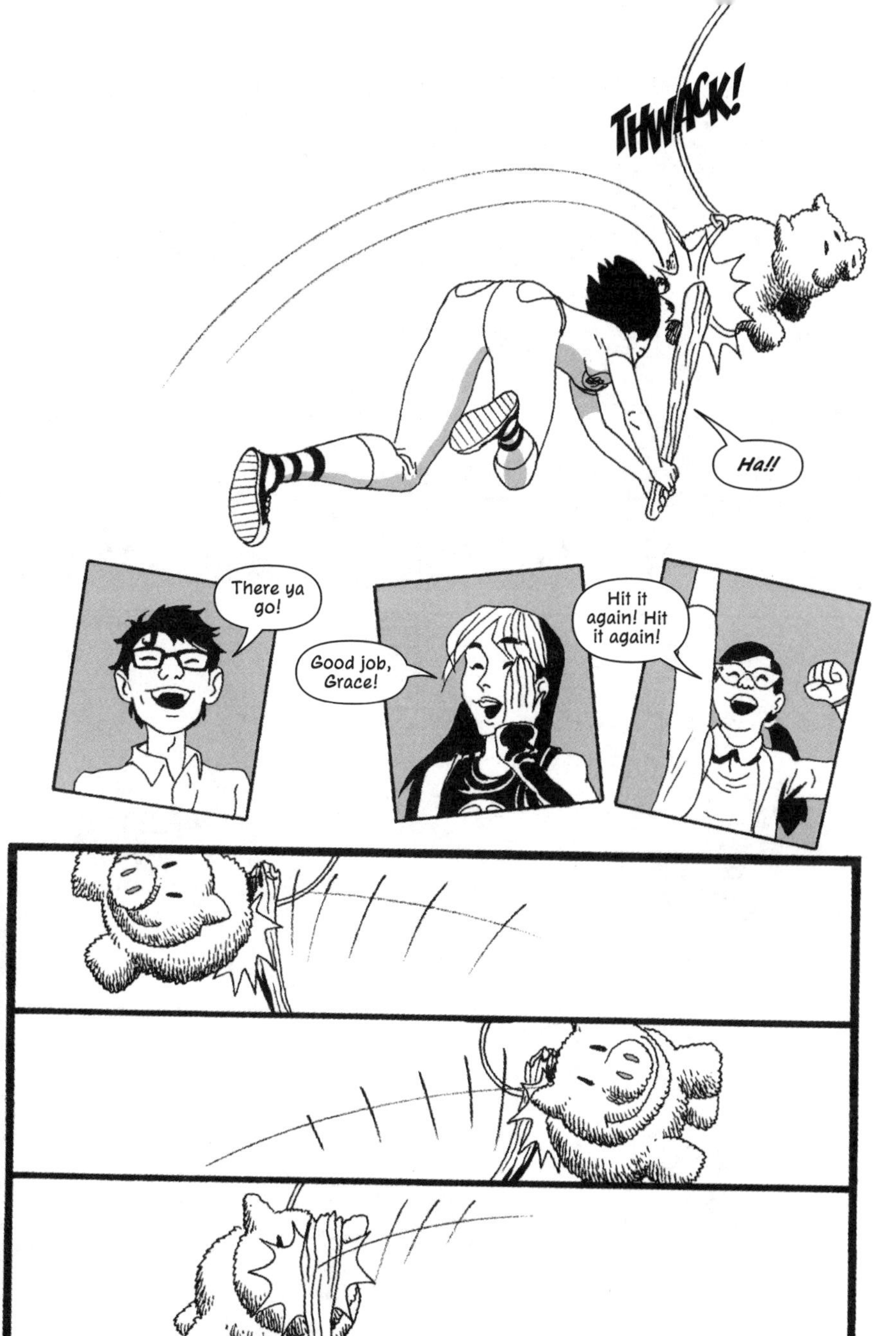
THWACK!
Ha!!
There ya go!
Good job, Grace!
Hit it again! Hit it again!

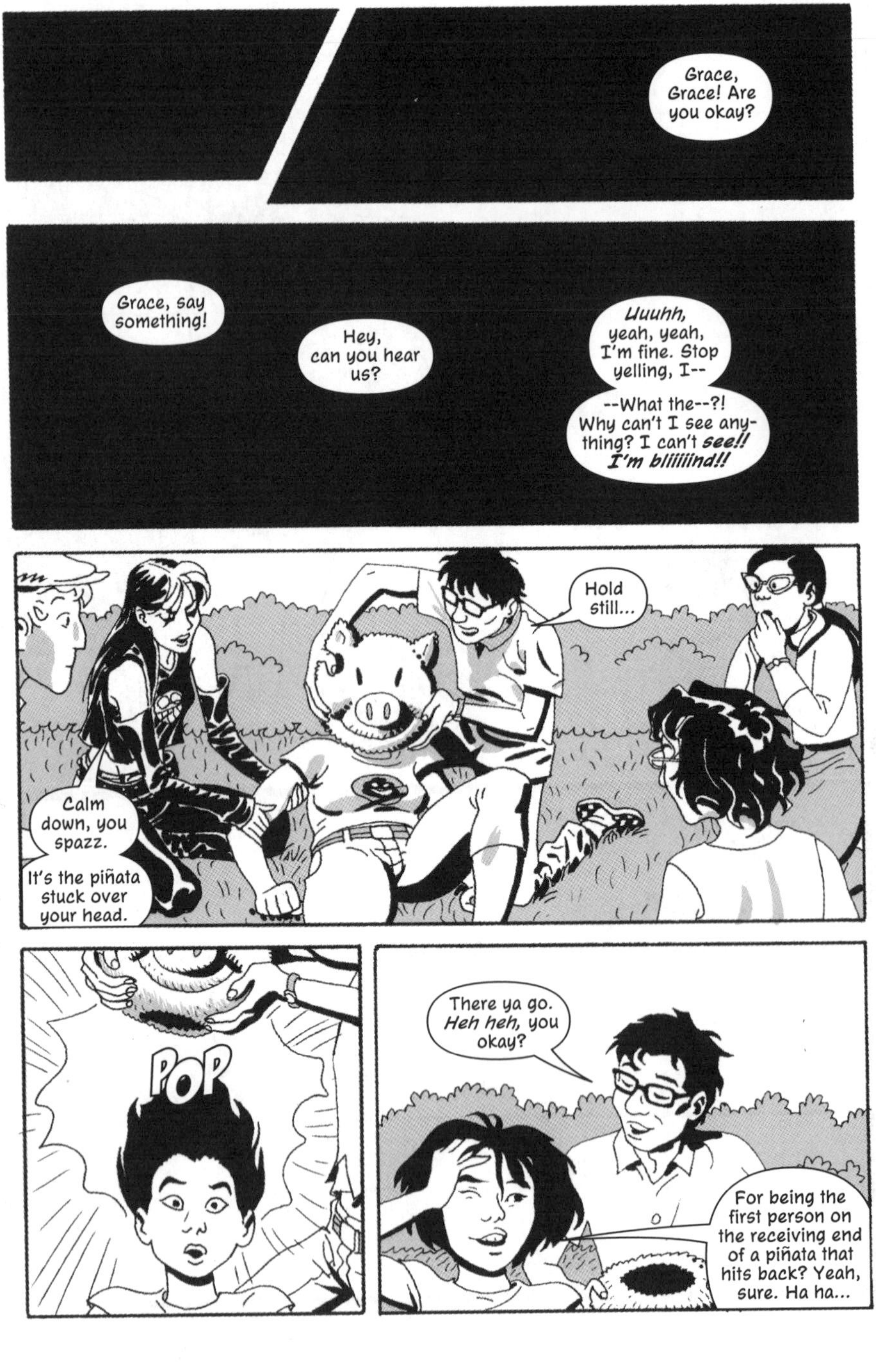
Grace, Grace! Are you okay?
Grace, say something!
Hey, can you hear us?
Uuuhh, yeah, yeah, I'm fine. Stop yelling, I--
--What the--?! Why can't I see any-thing? I can't ***see!! I'm bliiiiind!!***
Hold still...
Calm down, you spazz.
It's the piñata stuck over your head.
POP
There ya go. *Heh heh,* you okay?
For being the first person on the receiving end of a piñata that hits back? Yeah, sure. Ha ha...

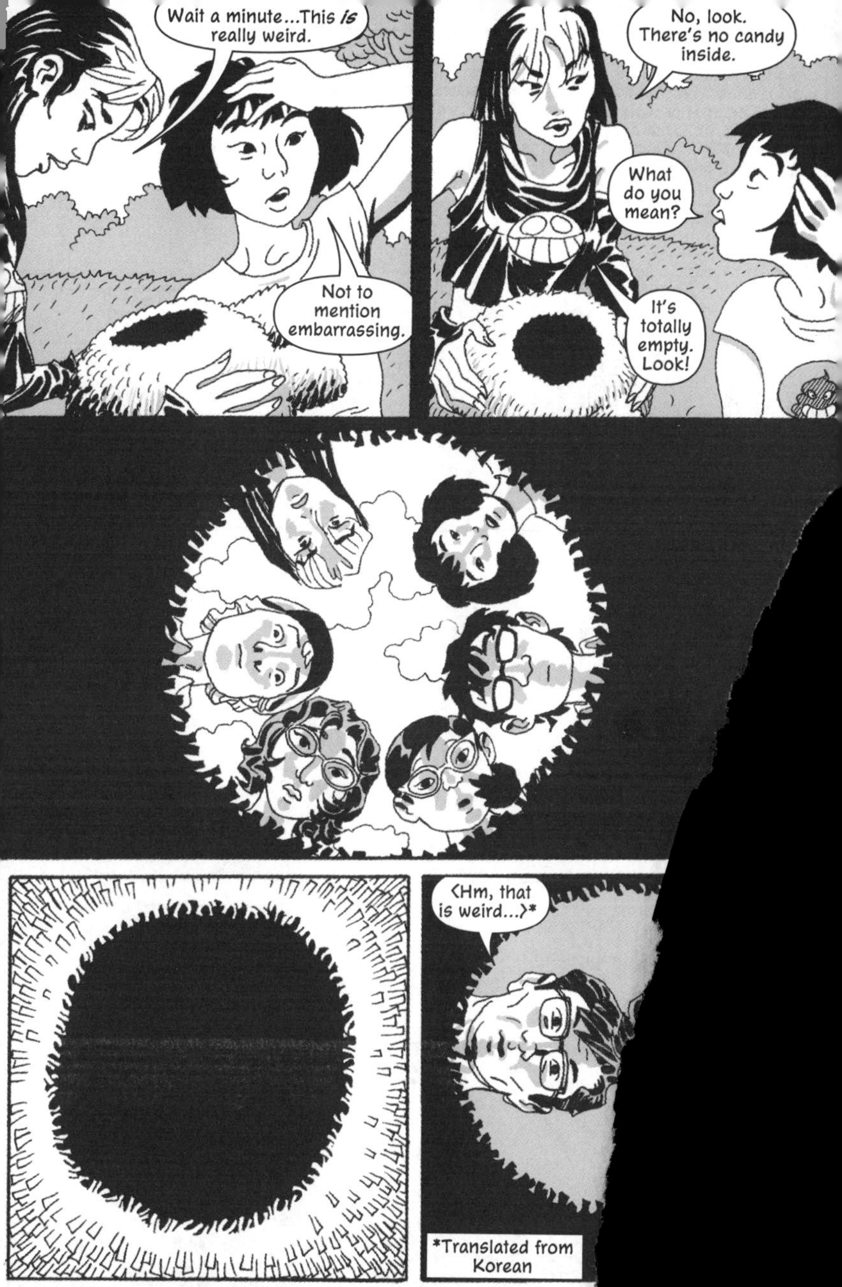
Wait a minute...This *is* really weird.
Not to mention embarrassing.
No, look. There's no candy inside.
What do you mean?
It's totally empty. Look!
<Hm, that is weird...>*
*Translated from Korean

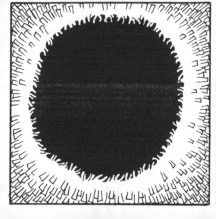

So there I was, about to blow my stack. But as I looked at the three of them, I suddenly started to feel dizzy. The total craziness of what was before me was hitting me full force again. There I was, standing in my room with... myself... at the age of 6, 29, and 70. I felt like I was in a dream, surrounded by distorted mirrors in an impossible funhouse.

...I can't stop staring... My room...My old room...

Okay, I wanna know one thing. What happened on your 18th birthday after you got hit on the head with the piñata?

...ver had a ...on my 18th ...thday...

Yeah, what piñata?

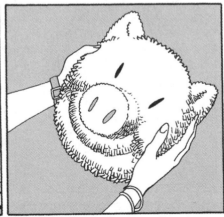

Don't miss any of the upcoming minx books of 2007:

confessions of a
blabbermouth
MIKE CAREY LOUISE CAREY AARON ALEXOVICH

CONFESSIONS OF A BLABBERMOUTH

By Mike and Louise Carey and Aaron Alexovich

October

When Tasha's mom brings home a creepy boyfriend and his deadpan daughter, a dysfunctional family is headed for a complete mental meltdown.

WATER BABY
Ross Campbell

WATER BABY

By Ross Campbell

November

Surfer girl Brody just got her leg bitten off by a shark. What's worse? Her shark of an ex-boyfriend is back, and when it comes to Brody's couch, he's not budging.

kimmie66
AARON ALEXOVICH

KIMMIE66

By Aaron Alexovich

December

This high-velocity, virtual reality ghost story follows a tech-savvy teenager on a dangerous quest to save her best friend, the world's first all-digital girl.

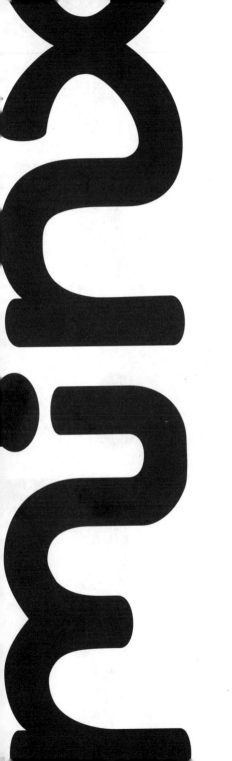

Go to

www.titanbooks.com

for exclusive interviews

and bonus artwork!

The Face of Modern Fiction